INVITED TO WITNESS

INVITED TO WITNESS

SOLIDARITY TOURISM ACROSS OCCUPIED PALESTINE

JENNIFER LYNN KELLY

DUKE UNIVERSITY PRESS DURHAM AND LONDON 2023

Printed in the United States of America on acid-free paper ∞
Designed by Aimee C. Harrison
Project editor: Ihsan Taylor
Typeset in Minion Pro and Canela Text
by Westchester Publishing Services

Library of Congress Cataloging-in-Publication Data
Names: Kelly, Jennifer Lynn, [date] author.
Title: Invited to witness : solidarity tourism across occupied Palestine /
Jennifer Lynn Kelly.
Description: Durham : Duke University Press, 2023. | Includes
bibliographical references and index.
Identifiers: LCCN 2022026708 (print)
LCCN 2022026709 (ebook)
ISBN 9781478019299 (paperback)
ISBN 9781478016656 (hardcover)
ISBN 9781478023920 (ebook)
Subjects: LCSH: Tourism—Social aspects—Palestine. | Tourism—
Palestine. | Solidarity—Palestine. | Volunteer tourism—Palestine. |
Palestinian Arabs—Social conditions. | BISAC: HISTORY / Middle
East / Israel & Palestine
Classification: LCC G156.5.S63 K455 2023 (print) | LCC G156.5. S63
(ebook) | DDC 306.4/819095694—dc23/eng20221003
LC record available at https://lccn.loc.gov/2022026708
LC ebook record available at https://lccn.loc.gov/2022026709

Cover art: Tanya Habjouqa, photograph from the series *The Sacred
Space Oddity.* © Tanya Habjouqa/NOOR.

Duke University Press gratefully acknowledges the Critical Race
and Ethnic Studies Department and the Feminist Studies
Department at the University of California, Santa Cruz, which
provided funds toward the publication of this book.

Dedicated to my mom, who has read every word of this more than once, continuing a long tradition of always being invested in my take on the world

CONTENTS

ACKNOWLEDGMENTS

This book emerges out of collectivity and love. It would not be possible without the world of interlocutors, mentors, colleagues, friends, and family who supported this work—and me—over the past decade of research and writing.

My debt of gratitude is owed first to my interlocutors in Palestine. To every tour guide and organizer who took the time to meet with me, let me sit in on so many of your tours, and talked with me about the past and present of tourism in Palestine: I am so grateful for your time and I hope the narrative I provide here resonates with the work you do. To every shop owner, farmer, and community member I spoke with, thank you for letting me know how you experience tourism in your homeland. And to every tourist who spoke with me about your experience: thank you for your care and time in thinking through your role as witness and delegate with me. This work only exists in the way that it does thanks to your engagement with my many questions about solidarity and tourism in Palestine. I want especially to thank those of you whose words animate the bulk of entire chapters: Sherna Gluck on first intifada delegations; Baha Hilo on the contours of Israeli state practice; Yazan Al-Zubaidy on acts of witnessing; Bisan Kassis on organizing; Fayrouz Sharqawi on Jerusalem as a beloved and multiply occupied city; Umar al-Ghubari on return; Bilal Dirbas on settler colonialism and Haifa; and Sarah Alzanoon, Maggie Goff, Yvonne Lory, Marietta Macy, Addis Green, Olga Negrón, RL, and Noelle Farasha on the fraught acts of touring Palestine. Maria Lebron, thank you for asking questions, as a tourist in Palestine, that stayed with me. Baha, in particular, your brilliance and friendship since Spring 2012 has meant the world to me and has strengthened this book in every way. Thank you also to the artists who allowed me to engage their work here. Julien Bousac and Tanya Habjouqa, in particular, thank you for your beautiful work and for your long support of mine. Tanya, I'm honored to include your powerful work on the cover of this book—this image so beautifully speaks to the labor of remembrance, pedagogy, and freedom dreaming from within a colonial present that the tour guides I interviewed do every day.

I had many mentors who shepherded this project through its different iterations. During my master's program, where the beginnings of this project started to make themselves known: Ella Shohat, thank you so much for seeing a future scholar in baby graduate student me, for making your classroom a space for the rigorous and careful study of Palestine, and for supporting my project through its many stages before and after graduate school. Ann Stoler, thank you for drawing me out in your graduate classes, for teaching me about colonial ruination, for providing the space for me to study Zionist afforestation as a strategy of state violence. During my PhD program, thank you forever to Barbara Harlow, my dissertation cochair, whose respect I had to earn, who always made time for cigarettes and conversation, and who taught me how to do honest and meaningful work on Palestine; every January 28 is a painful reminder of a world without your incisive critique, wild stories, and signature style. Naomi Paik, dissertation cochair extraordinaire, thank you for supporting this work from its very first moments and for helping me navigate graduate school and beyond with precision and care. Steve Marshall, thank you for gifting me hard questions you knew I could answer; the faith you had in me as a scholar had everything to do with the confidence I was able to cultivate in graduate school. Katie Stewart, thank you for modeling teaching that takes the craft of writing seriously; I try to make that kind of space in my own classes and am grateful to you with every syllabus I craft. Tarek El-Ariss, thank you for your many insights on my dissertation, from proposal through the defense. And Shirley Thompson, thank you for teaching me about archives and guiding me through exams; I learned so much from you.

To those mentors not on my committee(s) but who helped shape this project during graduate school: Amy Kaplan, thank you for teaching me about US empire before we met and for supporting my work so consistently after; you are so deeply missed by all of us. Sara Kaplan, Kirstie Dorr, Deb Vargas, and Erica Edwards—I can't thank you enough for your mentorship and friendship throughout the tumultuous path of graduate school, postdocs, partner hire negotiations, and navigating life as a junior scholar on the tenure track; you were anchors in so many storms. Vernadette Vicuña Gonzalez, thank you not only for teaching me so much about tourism through your work but also for providing the home for my first publication, supporting my work ever since, and offering me as a junior scholar many opportunities to grow and share my work. Gary Fields, thank you for your mentorship while I was a President's Postdoctoral Fellow at UC San Diego, and thank you to the broader PPFP community of mentors for the collectivity in mentorship you model. Mimi Thi Nguyen, Junaid Rana, and Martin Manalansan, the Chancellor's Postdoctoral Fellowship in Asian American Studies at UIUC and your mentorship were integral to my growth as a scholar. This was one of the first spaces in which my work on Palestine needed no prefatory explanation for why it belonged. Mimi, in particular, thank you for showing me what my book was doing; so much of what is clear here is thanks to the insight and care you took with my project. Nadine Naber and Rebecca Stein, thank you both for so carefully workshopping my book manuscript at UIUC. I remain so grateful for your thorough feedback on each chapter and the insights you offered for revision; this book is far better because of your time and care.

My colleagues and friends along the circuitous route of writing this book deserve all there is to give. At UT, in American Studies, thank you to Eric Covey, Irene Garza, Jake Maguire, Susan Quesal, and Elissa Underwood; your insights, jokes, and important work has sustained mine well beyond the narrow confines of grad school. In the Anthropology Department, thank you to Claudia Chavez, Sarah Ihmoud, Chelsi West Ohueri, Elizabeth Velasquez, and Mathangi Krishnamurthy; I am so grateful we got to grow in our writing together. In my adopted cohort at NYU, thank you to Leticia Alvarado, Eva Hageman, Emily Hue, Ronak Kapadia, Zenia Kish, Justin Leroy, Liz Mesok, and Elliott Powell. Emily, hypebuoy forever, I can't imagine doing any of this without you and our text thread, spa days, balcony talks, tourist trap adventures, eye rolls, everything; you make academia a place I want to stay. Liz, growing as a scholar and a mother alongside you is a gift I never take for granted; I look forward to a lifetime of milestones in tandem with you. At Dickinson, where I spent the last two years of dissertation writing, thank you to Poulomi Saha and Crystal Moten for all the love and laughs, from your living rooms to booths at Chili's and Applebee's.

After graduate school and before my first tenure-track position were years of working on my monograph amid job-market-induced fear and uncertainty that were made beautiful by the dearest of friends. At UC San Diego, during my first postdoc, thank you to my writing group and its honorary members: Josen Masangkay Diaz, Emily Hue, Davorn Sisavath, Ashvin Kini, Victor Betts, and Yumi Pak. Our retreats—from Lake Arrowhead to Palm Springs to Gossip Grill—made everything manageable. Thank you, also, to Patty Ahn, Mathilde Córdoba Azcárate, Yelena Guzman, Cassandra Hartblay, and Louise Hickman for making UC San Diego a welcome, if brief, home. During the second year of that postdoc, in Durham, where I first turned the dissertation into a book manuscript, thank you to Liz Ault (more on you later!), Mike Blank, Yuridia Ramírez Rentería, Eli Meyerhoff, and Jecca Namakkal: I miss our backyard laughs and coffeeshop "work" dates the most. Finally, during my second postdoc at UIUC, in addition to the mentorship I will forever appreciate, thank you also to Mike Atienza, Eman Ghanayem, Maryam Kashani, Soo Ah Kwon, and Patricia Nguyen for being lights in the midwestern winter. And to my dearest Lila Sharif, I am so grateful for your presence in my life; I cannot imagine what our lives would look like if we didn't lock eyes across the room on that olive-planting tour in 2012, two awkward graduate students finding each other amid a sea of tourists, awaiting one million inside jokes, lots of tears, so many meals, and a world of future collaborations.

I am so lucky to have landed at UC Santa Cruz, where this all began, where I am gifted with a community where the line between colleague and friend is beautifully blurred. Thank you to my dearests who have read my work and shared theirs, who have buoyed me with treks for good food and tide pools, who have shared so much on beach walks, who have welcomed me into their homes and lives, who have told endless stories from kitchen counters to the Humanities parking lot: Zsuzsi Abrams, Neel Ahuja, Taylor Ainslie, Neda Atanaososki, Karen Bassi, micha cárdenas, Vilashini Coopan, Muriam Haleh Davis, Jennifer Derr, Amy Mihyang Ginther, Camilla Hawthorne, Christine Hong, Shauntay Larkins, Cynthia Ling Lee, Xavier Livermon, Nidhi Mahajan, Megan McNamara, Nick Mitchell, Madhavi Murty, Marcia Ochoa, Eric Porter, Felicity Amaya Schaeffer, Tomas Serres, Savannah Shange, Alice Yang, and Jerry Zee. Santa Cruz is a warmer place, despite the fog, because of you. Thank you also to Bettina Aptheker and Gina Dent, for welcoming me—their former student—back to Santa Cruz with enthusiasm. And to my student interlocutors on Palestine at UC Santa Cruz: Samar Al-Salah, Robin Gabriel,

Yulia Gilichinskaya, and Noya Kansky, I learn so much from you and your work. Thank you, also, to all of you I haven't yet named at UC Santa Cruz, in CRES and Feminist Studies and beyond, for making this place such a vibrant intellectual home. Christine, thank you for your deep and loyal friendship, for fighting so hard for all of us in CRES, and for making sure Marisol and I could put our roots down here. Camilla, thank you for every supportive call or text, every cat meme and recipe, every coauthored word, every collaborative idea, every edit, every conversation over good food and better views; I am so grateful for you. Apart from UC Santa Cruz but also with Nick and during this timeframe: SA Smythe, our real-life and then virtual escape rooms got me through when I wanted to escape; and David Stein, thank you for all our very necessary text threads and Zoom debriefs. And Nick, after much internal debate, I moved my constellation of thank-yous to you to "family" for definitional precision and accuracy.

Throughout the entire journey of graduate school and my tenure as an early career scholar, I especially want to thank the colleagues and friends who have carved out a space for Palestine in all corners of our scholarship and organizing: Bayan Abusneineh, Sa'ed Atshan, Nadia Awad, Sara Awartani, Sophia Azeb, Ryvka Barnard, Tallie Ben Daniel, Lisa Bhungalia, Amahl Bishara, Umayyah Cable, Chandni Desai, Evyn Lê Espiritu, Maryam Griffin, Yara Hawari, Sarah Ihmoud, Haneen Maikey, Jennifer Mogannam, Loubna Qutami, Kali Rubaii, Noa Shaindlinger, Lila Sharif, Mejdulene Shomali, Somdeep Sen, and Sophia Stamatopoulou-Robbins; both my work and I have grown so much because of you and yours. Thank you for all the panels we've shared, all that you've taught me, and all the ways you've modeled support and care for one another and for me within and beyond the institutions—and the people who populate them—that silence scholarship on Palestine. Umayyah, I love you and am so grateful for all of our adventures, from Portland to Istanbul, and all our heart-to-hearts in hotel rooms everywhere. Mejdulene, you are my heart. What a gift it is to know you, to spend time with you, and to share space with you, from Baltimore to Beit Sahour. And to the mentors of so many of us: Rabab Abdulhadi, Evelyn Alsultany, Noura Erakat, Sarah Gualtieri, Nadine Naber, Sherene Seikaly, and Ella Shohat; thank you for making the space for feminist scholarship on Palestine, teaching us so much through your research, chairing our panels and giving us feedback, and supporting us in myriad ways as we do this work. Thank you also to the many senior scholars in and in proximity to American Studies—among them Maylei Blackwell, Keith Feldman, Cynthia

Franklin, Ruth Wilson Gilmore, Alyosha Goldstein, Caren Kaplan, Kēhualani Kauanui, Randolph Lewis, David Lloyd, Alex Lubin, Sunaina Maira, Curtis Marez, and Sarah Schulman—who have long supported my work and affirmed that a project on Palestine and tourism does indeed belong in our field.

Finally, during my last year of book edits—in Austin, Texas, during quarantine—thank you to my dear friends, some newer colleagues and some from childhood. Jenny Krones, thank you for the lake walks, laughter, and listening to the rollercoaster of the academic job market. Iván Chaar-López and Francheska Alers, thank you for our long talks and charcuterie boards. Ashley Farmer and Ade Adamson, thank you for your constant thoughtfulness. And Simone Browne, thank you for the laughs, support, and reunions we got to have this year. Roger Reeves and Mónica Jiménez, thank you for all the late-night backyard hangs, for supporting us at every turn, and for always checking in. Elizabeth Christie, thank you for always being there—in person or from afar—since the beginning, for listening during the losses and cheering me on during the wins.

Located across disciplines, and thus without access to disciplinary grants, this book would not have been possible without threaded-together funding from multiple different sources. My dissertation research was funded by the University of Texas at Austin's College of Liberal Arts Louann Atkins Temple Endowed Presidential Scholarship in American Studies; the Palestinian American Research Center (PARC); the David Bruton Jr. Graduate School Fellowship; and the Department of American Studies short-term Dissertation Research Grant and yearlong Dissertation Completion Fellowship. My work on the book during my postdoctoral fellowships was funded by the University of California President's Postdoctoral Fellowship, where I was in residence in the Department of Communication at UC San Diego, and by the Chancellor's Postdoctoral Fellowship at the University of Illinois at Urbana-Champaign, where I was in residence in the Department of Asian American Studies with affiliation in the Department of Gender and Women's Studies.

At UC Santa Cruz, my follow-up research for book revisions and the time to write were funded by a 2019–2020 University of California Humanities Research Institute (UCHRI) and University of California Office of the President (UCOP) President's Faculty Research Fellowship in the Humanities; a 2019–2020 Field-Based Research Fellowship from PARC; Faculty Research Grants from the UC Santa Cruz Committee on Research; the 2020–2021 Hellman Fellowship for Junior Scholars; and a generous Book Subvention Grant from Critical Race and Ethnic Studies and Feminist Studies. A special note of appreciation to PARC's executive director Penelope Mitchell, who continues to support my work, facilitate connections with other scholars, and circulate updates about my research. Lastly, thank you to the Freedom Archives in San Francisco, without which I would not have been able to write the first chapter, which is so integral to my larger argument.

At Duke University Press, I want to thank Ken Wissoker, who engaged my project since its earliest drafts, and my editor, Liz Ault, who supported this project and me at its early stages and so carefully and beautifully ushered it into being in its final stages. Thank you, Liz, for seeing my work so clearly, helping me clarify what it is doing, and choosing anonymous reviewers who so completely understood my project and took great care with their feedback. To those reviewers, this book is not the same as the one before it was in your hands. Your care and precision helped me anchor this book in the region and its history, refusing to isolate Palestine as an island in the present, and helped me clarify the stakes of my analysis of tourism in a context of military occupation and colonial plunder. Your comments also grounded me in knowing this book has something important to teach for the study of Palestine, tourism, and solidarity. Thank you also to Aimee Harrison, Benjamin Kossak, and Ihsan Taylor for all your work at the final stages in moving the book into production. Finally, to Cathy Hannabach and the other editors at Ideas on Fire, thank you for all the assistance with copyediting and the index; you made the final stages of publication and production far less stressful than they would have been otherwise.

Finally, to my family: thank you to my dad, David L. Kelly, for teaching me the value of clear writing; it is a lesson I've carried with me and work to pass on in all my classes. To my sister, Scharlet Kelly, thank you for supporting me in this long journey and providing a beautiful distraction—in Ronan, Cyrus, and Stella—from the book, the job market, and all the ups and down of this profession. Karla R. Kelly, Little Mom, there are not enough words to thank you for your steadfast support, your questions, your interest in my research, your advice on beach walks, your enthusiasm for the beautiful, and your refusal to turn away from the ugly. Your ability to see things in this nuanced, prismatic way—cognizant of their potential and clear-eyed about their problems—is the ethos that guides how I do research.

Nick Mitchell, we out here. Thank you for making my job materialize, for recruiting me to Santa Cruz, for sharing office hours and inside jokes and family dinners and beautifully planned day dates and late-night talks. Thank you for modeling how to do this work ethically. And thank you for seeing in me depths and heights I often fail to see in myself. I am so lucky to be in your orbit.

Marisol LeBrón, and our sweet Isla, sitting across from me at a café in Texas as I wrote the first draft of these acknowledgments and playing downstairs at our home in California as I edited them: you are everything. Marisol, you saw this project take shape before I did, you read every word as many times as I have, you shortened my sentences, you sharpened my critique, you provided a safe space to retreat. You kept us afloat during the most tumultuous of times. And you remind me of the value of my work every chance you get, especially when I most need the reminder. I love you with all of me and it is a gift to study and struggle alongside you. Isla, our moonbeam, you came onto the scene right as this book was making its exit. I submitted the manuscript on the way to the hospital to clear space for you—and what a beautiful gift you've been since you arrived. Your presence has served not as a break from this work but as a steady reminder to craft a world where all babies are free, from Puerto Rico to Palestine, and to make space for joy while crafting it.

INTRODUCTION

Invited to Witness and Invited to Go Home

"They called me a tourist, which I found insulting." So began a reflection by a delegate I interviewed who had gone on solidarity tours to Palestine during the first intifada. She grappled with her discomfort in occupying this term: *tourist*. She outlined her rationale, explaining that the designation *tourism*, attached to what she did in Palestine, felt derisive of her work, as though it wasn't serious and diminished the connections she made, connections seldom possible via tourism writ large. On a delegation during the summer of 2019, as we sat on the porch of the Tamimis' house, in Nabi Saleh in the West Bank, I navigated a similar sentiment. Ahed Tamimi, eighteen years old at the time of our visit, was arrested in December 2017 for famously slapping an Israeli soldier, sentenced to eight months in an Israeli prison, and released in July 2018. The delegates had just heard a lecture by her father, Bassam Tamimi, which outlined what they, as a family and a people, needed. As Ahed rounded the circle of thirty delegates, perfunctorily shaking each one's hand, Bassam told the delegates that what Palestinians needed was not tears ("We have enough tear gas," he wryly joked) but solidarity. After a dinner hosted by the Tamimis, the delegates circled around Ahed, taking incessant pictures and videos for their social media feeds and asking her a series of questions: What was prison like? What were the conditions? What did you do there? What was it like to finish high school in prison? Do you think you got a lighter or harsher sentence because of your notoriety? How has fame changed your life? One tourist tried to break up this line of questioning, posing a question an eighteen-year-old girl might rather answer: What do you do for fun and what kind of music do you like? The delegates ignored this derailing and returned to their questioning: Was the food in prison edible? What were other people in for? Another interlude: How do you feel about people coming here all the time asking you questions? And another return to the previous line of questioning: Can you drive around to places? Do you pass checkpoints when you go to school? Do you want to stay in Nabi Saleh? Really, for the rest of your life?

Gathered around a set of hookahs after this interrogation of a different sort, some of the delegates began asking me about my research: "So what exactly is your book about?" one tourist, active with the Dream Defenders, asked. I answered, "It's a study of solidarity tourism in Palestine. So, I go on tours like these and interview delegates, tourists, guides, and organizers about their experiences." Another tourist, a lawyer and prison abolitionist, balked, "Don't you think calling it tourism implies that there is a power dynamic going on?" "Yes, absolutely," I answered. The first tourist responded, "But don't you think it's different, because they are *tourists* and we are *delegates*?" I paused, then said, "Well, you're going to the same sites, meeting with the same people, hearing the same histories, and being asked to do the same things." Silence followed, but as the week progressed, it became clear that my presence as a researcher, returning the gaze toward tourists and delegates who were used to doing the observing, was upsetting the dynamic but in generative ways that asked activists to think about the power dynamics of their own presence.

This book takes as its subject what solidarity tourists are being *invited* to do in Palestine, despite their frequent disidentification with that category.[1] I argue that solidarity tourism is a fraught anticolonial strategy in Palestine that follows a series of conventions. It is, first, an appeal to the commitment of solidarity tourists, acknowledging the work they have done in coming to Palestine to begin with. Second, it is a reminder that their presence is a responsibility, which guides communicate through an emphasis on international—particularly US—complicity in Israeli occupation. Third, as tourists and delegates alike are repeatedly reminded that their work is not in Palestine but at home, it is a reminder to tourists that while, yes, they have been invited to Palestine, they are now being invited to go home. This daily labor, on the part of Palestinian hosts, who control neither the narrative about Palestine nor the borders to Palestine, is a project of repeatedly inviting tourists to come to Palestine *as tourists*: to come for a truncated amount of time, listen, learn, and, ultimately, go home. It is there where guides hope that tourists will do their work, in solidarity with Palestinians and—for most tourists—from a place of complicity in their subjugation. I say most because the "solidarity tourist," like the "solidarity tour guide," is an incoherent category; delegations and solidarity tours are made up of multiple people who come to Palestine for many different reasons, among them Palestinians in exile who can only return to Palestine *as* tourists.

Invitation as Keyword and Solidarity Tourism as Genre

The invitation extended via solidarity tourism is a genre marked by the repetition of certain conventions. Key to understanding how solidarity tourism functions is thus *studying* it: being willing to understand how the invitation emerges, who the invitation is for, what it is meant to do, and how those who are otherwise understood as "toured" redefine the invitation to confront and resist settler-colonial contexts that are nowhere near "settled." "Invitation" is not immediately understood as a cultural studies and comparative colonial studies keyword, nor is it a concept that is centrally theorized in the literature on tourism. But in Palestine, a site marked by occupation, displacement, and exile, and under the constraints of colonial military occupation, the politics of invitation, the genre of the direct address, and the disciplining of the tourist are interpellations that structure tourist and colonial encounters. The "contact zone" that animates solidarity tourism in Palestine, wherein tourists meet hosts, internationals meet Indigenous guides, and asymmetrical power relations collide, is one made possible *not* by the refusal to invite but by what constitutes the invitation itself.[2] In sites structured by US imperial expansion and extraction, multiple forms of settler colonialism, and colonial desire(s) shaped by the coalescence of tourism and militarism (for example, in Hawai'i), some Native scholar activists have asked tourists not to come.[3] Other collaborations between Native and not-Native tour guides have reworked the tourist encounter to craft itineraries that resist commercial and gentrifying forms of tourism in the archipelago to envision Hawaiian self-determination.[4] In Palestine, another site of military occupation *and* tourism, a site shaped by US imperial interests in the Middle East, Israeli settler colonialism, and Orientalist tourist desires, there are some who have asked tourists not to come, some who invite tourists to come and intervene in sustained and more long-term ways, and many more who invite solidarity tourists to Palestine—and then invite them to go home.[5] Palestinian tour guides, in a context in which they do not control their borders or the historical narrative, thus wrest both the capacity to invite and, in Edward Said's words, "the permission to narrate," from Israeli control.[6] Even more, they redefine the terms of the invitation, letting tourists know that despite their unease with the category, they are being asked to be *tourists of a particular kind* and also to shoulder the responsibility that accompanies that invitation.

This book takes this daily labor of Palestinian tour guides as its central subject to explore what happens when tourism understands itself as solidarity and when solidarity functions through modalities of tourism. Specifically, I ask what kinds of anticolonial imaginings are made both available and impossible through solidarity tourism. I use the term solidarity tourism to refer to forms of travel that are animated by the tour guide's desire to cultivate solidarity with their cause and tourists' desires to establish a deeper connection to or understanding of a particular social movement. I argue that, through solidarity tour initiatives, Palestinian organizers refashion conventional tourism to the region to advance three specific political goals. First, by staging tourist encounters with everyday Palestinian life, organizers seek to challenge Israeli state-sanctioned narratives and popularize Palestinian accounts of Israeli occupation. Second, organizers employ tourism to keep Palestinian shop owners and farmers on land that is under threat of expropriation. Finally, organizers confront the racialized asymmetries in their profession that privilege tourists' accounts of what they witness over Palestinian narratives of their own displacement. Taking as my subject a phenomenon that is too often relegated to one side of a "good tourism/bad tourism" binary, I instead analyze the complex ways in which solidarity tourism has emerged in Palestine as a viable organizing strategy—and a commercial industry—that is both embedded in and working against histories of sustained displacement.[7]

I resist advancing an evaluative analysis of whether or not solidarity tourism "works." Such an assessment, I argue, hollows out the everyday labor of tour guides and empties solidarity tourism of its nuance, contradictions, and import. Instead, I consider what work solidarity tourism does and for whom. The book details what tourists do in Palestine and after, taking into account their reflections on the ethics of their presence in Palestine and charting the extent to which tourism catalyzes their activism. However, rather than focus solely on the tourist encounter or whether tourists become activists, I focus on what change solidarity tourism effects in the West Bank, East Jerusalem, inside Israel's 1948 borders, and in Gaza. In this way, I show how the story of solidarity tourism in Palestine not only traces emergent and sedimented forms of international movement building but also reveals how Palestinian organizers are strategically using tourism to transform the "facts on the ground" in Palestine.

In the chapters that follow, I chart the conditions that led Palestinians to make their case to the international community through solidarity tourism in the first place. I also detail the ambivalences, asymmetries, and affective ties that take shape in solidarity tourism's orbit. In this way, the book is a "history of the present" that asks why Palestinian organizers have turned to tourism as both an organizing strategy and an income-generating business. It asks why they have done so despite the fraught asymmetries of tourism as a strategy. And it shows how, through this fraught strategy, tour guides and tourists have worked, albeit unevenly, to craft an anticolonial movement outside of a strictly witness/witnessed relationship and despite the epistemic violence and settler logics that structure their encounters.[8]

Solidarity Tourism and Its Discontents

The emergence of contemporary solidarity tourism in Palestine was made possible by the US-brokered Oslo Accords and their afterlife. The Oslo Accords both fragmented the West Bank and simultaneously enabled unforeseen possibilities for commercial tourism in Palestine. The Oslo Accords, and specifically Oslo II in 1995, initiated the fracturing of the West Bank into discrete "areas," with varying Israeli and Palestinian administrative and security control, though *everywhere* is subject to Israeli raids, Israeli control, and Israeli state violence. These taxonomies, and the subsequent land expropriation by the State of Israel, both animated the Oslo Accords and introduced and institutionalized a collection of curfews, closures, roadblocks, and checkpoints that led to increased Palestinian immobility in the Occupied Territories.[9] Along with the proliferation of Israeli settlements—the population of which doubled during the Oslo years—came bypass roads connecting settlements, turning the West Bank into an archipelago with expanding Israeli settlements connected by Israeli-only roads and islands of Palestinian cities and villages disconnected from one another or connected by roads that can be entirely shut down by the presence of one soldier.[10]

Alongside this fragmentation of Palestinian land, the Occupied Territories saw dramatic changes to the possibilities of tourism in Palestine/Israel with the

Oslo Accords' establishment of the Palestinian Authority and its Ministry of Tourism and Antiquities. Between 1967 and 1994, Palestinians were prohibited from becoming licensed tour guides in the West Bank or Gaza. Indeed, Israeli military leader and politician Moshe Dayan allegedly quipped that he would "be more willing to license a Palestinian fighter pilot than a Palestinian tour guide," demonstrating the profound political importance of the ideological narrative Israel was advancing through tourism.[11] Because of these prohibitions against Palestinian tour guiding, solidarity tours before Oslo were mostly composed of small groups of international activists seeking to show solidarity in the form of informal delegations—delegates, like the one who bristled at being called a tourist, sought to distance themselves from the moniker *tourism* even while the archives show both celebrations and critiques of their presence in the West Bank and Gaza.[12]

After Oslo, however, when the establishment of the Palestinian Authority's Ministry of Tourism made it possible for Palestinians to be trained as tour guides, these same delegate leaders alongside newly licensed guides began to launch feasibility studies to explore the possibilities of using tourism, in all its fraught inconsistencies, as an anticolonial strategy. They sought to design and develop tourist initiatives that foregrounded military occupation instead of solely highlighting the depoliticized sites the Palestinian Authority deemed national heritage sites. Organizers began to bring delegations to Palestine, particularly from the United States, with the expressed goal of teaching them about the contours of Israeli colonial violence.

This alternative tourism subsector grew in a context where general tourism to Palestine was also increasing as a result of the newly established possibilities for Palestine to host tourists.[13] Between 1994 and the beginning of the second intifada in 2000, the number of total tourists in the West Bank doubled, exceeding 105,000 per month.[14] Hotel capacity rose from 2,500 to 6,000 rooms, and occupancy rose to 60 percent.[15] Tourism employed approximately one thousand people and came to account for 7–10 percent of Palestine's gross national product.[16] During the second intifada, between 2000 and 2005, the alternative tourism sector experienced substantial setbacks, as checkpoints barred tourists from entering Palestinian areas, and 95 percent of those who had been employed by the tourism industry became unemployed.[17] This constellation of statistics partly reiterates Debbie Lisle's argument that "the tourist gaze requires a widely accepted cessation of military activity before the operations of tourism can be introduced."[18] Yet in Palestine there has been no real cessation of military activity. Palestinian guides and organizers, both during the first and second intifadas and now, do not structure their tours as a remembrance of violence that is relegated to the past; rather, their tours position the colonial violence of Israeli occupation as an uninterrupted stream of dispossession, an "ongoing Nakba."[19]

During the second intifada, some solidarity tourists still visited Palestine, and guides worked to create alternative itineraries during curfews and closures, always having, as one guide put it, a backup plan.[20] By 2013, there were about 290 officially licensed Palestinian tour guides, a minuscule number compared with Israel's 5,400 tour guides.[21] Of the Palestinian tourism sector, about 5 percent constitutes alternative or solidarity tourism, which speaks to the development of solidarity tourism as part of the larger economic sector and, on a smaller scale, an organizing strategy.[22] These statistics reveal not only the monopoly Israel holds over the Palestinian tourism sector and Israel's control over Palestinian borders, airspace, and entry and exit from Palestine/Israel but also how the Palestinian tourism sector, in some ways competing with Israel's, responds to market logics that necessarily privilege Christian pilgrimage sites over the exposure of Israel's militarized occupation. Nonetheless, the Palestinian tourism sector makes space for a solidarity tourism subsector that is comparatively small in scope but still results in rotating scores of curious international tourists and year-round employment for Palestinian tour guides and organizers. Thus, while the Oslo Accords enabled the possibility and professionalization of Palestinian-led tourism, the business of solidarity tourism in the West Bank emerged as both a product and a critique of the Oslo Accords.

Deliberately Truncated Visits and the Ambivalence of the Invitation

While early forms of commercialized solidarity tourism emerged in response to post-Oslo possibilities for Palestinian-led tourism in the West Bank, more recent forms of commercialized solidarity tourism have emerged in response to the perceived failures of other kinds of international presence in the West Bank and Gaza. As Palestinian guides and organizers repeatedly articulate to tourists, "You do far more for our movement by writing your members of Congress than you do by getting shot by a rubber bullet at a demonstration." This sentiment is a clear pushback against the desire on the part of internationals to "get shot by a rubber bullet," or what would otherwise be a feature of both disaster tourism and adventure tourism—tourism defined, respectively, by visiting sites of destruction and the desire to be part of the action.[23] As one of several examples during my research, I heard a Swedish youth—who was volunteering on his gap year with one of the solidarity tour campaigns—tell a tourist, "You can't leave Palestine without going to at least one demonstration." Here, in some ways like the circling of Ahed and interrogation about her prison experience, demonstrations become a "must-see" show internationals have to catch (and document) before leaving the West Bank.

This critique of international desire to participate in protests, or engage in a politics of confrontation with Israeli soldiers, indexes a substantive shift from the days when the International Solidarity Movement (ISM) began asking internationals to come to the West Bank and Gaza to serve as a protective presence for Palestinians under siege. The guides and organizers I spoke to positioned solidarity tourism in Palestine as a move *away* from direct action and protective presence and deliberately *toward* tourist itineraries meant to educate internationals—and then ask them to leave. Through this reframing of the role of internationals in Palestine, guides and organizers articulate a disciplined attempt to disrupt white savior narratives, wherein (mostly) white US and other international tourists come to Palestine to protect Palestinians. Even when they schedule moments of protective presence into their tours, solidarity tour guides and organizers resist positioning protective presence as the central feature of any of their tours. They repeatedly advise internationals *not* to provoke settlers or talk back to soldiers at checkpoints, and they rarely schedule Friday demonstrations into their itineraries. It is clear, from the fatigue of their narration, that this is something they have to reiterate often, repeatedly reminding tourists that it is Palestinians who pay the price for these forms of activism.

In her analysis of the digital archives of the ISM, anthropologist Sophia Stamatopoulou-Robbins analyzes how ISM workers relate to Palestine and narrate their relationship with Palestinians. She reads ISM workers' identification with Palestinians as a "prosthetic engagement" in which ISM workers see their own experience in Palestine as an extension or microcosm of Palestinians' experience.[24] In the way that ISM workers frame their work, she argues, they identify with Palestinians as "experiencing" occupation rather than acknowledging an identification with Israelis based on complicity in the occupation as US citizens whose tax dollars and government support Israeli state practice. ISM workers' identification as "occupied," even temporarily, Stamatopoulou-Robbins shows, allows them to deny their own privilege in their capacity to *leave* Palestine. Such critiques of international presence in Palestine that resembles ISM have made their way into the itineraries of solidarity tours. While there are some endeavors to show internationals "what it's like," there is a palpable turn away from allowing internationals to believe that they are "experiencing occupation" and toward an attempt to make them aware, at every turn, of their own privilege in Palestine.[25]

The shift away from direct action is also a reaction to the 2003 murders of Rachel Corrie, crushed under an Israeli military bulldozer, and Tom Hurndall, shot in the head by an Israeli sniper, which made Israeli impunity against internationals clear and necessitated a different approach to antioccupation strategizing.[26] Israel's willingness to murder international activists, like Corrie, who attempted to obstruct the occupying forces' destruction of Palestinian homes and Palestinian lives, called, in some ways, for a reassessment of the role of internationals in Palestinian resistance movements. In today's post–second intifada political climate, it is clear that solidarity tour organizers route internationals toward tourism and away from direct action and prolonged presence in Palestine. They repeatedly invite internationals to come—and then invite them to go home.

In this way, solidarity tourism has also emerged as a response to the proliferation of sustained volunteer work and voluntourism in the West Bank, wherein tourists, mostly on gap years or breaks from school, come to Palestine to work in schools or with organizations for a limited amount of time (usually a year, pieced together by three-month shifts to accommodate the tourist visa Israel allows internationals). The act of inviting tourists to Palestine, and then inviting them to go home, is thus a formulation that redirects tourists' desire to "see action" in the West Bank or stay for demonstrations and rallies. It is also a formulation that redirects tourists' desires to become fixtures in Palestine, to remain and volunteer either their time or their labor. There is an appreciation for internationals who help rebuild demolished Palestinian homes, who volunteer in Palestinian preschools, and who walk Palestinian children to school in places like At-Tuwani and Hebron to protect them from settlers, especially since these acts of protective presence are constantly being prohibited and policed by the Israeli state. Palestinian solidarity tour organizers' work is often made possible by a handful of volunteers, and their labor itself is rendered necessary because tourists have to *see it to believe it* because Palestinians are too often not treated as reliable narrators of their own condition. Fully aware of the contradictions of their labor, Palestinian tour guides extend invitations to tourists yet simultaneously redefine the parameters of that invitation, inviting internationals to Palestine but refusing their missionary relationship to the place and rejecting either narratives that position internationals in the benevolent role of helping Palestinians pick up the pieces of their lives or narratives that position seasoned activists as more capable of articulating the Palestinian condition than Palestinians themselves. International presence in Palestine is requested, but only for a structured and curtailed amount of time and only under conditions that don't replicate the colonial calculus of veracity that positions only tourists and delegates as truth-telling subjects, only tourists and delegates as witnesses to colonial violence in Palestine.[27]

This limiting of the time internationals spend in Palestine also emerges in a context wherein Palestine is flooded by internationals working in Ramallah NGOs, interns in Bethlehem, scholars studying conflict zones, and budding professionals learning to develop their skills. For instance, on a sardonic Tumblr popularized in 2014 titled "Ajanebed Out: The Tragedy of Foreigners in Palestine," the creators underscore the relationships between white privilege, international mobility, and career building in Palestine through GIFs, memes, and conversation fragments that expose the hypocrisy of "wanting to make a difference in Palestine" and using Palestine as a space for one's own personal fulfillment or career aspirations. One 1950s-esque advertisement, titled "Palestine: For all your professional and academic career needs!" mocks internationals' travels to Palestine to intern, build their CV, get into a PhD program, work in an NGO, and earn a salary doing so.[28] Another simply asks, "Need a purpose in life?" and answers "Visit Palestine!"[29] pointing to the many ways in which foreigners use Palestine to give their own lives a sense of purpose. While this was a short-lived project, it pointed to an exhaustion with foreigners' treatment of Palestine as a place for their personal and professional growth.

This exhaustion with internationals in Palestine also extends to those who overestimate the importance of their presence in Palestine for Palestinians. Much of this criticism is directed at those who believe that their presence alone is doing something to better the situation in Palestine. My discussions with community members affected by solidarity tourism in Palestine repeatedly reflected the paradox of escalated international presence in Palestine yet continued overwhelming silence on the part of the international community. They would ask, "Why, when so many solidarity tourists come to Palestine, does nothing change?" and "How many people have to come here and see, for it to make a difference?" This book probes fault lines of this sort. It asks what the movement-building limitations and possibilities of this kind of international presence are. It shows how solidarity tourism in Palestine is formulated in contradistinction to other forms of international presence at the same time that it rehearses and recapitulates them. And it demonstrates how solidarity tourism is rendered necessary by colonial logics that position "witnesses in Palestine" as the only ones capable of furnishing Palestinian accounts of Israeli occupation and settlement with evidentiary weight.

Through repetition to the extent that it forms a genre, solidarity tourists in Palestine/Israel are repeatedly told that their work is not in Palestine but back in their home countries. In this context, my book reads the ambivalence written into the two invitations that structure the solidarity tourist encounter: *Welcome to Palestine* and *Your work is not here*. Solidarity tourism is an invitation to visit Palestine followed by an invitation to leave. It is, simultaneously, a pedagogical exercise, an anticolonial praxis, an income-generating industry, and a voyeuristic and exploitative enterprise. I position solidarity tourism in Palestine as not reducible to only one of these categories; instead, I explore the contradictions that inhere within solidarity tourism to think through the *work* of tourism, and tour guiding, when it coexists unevenly with the *work* of resisting military occupation, staying on land under the threat of exile, and negotiating the circumvented mobility and fragmented geographies of settler states.

A Subjectless Critique of Solidarity Tourism: Feminist Readings of Literature, Methods, Citations, and Ethnography

This project is a multisited interdisciplinary ethnographic study grounded in transnational feminisms. Postcolonial and anticolonial feminist engagements with race, space, and (im)mobility have both shaped how I theorize the disparities in power and privilege between tourists and their hosts and enabled me to detail how tourism often facilitates and conceals past and present colonial violence.[30] These works are woven throughout my readings of asymmetrical mobility in Palestine, Palestinian tour guides' theorization of their own labor, tourist expectations and negotiations of the ethics of their presence in Palestine, and the colonial logics that structure tourist encounters. Jamaica Kincaid's direct address to the tourist in *A Small Place* informs how I write about tourist mobility: Palestinian tour guides' acts of reminding tourists of their stark mobility in contrast to Palestinian immobility echo how Kincaid challenges the tourist to consider their parasitic role in the global economy, as someone who "moves through customs quickly," whose whiteness shields them from being searched and interrogated at customs, whose mobility is enabled by the colonial present.[31] Jacqui Alexander's critique of the "Native friendliness" required of tour guides and hosts in colonial contexts structures how I write about Palestinian hospitality.[32] Teresia Teaiwa's and Vernadette

Vicuña Gonzalez's respective feminist readings of militourism—or, in Teiawa's words, when "military or paramilitary forces ensure the smooth running of the tourist industry, and that same tourist industry masks the force behind it"— have shaped how I understand how tourism functions in contexts of colonial military occupation.[33] These analyses of the routinization and coalescence of militarism and tourism, while in different colonial contexts ranging from Antigua to Trinidad and Tobago to Guam to Hawai'i to the Philippines, not only have shaped how I read my ethnographic data but also point to the larger stakes of this project: namely, that the study of solidarity tourism in Palestine does not only matter *to* Palestine. Solidarity tourism is a transnational phenomenon that asks us to consider how people under the strictures of colonial military occupation strategically use tourist forms and tropes to critique the colonial asymmetries of the tourist encounter, stay anchored to land receding from their grip, and envision decolonized futures.

This project exists at the interstices of feminist studies and tourism studies, American studies, Asian American studies, critical ethnic studies, and Palestinian studies. I chart questions of privilege and leisure on solidarity tours, the distance(s) between solidarity tourists and their hosts, the pitfalls of voluntourism, and the ethics of "sightseeing" itself.[34] I labor to put solidarity tourism in Palestine in conversation with research on domestic tourism's role in race making in the United States, militourism, and the intersections of tourism and US empire.[35] Indeed, this project emerged in American studies and has remained invested in studying the structuring forces of US empire, militarism, and war making, naming and writing against the unconditional support of the United States for Israel and charting the movement—and potential movement building—of US tourists. Further, careful ethnographic, archival, and interdisciplinary studies of forced migration, diaspora, war, occupation, and exile guide my understanding of not only how solidarity tourism functions in Palestine in a context of past and present displacement but also how the displaced are asked and expected to narrate their stories.[36] At the same time, I follow those scholars who have recently asked *if* tourism *can* advance an anticolonial and antiracist praxis.[37] I explore the contradictions, exploitations, and voyeurism that inhere in solidarity tourism, alongside the strategic uses of mobility in a context of restricted movement and the moments when tourism functions, if only aspirationally, as a site of anticolonial praxis.

Palestine has long been a historic site for tourism and the study of tourism, from colonial land surveys to the many forms of fiction that justified colonial pursuits in Palestine in advance of colonial acts—across multiple historical periods and under different colonial powers.[38] There have also been those who researched regional tourism in the aftermath of World War I, when British and French mandates partitioned the Ottoman Levant, some of whom focused on Zionist tourism to Palestine and some of whom focused not on tourism to Palestine but on Palestinian tourism to neighboring countries in the region.[39] In describing the role of tourism in Israel's occupation of Palestinian land—a history of the colonial present that this book centers—there is a great deal of scholarship and reporting that details how, since the establishment of the state, Israel has deliberately and strategically monopolized the tourism sector at the same time that it has expropriated land, homes, and businesses from Palestinians.[40] Scholars have also analyzed the tourist industry's role in the "business of peace," the "consumer coexistence" that shaped the Oslo period, and the role of domestic tourism in shaping Israeli national identity.[41] There is also an emerging body of literature on "alternative" tourism in Palestine/Israel, which I refer to here as solidarity tourism.[42] Some of this work tends to excoriate solidarity tours for clashing with the goals of locals, or celebrate alternative tourism's role in the Palestinian economy, or otherwise assess whether solidarity tourism "works" in its capacity to change hearts and minds. I learn from and engage with these extant studies, but rather than advance an evaluative claim, I analyze *why* Palestinian organizers are choosing tourism as a vehicle for activism and *how* organizers are negotiating, and even utilizing, the asymmetries that inhere within their profession.

Undergirding my reading of solidarity tourism across each of these fields is also the feminist critique of epistemic violence, or violence at the site of knowledge production. I show how violence at the site of knowledge production *shapes* solidarity tour itineraries. On solidarity tours, Palestinians are expected to provide evidence of their own, extremely well-documented dispossession against a constellation of US and Israeli state-sanctioned narratives that have rendered them unreliable narrators. For this reason, pivotal to the feminist analytics that shape this work is a feminist citational practice that not only centers women of color but specifically centers Palestinian authors. Following Sara Ahmed's contention that citation is a "successful reproductive technology, a way of reproducing the world around certain bodies," this book is built on a citational practice that honors the intellectual labor of women of color and structured by a commitment to citing Palestinians—both scholars and interviewees—as theorists of their own conditions.[43] In addition to describing the restricted mobilities and fragmented narrations of tour guides, I also describe the movement and listening practices of US tourists. I write about how

Indigenous guides and organizers structure their itineraries and how tourists move on land that is not their own; my work here is thus shaped by women of color feminist analyses of race and mobility, feminist and queer scholarship on US racism within its borders and within its imperial reach, Indigenous studies research on the shared logics and practices of settler-colonial states, and feminist analyses of the death-dealing violence that feminism without intersectionality and devoid of critiques of militarism can enact.

Further, coupled with Edward Said's contention that citational practice is central to the circulation and repetition of Orientalist knowledge production, this book is structured by a citational practice that *cites Palestinians*.[44] In writing about solidarity tourism in Palestine, I am writing about a phenomenon that has too often been shaped by tourists' refusal to read or cite Palestinian scholarship on their own displacement. Tourists articulate a desire to *see* instead of *read*, to allow witnessing to stand in as an alibi for research. For this reason, central to my political and intellectual project is a commitment to citing Palestinian authors, theorists, scholars, journalists, artists, novelists, tour guides, farmers, and shopkeepers. Palestinian intellectual production animates this work; Palestinian descriptions of settler colonialism—when it does and does not travel by that name—shape how I read the landscape and those who traverse it. In this way, Palestinian literature on their own displacement, and Palestinian tour guides' descriptions of their own labor, is the theory on which this book hinges.

For this reason, in my research, I also crafted a feminist ethnographic practice not only in the subjects I chose to interview but also in how I chose to interview them. In my interviews, I did not ask Palestinians to relive their trauma of displacement in their retelling. I did not ask them to share their wounds with me for my (and my readers') consumption. I did not ask them to share with me the "authentic" inner workings of Palestinian life or Palestinian thought. I did not ask them to reflect on what Palestinians—as some homogeneous singular entity—"think" about solidarity tourism. Instead, following Audra Simpson's theorization of what her interlocutors refuse to say and what she as an ethnographer refuses to write, I do not tell a story here that recovers a singular Palestinian "stance" on solidarity tourism; nor do I tell a story that asked my interlocutors to rehearse their own trauma of exile. In fact, I show how tour guides also refuse to participate in the performance of reliving their trauma for tourists. Though solidarity tours are, in many ways, predicated on the performance of subjection, I document moments when tour guides *reject* performing subjection for the tourist gaze.

My ethnographic practice centered on asking tour guides to tell me about their jobs, their daily labor, their thoughts and theorizing on the tourist industry in Palestine, their relationships with tourists, the impetus behind the pedagogical work they do, and the changes they witness in their own landscape. I asked tourists to reflect on the ethics of their presence in Palestine, the asymmetries that shaped their itineraries, what brought them to Palestine, what they brought with them, and what they did when they returned home. In this way, my project is a feminist one not because it centers women, though I interviewed tour guides and tourists who identified as women, men, trans*, genderqueer, and nonbinary. My project is a feminist one because, borrowing from women of color and queer of color writings that underscore the importance of subjectless critique, which endeavors to decenter "women" as the sole subjects of feminist studies, it takes up a feminist analysis that is grounded in the transnational study of race, gender, and settler colonialism and foregrounds a feminist ethnographic and citational practice in its study of the fraught anticolonial project of crafting lives and livelihoods in contexts of state and settler violence.

To demonstrate how and why Palestinian organizers are treating tourism as a viable anticolonial tactic despite the problems that tourism poses as an organizing strategy, I drew from interviews with guides, community members, tourists, and activists and from participant observation of solidarity tours in Palestine/Israel. I interviewed tour guides, rather than directors of programs, to get a sense of what the quotidian labor of guiding solidarity tours looks like, to understand how tour guides differently envision their work, and to explore the tourist expectations solidarity tour guides negotiate on a daily basis. I interviewed Palestinian organizers in the West Bank, in East Jerusalem, and inside Israel to learn more about how they set up their tours and why. I interviewed Ashkenazi Jewish Israeli organizers and tour guides doing work in East Jerusalem and inside Israel to understand how they construct their itineraries and how they see the politics and ethics of their solidarity work. I also interviewed Palestinian citizens in Israel who lead tours to villages that were depopulated in 1948 to gain an understanding of how they see their labor and how they articulate the effects of the work they do. Finally, I interviewed US solidarity tourists across multiple different demographics—white Presbyterian youth ministers, queer Black solidarity activists, tourists who identify as mixed race, diaspora Palestinians returning to Palestine for the first time, for instance—to demonstrate the multiple and varied reasons tourists come to Palestine. The interviews that form the basis of this book thus detail the phenomenon of solidarity tourism at the same time that they disrupt the coherence of "solidarity tour guide" and "solidarity tourist" as its central categories.

Over the past decade, I have participated in one hundred different solidarity tours—day trips to Hebron, thematic solidarity tours of West Bank cities and villages, weeklong advocacy workshops straddling the West Bank and East Jerusalem, bus tours through East Jerusalem, walking tours in villages and city centers inside Israel, and virtual tours to sites in Gaza and elsewhere across Historic Palestine. By Historic Palestine, I mean *all* of Palestine. In studying solidarity tourism across all of Palestine, I am referring to Historic Palestine, a shorthand for the Palestinian lands of what constitutes today's State of Israel, the Occupied Palestinian Territories of the West Bank and Gaza Strip, and the (also occupied) city of Jerusalem. In doing so, I am also refusing to define Palestine solely through shifting definitions and newly policed borders that emerged in 1948, with the Nakba; or in 1967, with further entrenched occupation; or in 1993, with the categorizations of the Oslo Accords. I also treat all of Palestine as occupied, albeit in radically different ways. Tourists, too, learn this on solidarity tours, from Hebron to Haifa, where occupation takes different forms but also works toward the incremental and sustained expulsion of Palestinians from city centers, towns, and villages across Palestine.

This research method allowed me to follow the itineraries of organizers in the West Bank, in East Jerusalem, and inside Israel as they worked to reject the borders and checkpoints crafted to divide them. It also allowed me to detail how guides and organizers collectively attempt to use tourism to both expose the continuity of past and present Israeli settler colonialism and imagine a future without colonial occupation in Palestine/Israel. My research drew from participant observation; interviews with guides, organizers, community members, and tourists; Palestinian cultural and literary production on displacement and return; and archival material activists have compiled in the wake of solidarity delegations to Palestine since the first intifada. In this way, this book is not a straightforward ethnography;[45] it is, instead, deeply interdisciplinary and committed to the ethos that the research questions we ask should determine the methods we use and not the inverse. This interdisciplinary ethnographic approach enabled me to contextualize the emergence of solidarity tourism as both an industry and an organizing strategy and to explore the promise and pitfalls of solidarity tourism as an anticolonial praxis across Palestine/Israel.

As a researcher in Palestine, I traveled with the mobility of a tourist. Unlike my Palestinian colleagues who have been denied entry to Palestine, I was let through after bored and distracted Israeli agents at Ben Gurion Airport engaged in multiple lines of questioning and much confusion as to why I, a young non-Jewish and non-Arab woman, ostensibly straight (a misreading) and unaccompanied, was traveling alone to Israel without a return ticket. Unlike Palestine solidarity activists with less common names and more visible profiles, I was not placed in detention or denied entry. Nor did I receive the stamp, doled out to both international activists and Palestinians in the diaspora, that denies entry to Israel for five to ten years. Unlike the West Bank Palestinian tour guides with whom I worked, I followed the tourists wherever they went and traversed checkpoints, green lines, and arbitrary borders. With barely a glance at my documents, I was (mostly) allowed to pass. My ability to pass through this racialized surveillance and border policing—to be read as solely a tourist—enabled research that would otherwise have been foreclosed. These racialized injustices deny Palestinians the ability to move and live in their homeland and to visit and explore other parts of their own inherited geographies; they also deny many Palestinian researchers in the diaspora the right to do place-based research on their own histories. I thus tell this story as a settler in two places, a non-Indigenous faculty member working on Amah Mutsun Tribal Land at my institutional home of University of California, Santa Cruz, and a non-Palestinian researcher in Palestine who was able to move freely on land that is not my own. My research, in this way, documents, archives, and indicts the shared settler-colonial practices that have enabled it.

A Narration in Seven Parts

Again, in a refusal to tell the story of solidarity tourism in Palestine via a time line punctuated only by 1948 and 1967, I construct a historical chronology in the book that traces the material of contemporary solidarity tours to Zionist land expropriation that began as early as 1908, positioning displacement in Palestine as ongoing and sustained. The book draws from ethnographic fieldwork in the West Bank, in East Jerusalem, and inside Israel's 1948 borders, alongside secondary research on Gaza, yet resists dividing these spaces from one another by chapter and thus mirroring the fragmentation of Palestine itself in book form. Instead, the manuscript begins the story of solidarity tourism in Palestine with delegations during the first intifada but also travels from 1901 to 2021, and crosses borders, checkpoints, and green lines, to narrate the continuities in displacement, sustained exile, and the shifting strategies in organizing against expulsion that have animated solidarity tourism, first as a strategy and then as an industry, in Occupied Palestine. In this sense, my project not only reveals the fragmented terrain to which Palestinian guides invite tourists but also seeks its own alternative structure, beyond fracture and fragmentation and beyond a straightforward chronology, to tell this history.

The first chapter draws from pamphlets, report-backs, speeches, and artist statements from solidarity tours to Palestine during the first intifada (1987–1993) to chart how this phenomenon emerged as a political strategy in Palestine. I show how these archival materials are characterized by a studied—and curious—unwillingness to cite Palestinian literature as well as tourists' need to "see for themselves." I argue that this phenomenon, wherein tourist witnessing functions as an alibi for research, became institutionalized in solidarity tourism before it became a legalized profession in Palestine and persists in contemporary solidarity tour itineraries. In chapter 2, I chart the emergence of solidarity tourism as both a product and a critique of the 1993 US-brokered Oslo Accords and the attendant establishment of the Palestinian Authority and its Ministry of Tourism. In this chapter, I show how solidarity tourism emerged as a viable practice—and industry—for garnering international support for Palestinian freedom from occupation. This leads into chapter 3's analysis of post-Oslo West Bank solidarity tours and the displacement across Historic Palestine that the tours trace, where I focus specifically on Palestinian olive-planting programs that connect contemporary settler destruction of olive trees in the West Bank to the long history of Zionist afforestation in what is now Israel.

Chapter 4 analyzes solidarity tours of Jerusalem as a multiply occupied city. Some of these tours cover the eastern part of Occupied Jerusalem, with settlements extracting land and resources from Palestinian neighborhoods that are not granted municipal services. Others focus on the Old City of Jerusalem, with settlements taking over the top floors of Palestinian apartment buildings and Israeli archaeological and tourist projects excavating the tunnels beneath Palestinian homes. Still others take tourists to West Jerusalem neighborhoods, with Israelis occupying mansions that belonged to affluent Palestinians before their exile in 1948. Together, they reveal three differently occupied sites across the same city, resulting in the combined isolation, fragmentation, and expulsion of the Palestinians who live there.

Chapter 5 takes Palestinian solidarity tours inside Israel's 1948 (and 1967) borders as its subject and describes what the return of Palestinian refugees could look like in this space. Studying tours that span the Palestinian village Imwas, razed in 1967 and now named Canada Park; the Palestinian village 'Ayn Hawd, now Dada artist colony and tourist site named Ein Hod; and segregation in "mixed cities" like Haifa, Jaffa, and Nazareth; this chapter refuses to use "solidarity tourism in Palestine" as a shorthand for "solidarity tourism in the West Bank" and instead looks at how these tours take shape, and what work they do, across Historic Palestine.

Chapter 6 turns to forms of virtual tourism, celebrity tourism, and guerrilla art installations in Gaza, and the response to each by Palestinians elsewhere in Palestine and Palestinians in the diaspora. Charting these initiatives that resemble tourism, forged under the Israeli siege on Gaza that has now lasted fifteen years, this chapter intervenes in narratives that circumscribe Palestine to the geographic borders of the West Bank at the same time that it shows how Palestinians and internationals alike have sought to circumvent the borders erected to sever Gaza not only from the rest of Palestine but also from the rest of the world.

The seventh and final chapter returns to interviews with US tourists about how they interpret the ethics of their fleeting moments in Palestine as tourists and their role as witnesses back home. In this chapter, I focus on the many different "tourists" who participate in solidarity tours, including displaced Palestinians in exile who can only return to Palestine *as* tourists. I detail not only the logistic difficulties of diaspora tourism in Palestine, where Palestinians in exile are criminalized and racially profiled at the airport, detained, deported, or otherwise intimidated into not trying to enter at all but also the joy and trauma diaspora Palestinians experience when they *are* able to enter Palestine via a tour and the many ways in which the tours struggle to make space for this multiplicity. In this way, Palestine, in the story I tell, is not circumscribed by the geographic borders of the Israeli nation state and its Occupied Territories *or* by Historic Palestine. Palestine is, instead, defined by its people, including the six million in its diaspora.

Building from literature in queer and affect studies that has outlined the contradictory project of hope in the face of despair and work on Palestine that has outlined the generative potential of Palestinian cynicism, I conclude the book by exploring the paired questions of hope and futurity as they are articulated through solidarity tourism in Palestine. I call these questions not as a rhetorical device to index themes but as real questions: articulations of a futurity that is consistently under threat of erasure and descriptions of a hope that is precarious but unyielding. I detail not only how tour guides think about their labor in a context in which the "future" of solidarity tourism would render it obsolete but also how they see their work as a potential, if uncertain, safeguard for the future of their presence in Palestine. In this way, the book concludes by demonstrating how Palestinian guides and organizers position hope, like solidarity, as an incomplete and sometimes impossible endeavor, yet one that is altogether necessary.

In total, *Invited to Witness* explores the varied uses of tourism, the strategic uses of mobility in a context of restricted movement, and the shifting strategies of anticolonial labor that converge in solidarity tourism in Palestine. It also explores the contradictions, exploitations, and voyeurism that inhere in solidarity tourism. I look at how solidarity tourism both effects change and traffics in promises of change that it cannot deliver and contains all the trappings of tourism at the same time that it critiques them. Accepting the invitation to *study* solidarity tourism, my work resists easy definitions, and evaluative assessments, of what solidarity tourism is and does. I ask what happens when tourists are simultaneously invited to Palestine and invited to leave, when they are asked to be witnesses yet also asked to interrogate their voyeurism, when tourists and tour guides alike commodify Palestinian culture while resisting its erasure, and when solidarity tourism is predicated on the performance of subjection but tour guides refuse to reenact it for tourists. Refusing the desire, and invocation, for me to position solidarity tourism as either wholly redemptive or wholly exploitative, I instead show how solidarity tourism troubles how we understand both "solidarity" and "tourism," looking not only at the limitations of each, nor only at their radical potential, but at the asymmetrical ways they take shape in settler-colonial contexts.

ONE

THE COLONIAL CALCULUS OF VERACITY
DELEGATIONS UNDER ERASURE AND
THE DESIRE FOR EVIDENTIARY WEIGHT

Charting a history of solidarity tourism in Palestine is a project that unearths its tropes, its rhythms, its repetitions, and its precedent. For that reason, I begin where so many of today's solidarity tours started—with delegations during the first intifada.[1] Delegations during the first intifada were not the professionalized tours they are today. They were informal, clandestine, and, typically, unpaid, since it was only after the US-brokered Oslo Accords that Palestinians in the West Bank were formally "allowed" to be tour guides and hosts on their own land. These tours/delegations/political education trips varied as much as the hosts and delegates who populated them. People came to Palestine to learn more about nonviolent resistance, like the tax boycotts of Beit Sahour and the intifada gardens on rooftops in Bethlehem; they came as comrades, as colonial subjects from elsewhere seeking to craft solidarities; they came as teachers, students, and tourists. While it is tempting to romanticize this moment in the history of delegations as one that was more politically pure and less sutured to "tourism," this kind of nostalgia lionizes a moment when Palestinian hosts were not paid for their labor and international guests brought to Palestine many of the same assumptions, desires, and asymmetrical power relations that they bring with them today.

This chapter takes as its subject one trope that emerged during first intifada delegations and that persists and continues to shape the itineraries of today's solidarity tours: the tourist/delegate's desire for evidentiary weight. Tourists rely on their own experience of witnessing as evidence of the realities of occupation despite the volumes of Palestinian scholarship that have narrated colonial displacement. This desire also persists in tourists' studied—and curious—unwillingness to cite Palestinian literature in what has become a "report-back" genre. In report-backs, witnessing functions as an alibi for research. In this formulation, those who have visited—but are not from—Palestine need not engage with or present their audience with the work produced by Palestinian writers, artists, and cultural producers. Instead, they need only describe what they *saw*. Drawing from archives of report-backs and literature solidarity tour alumni produced during the first intifada, I show how this need to "see it to believe it" became institutionalized—and cyclically repeated—in solidarity tourism before solidarity tourism became a legalized profession in Palestine.

A second, but related, pattern endemic to report-back literature from the first intifada is a trope in which solidarity tourists and delegates describe their time in Palestine as putting a human face to what had previously been abstract. Rather than take this conversion from statistic to human for granted, or as simply a linguistic shorthand for a meaningful experience, I explore what it means for Palestinians to not be rendered human until the tourist witnesses their condition with their own eyes. Both the tendency to believe Palestinians only after witnessing their plight and the conversion of Palestinians from statistics to humans only through witnessing set a precedent for contemporary solidarity tours that tour guides continue to confront. This need to see it to believe it, and to render real what was previously abstract, is born not only out of a long history of Palestinians being considered unreliable narrators of their own condition but specifically, as the interlocutors in this chapter will show, out of a history of US media and knowledge production that routinely invalidates Palestinian narratives of their own displacement. The choice to underscore what tourists and delegates *see* is thus a strategic one, but one born out of the coalescence of racism, Orientalism, and Zionism that has rendered the Palestinian narrator unreliable and the witness objective.

The narratives that circulate about Palestine/Israel construct Palestinians as unreliable narrators, making international witnesses, having seen it with their own eyes, reliable interlocutors, able to translate what they witnessed into truths for US audiences. At the time of the first intifada, Israel both criminalized and penalized Palestinian-led tourism. Palestinian-led tourism was not legal in the Occupied Territories until 1993 with the establishment of the Oslo Accords and its attendant Ministry of Tourism and Antiquities. Palestinian tour guides crafted an encounter that was both dangerous—they invited and hosted tourists at great personal risk to their own lives—and structured by a colonial calculus of veracity that refused to position them as truth-telling subjects. In this way, on these informal, clandestine, and criminalized delegations of the first intifada, solidarity tour guides in Palestine used tourism to intervene in the knowledge produced about Palestine. They also used tourism to refuse to perform (only) subjection for tourists even in a nascent profession that was ostensibly contingent on that performance. Finally, they used tourism to intervene in tourists' tendency to distance themselves from what they witnessed by underscoring tourist complicity. This chapter will show that, during these first intifada delegations, so often held up as a foil to contemporary solidarity tourism, Palestinian guides and hosts, like today's solidarity tour guides, negotiated the unevenness that inheres in delegations of this sort by extending truncated invitations to internationals to come to Palestine to learn from Palestinians and witness their repression while simultaneously reminding tourists of their own role in Israel's occupation and refusing to perform (only) subjection, thus subverting the expectations that tourists bring with them to Palestine. In this way, Palestinian hosts have worked since the first intifada to restructure leftist investment in Palestine through tours; they have worked to turn the curiosity and desire for corroboration that animates solidarity tourism into decolonial investment and praxis.

Witnessing and Its Alibis: On Context and Critique

In 1994, Sherna Berger Gluck, a white Jewish American author, activist, and oral historian, authored a memoir about her time in Palestine between 1988 and 1991.[2] Her book, *An American Feminist in Palestine: The Intifada Years*, traces her experience on four different trips to Palestine, each one lasting between two weeks and a month. She narrates her travels, her time in Palestine, and her often-thwarted expectations of Palestine as she experienced it on these trips. Her book functions as an early, and exemplary, text in what I have come to understand as the report-back genre of solidarity tourism in Palestine. In many ways, it reflects a formula that has become embraced by many activists and travelers to Palestine in the wake of their trips. In what follows, based on both the text and a 2019 interview with the author, I remain attuned to the context in which this book was written, and I also unpack this narrative formula, both for what it reveals about tourists' incapacity to believe it until they see it and for what it reveals about the construction of Palestinian narrators as suspect, only trustworthy if and when their histories are filtered and translated through a US non-Palestinian interlocutor—a construction Gluck both acknowledges and laments having to work within.

Gluck's book was published in 1994. In a blurb for the book, Palestinian scholar and activist Rabab Abdulhadi, then on the national board of the Union of Palestinian Women's Associations in North America and now professor of Race and Resistance Studies and Founding Director/Senior Scholar of the Arab and Muslim Ethnicities and Diasporas Initiative at the College of Ethnic Studies at San Francisco State, called the work "a serious and conscious effort to grapple with the diversity in feminist thought and practice while resisting the imposition of her own brand of 'Western' feminism on Palestinian women." Barbara Harlow, longtime ally of Palestinian freedom struggles and professor of English Literature at the University of Texas at Austin (until we lost her in January 2017) wrote, "The critical questions raised by Gluck—a feminist, a Jew, a US academic and activist—in the course of four visits to the Israeli-occupied territories of the West Bank and Gaza Strip loom no less large and significant, even now as Israel and Arafat's PLO seek to implement the terms of their 1993 agreement."[3] These endorsements of Gluck's text point to its specific contributions at the time of its publication. For Harlow, the book's contributions lie in its sustained relevance on the eve of the Oslo Accords, which would prove to further fragment the West Bank and render impossible a two-state solution. Harlow also emphasizes Gluck's position as "a feminist, a Jew, a US academic and activist," the subtext of which speaks to the narratives that circulate about Palestine and who is read as having the credibility to intervene in them—a facet of "witnessing" that Gluck would speak to in her interview with me. For Abdulhadi, it is Gluck's disciplined attempt to interrogate her ethnocentrism and refusal to write Western feminist norms onto Palestinian women's organizing that is worthy of praise.

Gluck's book emerged alongside a cluster of texts on women and Palestine as well as feminist theory imploring scholars to reject colonial feminisms. Indeed, Gluck's book was published in the same year and amid the same debates in the field as Inderpal Grewal and Caren Kaplan's *Scattered Hegemonies: Postmodernity and Transnational Feminist Practices* (1994), which was, in so many ways, a critique of cultural imperialism in the form and shape of Western women's liberation. It also came out alongside Simona Sharon's *Gender and the Israeli-Palestinian Conflict: The Politics of Women's Resistance* (1995) and Tamar

Mayer's *Women and the Israeli Occupation: The Politics of Change* (1994), which were, in turn, read and reviewed together.[4] Of these texts by Jewish American and Israeli women, Therese Saliba, then a Fulbright Scholar at Bethlehem University and now academic dean of Evergreen State College, lauded Gluck's refusal to draw parallels between Israeli and Palestinian women as though their struggles and the obstacles to their organizing were comparable.[5] Saliba points also to the emergence (and importance) of texts on Palestinian women's organizing authored *by* Palestinians, citing Souad Dajani's *Eyes without a Country: Searching for a Palestinian Strategy of Liberation* (1994), Amal Kawar's *Daughters of Palestine: Leading Women of the Palestinian National Movement* (1996), and Lisa Taraki and Penny Johnson's *Approaching Gender: Studying Gender Relations in Palestinian Society* (then forthcoming).

Indeed, this moment could be characterized as one in which Palestinian women's organizing emerged as a central research topic for scholars trained in feminist studies. In a short but scathing critique in the *Middle East Report* of the efflorescence of researchers and tourists in Palestine in the mid-1990s—one that reads as though it could be written today—Salim Tamari wrote, "There is a substantial amount of money available to people 'doing Palestine,' especially if the focus is one of the current hot topics: Islamic fundamentalism, women's movements, Arab-Jewish dialogue, economic development and health all attract legions of academic and semi-academic hustlers in addition to bona fide researchers. The thin line separating these two groups begins to blur as serious scholars, thirsty for funding, adjust their research to focus on areas that are in demand."[6] Here, Tamari identifies a phenomenon that still shapes the presence of internationals in the West Bank. Citing the ubiquity of foreign researchers hiring local translators, who abandon their own work to get paid for others', Tamari flags how these funding initiatives indeed shape the research questions asked, funneling all knowledge production through limited and ultimately more palatable frameworks. In this way, Gluck's book appeared among others interested in women's movements, part of a robust—in Tamari's estimation, too robust—conversation around Palestinian women's organizing and also deeply self-conscious about the ethics of its own contribution to that literature.

In this context, Gluck's book was a disciplined attempt to intervene in two then (and, often still) prevalent discourses: (1) the ubiquity of feminist knowledge production that eclipsed local contexts and imagined white—and, in the case of Palestine, Jewish—US feminism to have a monopoly on feminism writ large; and (2) the absence of Palestine from discussions about US Left investments in the world. Gluck's text thus makes an important intervention in the

1994 terrain of feminist studies, particularly in positioning Palestine—and not just Palestinian women—as a feminist issue. As feminist scholars and activists argue today whenever there is a bombing on Gaza and an uptick in articles about "womenandchildren," in Maya Mikdashi's formulation, the emphasis on Palestinian women presupposes that Palestinian men are always-already terrorists.[7] Though she set out to work on "women's issues," Gluck, too, wrote about a Palestine that was gendered by colonial appellations that defined Palestinian men as terrorists and Palestinian women as victims *of* Palestinian men and not of Israeli state practice. While she had plenty to say about gender politics in Palestine, she also read the military occupation of Palestine itself—and not just Palestinian women's organizing—as a deeply feminist issue.

While *An American Feminist in Palestine* anchors its analysis in a refusal of "feminist" approaches to Palestine that sediment stereotypes about Palestinian men and privilege critiques of patriarchy over critiques of military occupation, it also evidenced two central tropes that tend to animate the power dynamics of solidarity tours. The first narrative trope is the repeated refrain that tourists, delegates, and scholars could not believe what they saw in Palestine until they saw it. The second narrative trope is the author's description of her time in Palestine as rendering concrete what had previously been abstract. Turning up the volume on the ubiquity and underlying meaning of these two narrative tropes is not to discount the work that these scholars and tourists, like Sherna Gluck, do in the wake of their delegations to Palestine. It is, rather, to call attention to a convention in narrative form that emerges from a milieu in which Palestinians are not believed when they speak. When a tourist or delegate repeats, several times, that they could not believe what they heard about Palestine until they saw it, they are privileging witnessing over research. In this formulation, witnessing *supplants* citational practice. Tourists, activists, and scholars need not cite the volumes of literature Palestinians have produced about their own displacement. They need only describe what they saw. Their witnessing stands in as the "truth" about the occupation, the facts that need to be circulated in order for the occupation to come to its necessary end. The circulation of this formula, without reflection on why Palestinian narratives were unbelievable to them in the first place, can serve to eclipse Palestinian voices and render the tourist as the default expert.

This formula, however, is also not reflective of stubborn defiance or sheer refusal to believe Palestinians; it has everything to do with the urgency of circulating information on the conditions of Palestinians under occupation and in exile as well as the long and storied refusal of the US Left to consider justice in Palestine as one of its central platforms.[8] In her book, Gluck writes with an urgency that employs both of these formulas—"I didn't believe it until I saw it" and "Palestine rendered human what was once abstract"—to make the case that justice for Palestine should be central not only for the US Left writ large but for US feminists in particular. In this way, the tone of her narration is also about audience: her audience is unfamiliar with Palestine; her audience needs to be convinced, and her tool to convince them is telling them what she saw. As feminist critiques of epistemic violence have shown how the violence of knowledge production shapes how we know what we know, I argue that here and throughout this book, the suturing of witnessing to evidence is a central problem of solidarity tourism. What Palestinians confront is not a question of evidence but a question of epistemology.[9] It is not that more facts need to be circulated about the occupation and its myriad forms of violence. It is that Palestinian narrations of the violence they experience need to be believed in the first place.

Shock as Rhetorical Device and the Affect of Disbelief

An early scene in Gluck's book finds her in East Jerusalem in December 1988 and January 1989. This scene is one of many in which Gluck articulates *disbelief* as both a rhetorical device and a depiction of her transition, in Palestine, from disbelief to a reckoning with the narratives she had internalized about Palestine/Israel. She describes shopping among other tourists in the Old City, when Israeli police suddenly swarmed Salah Al-Din Street. She explained, "Suddenly the blue-uniformed police began to unleash a volley of tear gas canisters. People began to scream and ran back down the street or into the shops. Already overcome by the initial release of tear gas, we stood there, confused and disbelieving."[10] She continued, "A shopkeeper who came out to assess the situation on the street rescued us, pushing us into his simple tea shop as he partially pulled down the heavy metal shutter behind him."[11]

As she sat in the shopkeeper's store, wrapped in a *keffiyeh* she had bought in Palestine, she attempted to reconcile her understanding of her situation: "I am fleeing from Jews—Israelis—and being protected by Arabs—Palestinians. Everything was turned upside down."[12] She explained this reversal in clear terms: "In the United States, in the face of anti-Semitism, I had sought solace from other Jews. Never would I have expected to seek protection *from* Jews and be given safe haven by non-Jews, particularly by those who allegedly hate me."[13] Here, Gluck unpacks the contours of her disbelief. She describes the coalescing narratives she had internalized—not only that Palestinians would hate her as a Jew but also the "upside-down" world in which Arabs would protect her from Jews. As Palestinians on Salah Al-Din Street protected her from Israeli police lobbing (US-made) tear-gas canisters into Palestinian neighborhoods and shopping districts, Gluck searched for ways to understand what she at first refused to believe, laying bare two deeply ingrained assessments: that Arab is the antithesis of Jew—rendering Arab-Jews invisible and structuring Jews and whiteness as synonymous—and that Jews always-already need protection from Arabs—bolstering Zionist logics that rename colonial state practice as a "conflict" between "Arab" and "Jew."

Gluck's transition from disbelief to understanding parallels the refrain, repeated by Gluck and so many other tourists, that *nothing could prepare them for what they saw*. In Gluck's introduction to *An American Feminist in Palestine*, written retrospectively, she reflects:

> Our eyewitness tour immersed us in life under occupation and left me feeling quite overwhelmed. It was one thing to see pictures of Deheisheh or Jabalya refugee camps and quite another to slog through the muddy lanes and avoid the patrolling soldiers; it was one thing to hear reports about demonstrators shot by soldiers and another to see their wounds; it was one thing to read casualty figures and another to go to a wake for a youth shot at the funeral of his friend.[14]

This narration positions witnessing as more real and reliable because of its visceral impact. This fealty to witnessing inadvertently constructs scholarship and reporting produced out of and about Palestine as inadequate when compared with a real-life tour. For Gluck, and those who would follow her, witnessing the suffering of Palestinians makes their suffering both real and legible, particularly up against the Israeli state-sanctioned narratives that render Palestinians as either not suffering or, if suffering, deserving of it.

In another example, in reference to meeting internally displaced Palestinians from the village of Lydda (now Lod) in 1990, she writes: "We slogged through the foul-smelling mire that served both as drainage ditch and as a sidewalk and stopped at a few other houses. Reading about the reduced budget for services for Israeli Arabs in contrast to the Jewish population was one thing. Seeing the results was quite another."[15] And, again, when preparing to lead a seminar on feminist oral history at Birzeit University, she writes, "It was one thing to hear about the underground classes and another to participate more directly in the intellectual life of the institution."[16] These declarations, while earnest in their attempt to position the occupation as *real* for potentially skeptical readers, invalidate the volumes of literature produced both about Palestine, and, more importantly, by Palestinians, positioning this literature as less capable of revealing the "truth" of military occupation than American witnessing.

The refrain that it was a superior and more accurate thing to witness Palestinian plight than to read about it circulates in spite of the volumes of literature on Palestinian displacement. As a chronicle of her time in Palestine, Gluck's 226-page book has no citations nor a bibliography. There are footnotes, which serve to explain, for example, the meanings of Arabic words or moments in the timeline of Palestine/Israel. The only scholar referenced in the text is the Israeli historian Benny Morris, and even in his case, she does not offer a citation. This is not an oversight on Gluck's part—it is clear by how she crafts her argument that she is deeply engaged in feminist studies literature and indeed that she has read plenty about Palestine in general ("*it is one thing to read about . . .*"), but she makes a narrative choice to not include Palestinian scholarship in her work. She does not include the Palestinian scholars, lawyers, or journalists whose work she had read and cites only her own witnessing. In doing so, Gluck does not corroborate her own analysis via citational practice; instead, she uses her witnessing to corroborate Palestinian narrations of displacement.

In literature like Gluck's—and far beyond it—there is also a tendency to point to human rights agencies as more capable of corroborating Palestinian narratives than Palestinians themselves. When visiting the village of Jiftliq near Jericho in the Jordan Valley, she reflected on what she had read about the village and what she had heard from her host, Hassan. "It was inconceivable to me that an unarmed village of two hundred families could pose such a threat to the Israelis that it would bring down such treatment. Had I not been reading reports from the human rights agencies, I would have thought Hassan's claims were grossly exaggerated."[17] Here, as much as Gluck is learning from her Palestinian hosts, she still positions human rights agencies as the truth-telling subjects, not the Palestinians about whom they write.

In another instance, a Palestinian mother in Gaza recounted to Gluck the violence visited upon her family by the Israeli military:

> The mother recounted how nine months earlier, carrying her infant in her arms, she was shopping in the open market during the brief lifting of the curfew. A volley of tear gas had been unleashed, and the next thing she knew, the baby was hit in the eye by a rubber bullet. Inexplicably, the soldier who had fired the bullet tried to remove it, an act that might very well have

precluded the possibility of saving the eye. For the rest of her life, Fida al-Sharafi will wear the glass eye, which her *mother took out to show us.*[18]

In a footnote to augment this anecdote, Gluck added, "The mother's account was corroborated by a UN officer the next day."[19] Even here, this literal evidencing, the glass eye on display, this spectacle of the aftermath of violence, is not evidence in and of itself. Or, while it is evidence for Gluck, she presupposes that it will not stand as evidence for her reader. In accounts like these, UN officers and human rights agencies corroborate Palestinian stories for tourists and their audiences, even when tourists are ostensibly in Palestine to learn from Palestinians. The inability of literature, news reports, histories, and images emerging from Palestine and its diaspora—in other words, Palestinian accounts of their own displacement and the violence of Israeli occupation—to prepare tourists for what they witness is intimately related to the fact that they viewed what they had read as abstract before their time in Palestine made it concrete, tangible, and real.

Conversions and the Subtext of (In)humanity

Another central piece of the formula of the report-back genre is the process, for tourists, of reconciling what they witness with what they thought they knew about Palestine. In particular, this process—and the genre it has become—involves tourists' narration of their time in Palestine as concretizing their activism by converting what was once abstract into something concrete. This formula is less a narration of fact than it is a strategy, a move to reach an audience for whom Palestinians are, by and large, numbers in the news. Reflecting on this phenomenon, I want to ask, To whom were Palestinians merely "statistics" before? And what renders prewitnessed Palestinians "abstract"?

During the first intifada, with the routing of tourists through Palestinian homes and hospitals, with Palestinian hosts actually putting on display their maimed and wounded bodies, and with tourists meeting wounded Palestinians eager to tell their stories *and* Palestinians who critiqued tourists' presence in Palestine, solidarity tourism was wrought with the spectacle of visiting war-torn locales and also the imperative of forcing tourists to confront, face-to-face, the destruction caused by their governments. This collision of guiding logics—putting wounded bodies on display while simultaneously asking tourists to consider their role in that wounding rather than gasp at what they are witnessing—resulted in scenes where tourists, including but not limited to

Gluck, repeated the refrain that, now, after their tour, *Palestinians were no longer statistics*. However, the repetition of this refrain is directed at an audience: a reader, a viewer, a listener. In this way, this repetition is not Gluck insisting that Palestinians were statistics before she met them. It is, instead, Gluck asking her audience, by way of a biography of transformation, to consider why Palestinians might remain statistics for them.

During a late December 1988 visit to Dheisheh Refugee Camp, Gluck recalls that her host, Jawdat, abruptly brought her to a home in the wake of a murder. She writes, "Jawdat simply told us we were going to a house where a man had been killed."[20] She continues, "Although we had all heard and read stories about the killings of Palestinians, we were appalled by the story the thirty-four-year-old woman told of her husband's death."[21] Gluck frontloads this sentence, one of so many like it, with a clause that is subsumed by the one that follows it. *Although* she, and the other tourists with her, had read about the killings of Palestinians, it was another thing to meet the family members of those who had been killed. It does Gluck—and solidarity tourists and their guides—a disservice to read a refrain like this as simply an admission that the killings of Palestinians did not appall or move her until she heard their stories firsthand. Given Gluck's travel to Palestine and her life's work before and after, we know her commitment to Palestinian freedom struggles did not begin with her time in Palestine. However, it is important to unpack sentences like these as both rhetorical devices tourists employ to garner the attention of their (potentially indifferent) readers and, simultaneously, constructions of affective hierarchies, endemic to the report-back genre, that position the murder of Palestinians as a backdrop to the transformation of the tourists' understanding.

In more explicit terms, she describes hearing Palestinian stories and seeing a house demolition firsthand as concretizing what had hitherto been abstract. She describes her host, Saleh, and the stories he shared with her as insight into the lives of her hosts while the time they shared together brought their pain into sharp relief:

> Our day with the Saleh family offered us an intimate glimpse into Palestinian life. But the tale of their experience, along with the encounters we observed in Jerusalem earlier that morning, the story of the killing of Ibrahim Odeh, and the sight on our return route to Bethlehem of the hulking shell of an apartment building that the Israeli authorities had demolished, left me numb. I had read reports of the deaths, injuries, and demolitions, as well as accounts of the 1948 refugees, but these had been abstractions. Seeing the

real people, hearing their voices as they told me their own stories, drinking coffee and eating with them, *made their pain more concrete.*[22]

Gluck recounts the numerous machinations of Israeli occupation: expulsions, murder, injuries, house demolitions. Gluck and many of the other tourists I interviewed narrate what they knew about Palestine before they traveled to Palestine as "just" facts, abstractions. In Gluck's narration, spending time with Palestinians—eating, drinking, talking—made their pain more concrete. In this formulation, the pain and suffering of Palestinians is made real through their narration—but not their narration to journalists or their narration in the form of testimony, research, or memoir, only their narration in person: hearing their voices as they told their own stories. Here, Palestinian recitation concretizes their pain for tourists. Only through narration is their pain rendered tangible. This affective hierarchy positions witnessing via tourism as providing access to "the real"—the most moving. It furthermore places the onus on Palestinians to provide more evidentiary weight of their own, already extremely well-documented dispossession.

Gluck narrates for her reader how she negotiated the conversion of Palestinians from statistics to real people. She reflects on her time in Palestine: "The facts and figures about the conditions of Palestinians under occupation were no longer abstractions. The faces and voices of the people with whom I drank coffee and ate were now attached to these statistics."[23] She adds that Israelis, too, were no longer merely abstractions: "Furthermore, the Israeli occupiers were no longer an abstraction either."[24] She continues, "They were the members of the Border Patrol in Jerusalem who stopped the school girls, the couple who performed the bump and grind on the steps of the post office, the sharpshooter who killed Ibrahim Odeh as he stood at the window of his house in Dheisheh, the soldier who fired the rubber bullet that destroyed little Fida al-Sharifi's eye."[25] Gluck describes being moved to anger *through* witnessing, and she narrates this transformation to her reader under the assumption that they can't, themselves, witness. By attaching human faces to Israelis and Palestinians, she explains, she could have clarity about what military occupation looked like, what its costs were, whose lives hung in the balance. The implication, however, is that only through witnessing did they become human.

This is neither to invalidate Gluck's time spent in Palestine and lifetime spent organizing afterward nor to suggest that Gluck, or any other delegate to Palestine, is deliberately working to devalue Palestinian narrations of their experience of colonial displacement and occupation. It is, instead, to ask *why*:

Why is it that tourists routinely narrate that they could not believe it until they saw it? Why is it that Palestinians are rendered "abstract" in these narrations until they are seen? And why do tourists and delegates to Palestine often repeat these tropes in ways that preclude a thorough examination of what these tropes imply? If Palestinian pain and suffering is only made real when an international, particularly US, tourist sees it, how else, other than tourism, are Palestinians supposed to garner international support? This tourist pattern of disbelief, reconciled by outrage, points to how tourists render *incomplete* the volumes of literature produced by Palestinians on their own condition. In this formula, witnessing *completes* this archive. In other words, witnessing corroborates Palestinian historiography.

Near the end of the book, Gluck reflects on her own privilege: the world she inhabited where war felt far enough away so as not to feel relevant and urgent. Reflecting on the news of 100,000 Iraqi troops on the Kuwait border in the summer of 1990, she thinks about the people she met in Palestine. "War," she writes, "was no longer just an abstract horror."[26] She continues, "It had taken on a personal face. I was so concerned about Rayna Moss in Tel Aviv when the news of the first SCUD attack was broadcast. And I worried about Suhara and her family in Jabalya Refugee Camp as the curfew imposed on the Palestinians stretched to forty days."[27] Here, Gluck details the contours of this conversion from abstract to personal. She describes how, after her trip(s), these were not just reports on abstract individuals in a far-away place with no connection to her. Rather, they were reports on Palestinians and Israelis who were potentially friends and colleagues, people she might know or could know, in unsafe conditions with their lives threatened.

Gluck's trip was crucial to her understanding of what was happening in Palestine/Israel at the same time that it enabled her to see clearly the horrors of war. This revelation brings Gluck's insulation from witnessing state violence into sharp relief at the same time that it reveals how Palestinian literature on their displacement circulated in the United States. Gluck's trip was necessary for her to understand Palestine *in spite* of the literature she read, as a scholar, activist, and oral historian, in preparation for her trip to Palestine. This act of rendering incomplete the scholarship on Palestine reflects how Palestinian narrations of their own conditions, especially in the late 1980s and early 1990s, did not circulate widely enough in the United States. And, if they did, as now, they were often met with a request for "balance" in the form of a Zionist counterperspective. Think only of the attacks on student activists leading up to this moment when they dared to equate Palestinian freedom struggles with anticolonial Third World left organizing in other sites. In her history of the Arab American left in the United States, Pamela Pennock charts these attacks on student activists, from the Anti-Defamation League's infiltration of the Organization of Arab Students (OAS) convention to then-Congressman Gerald Ford's attack on Arab students as radical agitators and potential terrorists in a speech to the American Israel Public Affairs Committee (AIPAC). In her archiving of these attacks, Pennock includes New Left flyers likening Palestine to Vietnam, Algiers, and Angola, and describes coalition building between Black radicals and Palestinians but also traces how OAS chapters partnered with Third World liberation campus organizations in ways that were often tenuous, characterized more by shared ideological commitments to anti-imperialism than to in-person coalitional organizing. The broader American Left's commitment to Palestine, she reminds her readers, remained "soft and somewhat perfunctory" at best, with an idealized image of Third World guerrillas that they applied superficially to Palestine in lieu of nuanced historical understandings of the region.[28] For a left, Jewish American feminist scholar like Gluck, grappling with the justificatory logics for Zionist displacement that circulated around her growing up, alongside the US Left's vacillation between indifference toward and romanticization of Palestine, Gluck traveled to Palestine in many ways to set the record straight, for herself and for her readers.

Indeed, in an interview with me in the spring of 2019, Gluck reflected on this moment and the ethical conundrum witnessing posed—and continues to pose—regarding Palestine. Reflecting on her own invitation to witness, she filled out the contours and context of her trip to Palestine. At the time of her delegation, Gluck was a faculty member at California State University, Long Beach. She was active in organizing in defense of the Los Angeles 8: eight Palestinians arrested for McCarthy-era McCarran-Walter Act charges of "World Communism" because of their affiliation with the Popular Front for the Liberation of Palestine (PFLP). Deportation attempts against the two US citizens, who were students where Gluck taught, lasted twenty years.[29] Having started Students and Faculty against Israeli Occupation, she "decided she really needed to go to understand the situation." Setting out to interview leadership in women's activism during the first intifada, she felt a specific responsibility as an American Jew. "I felt like it was important to travel as a Jew," she explained, "so I could come back as a Jew and make my statements."[30]

Later in the interview, reflecting on this—her place as both Jew and US citizen—as a racialized privilege and a responsibility, she explained: "It's clear that we're using [racialized privilege]. And it's the only way to get heard. Especially in those days, more so than now I think. And it's exerting privilege that I don't want to have."[31] Gluck was not unaware of the contradictions of solidarity tourism; nor was she unaware of the weight of her words in relation to those of her hosts. Indeed, she was reluctantly strategic in employing her voice—then and now—as a Jewish American feminist invested in the liberation of Palestine. She continued, "So it's the same thing as the entry issue . . . does not feel good. Yet, would I have been heard? I don't know." Reflecting not only on who is given a platform to speak but also on how people listen, Gluck connected this disparity in privilege and visibility—and, importantly, the veracity granted to her words—to her ability to enter Palestine when so many Palestinians in exile are barred from entering Palestine, even as tourists. She tied this to the ethics of telling these stories at all:

> But then there's the other issue where we never know how the people there feel about how we're representing their story and what they've told us. And that's always the moment with oral history generally. . . . You know, even the way they responded to me was again "because you're a friend and we trust you, it helps get our message across," but it doesn't tell me how they feel about it. I mean, I felt good that they didn't object to anything, but is it just one more way that they're being objectified? Even though they know that it is important for their story to be told and they trusted me to tell it, there's still that uneasy feeling.[32]

Rather than offer an analysis of Gluck's text that is either performatively critical or unmoored from the context in which it was produced, the ethics that went into the writing, the struggles over what to include and what to eschew, I want to read it alongside the genre of the report-back. It is an uneasy genre; it is a strategy reluctantly employed; it is an uncomfortable performance. It is also an act that—knowingly and reluctantly—both deploys and relies upon the racism it critiques.

The report-back traffics in a tacit and shared understanding that witnessing supplants the extant archive of Palestinian displacement. It relies on an understanding that the words of the witness to Israeli state violence carry more weight than those of the Palestinian victims of that violence. And it circulates and recycles the tropes that state violence in Palestine cannot be understood until it is *seen* and *felt*, which invalidates any retelling that is not paired with witnessing, at the same time that it successfully and strategically intervenes in narratives that justify the colonial and military occupation of Palestine. To offer only a wholesale critique of the report-back genre undercuts the labor of guides and hosts, and the thoughtfulness of tourists and delegates. Yet it also undermines Palestine solidarity work to obscure the hierarchies of the genre and ignore the narratives it repeatedly and routinely sediments.

Witnessing and/as Corroboration

Gluck is not alone in her reflections on her time in Palestine during the first intifada *making real* Palestinian histories. In the edited volume *Occupation and Resistance: American Impressions of the Intifada*, curators, organizers, and artists share their reflections on their delegation to Palestine between March 28 and April 24, 1989. Writer and curator G. Roger Denson begins the volume with an essay titled "Know Thine Enemy: Americans Face the Palestinian Intifada," which immediately flags the construction of Palestinians as "enemy" and uses the verb "face" to index Americans confronting Israeli state violence as something they would prefer to ignore and something in which they are deeply implicated. He, too, describes the conversion of Palestinians from statistics to human beings. Denson first writes, "Before making the trip, the Americans knew only statistics. These numbers show that between December 7, 1987, at the beginning of the intifada, and April 1989, 681 Palestinians from the West Bank and the Gaza Strip had been killed. Another 34,000 were listed as wounded, 5,800 permanently disabled, 30,000 detained or imprisoned, and 3,700 miscarriages reported as a result of the gas."[33] He continues, underscoring the complicity of the US delegates and the US citizens who would potentially view the art exhibit and read the edited volume: "What every American should know is that this had been accomplished with the aid of 3.1 billion American dollars—1.8 billion of which is apportioned strictly for military operations—in addition to American-made artillery."[34]

Having outlined the statistics and underscored the US role in Israeli military occupation, Denson describes how the delegates came to understand what they were witnessing:

> But by the trip's end, these statistics no longer reflected *impersonal numbers*; now the Americans thought of the statistics entwined with the names, faces, families, homes, and friends they met while in the West Bank and Gaza Strip. One of the delegates, Deborah Willis, a writer and exhibitions coordinator at the Schomburg Center for Research in Black Culture, noted, "the news never gave the names or showed the faces of the Palestinians. But on the trip, everything was one-on-one. I saw people's faces and knew

their names. I heard their stories personally. Some of the Palestinians even became my friends."[35]

Denson uses Willis's account to narrate how the delegation transformed Palestinians from "impersonal numbers" to people with faces and names. The language of this repeated account of the conversion from statistic to human highlights how forms of war and conflict reporting render invisible and homogeneous those who lose their lives. Deborah Willis points in particular to the US news media and its failure to give names and faces to Palestinians, constructing the population en masse as one uniform group of individuals vacillating between "victim" and "terrorist." On the trip, Willis explains, she began to see Palestinians as her friends. In this conversion, however, the question remains: Why do people in the United States need to *know* Palestinians in the West Bank, Israel, and Gaza to understand their subjection to the military rule that the US bankrolls?

Another first intifada report-back in the archives of solidarity delegations to Palestine pivots to ask how Israelis corroborate the violence they witness. The report describes a weeklong February 1988 delegation of Physicians for Human Rights (PHR) to Gaza. The delegates included twelve Israelis—ten physicians and two psychologists. Reflecting on their delegation, the authors explain, "The stories are difficult, and even we, who listen with some suspicion and reservations, are unable to deny them."[36] Readily admitting their suspicion, these Israeli doctors also admit their desire to ignore the conditions to which their government subjects Palestinians in Gaza. Even more, they describe the revelation that they have not, before now, actually listened to Palestinians. "We have been sitting in Gaza for three hours now," the report-back continues. "Some of us are very surprised and have a first experience: 'For the first time I hear a Palestinian who is prepared to recognize us and make peace with us.' Is it possible that we have not heard this until now?"[37] The report continues, articulating the Palestinians' response to their shock. "The Palestinians cannot believe their ears: 'We've said this many times, in different ways, the PLO as well, it's not possible that you haven't heard. You didn't want to hear!'"[38] Here, Palestinian hosts in Gaza ask Israeli delegates to directly confront the politics of their surprise: What does it mean that they are shocked when they see the conditions in Gaza hospitals? What does it mean that they are experiencing as a "first" the notion that many Palestinians, in 1988, want to recognize Israel and live in peace with Israelis? Their Palestinian hosts extend them the generous reminder that they have not wanted to hear Palestinians, that they have ignored both the conditions in which Palestinians in Gaza live and Palestinians' desire to coexist in real and just peace with Israelis.

Palestinian tour guides and hosts, as a practice, repeatedly negotiate tourist shock. Tour guides routinely confront tourist surprise and calmly repeat the same stories they have been telling for decades. The patience, and indeed creativity, required to find ways to help tourists—Israelis, in this case, but far more often internationals—confront their own ignorance and inaction and recalibrate these tourists' desire for *knowing* into a desire for *doing* has marked Palestinian delegations since the first intifada. Yet, during the first intifada, tour guiding was prohibited and heavily policed; Palestinians were not allowed to be hosts, and retribution could be meted out in the wake of tourist delegations. It is thus worth asking how and why Palestinians during the first intifada took on this precarious labor, in spite of the repeated act of witnessing their own conversion, in tourists' eyes, from statistic to human.[39]

The Cost(s) of Delegations during the First Intifada

The intifada years, beginning December 9, 1987, and ending September 13, 1993, were years in which Palestinians in the West Bank and Gaza looked not to Palestinian leadership or to solidarity from Arab states but to each other for anticolonial movement building. Occurring twenty years after the 1967 war and subsequent occupation of the West Bank, Gaza, East Jerusalem, the Sinai Peninsula, and Golan Heights, the first intifada was made famous by strikes, boycotts, demonstrations, and coordinated popular organizing against entrenched Israeli settler state practice, warfare and its aftermath, and sustained land expropriation.[40] The year 1967 also marked a sea change in both US foreign policy and the US body politic's engagement with the question of Palestine.[41] In particular, as Melani McAlister has labored to show, Israeli state expansion through the 1967 War—named the so-called Six-Day War to celebrate the swiftness of Israel's "military prowess"—marked a critical juncture in bolstering Ashkenazi Jewish American claims to both whiteness and a form of "masculinization" defined by Israeli military gains, a racialized and gendered allegiance to US and Israeli militarism amid the perceived failures of the Vietnam War.[42] In this way, the 1967 War served assimilation efforts by (white) American Jews in the wake of palpable antisemitism in the United States and via a proxy relationship to Israel that saw Israeli military "gains" as making up for US military "losses." This context reveals the deeply racialized and gendered political investments in Israeli state practice mediated by US popular culture and bolstered by US foreign policy; it also reveals the terrain to which delegates like Gluck traveled, working not only to disrupt Zionist allegiances to which they had become acculturated but also to craft alliances with Palestinians against more rewarded investments in whiteness and masculinized militarisms.

At the same time, as they are reflected in tourist report-backs from the 1980s and 1990s, during the intifada years Palestinians put themselves in danger to lead delegations and guide tourists toward rejecting both Zionism and US and Israeli state-sanctioned narratives about Palestinians. As Israel criminalized Palestinian-led tourism before the Oslo Accords in 1993 and forbade Palestinians from being legally sanctioned guides of their own territories, Palestinians led delegations at great personal risk. Repercussions for hosting tourists included lengthened curfews and retaliatory attacks on villages suspected of hosting tourists, sometimes resulting in the imprisonment and even deaths of Palestinian hosts. Tourists' report-backs, both in and beyond Gluck's, include narrations of ducking past Israeli guards near refugee camps in the West Bank, clandestinely hurrying through alleyways in Gaza, and seeking shelter in storefronts to get away from tear gas and not be seen by Israeli soldiers.

After visiting Dheisheh Refugee Camp in the central West Bank, Gluck notes that the Israeli army, even in the absence of a formal curfew, would declare an area a "closed military zone, especially as a way to keep out foreign observers."[43] Referencing the racialized difference in the repercussions for this transgression that would be felt by her versus those that would be felt by her host, she writes, "They probably would have done no more than expel us from the camp, but *Jawdat might have been detained and even imprisoned again.*"[44] While she would merely be kicked out, her guide Jawdat could have been detained and imprisoned yet another time. On a return trip to Gaza in June 1989, she writes, "If I were detected, it would mean trouble for all of us: the camp would very likely be punished by the imposition of another curfew, and I would surely be escorted out."[45] In each of these scenarios, Gluck reflects on what would happen—to both her and her hosts—if she were caught on a solidarity tour of Palestine. She acknowledges that the personal risk to her—being escorted out of either the camp or out of Gaza or Palestine/Israel altogether—is far smaller than that which would be experienced by Jawdat or the refugee camp they visited in Gaza.

In another example, Gluck describes an early morning visit from one of her host's neighbors in Kufr Nameh in the summer of 1991. Upon hearing the neighbor knocking frantically at the door, Gluck mistook her visit for a raid. Reflecting on her own fear, she explains the following:

While I feel the same visceral fear whenever I see soldiers or police amass anywhere, it was also a much more complex reaction. True, I was concerned that my presence might bring retribution on my hosts. But I also believe that I had not totally stilled the little voice that I had heard since childhood, the one that warned me not to betray "my people." At some level, regardless of how righteous I felt, I was not fully prepared to be discovered there by other Jews.[46]

Gluck's analyses mirror the multifaceted, complex, and contradictory ruminations of solidarity tourists writ large. Her concern for her hosts, and the violence that might be visited upon them in the wake of her visit, is, she admits, subsidiary to her concern that she would be found: a Jew among Palestinians. Gluck's reflections are unfiltered and honest; she readily concedes that her concern about retribution was secondary to her concern of being discovered by "her people," with the phrase in scare quotes. Her sentence structure, "*True, I was concerned that my presence might bring retribution on my hosts*," reveals how many solidarity tourists during the first intifada saw clearly that their presence in Palestine was not an innocuous learning expedition. It was an invitation on the part of Palestinians, at the expense of retribution, where tour guides negotiated this risk and danger on a daily basis and ultimately bore the cost for guiding tourists through the occupied West Bank.

Palestinians who hosted thematic delegations during the first intifada also experienced Israeli retribution in the aftermath of the tours. On March 27, 1988, for example, after a tour of Birzeit University where several academics gave talks, including well-known scholars of Palestine/Israel like Zachary Lockman, Israeli soldiers shot and killed two Palestinian youth from Salfit.[47] A 1988 *Al Fajr* piece documenting the bloodshed in the wake of the conference cited an Israeli army spokesperson, who explained that "clashes developed" after the army attempted to aid a group of tourists that had mistakenly entered the town. Following their visit, the scholars insisted that the violence against Palestinians in the wake of their tour was unprovoked and indeed instigated by the Israeli army, which had been surveilling them via helicopter since they entered the village. Zachary Lockman spoke at a press conference at the American Colony Hotel in Jerusalem on March 28, one day after the murders: "We were outraged by how our trip was used," he emphasized, adding that, in contradistinction to Israeli reporting, the population of Birzeit had been peaceful.[48] Ann Lesch, of Villanova University, added that residents had helped the group clear stones blocking the street so that they could pass.

The following issue of *Al Fajr* covered the conference at Birzeit in fuller detail. Because of the three-month closure of Birzeit, much of the conference was held at the Ambassador Hotel in East Jerusalem. Edward Said, whose family is from Jerusalem, was scheduled to give the keynote but was denied entry to Palestine/Israel.[49] Gaza attorney Raji Sourani was scheduled to present a paper on human rights violations in Gaza; instead, he was placed on a six-month administrative detention order on the first day of the conference.[50] Dr. Haidar Abd al-Shafi, head of the Red Crescent, was prevented from leaving the Gaza Strip for Jerusalem.[51] Many other Palestinians, the conference organizers noted, were unable to attend. Even more, "as [participants] presented their papers, they were receiving fresh news of Palestinians being killed or injured, and of curfews and sieges."[52]

The restrictions on Palestinian movement, including the movement of Palestinians in Gaza and in the diaspora, like Edward Said, indeed shape conferences of this sort. The absence of Palestinians from anywhere outside of Jerusalem, the West Bank, and inside Israel's 1948 borders was palpable as the conference-goers gathered at the hotel. Further, not only were Palestinians attacked and murdered in the wake of the delegates' visit to Birzeit, they were attacked and murdered throughout the duration of the conference, with reports pouring in as Palestinian and international scholars presented their work. In this way, the bodies at risk before, during, and after international delegations, of tourists and academics alike, are Palestinian. Those denied entry are, on the whole, Palestinians whose families have already been exiled. In this way, the invitations extended, the entrances denied, and the costs incurred were by differently positioned Palestinians in Palestine, under siege, and in the diaspora.

Other report-backs that make up the archive of first intifada solidarity tours similarly catalogue the human costs of delegations. At al-Am'ari in the West Bank, a Palestinian refugee camp near Ramallah and al-Bireh, Alternative Museum delegates described the retribution that they suspected was meted out on the camp after their visit. G. Roger Denson writes, "It was at Al-Amaari, in the first house to host the delegates, that they met Amel Habid, a sixteen-year-old boy active in the intifada who would end up dead just four days after their visit."[53] He continues, "There was some fear on the part of museum director Rodriguez that the boy may have been killed in retaliation for having welcomed the Americans into his home and informing them of the camp's plight under military occupation. Ms. Sachs, however, stated that she was not given that impression by the boy's family."[54] Palestinian playwright and delegate Magda Dajani reflects on this moment, explaining that the American "obvious entrance" was to blame: "It was such an obvious entrance. We just marched in there, fifteen Westerners."[55] "Gradually," Denson concludes, "the delegates realized they might be endangering the Palestinians when taking such liberties."[56] While impossible to ascertain direct causal relationships given the ubiquity of Israeli military violence, narrations via witnessing and speculation of Palestinians experiencing retribution in the wake of delegates' visits to the West Bank pepper solidarity tour report-backs during the first intifada.

Roadshows, Solidarity Tourism, and Spectacle during the First Intifada

In Gaza, too, Palestinians who hosted tourists were subject to retribution. Writer and Schomburg Center exhibition coordinator Deborah Willis explains that "the residents had no preparation at all for their arrival and didn't trust the delegation."[57] She recalls the resentment expressed by a Palestinian woman in Gaza toward American delegates. Willis remembers: "One woman came to a few of us as we were on the beach. She didn't like the fact that some of us were taking photographs and asked in an irritated manner, *'What is this road show all about? This isn't a picnic here. Why are you in our homeland?'*"[58] Here, Willis describes a Palestinian woman refusing to play the role of the host, refusing to perform subjection for tourists, and refusing to congratulate American tourists on their presence in Palestine.

Further, this (nameless) Palestinian woman in Gaza calls attention to solidarity tourism's role in rendering Palestine a spectacle: *What is this roadshow all about? This isn't a picnic here.* The report-back continues to explain that "once delegates left, the soldiers would enter the camp and punish the people who lived there."[59] Even more, Willis explains, "Once a television crew had come into the Beach Camp and filmed. After the crew had left, the soldiers came into the camp and a child was killed. The camp's residents thought the killing was the result of the television crew's visit. The woman told us that they didn't need the media there and they didn't want the media there."[60] Willis's repetition of this Palestinian woman's words, and the fact that she herself is not interviewed here, speaks to how there was (and is) no "Palestinian consensus" on the futility or efficacy of solidarity tours. In this scene alone, there are Palestinians inviting internationals and leading delegations, Palestinians hosting delegates, Palestinians critiquing international presence, and Palestinians from the diaspora on the delegations themselves. Some Palestinians across Palestine invited tourists to witness the clandestine businesses, alternative farming practices, and daily resistances of the first intifada, and some Palestinians across Palestine resented international presence in their homeland, not only for its potential futility but also for the retribution it brought upon its hosts.

On solidarity tours during the first intifada, delegates described their outrage, like Zachary Lockman, at the cynical ways that the Israeli military used their presence in Palestine to punish Palestinians. Palestinians hosted tourists at great personal cost to themselves and their communities. Like today, not all Palestinians were willing to host delegates, nor were they all in support of the project of inviting internationals to Palestine to witness the devastation wrought by the Israeli army with US-made weapons and US support. Yet those Palestinian guides and organizers who *did* invite tourists did so, notwithstanding the risk to their own lives, to underscore the complicity of US tourists in their suffering and to ask tourists to confront the violence visited upon Palestinians in their name. And on these first intifada delegations, questions of complicity and reparation took center stage as Palestinian hosts and US delegates, respectively, and sometimes collectively, envisioned reparation in Palestine, asking us to consider where, if anywhere, tourism fit into this vision.

Tourists, among them scholars, colleagues, friends, and delegates like Sherna Gluck, brought (and bring) with them a host of motivations as varied as sheer curiosity, thrill-seeking impulses, putting a "human face" to "abstractions," intervening in knowledge production about Palestine that invalidates Palestinian perspectives, corroborating Palestinian narratives, and seeing Palestine firsthand to legitimate antioccupation and anti-Zionist organizing back home. For this reason, hosts, unwilling to wash their hands of tourists' misguided intentions or uninformed questions, consistently seek ways to intervene in delegates' expectations of what they will find, and what they are there to learn, in Palestine. During first intifada tours in particular, tour guides consistently sought ways to intervene in delegates' expectations. They did this, first, by subverting spectacles of suffering into invitations for US travelers to participate in potential acts of reparation, and, second, by underscoring Palestinian joy. Here, I take one staple "destination" on solidarity tours and delegations during the first intifada: Palestinian hospitals. More than just war tourism, these hospital trips were characterized by voyeurism, subjection, and subversion; they were moments when tourists gawked at Palestinian injury and simultaneously moments when Palestinians, instead of performing solely subjection for tourists, invited tourists to both participate in their sustenance and partake in their cultivation of joy under occupation.

In *An American Feminist in Palestine*, Gluck describes her visit to al-Ittihad, a private hospital in Nablus. Her first sentence reveals the ubiquity of delegate visits to hospitals: "Al-Ittihad, one of two private hospitals in the Nablus area, is an obligatory stop on any tour of the Israeli-occupied West Bank."[61] The construction of a hospital visit as obligatory underscores one of many differences between solidarity delegations thirty years ago and delegations today: not one of the one hundred tours I went on while doing the research for this book would ever bring tourists to a hospital, not because Palestinians are no longer maimed and injured by Israeli forces (they are), but because many tour itineraries today endeavor to disrupt the voyeurism that can too often characterize solidarity tours.[62] In this, as in organizers' rerouting of internationals in Palestine *from* protective presence and *toward* tourism, solidarity tourism is a shifting and evolving strategy, a pedagogical project that takes inventory of its past flaws and endeavors to move toward a more just enterprise.

In her description, Gluck herself critiques the voyeurism of visiting hospitals: "The visits to the wounded helped us to see the flesh and bones behind the statistics of the intifada casualties; but it was hard to shake the uncomfortable feeling of being a voyeur as the patients exposed their wounds and their amputated limbs and recounted their experiences."[63] This discomfort stayed with her thirty years later. In an interview in her living room, she reiterated, "The hospital visits were probably where you got the most uncomfortable feeling of voyeurism. . . . [They] just felt so voyeuristic and exploitative of the patients and their families. Very often the family member was there too. And it felt . . . Like I a couple of times would leave the room. Not just because of how awful it was, but how voyeuristic it felt."[64] In the book, she describes these visits in more detail:

> An old, ill equipped facility, it reminded me of Cook County Hospital in Chicago forty years ago. The hospital was crowded with shooting and beating causalities of the *intifada*, young and old, male and female. While the older victims were angry and bitter, there was still a kind of innocent sweetness about the younger ones, like the ten-year-old and the twelve-year-old who shared a room with several adult patients. Both were victims of high-velocity bullets. The younger boy had a cast on his arm, the older boy, one on his leg. Nuzzling up against his cast-covered leg was the spotted white hospital cat the boys had adopted. Posing for a picture, the ten-year-old grabbed a newspaper and carefully folded the front page to display a photograph of Yasir Arafat. With his free arm he made the "V" sign.[65]

The description of (some) Palestinians as "bitter," or more specifically, the comparison between innocent/welcoming Palestinians and bitter/angry Palestinians, is threaded throughout many solidarity tour report-backs. Though US tourists repeatedly describe US complicity in Israeli occupation, the devastation wrought by the Israeli military and US weapons, and the conditions of life under occupation, these tourists still frequently resort to descriptors that construct Palestinians who are not excited at international presence in Palestine as excessively resentful, bitter, and angry. Yet there is also something else in Gluck's description: rather than performing subjection and victimhood for the camera, this ten-year-old Palestinian boy performs pride and victory. Gathering up his affections—the stray hospital cat and newspaper pictures of Yasser Arafat—this Palestinian youth poses triumphantly, performing joy and pride rather than despondency and subjection. In this small way, he narrates the terms of his representation, and Gluck archives his representation on his terms, even as he remains the subject of a voyeuristic hospital visit.

Gluck's next description, echoed in several other report-backs from the era, underscores one surprising phenomenon that characterized first intifada solidarity visits to Palestine. Frequently, while Palestinians were sharing stories of their injuries with tourists and displaying their wounds, tourists were invited, and/or sometimes felt compelled, to donate blood to wounded Palestinians. Gluck, for one, writes about visiting hospitals during her time in Palestine to donate blood alongside descriptions of the health committees mobilized in response to the intifada, which trained thousands of people to administer first aid and blood-typed tens of thousands of people to prepare for the necessity of blood transfusions resultant from serious injuries.

In a 1989 article titled "From the Diary of an American in Occupied Palestine" in the *Link*, a journal published by Americans for Middle East Understanding, the (anonymous) author describes giving blood to a youth shot by an M-16 in the village of Birzeit: "He was in critical condition and needed blood. We went. The youth had been in the operation room for over four hours and he had already used twenty-five pints of blood from twelve donors."[66] She describes waiting in line to donate among Palestinians and internationals, since "community blood-typing for such emergencies had mobilized dozens more who were ready to donate."[67] She continues, "The room was filled with people anxious to give their blood. We waited our turn."[68]

In *Occupation and Resistance*, C. Roger Denson describes participants on the artists and activists delegation giving blood while in Palestinian hospitals. He describes a twelve-year-old boy who had been shot in the back while playing soccer: "He was brought into the emergency room still clutching his soccer ball,"[69] a description that, for today's readers, brings to mind Ismail, Zakaria, Ahed and Mohamed Bakr, four cousins between the ages of nine and eleven murdered by Israeli forces while playing soccer on a Gaza beach in 2014.[70] The delegates watched from the ICU as the surgeons attempted to remove the bullet. "Outside the corridor," Denson explains, "his mother wept and talked with some of the Americans who chose not to watch."[71] Many delegates broke down in outrage. "Some artists," Denson continues, "were so moved that they volunteered to give blood to the hospital."[72] One photographer, Gary Nickard, claims: "I had never before given blood. . . . But I had never before been faced with such tragedy. I felt that I had to do something because I was so appalled. I just couldn't stay there and do nothing."[73] Here, Nickard transforms his feelings of outrage and helplessness into *doing something* while witnessing. He simultaneously positions Palestine as the first time he is confronted with tragedy of this magnitude, which speaks to his own insulation against suffering in the United States.

Denson provides further context for this phenomenon of delegates and tourists, in outrage and solidarity, donating blood to Palestinians in the West Bank:

> In most of the West Bank, blood is an essential resource guarded cautiously by the Palestinians. West Bank medical professionals are so afraid that the Israeli military patrols will confiscate any blood supplies found on a hospital's premises that blood is, instead, kept in floating blood banks. Such banks are mobile, never kept in one spot, and are always ready to transfer within the Occupied Territories. Hospitals also keep lists of donors who profess readiness when and if their blood is needed.[74]

For this reason, delegates, when able, were encouraged to donate blood to evade Israeli regulations on sustaining Palestinian life. While solidarity visits to hospitals are no longer obligatory, or even offered, this first intifada ubiquity of Americans donating blood to Palestinians wounded by US weaponry deployed by Israel raises a different set of questions. What does it mean for US citizens, upon witnessing the injury done with their tax dollars, to donate blood to injured Palestinians? Can this act—though motivated by a guilt that tourists continue to articulate as they describe their time in Palestine—potentially be understood as a step, if meager and fraught, toward reparation? This act, which could be characterized as a mobilizing rather than stultifying guilt, is one where Americans, recognizing both their role in the devastation they are witnessing and circumventing the restrictions Israel places on Palestinians helping other Palestinians live, take from their own bodies to sustain Palestinians, to offer what they can in Palestine in spite, and perhaps because, of the other kinds of injuries their presence in Palestine may be causing.[75] They also donate blood to negotiate their own "ugly feelings" around the voyeurism endemic to tourism, which feminist theorist Sianne Ngai defines as negative affects marked by a *suspended agency*.[76] What, then, to make of this agential act amid the other simultaneous, and violent, acts of international tourists watching the spectacle of Palestinians having their wounds dressed and their bodies salvaged?

While tourists did not expect to give of themselves while in Palestine, neither did they expect to be "confronted" with Palestinian joy. While (too) many tourists read this joy as solely a welcome absence of bitterness, tour guides' and hosts' acts of introducing tourists to Palestinian cooking, dancing, gardening, and celebrating is a reversal of tourists' expectations that they are in Palestine to witness abject suffering. In the *Link*'s "From the Diary of an American in Occupied Palestine," the author describes entering the village of al-Mughayer, northeast of Ramallah. There, the first thing she saw was a huge banner draped at the entrance to the village that specifically interpellated tourists. She writes, "A huge banner stretching across the road eases us back into human society [after a length of travel time with solely landscapes] with its friendly, yet defiant greeting: *'Welcome to the independent village of al-Mughayer.'*"[77]

With this welcome to tourists traveling through the West Bank, the villagers of al-Mughayer defied the restrictions placed on their capacity to host international tourists. In this banner, they first stake a claim to their independence, and second exercise their *right to invite* tourists despite Israel's attempts to foreclose the possibility of Palestinian-led tourism. The anonymous author continued to describe the scene: "Children in a house on the hill proudly wave their slingshots in greeting rather than warning. Another one hundred meters down the road a string of flags hangs across the road. Flags and pictures of Arafat are posted on telephone poles along the main street. Someone has even turned the local bus stop into a Palestinian flag."[78] Here, the author describes a scene of Palestinian joy in resistance: a celebration of Palestine under an occupation that wants to eradicate all semblances of Palestinian nationalism. Following the 1967 Israeli occupation of the West Bank, East Jerusalem, and Gaza, Palestinian flags, much like Palestinian-led tourism, were outlawed; the ban on Palestinian flags persisted until after the signing of the Oslo Accords in 1993.[79] Palestinians responded with scenes like this, brandishing the flag in defiance, alongside painting the colors of the flag and sewing Palestinian flags into the *tatreez*, traditional Palestinian embroidery, on *thobes*, traditional Palestinian dresses. Moments after this introduction to the village, the author describes yet another invitation by her host in al-Mughayer. "He invites us," she explains, "to look at the forest of flags marking the town center."[80] In the midst of military destruction of flags and penalization of tourism, villagers at al-Mughayer invite tourists to witness not (only) their suffering at the hands of Israel but also their joyful defiance of its arbitrary rules and their rejection of its colonial prohibitions and appellations.

Everything about these tourists' movement through Palestine at this time was illegal: Palestinians were forbidden from being tour guides of their own territories, yet they regularly hosted tourists—and even hung banners announcing their defiant invitations to and welcome of tourists; Palestinians were prevented from donating blood to one another, yet when tourists came to Palestine, they sometimes donated blood to wounded Palestinians to circumvent these prohibitions; Palestinian flags were illegal, yet they peppered the West Bank and animated both hosts' invitations to tourists and the itineraries of the tours themselves. The politics of invitation in this context belie any claim that solidarity tourism, then and now, is merely voyeurism or inescapably futile. These moments on the tours are not detours but scripted stops on the itinerary. They reveal the multiple ways Israel tried to stamp out Palestinian life and Palestinians; they also reveal how tour guides and organizers mapped out a flawed but meaningful and deliberately decolonial tourism, working to provide not only evidentiary weight of their suffering under Israeli occupation—which tourists expected as part of their trip—but also evidentiary weight of the many ways they were living, and not just surviving, in their homeland.

First Intifada Transactions

In 1999, Edward Said, in collaboration with photographer Jean Mohr, published a photo essay called *After the Last Sky: Palestinian Lives*.[81] In it, Mohr and Said produce an archive of Palestinians living and, in Rafeef Ziadah's words, "teaching life" under occupation.[82] Said explains the reason for the essay, writing, "For it is not as if no one ever speaks about or portrays the Palestinians. The difficulty is that everyone, including the Palestinians themselves, speak a very great deal."[83] He describes, in 1999, the enormous body of literature that emerged on Palestine, most of it "polemical, accusatory, denunciatory."[84] Indeed, he adds: "At this point, no one writing about Palestine—and indeed, *no one going to Palestine*—starts from scratch: We have all been there before, whether by reading about it, experiencing its millennial presence and power, or actually living there for periods of time. It is a terribly crowded place, almost too crowded for what it is asked to bear by way of history or interpretation of history."[85] When Said writes, *We have all been there before*, he is flagging the representational practice—even of the US Left—that positions Palestine as both known and always-already characterized by irrational and uncontained violence. Outlining the purpose of his text—to represent Palestinians living life—he explains, "Yet, for all the writing about them, Palestinians remain virtually unknown. Especially in the West, particularly in the United States, Palestinians are not so much a people as a pretext for a call to arms."[86]

Here, Said outlines precisely the problem from which (past and present) solidarity tourism emerges. Solidarity tourism, in its proto-professionalized form during the first intifada, emerged not because of a paucity of literature on Palestine or a lack of evidence but because of its excess: an abundance of knowledge produced about Palestinians. It is not that solidarity delegates did not read about Palestine; it's that they needed to *see* it despite having re- searched it. This insistence on witnessing, with an industry about to emerge to ensconce it, is, at its core, about Palestinians speaking and not being be- lieved without corroboration. And Palestinians not being believed is due to the imaginative geographies Said outlines here, a Palestine to which everyone, especially tourists, has been before, a Palestine populated by images of a people who "are visible principally as fighters, terrorists, and lawless pariahs."[87]

In this way, tourists' demand for evidence cannot be dismissed as a gauche tourist trait, the "ugly American" personified. This search for evidence lays bare the myriad ways Palestinians consistently labor to intervene in the epis- temic violence that has animated how stories about Palestinians move in the world. Tourists seek, through their time in Palestine, to gather the tools to return home and intervene in the narratives that construct Palestinians as ter- rorists, as ungrateful, as unwilling to compromise. At the same time, tour guides seek, through tourists' time in Palestine, to intervene in the ease with which tourists often want to construct Palestinians as victims and nothing more.

Tour guides during the first intifada—and Palestinians whose homes, cities, and villages were toured—demanded that tourists grapple not just with the question of empathy but specifically with the question of complicity. Tour- ists report-backs from the first intifada are rife with scenes where Palestin- ians (rightfully) demanded to know what tourists would do with what they were learning in Palestine. Sherna Gluck describes a shopkeeper who inquired about a protest she and roughly fifty other Americans had held at the American consulate. The shopkeeper said that was a start but he urged her "to do something about the unquestioned American support of Israel."[88] Gluck recalls that he implored, "Don't they know what is being done to us?"[89] She describes her encounter with another displaced Palestinian, in Lod: "As we were leaving her house, the woman squatter accompanied us to the muddy front yard, beseeching: 'Don't forget about the Palestinians inside Israel. Write about us in the newspaper.'"[90] Here, she explains to Gluck that her job is not done; her work will begin when she returns to the United States in the form of op-eds in newspapers explaining that Palestinian citizens in Israel are not "Israeli Arabs" with comparable rights but are subject to a completely different set of discriminatory laws and foreclosed opportunities alongside everyday racism.[91] Both of these encounters center on the demand that Gluck circulates what she witnessed to audiences that, potentially, do not know. And indeed, Gluck has done a lifetime of this work, as she taught about Palestine, worked with Palestinian students, organized in solidarity with Palestine, and started and ran Radio Intifada, a Los Angeles radio station devoted to Palestine and the region more broadly, for a substantive portion of her career.

Other examples show Gluck and her fellow delegates being excepted from interrogation from Palestinians, allowed to pass, or given items for free under the condition that they would widely publicize what they saw. One narrative, from when Gluck was in Gaza in December 1988, notes that some young Palestinians, who were initially suspicious of the delegates, decided to invite them into the area after talking to the guides:

> As the *shabab* relaxed their stance, the women came out to greet us. They were dressed in the blue-and-rose-striped *thaubs* typical of the region, their heads covered with white, chiffon-like scarves worn in various styles. They exuded strength and determination as they surrounded us, all shouting at once. Their voices sounded angry—it is not hard to detect anger, regardless of the language barrier. But their faces registered friendliness. They wanted us as Americans to do something about the tear gas that our country supplied to their Israeli rulers.[92]

Similarly, at the house of Fida al-Sharafi in Gaza, the little girl who lost her eye when an Israeli soldier shot a rubber bullet at her and then tried to remove the bullet, the mother initially did not want to tell her story. Gluck recounts, "Torn between the futility of *once again repeating the story* of what had befallen their little daughter, Fida al-Sharafi, and the hope that something good might come of their personal tragedy, the couple overcame their reluctance only at the urging of the other women of the household."[93] Here, Gluck again narrates a reluctance, a hesitation, a moment that potentially invites what Audra Simpson calls ethnographic refusal, when the author of an ethnography refuses to supply the reader with every last detail, a display of every wound.[94] Yet these subjects instead invite guests, tell their stories, and allow these entrances in hopes that their narration will not prove futile.

Further, Gluck is reminded in these moments that it is her government supplying the tear gas and the rubber bullets, alongside the diplomatic and monetary support, to the occupying forces. This repetition—a rhetorical strategy that will come to form the crux of narration on solidarity tours—serves a purpose. It is an act of *once again repeating the story* to intervene in the ubiquitous twinned imaginative geographies that somehow simultaneously render Palestinians either victims or their opposite—in Said's words, the historic image of the "helpless, miserable-looking refugee," which has come to be replaced by the image of a "man wearing a *keffiyeh* and mask and carrying a *kalachnikov*."[95] In this way, the book born out of Gluck's trip, along with her lifetime of activism and pedagogy for Palestinian liberation struggles, is her "repayment" for the stories she hears in Palestine, her promise fulfilled to the people who extended invitations to her, who hosted her, and who—at the risk of bodily harm and retaliation and/or the futility of repetition—again shared their wounds and stories.

Invitation, Repetition, and the Genre of the Report-Back

In the report-back genre, the imagined geographies that render Palestine known and understood, as either victim or terrorist or both, meet the solidarity tourist's desire to be accountable to their host. During the first intifada and today, these report-backs take the shape of lectures, articles, op-eds, performance pieces, song lyrics, and art installations. The Alternative Museum's delegation, for example, underscored cultural production in addition to knowledge production. Led by Puerto Rican artist and curator Geno Rodriguez, the delegation sought to cultivate solidarity between groups subject to racialized discrimination, bringing Latino and African American delegates to Palestine alongside first-generation Americans who came to the United States to escape oppressive regimes and dictatorship in their homelands.[96] In Palestine, Rodriguez hoped, delegates would see both commonalities and ruptures between their own experiences and those of the Palestinians they met in Gaza and the West Bank. Further, Rodriguez hoped, the delegates would create art in the wake of their delegation that would not only reflect their divergent and shared experiences of racism, displacement, and diaspora but also intervene in widely circulated images of Palestinians.

The edited volume accompanied an art exhibition by the same name—*Occupation and Resistance: American Impressions of the First Intifada*—housed at the Alternative Museum in New York City in the summer of 1990. New York artist Jay Murphy's contribution to the volume, "The Intifada Makes Many Artists," underscores how this delegation of artists, curators, and cultural workers witnessed the myriad ways Israel attempts to "quash the intifada" by "eliminating exhibition spaces in the Occupied West Bank."[97] Murphy quotes Palestinian artist Adnan Zobidy, who explains that "when political exhibitions can only be held in Jerusalem . . . only the wealthy of the community come."[98] Murphy surmises, "There are less branches out to the grassroots of the intifada."[99] Palestinian art, then, mirroring tourist mobility, circulates in places the artists themselves cannot go. As tourist movement in Palestine/Israel is far more expansive than that of their Palestinian hosts, so too is art. These delegates and artists traveled back to the United States, like Gluck, heavy with the responsibility of producing art that could reflect what they witnessed and the violence for which they were, in part, responsible as US citizens. With Geno Rodriguez as the curator of the exhibit, the artists included Terry Berkowitz, Bill Biggart, Magda Dajani, David Donahue, Ming Fay, Gadi Gofbarg, Tom Hayes, Marylu Meibers, Yong Soon Min, John Morita, Tariq Abu Sammie, Jos Sances, Coreen Simpson, Deborah Willis, and a collective piece by the Break the Silence Mural Project in San Francisco, in the wake of their delegation to Palestine.

Some pieces focused explicitly on the violent crackdown against the intifada and the arbitrariness of Israeli policing. Terry Berkowitz's piece, *Somebody's Brother, Somebody's Son (Homage to Hamad)* (1990), included video stills of youth in Palestine before they were murdered (figure 1.1). The stills show images of Hamad, a sixteen-year-old from al-Am'ari refugee camp, whom Berkowitz had interviewed two days before.[100] Magda Dajani crafted a piece titled *Mona Lisa Minus the Forbidden Colors of the Palestinian Flag* (1990), a mockery of Israel's dictate that Palestinian artists could not use the colors of the Palestinian flag—red, green, black, or white—in their work (figure 1.2).

Dajani's interview with artist Fathi Ghaban, who was beaten and imprisoned for using the colors of the flag, accompanied her piece. Dajana's Mona Lisa is rendered in black and gray, her facial features nearly imperceptible.[101] Other contributions labor to tie their pieces to a message about US foreign policy and unrelenting support for Israeli settler-colonial state practice. Marylu Meibers (*Untitled*, 1990) drew sketches of intifada scenes with lists of violent acts Israel

1.1 Terry Berkowitz, *Somebody's Brother, Somebody's Son* (1990). From Alternative Museum, *Occupation and Resistance: American Impressions of the First Intifada.*

1.2 Magda Dajani, *Mona Lisa Minus the Forbidden Colors of the Palestinian Flag* (1990). From Alternative Museum, *Occupation and Resistance: American Impressions of the First Intifada.*

visits upon Palestinians with the support of the United States: murder, injury, arrests, exile, closures, gunfire, tear gas, military exercises, bombings, home invasions, home demolitions, uprooted citrus and olive trees, land annexed, water diverted to Israel.[102] She writes: "As Americans, we support this outrage by our yearly donation of more than $3 billion to the government of Israel. Let us stop the occupation now. Our money could buy peace for Palestine."[103] John Morita, in *House Demolition II* (1989; figure 1.3), presents a photo etching of Palestinian children superimposed atop a house demolition. The only words accompanying his piece are "Only an informed public can prevent genocide," placing the onus on US viewers of the New York exhibition to prevent the genocide carried out in their collective name.[104]

Still others work to connect racialized violence against communities in the United States to that experienced by Palestinians living under Israeli rule. Deborah Willis references African American traditions of quilting in her quilted collaged piece of dolls, kuffiyahs, and photographs in homage to the mothers

1.3 John Morita, *House Demolition II* (1989). From Alternative Museum, *Occupation and Resistance: American Impressions of the First Intifada.*

who "birthed, raised, and lost" children in the intifada (figure 1.4).[105] Here, she uses the metaphor of stitching to connect African American struggles, and particularly—one can infer—the struggle of losing children to state violence, alongside resistance traditions in the United States, with those of Palestinians across Palestine.

The exhibition ends with a photograph of the mural created by the Break the Silence Mural Project in San Francisco. The accompanying text explains the Break the Silence project, wherein four Jewish women artists from the San Francisco Bay Area traveled to the West Bank and lived with a Palestinian family in a refugee camp in Ramallah: "In a collaborative effort with local Palestinian artists they created six murals and taught art classes as an expression

1.4 Deborah Willis, *Mothers and the Shebab* (1989). From Alternative Museum, *Occupation and Resistance: American Impressions of the First Intifada.*

of international solidarity with the Palestinian struggle for independence and for justice and peace in the region."[106] The Break the Silence Mural Project was founded at the start of the first intifada by a collective of Jewish women artists in the Bay Area—Marlene Tobias, Dina Redman, Susan Greene, and Miranda Bergman—who wanted to support Palestinian freedom struggles by supporting Palestinian artists.[107] Four members of the collective painted the first Break the Silence mural at the Popular Arts Center in Ramallah in 1989.[108] After the Oslo Accords, and the many ways they disrupted Palestine solidarity organizing with false promises of statehood and resolution, the project has since evolved into an artist and activist collective: Art Forces, headed by Susan Greene, which continues to raise awareness about the conditions in Occupied Palestine, including via participation in artist and activist delegations to Palestine today.[109]

Many of Break the Silence's projects were funded by the Middle East Children's Alliance (MECA), an organization that works for Palestinian rights and was itself established in 1988 after one of its cofounders, Barbara Lubin, went on her own solidarity delegation to Palestine.[110] She has since led nearly twenty other delegations to Palestine/Israel, Iraq, and Lebanon.[111] The incorporation of the Break the Silence Mural Project into Geno Rodriguez's exhibition, and the story of its emergence and continued relevance to international solidarity struggles, underscores how, for many, one solidarity trip to Palestine is not the work but the catalyst for the work. It is often the beginning of a lifetime of collaboration with Palestinians in their fight for freedom. Further, it is through the shared conventions of invitation and repetition—inviting tourists to witness and repeating narratives of both displacement and life-crafting—that tour guides seek to intervene not in the silence but actually in the volume of the knowledge produced about Palestine that render Palestinians unreliable narrators of their own condition. This phenomenon takes shape, solidifying during the first intifada, *through* tourism: a practice that relies on non-Palestinian internationals to corroborate Palestinian narration, recycling and intervening in that cycle simultaneously.

The Evidence and Epistemology of Witnessing

Solidarity tourism is in many ways a transactional process in which "evidence" is exchanged for a twinned reckoning with complicity and commitment to intervene in the knowledge produced about Palestine. US tourists during the first intifada were confronted with wounds, injuries, and hospital visits made possible by US-supplied weaponry. They walked through alleyways in Gaza, refugee camps in the West Bank, and forests of flags in Palestinian villages on clandestine delegations that sometimes brought harm upon their hosts. Delegates grappled with voyeurism, and tour guides grappled with tourists' demands for evidence in a context in which evidence abounds. Yet, as was true then and is too often true now, tourists demanded to *see for themselves*, throwing into question the veracity of Palestinian narratives—even in the name of solidarity—and refusing to corroborate those narratives until they witnessed scenes of violence with their own eyes. In response, tour guides and hosts often found ways to both subvert this tourist gaze and unsettle expectations of an endless barrage of suffering.[112] Guides, organizers, and hosts in these contexts redirected the tourist gaze to the tourists themselves, asking them to consider their role in what they were witnessing, asking them to ask themselves why they didn't believe Palestinians in the first place, and asking them to reshape Left investment in Palestine with their words, their art, their performances, chipping away at the images of Palestinians as either terrorist or victim, and nothing less or more, that populate US media.

Positioning the space of the solidarity tour as a way to invite tourists to grapple with what, at first, they could not believe, solidarity tour guides have long participated in a performance of their own suffering that is deemed necessary to demonstrate veracity. This is a product of colonial knowledge production that has elevated Israeli narratives as "truth" and relegated Palestinian narratives to "bias." It is clear, both then and now, that what Palestinian tour guides, organizers, and hosts confront is not a question of *evidence*. Evidence of the violence of Israeli settler colonial state practice is as accessible as it is abundant. What Palestinians confront is a question of *epistemology*. Violence at the site of knowledge production, what women of color feminists have long called epistemic violence, renders Palestinians unreliable narrators of their own histories. This epistemic violence both structures and necessitates solidarity tourism in Palestine.

When I have described my research on contemporary solidarity tourism to US activists and scholars who were involved in these early, informal, and clandestine delegations, or who were not, but look back on them fondly, I often sense a nostalgia for a purer form of solidarity, one less fraught with the commercialization that sometimes characterizes contemporary solidarity tourism. However, what this nostalgia eclipses are (1) the many and varied similarities between delegations during the first intifada and delegations today; (2) the exploitative and voyeuristic shape these tours took, with Palestinians putting their wounds on display for tourist consumption; (3) the violence visited upon Palestinian hosts during these delegations; and (4) the ways Palestinian hosts and guides on these early delegations were not paid for their labor. This nostalgic sentiment is shared by Palestinians who believe that doing this work should be a national duty, given for free, and not a compensated profession. This constellation of different stances toward solidarity tourism in Palestine brings me to another question I am often asked: What do *Palestinians* think about solidarity tourism? This question assumes that thirteen million people across Palestine and its diaspora have reached a consensus on a singular fraught phenomenon. It also assumes that the employed Palestinian tour guide is not representative enough of Palestine, which positions destitution and Palestinianness as merged, authentic, and synonymous.

The activist nostalgia for first intifada delegations, and their accompanied unpaid labor, seeks to create distance between "solidarity work" and its crass cousin "tourism" even though the distinction in Palestine is never quite so clear. While solidarity delegations have changed in terms of itinerary and content, they have not changed in terms of how tour guides grapple with tourists' demand for evidence or how they repeatedly labor to turn the lens back on the tourist. Tour guides, as I outline in the next chapter, continue to repeat their stories of displacement and continue to invite tourists to witness, reflect on their own complicity in Israeli state practice, and acknowledge their own expansive movement amid the growing restrictions on Palestinian movement and Palestinian movement building since the end of the first intifada and the signing of the Oslo Accords in 1993.

TWO

ASYMMETRICAL ITINERARIES
MILITARISM, TOURISM, AND
FRAGMENTATION UNDER OCCUPATION

In 2009, French artist Julien Bousac designed a map of the West Bank titled *L'archipel de Palestine orientale* (The Archipelago of Eastern Palestine; figure 2.1).[1] With a nautical anchor affixed in the upper left corner, the map transforms West Bank cities and villages into islands depicted in different shades of green to signify different levels of Palestinian autonomy. In the bottom right corner, Bousac explains that all areas in Israeli hands—*aux mains d'Israel*—were transformed into the sea, and white space representing Israeli settlements blends almost seamlessly into the sea-foam backdrop.[2] Jericho is its own island far off to the east; Ramallah is an island in the center of the archipelago; and Bethlehem is severed from Ramallah, with the Canal de Jérusalem and the islands of 'Anata and Ar-Ram peppering the waters in between. Israeli nature reserves, designated by green stripes, take up the space of some of the otherwise Palestinian landmasses, and Israeli military roads, signified by dotted shipping lines, function as the only connecting thoroughfares between the islands.

Bousac's map is based entirely on data from B'Tselem, an Israeli human rights organization. It is part utopia, populated by names like the Isle of Olive Trees and Honey Island. It is part dystopia, with dotted lines signifying shipping links that connect all the Israeli ports to one another. It is part maritime war-craft imagery, as tiny blue Israeli warships—*zone sous surveillance*—are positioned everywhere that there were permanent checkpoints in 2009. It also is part mockery of the existing regulatory regime of the West Bank, with tiny palm trees signifying protected beaches and highlighting how Israel uses the discourse of protected land to secure its own space.[3] Bousac's map illustrates—via a military and a tourist imaginary—how the US-brokered Oslo Accords fragmented the West Bank into enclaves separated by checkpoints and settlements that maintain Israeli control over the West Bank and circumscribe the majority of the Palestinian population to shrinking Palestinian city and village centers. His map details the impossibilities of both movement and any semblance of conventional tourism in the West Bank, demonstrating how settler-colonial state practice can create island formations without water, using checkpoints, walls, fences, and military outposts to disrupt any contiguity between Palestinian space.

I begin this chapter with Bousac's map because it asks us to consider the fragmented archipelago that the West Bank has become not just since 1967 but specifically since the 1993 Oslo Accords, which were ostensibly meant to bring an end to the first intifada and facilitate eventual Palestinian statecraft but were in actuality a formalized Israeli land grab. Like Bousac, I, too, want to chart the post-Oslo fragmentation of the West Bank and ask when and how those landmasses in between seas of checkpoints and military roads become navigable, and for whom. In this chapter, I explore what happens when subjects under occupation attempt to circumvent the archipelagic logic that divides them. What possibilities are made both available and impossible when tourism, militarism, and antioccupation activism occupy the same space? I show how, in the context of ever-shrinking Palestinian access to their land, Palestinian tour guides and organizers are using tourism, despite its limitations, to expose the fragmented terrain they have inherited and to attempt to stay anchored to the land they still have.

Drawing from interviews with Palestinian tour guides, many of whom have been organizing tours of Occupied Palestine since the first intifada, I detail how what began as informal, ad hoc, and clandestine tours of the West Bank and Gaza to supporters of the Palestinian struggle has grown into an income-generating, if somewhat provisional, enterprise. I trace how the Oslo I and II Accords, and the attendant establishment of the Palestinian Authority and its Ministry of Tourism and Antiquities, both changed the parameters of what was possible in terms of Palestinian-led tourism in the West Bank and also fragmented Palestinian land, ushered in a period of expanding settlements,

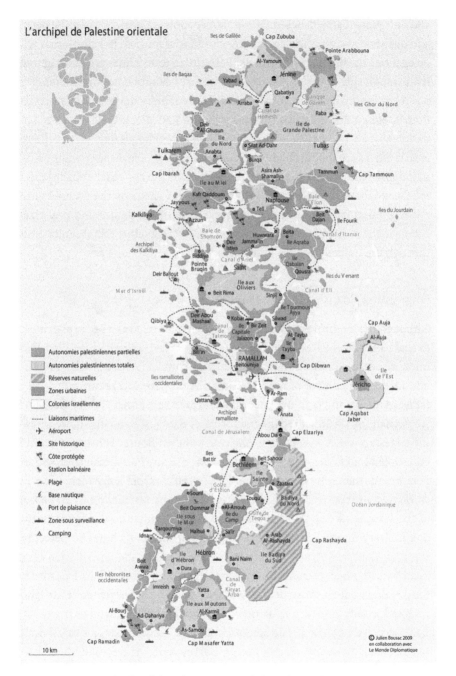

2.1 Julien Bousac, *L'archipel de Palestine orientale* (2009). © Julien Bousac.

and entrenched an aid-based Palestinian economy. I also focus on the deeply and deliberately asymmetrical nature of solidarity tourism in Palestine: as with delegations during the first intifada, Palestinian tour guides are guiding tourists through spaces that, often, they themselves cannot enter in an attempt to use tourist mobility to highlight their own immobility under military occupation. These guides and organizers have chosen to dedicate their energy to solidarity tourism, even when its role in movement building is difficult to delineate and its effects are shot through with contradictions, because they value its role in helping Palestinians—from shop owners to farmers—stay on their land in the face of forced exile. In this way, this chapter focuses on the fragmentation of Palestinian land and the fraught ways Palestinian guides and organizers have sought to demonstrate, negotiate, and work against this fragmentation through the unlikely vehicle of tourism.[4]

Fragmented Tourism in the Post-Oslo West Bank

Although the US-brokered Oslo Accords were presented as a peace plan meant to lead to eventual Palestinian statehood, they in fact splintered the West Bank into city centers under nominal Palestinian control (Area A), villages under administrative control of the Palestinian Authority and security control of Israel (Area B), and land under complete Israeli rule (Area C).[5] As the Oslo II Accords in 1995 sedimented the fracturing of the West Bank into these areas—the largest of which is Area C, or "the sea," as Julien Bousac constructs it and as Palestinian tour guides echo—Israel worked to secure Palestinian land, without Palestinians themselves, and transfer it to Israeli control.[6] Since then, Israel has worked to prohibit Palestinian development and construction in 40 percent of the West Bank and in 70 percent of Area C through legal, administrative, and military means.[7] Area C, under full Israeli rule, constitutes 60 percent of the West Bank.[8] In Area C, 63 percent of the land is under jurisdiction of the local and regional councils of the settlements and off-limits to Palestinians for development or construction, while 2.5 percent is designated "state land," reserved wholly for Israeli settlements, military, and infrastructure.[9] In late 1993, Israel stopped declaring state lands in the West Bank for several years; but in 1997, it enacted a regulation monitoring "survey lands" to keep undeclared lands as government property and enable their use by the state. Now, 20 percent of Area C lands are classified as survey lands.[10] Palestinians living in Area C thus cannot build their homes for fear of house demolitions. Area C also includes 165 "islands" of Area A and B land, the space to which the major concentrations of populations in the West Bank are circumscribed.[11] Ultimately, since Oslo, Israel has consistently worked, through legal, administrative, and military means, to render a Palestinian state impossible by acquiring more and more West Bank land and foreclosing Palestinian use of it.

The taxonomies of Areas A, B, and C, and the subsequent land expropriation by the State of Israel, were not a by-product of the Oslo Accords but were specifically written into the implementation of the "peace plan." Palestinian legal scholar Noura Erakat describes the Oslo Accords as having "engendered yet another specialized regime that has enabled Israel to continue its settler-colonial expansion, this time under the veneer of peacemaking."[12] In Israeli historian Ilan Pappe's words, this veneer of peacemaking produced a solution to a paradox Israel had long sought to solve: "how to have the land without its native people in a world that no longer accepted more colonialism and ethnic cleansing."[13] The solution, then, was to employ the discourse of peace while "creating facts on the ground that lead to the restricting of the native population to small spaces, while the rest is annexed to Israel."[14] In conjunction with annexation, Oslo also introduced closures, curfews, roadblocks, and checkpoints meant to contain and immobilize the Palestinian population.[15] The population of settlements doubled in the years after the Oslo Accords, with Israeli-only roads connecting settlements and severing Palestinian communities from one another.[16]

Palestinian lawyer and author Raja Shehadeh recounts how the post-Oslo militarization of the West Bank was accomplished largely via settlement expansion; he describes how "one hilltop after another was claimed as more and more Jewish settlements were established" on the land that once provided "the setting for [his] tranquil walks."[17] The roads connecting each hilltop settlement bloc—the *liaisons maritimes* in Bousac's formulation—formed, in Shehadeh's words, "a noose around Ramallah."[18] Even more, the violence that accompanied each settlement transformed the tenor and terrain of the land; Shehadeh describes his increasing encounters with militarized violence by both Israeli settlers and Israeli and Palestinian Authority security forces.[19] The fragmentation of Palestinian land brought on by the Oslo process was thus made possible only through the machinations of military occupation: a series of militarized immobilities in the form of checkpoints, closures, settlement roads, "firing zones," and roadblocks.

The "continuity of the settlement enterprise," in the words of Rashid Khalidi, continued throughout George W. Bush's "Road Map to Peace," throughout the construction of the Wall, and throughout Donald Trump's presidency;

and it is now supported during Joe Biden's presidency, most recently with his May 2021 authorization of a weapons sale—in the amount of $735 million—to Israel *during* its bombardment of Gaza.[20] Throughout various iterations of the "peace process," Palestinians have been asked to remain committed to US-led "negotiations." Indeed, as scholar and senior analyst at al-Shabaka Yara Hawari rightly notes, "Palestinians are consistently told that the two-state solution is the only possible outcome and that they must therefore concede on certain rights, including the right of return."[21] Palestinians have thus been expected to sustain a hope that the peace process will yield a discernible improvement in their lives, even as they continue to be told that new Israeli settlement homes will somehow "not affect the peace map."[22] The language of the peace process, not only the expressed goal of peace but also the emphasis on process, is meant to connote motion, produce hope, and foreclose Palestinian demands for resolution to issues that were deemed "final status" by the Oslo Accords, like Jerusalem and the Right of Return for Palestinian refugees. The process, in Edward Said's words as early as 1995, has functioned as a "distortion of hopes and rightful aspirations."[23]

"Israel, Israel, Israel": Wresting the Narration of Palestine from Israeli Control

After Oslo, once Israel lifted the prohibition against Palestinians becoming licensed tour guides of their own land, Palestinians took up tour guiding and work at tourist agencies while they began to professionalize solidarity tourism. Yet, while the Ministry of Tourism focused almost exclusively on promoting national heritage sites—like the Mount of Temptation and the Church of the Nativity—burgeoning alternative tourism organizations sought to focus on the occupation, turning what was once a non-income-generating method of movement building into an income-generating business. This professionalization of solidarity tourism, then, employed the language of business, from image branding to marketing, at the same time that it employed the language of liberation—from freedom from occupation to anticolonial resistance. The merging of these two goals—business acumen and liberation from colonial rule—sits uncomfortably together with and lays bare the tensions that continue to animate solidarity tourism in today's post-Oslo moment.

Michel Awad of the Siraj Center, which provides training in tourism development under the ownership of local communities and promotes Palestine as a sustainable tourist destination, explained the relationship between "alternative" modes of tourism and tourist-to-host accountability. Preferring the phrase "responsible tourism" to "alternative tourism" ("because alternative to what?" he asks), Awad noted, "Our first aim is to create rural development, the other is to change the perception about Palestine. People look at Palestine as part of Israel. We try to brand Palestine as [a site for] experiential tourism itself."[24] Siraj Center positions itself as having helped drive the development of responsible tourism in Palestine, "*rebranding* Palestine as a destination for experiential travel and human connection."[25] In the wake of Oslo, and in conjunction with the contemporary Israeli political strategy to "Brand Israel" as a liberal, multicultural, and gay-friendly space in response to critiques of Israeli human rights violations, it is important to emphasize not only the ways solidarity tourism is indebted to strategic forms of tour guiding during the first intifada but also how solidarity tourism in Palestine has also become an income-generating business competing in a field of battling narratives over Palestine.[26] In a cultural sphere where, through rituals of repetition and citation, Israel is routinely positioned as an evolved and modern democracy and Palestine is positioned as both inhospitable and violent, Palestinian tourist agencies—solidarity and otherwise—seek to reframe the *image* of Palestine as a space that can, and will gladly, host tourists.

As an industry, then, solidarity tourism has necessitated a recognizable image and a marketable "brand." In the same breath as he described the political and economic situation in Palestine as one characterized by corruption, unemployment, loans, debt, and aid, Awad lamented the lack of a Palestinian brand:

> We don't have a Palestinian brand. What we promote is pilgrimage; that's what Israel promotes. So, if you promote like your competitors, then you are doing a favor for your competitor; if you promote the same product that your competitor's promoting, you are providing the knowledge about the product and [the customer] may buy it from you and he may buy it from your competitor. The problem is that we don't have a branding; we don't do marketing.[27]

To say "we don't do marketing" and "we don't have a Palestinian brand," to speak of tourists as customers, to speak of tourism as a product, and to speak of Israel as a competitor clearly reveals how solidarity tourism in Palestine is in no way solely a movement-building, grassroots initiative. This language is the language of production, consumption, marketing, and profit. However, to emphasize the importance of Palestine's "brand," and to caution against both Israeli representational practice and Israeli theft of Palestinian knowledge, does more than cynically position solidarity tourism as circumscribed to a profit-generating endeavor. Instead, Awad revealed how solidarity tourism is, at once, an initiative to provide resources, training, and income to Palestinians and an endeavor to change international perceptions of Palestine, to rebrand Palestinians. This is particularly true, Awad added, in the wake of 9/11 when internationals, especially Americans, including those who come to Palestine, collapse anything having to do with Islam with notions of a terrorist threat and believe that "if Israel is being threatened, America is being threatened."[28] Awad thus delineated a landscape of competing narratives—not of two equal "sides" of a conflict with parity in positioning and power but a battle over narrative in which Palestinian tour guides are attempting to wrest, in Edward Said's words, the "permission to narrate" from Israeli control.[29]

At the same time, there is of course no uniform stance belonging to Palestinian tour guides and organizers writ large. Baha Hilo, a fieldworker for the Joint Advocacy Initiative and the Alternative Tourism Group's Olive Tree Campaign at the time of my initial research and cofounder of an organization that runs geopolitical tours today, instead reframes this "rebranding" and describes it as a crucially important intervention in Israeli state-sanctioned narratives. In his words, "From the very beginning of the Palestinian issue, there has been so much effort put into discrediting the Palestinian realities and making sure Palestinian voices always have no credibility."[30] Tying this discrediting specifically to diplomatic interest and foreign policy, he said, "It's not in the best interest of any Western government that its public finds out about the atrocities committed by their good friend Israel against a native population that is the Palestinians, so it's not in the best interest of Western government or media to expose what is happening to the Palestinians."[31] He elaborated: "You'll always find one narrative that is being shared, one narrative that is being exposed, one narrative that is being supported, and that is 'our' narrative, the narrative of the governments, which says basically that Israel is one of the best achievements of the twentieth century, that Israel is the only democracy in the Middle East, Israel is the only civilized [country]. . . . Israel, Israel, Israel."[32]

Here, Hilo pointed to the ubiquity of the celebratory narrative of Israel that positions it as an island of democracy in an otherwise backward sea. He also pointed to the complicity of Western governments in Israel's occupation and, more, the complicity of internationals—perhaps especially those on the tour itself—in perpetuating and circulating this narrative. Paralleling Edward Said's 1978 analysis of Orientalism as a citational practice that positions "the

East" as static and "the West" (which, in this formulation, includes Israel) as dynamic, Hilo explained:

> And then you have no room whatsoever for the Palestinian's voice, simply because everything we say in the West, or everything that is being said in the West, about Israel, happened at the expense of the Palestinian population and you don't want that to be seen. "Israel is the only democracy in the Middle East." . . . It's a democracy for immigrants that happens at the expense of Palestinians who are not part, or not allowed to be part, of this so-called democracy. "Israel made the desert bloom." . . . We all know that the land that was made to bloom already bloomed because there is a Palestinian population [living] here.[33]

"Palestinians have found themselves," Hilo continued, in a situation where "they have to challenge a Western media that is completely taking the side of the oppressor in this conflict."[34]

Describing his labor, he elaborated, "From this need for sharing information, exposing reality, we found out that the best way to do it is by having people here, expose them to the reality, and let them decide [for] themselves."[35] In doing so, Hilo repeatedly extended an invitation to tourists: come and see and decide for yourself. This invitation, truncated and circumscribed as it is, emerges in a context where Israel has commandeered not only tourist itineraries in Palestine/Israel but also the tourist story. "What Israel tries to do, through tourism," Hilo explained, "is sell its own story, where the Palestinian is not part of the story. The Palestinian is the problem in the story. The Palestinian is scary in the story. So, what has emerged today is that you find Palestinian people who are under Israel's control trying to take over this job by themselves, trying to correct the story that the State of Israel sells about us."[36] This language of erasure, exposure, and correction parallels Said's descriptions of the "permission to narrate," as Hilo noted that Palestinian refugees, in particular, have had to watch the "modern spectacle" of Israel and the "unending ceremony of public approbation" for the force that dispossessed them, while simultaneously being asked to "participate in the dismantling of their own history."[37] In this way, while Awad positioned solidarity tourism as a necessary endeavor to reposition Palestinians and Palestine in the context of an industry under occupation, Hilo positioned solidarity tourism as, in large part, a disruption of a colonial logic that dispossesses Palestinians of both their land and their capacity to narrate.

"A Noose around Ramallah"

While contemporary solidarity tourism in Palestine traces its beginnings to solidarity tours during the first intifada, it was modeled into an income-generating
business in the wake of these divisions and taxonomies that characterize the
Oslo Accords. On their tours, guides work not only to intervene in Israeli state-
sanctioned narratives, as outlined by Hilo, but also to reveal the deliberate ways
the Oslo Accords have thwarted the growth of Palestinian economy (including its tourism sector) by separating Palestinian communities into distinct
enclaves and denying them access to land and resources. After Oslo, while
Palestinian-led tourism was now possible—in Palestinian territories, with Palestinian guides, flags, maps, and political perspectives—Palestinian movement
remained circumscribed to Palestinian "areas." Michel Awad explained that,
"before Oslo, people had more accessibility."[38] Guides could go between Bethlehem, Jerusalem, and Ramallah; they could meet their groups at the airport.
Awad also described the transition from pre-Oslo to post-Oslo tourism as one
bound by the expectations of potential statehood: "Before Oslo, Palestine was
under Israeli authority, so [guides] were working in tourism, but mostly in
pilgrimage. After Oslo, Palestinians were looking to have an independent state.
To have an independent state, you should rely on your own resources."[39] It was
this shift, in part, that enabled Israel to position solidarity tourism as somewhat
permissible (though still heavily policed on exit and entry into the country), if
only because it simultaneously became containable.[40]

Tour guides' work was contained and circumscribed within the West Bank
under the auspices of eventual statehood. As such, it followed the shape and
forms of first intifada delegations but was also predicated on questions of
marketing and business. While Hilo asked how we could use tourism to intervene in colonial knowledge production, Awad asked what alternative forms
of tourism—hiking and political tours, for example, rather than pilgrimage—
could compete with Israel's tourism sector. He explained:

> Most of the Palestinian travel agents in Bethlehem, Jerusalem, Ramallah,
> who work in pilgrimage, feel huge competition because [Israelis] own
> the airport, they have charter flights, and they have more accessibility to the
> tourist areas inside than we do, so it's very hard to compete with them.
> So that opens new options for the people. So that's the story of how alterna-
> tive tourism started; after Oslo, people started to think about new options.[41]

These "new options," then, were organized around changing international perceptions of Palestine, creating jobs and training for Palestinians, contributing to rural development, and working within and, later, against the confines of what was promised to eventually be a Palestinian state.

Moreover, the (im)possibilities of Palestinian tourism and constricted access that Awad describes were written into the negotiating at Oslo. While much has been written on the ways Palestinian negotiators had no knowledge of settlement expansion, no knowledge of resources, and no knowledge of the land, much less has been written on the lack of emphasis they put on tourism.[42] Israeli negotiators, for instance, brought a tour guide with them, while Palestinian negotiators did not. Awad explained, "If they don't know about the other issues—waters, aquifers, resources, land—for sure they don't know about tourism. They never thought tourism was important to know about."[43] Awad emphasized this refusal to prioritize tourism on the part of Palestinian negotiators via an anecdote:

> You know I met a guide. . . . He's in the sixty age range, or seventy-five. I met him in Jerusalem. He's an Israeli guide. And I was talking with him. And at the end of our chat, he told me, "Michel, I was part of the Israeli negotiating team in Oslo." A guide. They took a guide with them! . . . Did the Palestinians think to bring a guide with them? At least, when they asked for a site? This is the issue I think we really face.[44]

This story, even if and when it circulates solely as anecdote, reveals the centrality of tourism to the political terrain in Palestine/Israel. That an alternative tour organizer would underscore Israel's cunning and calculated approach to negotiations, specifically around tourism, demonstrates how the land divisions that inhere in "negotiations" between Israelis and Palestinians are contingent on Israel's commandeering of natural resources like aquifers, cultivated resources like olive groves, and natural and cultivated resources *for* tourism.

Sebastia, near Nablus, provides a telling example: "In Sebastia," Awad explained, "when people went to negotiation and put the lines of A and B and C, Israel knew that Sebastia was a very important site. So they put the city in Area A, and the heritage sites they put in Area B or C."[45] He continued: "So now, if you are at the entrance to Sebastia, at the site, it's Area A. If you move two meters, it's Area C. Two meters! And Palestinians are not allowed to build in Area C. People are stealing things in Sebastia, and no one can talk with them because the Palestinian Authority doesn't have any control."[46] In this way, it was not only that Oslo divided the land, fragmenting Palestinian communities from one another, partitioning the cultivable land into Israeli hands, weakening the Palestinian economy, and confining Palestinian city centers to Area A as Israel gathered the land into Area C. It is also that Oslo helped bring valuable tourist sites into Israeli control, allowing Palestinian tourists to be guides "of their own territories" but denying them access to sites that would both index heritage and generate income. Further, both of these characterizations—that "what Palestinians face" is a political landscape that refuses to see the value in tourism and that Israeli negotiators during Oslo deliberately crafted a geographical landscape that gave Israel control of the most valuable sites and the Palestinian Authority only nominal control—illustrate the Palestinian Authority's past and present misunderstanding of the importance of tourism in Palestine.

Some tour guides and organizers with whom I spoke explained that promoting tourism in Palestine and ensuring that it be responsible and not predatory should be the work of the Ministry of Tourism, not that of civil society. In one organizer's words, "The work I do should be the work of someone sitting in the Ministry of Tourism! Not me, doing it for free. If I don't want my work to replicate NGOs [nongovernmental organizations], I have to have some stake in it. Otherwise I can't justify the time I spend away from home, away from my kid." These sentiments are shared by those I interviewed who had been involved in creating the "Code of Conduct for Tourism in the Holy Land: A Palestinian Initiative," which outlines a set of terms through which responsible and just forms of tourism and solidarity in Palestine can be cultivated.[47] Yet it is members of the public, tour guides and organizers, and not the Palestinian Authority's Ministry of Tourism, who are working to fashion tourism in Palestine that resists exploitation and commodification in the context of an already relentless military occupation. Solidarity tourism, as a contemporary industry in Palestine, thus began with informal delegations during the first intifada, became a business in the wake of the Oslo Accords, and, on the majority of tours, showcases the state violence written into the Accords. The Oslo Accords, tour guides labor to emphasize, divided Palestinian communities into distinct enclaves and denied them access to land and resources, but they also distributed tourist sites directly into Israeli control with the cooperation of the Palestinian Authority.

As the rest of this chapter will map out, this work of professionalizing solidarity is not without the problems endemic to other kinds of tourism—from leisure tourism to disaster tourism to adventure tourism and even, as we saw in chapter 1, to intifada tourism. Even a tourism grounded in attempts to show-case inequality, privilege, and (im)mobility will simultaneously—and perhaps inevitably—traffic in asymmetries that privilege the position of the tourist at the expense of the host. Still, as they walk tourists through spaces they will characterize as a catastrophe that began, but did not end, with partition, the work of Palestinian tour guides is about upending the assumptions tourists bring with them. The work of Palestinian tour guides is to ask tourists to re-consider the reliance on the United States as an "honest broker," to reassess what they are in Palestine to do, and to rethink what they've learned about Israel, about Palestinians, and about the territorial contours of Palestine/Israel. Guides aim to rearrange these international assumptions while they simulta-neously encourage internationals to rethink their desire to either do work in Palestine or, worse, to consider their time in Palestine as the extent of the work they need to do.

"A Nice Evening in Bethlehem": The Right to Tourism as Tourism

At the same time that guides do the work of hosting tourists and guiding them through the fragmented post-Oslo landscape, there are also endeavors to craft platforms for tourism in Palestine that are not explicitly political tours but in-vestments in the concept of Palestine *as* a tourist destination. Hantourism, for example, is a platform for community-based tourism in Palestine. Named after a *hantour*, the Arabic name for a horse-drawn carriage, which farmers in Pales-tine used to use to cultivate their fields, the platform began with a guesthouse in Jericho as an environmentally friendly effort to add value back to the local com-munity. Pairing business with self-determination, Hantourism reached out to farmers, guides, guesthouse owners, businessowners, local chefs, and other com-munity members. According to one of its organizers, the platform was based on an understanding that tourists bring to Palestine an image of Palestine that is already sedimented. In his words, "We know that in a lot of incoming travel-ers' minds, this is only a place of trouble, of war, and people know us only through that channel first. And we wanted to have a way to have a platform that's inclusive of a lot of other things, including but not exclusive to solidarity tourism."[48]

He explained that it is not only that travelers need political tourism from Palestine but that, often, it is also necessary that travelers experience Pales-tine *as* a tourist. He said that Palestinians do not have the luxury of "neutral" tourist initiatives and must stay abreast of Israeli tourist initiatives: "We can't keep living in this ecosystem of ours that's basically in the shadow of the occupation, and our daily struggle as Palestinians living under occupation." He continued, "We have to be very aware of what's happening on the other side of the wall, what kind of activities, how hummus is being sold as an Israeli experience, how shakshuka . . ."[49] He trailed off, gesturing toward how Palestinians must contend with land theft and cultural theft—the theft of what would otherwise be offered as part of a Palestinian tourist experience. Without the luxury of being neutral, Palestinian guides still, even in their support for solidarity tourism, maintain that solidarity tourism is not the only ethical or anticolonial way to experience Palestine. In fact, they argue that Palestinians have the *right to tourism*, the right to share Palestine with the uninformed, even under an ecosystem of occupation. It is precisely that ecosystem, where the Israeli tourism industry profits from everything Palestinian—from touting "ancient ruins" to hummus to shakshuka—on the other side of the wall, that necessitates multiple forms of tourism under occupation. In this context, even sharing with tourists a Palestine that is not defined by Israel is an act that resists Israel's monopoly on the narrative of Palestine/Israel as well as everything Palestinians have produced before and during Israel's colonial reign.

Hantourism, then, as one example, discovered that, for tour guides and other individuals interested in innovating in this sector and doing something other than strictly heritage sites or political tours, there was no platform through which to collaborate, meet each other, and gain clients. Instead of having an umbrella tourism initiative, with Hantourism in control of the guides, the buses, the sites, etc., they instead created a network to simply connect people doing different things with and through tourism across Palestine, from Jericho, to Nablus, Nazareth, Ramallah, Jerusalem. Thus, tour guides become local partners through a revenue-sharing model, but the guides do not have to pay to be on board; they just have to share Hantourism's values in fair trade employment and crafting tourism initiatives that benefit local communities. This example reiterates that there is no Palestinian consensus on solidarity tourism. Instead, there are multiple forms of tourism functioning in Occupied Palestine with varied relationships to markets, space, and local workers—some explicitly anticolonial and some anticolonial by virtue of celebrating a Palestine that Israel has attempted to condition the world not to celebrate.

This push to celebrate different forms of tourism in Palestine—aside from solely solidarity or political tourism—is also a push for creativity and, in business terms, "innovation" in a way that resists the NGO-ization of West Bank initiatives and the forms of tourism NGOs are interested in seeing. Local guidebooks, one organizer explains, parrot the language of NGOs, which would appeal to a delegation but not to "somebody just a few miles from here sitting in Jerusalem deciding if tonight they should go party on Jaffa Street or come to Bethlehem to have a nice evening."[50] Because the concept of a "nice evening in Bethlehem" is so foreign to so many, platforms like Hantourism want to re-cuperate the idea that Palestine is a nice place to visit, even if you are not doing so through an explicitly political tour. As will become clear as these narratives of solidarity tourism unfold throughout the book, solidarity tours are almost al-ways spliced with moments of reprieve—"nice evenings in Bethlehem"—when tourists not only witness the violence of occupation but also witness Palestinian beauty and joy against a narrative Israel produces and circulates where every-thing joyful and beautiful that emanates from Palestine is, in fact, Israeli.

Walking Tours of Occupied Land and the Spectacle of Immobility

On explicitly solidarity tours, meanwhile, guides pose a challenge to tourists' expectations that they are coming to Palestine to understand "what it feels like" to live under occupation, asking tourists to confront their own privilege in Pales-tine and complicity in its subjugation. As a result, what many solidarity tourists take away from their experience in Palestine is not a belief that they know what it feels like to be under occupation but rather a profound sense of shame and guilt. These alternating sentiments can be understood as sometimes productive and sometimes incapacitating for tourists' attempts to be in solidarity with Pal-estinians under occupation. In a similar vein, in *Postcolonial Melancholia*, Paul Gilroy distinguishes between paralyzing guilt and productive shame. Writing of the work of decolonization, he suggests that to confront one's complicity in imperial projects, one must take up "the painful obligations to work through the grim details of imperial and colonial history and to transform paralyzing guilt into a more productive shame that would be conducive to the building of a multicultural nationality that is no longer phobic about the prospect of exposure to either strangers or otherness."[51] While the tourists I interviewed did not distinguish between the guilt and shame they felt, they did articulate how their experiences of guilt and shame on the tours were resonant turning points in their understandings of settler colonialism in Palestine—moments that not only catalyzed their outrage but also ignited an urgency that disallowed any sense of apathetic complacency in imperial projects. In this way, they began to take up the work of transforming paralyzing guilt into productive shame—not as Israelis reckoning with building a multicultural nationality, as Gilroy might imagine here, but as US citizens rejecting US imperial interests in maintaining Israel's US-bolstered status quo. The shame and guilt tourists described are, additionally, directed at their governments, which enable Israeli occupation, and at their own mobility in Palestine in stark contrast to the restricted mobility of the Palestinians guiding their tours.

Written into solidarity tours is a negotiation of the fragmentation of the West Bank that includes, for example, handoffs of tourists at checkpoints between Bethlehem and East Jerusalem, separations between Palestinian guides and tourists in Hebron, and arbitrary searches at checkpoints and bus stops. In these moments, tour guides make tourists aware of their difference—not sameness—from Palestinians in terms of access, mobility, and privilege.[52] Tourists, then, are encouraged (despite the sentiment they bring to Palestine) not to feel like saviors who are making it possible for Palestinians to survive occupation and not to feel the same as Palestinians, as though, somehow, by their abridged visit to Palestine, they know what it is like to be occupied. Instead, solidarity tour guides and organizers are attempting to disrupt what Sophia Stamatopoulou-Robbins calls the "prosthetic engagement" that can mark forms of international presence in Palestine, wherein tourists/activists read their time in Palestine as an extension of the occupation, an experience of being temporarily occupied.[53] Instead, guides remind tourists of their privilege and ask them not to become a fixture in Palestine but to return home, where their work against Israeli colonial state practice has more impact.

"Your work is not here" is a refrain I heard tour guides repeatedly tell tourists during my research; they consistently redirected international desire to "stay" and "help" in Palestine and instead deliberately framed their invitation in Palestine as an invitation *to be* a tourist: to come to Palestine for an orchestrated and curtailed amount of time. I have come to understand the politics of this intentionally truncated invitation as a project of rearranging tourist desire. Contemporary solidarity tours attempt to "rearrange [tourist] desire" first by consistently critiquing the exclusive reliance on the potential of US-led negotiations and the celebration of the work of the Oslo Accords.[54] Second, they lead tourists through the post-Oslo fragmentation of Palestinian land and communities. Third, they labor to redirect the aspirations of international tourists, guiding them—through multiple different iterations—toward the understanding that their work is not in Palestine.

Solidarity tours are, in part, structured to make tourists witness or experience, if only fleetingly, the restricted mobility of Palestinians resulting from decades of occupation and sedimented by Oslo. Some of this structuring is inevitable, and some of it is deliberate. Because of Israel's unyielding restrictions placed on researchers, scholars, and activists—tourists with any connection, however tangential, to Palestine—solidarity tourists experience a version of restricted mobility and access from their arrival at Ben Gurion International Airport in Tel Aviv. Internationals entering Israel through Ben Gurion with the intent to spend time in the West Bank know that if they announce that they are going to Palestine, if they have an Arab last name, if they are Muslim, if they have family or friends in Palestine, or if they have spent time in any predominantly Muslim countries, they will be subject to a lengthy interrogation and possibly refused entry.

From their first moments in Palestine, solidarity tourists are made aware of how their itineraries, and the narratives provided on their itineraries, will differ from the scores of other tourists who form the backdrop of so many sites in Palestine/Israel. In this way, tour guides, from the start, instruct tourists on where they will be positioned in this battle over narrative that consumes not only the geopolitical terrain of Palestine/Israel but also the landscape of tourism itself. While solidarity tourists often visit many of the same sites that religious and heritage tourists visit—for example, sites of Christian pilgrimage like the Church of the Nativity in Bethlehem and Mount of Temptation in Jericho—the information they are given is substantively different. For example, if participants are taken to the Church of the Nativity, instead of hearing a narrative that focuses solely on the birth of Christ, they will also hear about Oslo's division of the West Bank, how Bethlehem is 87 percent Area C under Israeli control, and how Bethlehem suffers from land annexation. Solidarity tourists will hear about the lives lost in the forty-nine-day siege in 2002, about growing settlements encroaching on Palestinian lives and land, and about US and European silence on the settlement project. Meanwhile, they will witness the disjuncture between the large number of tourists from Israel entering the Church of the Nativity and the nearby towering Separation Wall severing Palestinians from their former land. By underscoring the historical and contemporary violence of Israeli occupation, the inherent failures of the Oslo Accords, and the US and European facilitation of Israeli occupation, solidarity tour guides and organizers stage a dissonance between what the tourists are there to witness and the narratives told to the scores of tourists filing in and out of the Church.

As part of their weeklong tours, guides will also take tourists to Beit Jala, where Israeli-only roads connecting settlements bisect and trisect Palestinian land. The bypass roads, guides explain, began to be constructed in 1993, through Palestinian lands with olive trees flanking both sides. Guides detail how these roads make "occupational sense" in that they seamlessly connect settlements that are in violation of the Fourth Geneva Convention, Article 49, stipulating that no occupying power can move its civilian population to live in the occupied territories. Tourists hear narratives of displacement, restriction of movement, and land expropriation in 1948, 1967, 1993, 2010, and now; organizers and guides frame these moments of displacement as an ongoing Nakba. Here, and throughout the week(s), guides frame contemporary house demolitions, settlement construction, and land expropriation as a Nakba that did not end in 1948 but continues today via forced displacement. Moreover, guides and organizers position Oslo as deeply a part of that ongoing Nakba and not anomalous to it.

Solidarity tour organizers also structure walking and bus tours to explicitly reveal the post-Oslo fragmentation of the West Bank. In Bethlehem, organizers lead tourists along the Wall, often leaving them on their own to read the solidarity messages written there, explaining that, for the most part, these are works by internationals, not locals. As the tour bus travels through the West Bank, guides tell tourists about how settlers steal water from Palestinians and then sell it back to them at exorbitant costs. Tourists are given a detailed visual explanation of how Oslo fractured the West Bank into Areas A, B, and C, calling attention to the disparity between the sprawling, built-up settlements, continually expanding and under construction, and the homes belonging to Palestinians prohibited from building extra rooms and knowing they would be under threat of demolition if they did. Guides explain how the Wall has killed the economic life of Palestinians, taking up 725 kilometers of the West Bank, extending 20 kilometers into the West Bank, a Wall of which only 10 percent is an actual wall, with the rest military road, electronic fences, and other means of constricting movement and expropriating land. Guides emphasize the impossibility of their travel to Jerusalem—a "final status" issue as decreed by Oslo—by way of analogy: one solidarity tour guide frequently explains to tourists, "I can get to Copenhagen easier than I can get to Jerusalem."

Guides further emphasize this gulf between Palestinians on both sides of the Wall by facilitating a trade-off of tourists at Checkpoint 300, which separates Bethlehem from East Jerusalem. Here, organizers make sure that tourists understand that their Palestinian guide, who has facilitated their movement around the Bethlehem area thus far, cannot go with them. Tourists walk through the labyrinthine corrals of the checkpoint and wave their international passports in front of the bulletproof glass while the Palestinians next to them have to show their wrinkled permits and ID cards and place their fingers in the biometric scanner. Armed teenagers serving in the Israeli military sit behind the bulletproof glass or pace above and around the tourists and workers corralled within the walls of the checkpoint.

Palestinian workers often hurriedly try to get through, while tourists sometimes slow down the process, marveling at the cage they—only momentarily—find themselves in. Israeli tourism posters adorn the walls inside the checkpoint, inviting passersby to visit the Dead Sea, to see the beach in Tel Aviv, to "experience Israel." In 2012, the posters read, in English, "Every Day Is a Vacation." In 2019, updated Israeli Ministry of Tourism ads, bigger and shinier, wallpapered the checkpoint's exits from floor to ceiling. Palestinians subject to Israeli rule crossing the checkpoint know that their entry is contingent on permits and the arbitrary permission granted by the soldier, a humiliation further exacerbated by the presence of tourists, who have unfettered access to all those spaces. This experience of the checkpoint demonstrates the ambivalent role of the solidarity tourist as one who both challenges and affirms racial and spatial inequalities in Palestine.

Tourists, in these walk-throughs, are presented with a checkpoint experience to, in some ways, simulate "the Palestinian experience." Yet they are also given detailed information on how this is only some Palestinians' experience: those who live in the West Bank, those who have work permits to enter Jerusalem, or those who do this daily. Simultaneously, they are meant to witness how their own checkpoint experience differs vastly from that of the Palestinians next to them. In this way, even in these moments wherein guides attempt to approximate a sense of the occupation, they simultaneously work to make sure that tourists take note of the disparity in treatment they both witness and enact. Tour guides do not flag this disparity or necessarily ask tourists to note the differences in their treatment compared to West Bank Palestinians, but, for many tourists—as will soon become clear—this discrepancy is impossible to ignore.

On the other side of the checkpoint, the internationals will have a new guide for the day in Jerusalem. On political tours through the Old City, tourists will see armed civilian settlers, settlers' armed bodyguards in plain clothes, groups of heavily armed young Israeli soldiers on every corner, homes settlers have taken over, and the grates above Palestinian markets to catch the trash settlers throw. Then they will file onto a bus to hear a thorough explanation of Israeli apartheid in East Jerusalem and witness its effects, from the lack of infrastructure and unpaved roads in East Jerusalem to the Wall cutting through Abu Dis and severing the route that had long served as a throughway from Jerusalem to Jericho. Standing near a Palestinian gas station, reading the antioccupation graffiti on the

Wall, situated in a Palestinian community severed from their former neighbors and their family across the Wall, guides will routinely pause so tourists have a moment to take in the last thing they see of Jerusalem before traveling back to their Palestinian guides and organizers on the other side of the Wall.

Guides and organizers deliberately force a confrontation with the restriction of mobility within the West Bank as well. They work to make tourists understand that the immobility they are witnessing is tethered to the racialized taxonomies of Israeli settler colonialism. At various military checkpoints restricting movement in the West Bank, a Palestinian guide may, at times, attempt to blend in with the internationals, allowing the Israeli soldier guarding the checkpoint to determine whether to let the collection of "just tourists" in. Tourists and guides alike pass through the checkpoint together, performing "normal" conversation and attempting to avoid looking suspicious, in hopes that the young Israeli guard will not ask for identification. If the soldier mistakes the Palestinian tour guide for a European, or is otherwise too busy or distracted to bother, the guide will pass through the checkpoint with the tourists unnoticed, or at least unflagged. Moreover, this "passing" is often only possible with a guide new to their post, as Palestinian tour guides in some of these spaces become recognizable to guards over time. Guides and organizers stress the arbitrary politics of identification in these contact zones; one tour guide routinely asks on his tours, when crossing the Qalandia Checkpoint with his yellow license plate that signifies Israeli citizens and residents of East Jerusalem, "Will they think I'm a Shlomo or an Ahmed?" He explains that usually he's a Shlomo, but if the soldiers are feeling bored, if it is a slow day, he may be an Ahmed. Through this anecdote and others, tourists are meant to understand the extent to which entrance is contingent on "not looking Arab" and all mobility is at someone else's discretion; more specifically, this anecdote is meant to connote the deeply racialized policing of Palestinian mobility.

As a central part of showcasing militarized and racialized (im)mobility in the West Bank, guides always bring tourists to Hebron. In Hebron, tourists walk alone down Shuhada Street, which once hosted a thriving market, a street so busy, one guide tells tourists, that he used to have to hold his father's hand to not get lost in the bustling marketplace. Shuhada Street is now closed to Palestinians, including those who still live on the street and have to enter their homes from the back, who have cages around their patios to protect them from settler violence, who have signs in their windows that read "You are witnessing apartheid." Tourists often take in Shuhada Street alone, rarely seeing anyone else, since it has become a ghost town.

The city's main road is closed to the 177,000 Palestinians who live in Hebron, with access only to tourists, the 500–800 settlers who live there, and the 1,500–2,000 soldiers who protect them.[55] Guides intend for tourists to witness some of the more than four hundred stores that have been closed under military orders, some of the almost two thousand others that closed because of all the closures and checkpoints, and some of the more than one thousand emptied Palestinian homes.[56] When tourists file out of Shuhada Street to reunite with their guides, they exit on a street solely for settlers and tourists, while Palestinians file onto a street one-quarter the size of the one they are walking on, having to go through yet another checkpoint, and then another. Guides include Hebron in their itineraries because it is such a starkly segregated space that unequivocally shows the violence of military rule while revealing the containment of Palestinian movement and tourists' comparative freedom to explore. Through their itineraries in militarized spaces like Hebron, tour guides use the expansive mobility of tourists to underscore the restricted mobility of Palestinians; further, guides and organizers frame this contingency and racialized precarity of movement as a constitutive part of the regime of military occupation.

"I've Seen More of Palestine Than Many Palestinians"

If one ostensible goal of tourism—solidarity tourism included—is to sightsee, part of the work of solidarity tourism in the West Bank is to show that what tourists see is often far more capacious and expansive than what can be seen by most Palestinians. When asked about what resonated most during her ten-day tour of Palestine in 2012, Maggie Goff responded: "As an American who grew up in the Midwest, just the overwhelming amount of militarism, and military presence, in the West Bank was really shocking. And the idea that I've seen more of Palestine than a large portion of the Palestinian population."[57] Here, much like Bousac's map, Goff demarcates the two things that most stood out on the tour: the spectacle of military occupation and the expansive vision and mobility of the tourist.[58] For Goff and other tourists I spoke to, the disparity between their own movement and that of the Palestinian guides and organizers orchestrating their movement is the starkest and most immediate memory they have of their time in Palestine. Yvonne Lory described her freedom of mobility at Checkpoint 300 and in Hebron as throwing into sharp relief both "the benefit and shame" of being a US citizen in Palestine. She recalled getting waved through the checkpoint while Palestinians were pulled aside and interrogated: "I would just get a smile and get passed right on by because of my passport."[59] In many ways, Lory was shocked more by the mobility and access she embodied than the discrimination she witnessed. Lory further described the guilt she felt in "touring" Palestine, as her "hard-earned money," in reference to her tax dollars, was "going to make life a living hell" for Palestinians.[60] In my interviews with them, tourists used the word *shame* with notable frequency to describe their tax dollars at work in constructing the geography of occupation in Palestine, to detail how they felt about the differential treatment they experienced and embodied as US citizens in Palestine, and to index their role as complicit subjects in the occupation.

Moreover, differently positioned tourists articulated their sense of shame in disparate ways. Sarah Alzanoon, a Palestinian American tourist who was on the same tour as Lory, also narrated the guilt she experienced as a US citizen in Palestine with the capacity to move throughout Palestinian space. However, Alzanoon's narrative differs markedly from Lory's and Goff's, demonstrating not only the complexity of solidarity tourism in Palestine but also the competing and multiple registers of complicity, familiarity, outrage, and shame that can inhere in a form of tourism that is structured as an anticolonial project. Alzanoon described her experience as the first Palestinian in her family—scattered, since 1948, across Jordan, Kuwait, Canada, and the United States—to see Palestine, outside of her relatives in Gaza, who have been unable to leave and whom she has never met. She described being detained at the airport for "somewhere between five and seven hours" before she was eventually allowed entry, kept in a room where they ostensibly "randomly check people" but which was populated, in her words, solely by "brown people like me."[61] Alzanoon's relationship to Palestine as a tourist is connected to both her brownness and her identity as a Palestinian American, coupled with the weight of being her family's emissary of return—if only for a fleeting moment. Her first moments in Palestine echo countless other experiences of discriminatory and racist policies at Ben Gurion Airport at the same time that they set her apart from many of the other participants on solidarity tours.

While Alzanoon's capacity for movement differed from her white counterparts with US passports upon her arrival in Palestine/Israel, once in Palestine and outside the airport, her mobility approximated theirs more than it did the Palestinians with whom she identified and felt a shared lineage. She describes one of the most resonant moments from her time in Palestine that continues to haunt her: when her bus was stopped at the checkpoint between Bethlehem and Jerusalem and all the Palestinians were ordered off the bus to be searched.

Alzanoon recounted a soldier carrying an assault rifle beginning the search process as Palestinians around her began exiting the bus:

> So they all get off the bus and then I get off the bus, too, because I'm [a Palestinian]. And this Palestinian lady looks at me, with this strong look, and she's like, "You don't have to get off; just stay," is what she was pretty much telling me, like, "You don't have to go through this." So I just stayed. So they all have to get strip-searched, pretty much all the Palestinian people, with Palestinian IDs, but because I was a foreigner—even though I'm just as Palestinian as them—but I have my American passport, I get more rights than the people that have lived there, and their ancestors who have lived here for hundreds of years, and they pay taxes to Israel.[62]

She rephrased this in more certain terms: "I have more rights than them, from being a tourist, even though I'm just as much a Palestinian."[63] Here, Alzanoon described her fear and anxiety, her confusion about her place as a Palestinian American in Palestine, and her inability to comprehend the level of movement this time not restricted by her brownness but granted by her citizenship. Her role as a tourist, and not as a Palestinian, was sedimented in moments like this as much as it was troubled by moments like her detention in the airport. She thus described her movement through Palestine as characterized by an expansiveness made possible both by her legal status as a US citizen and by her particular experience of diaspora, as a Palestinian American with the freedom to move around Palestine in contrast to West Bank Palestinians surrounding her, who are routinely subject to the violence and humiliation of checkpoints and whose movement is foreclosed at worst and surveilled at best.

Alzanoon further tethered her feelings of guilt not only to her tax dollars and her mobility within Palestine but also to her capacity to return home. She repeatedly explained how she can "go home and not worry that there's going to be an intifada the next day."[64] While earlier in the interview Alzanoon articulated her struggle to enter Palestine as a mark of her otherness in Israel, here she positioned her capacity to leave as indexing her privilege. Alzanoon's ability to "go home" punctuated her ambivalence about her position as a Palestinian American in Palestine: in her experience of diaspora, "home" both must be elsewhere and can be elsewhere.[65] Alzanoon's time in Palestine thus served as a painful reminder that while she could see more of Palestine than the Palestinians who live there, she was not recognized as Palestinian in the same way—by either Palestinians or the Israelis who police them. In this way, even her mobility in Palestine was a reminder of her exile.[66]

In this scene, "solidarity tourist" and "solidarity tour guide" prove, again, to be unstable categories. Palestinians are at once hosts and guides, allowed entry and denied entry, severed from one another yet temporarily in the same space, that space defined by an asymmetry predicated on exile and policed borders. Though differently positioned, and articulating radically different relationships to Palestine, the tourists with whom I spoke described these moments of their own asymmetrical freedom of mobility as the moments that most resonated with them and catalyzed their activism back home. These moments, in which they embodied and not only observed starkly racialized disparity in Palestine, animated their understanding of colonial violence and its effects. In solidarity tour itineraries, while tour guides are navigating and narrating the fragmented terrain they have inherited, tourists are rehearsing the segregation that inheres within it. Solidarity tours ask tourists to reenact and perform the very practices of apartheid that they are ostensibly in Palestine to critique. This is not an unfortunate contradiction of solidarity tours or an accidental hypocrisy of their structure. Instead, it is a strategic choice on the part of Palestinian organizers and guides to employ the asymmetries of both power and mobility that make possible the movement of tourists in the West Bank to underscore the difference—and not sameness—of internationals in Palestine. Solidarity tour guides are not trying to facilitate an adventure tour that enables tourists to play at being occupied, nor are they encouraging tourists to embark on a disaster tour that results in tourists asking, "What can we do?" Rather, solidarity tour guides are crafting starkly asymmetrical itineraries that force tourists to ask what they are already doing that makes possible the freedom of mobility they are embodying and the containment under occupation they are witnessing.

Exported Tear Gas and Reminders of Complicity

In December 2013, the US Agency for International Development (USAID) donated almost $400,000 to Christmas celebrations on Manger Square in Bethlehem, a move both the mayor of Bethlehem and the Palestinian Ministry of Tourism celebrated as a boon to Palestine's tourist economy.[67] The logic behind this donation was to boost Christmas tourism to Bethlehem and "increase the share of tourist dollars spent at the birthplace of Christ."[68] Signs peppered Manger Square that read "USAID—A gift from the American people."[69] Local activists, however, wanted to show tourists what else constituted a gift from the American people: spent tear gas canisters and stun grenades fired at youth in the Aida Refugee Camp less than a mile away. Activists affixed tear gas canisters with *Made in the USA* emblazoned on them to a small Christmas tree in Manger Square to show tourists what their tax dollars—$3 billion per year—were actually buying in Palestine/Israel. This method of exposing tourists to the violence visited on Palestinians in their name and with their money is echoed repeatedly on solidarity tours. In spaces like Bil'in, where the village's Popular Committee Against the Wall will host a tour group on a Wednesday and lead a demonstration against the Wall on a Friday, guides pick up spent tear gas canisters and make sure that tourists take note of the labels. In Aida Refugee Camp, a shop has emerged where local teenagers sell art made from tear gas canisters (figure 2.2). The canisters themselves are fashioned into vases. CTS is stamped on every canister next to a complete address: *Combined Tactical Systems, 388 Kinsman Road, Jamestown, PA 16134*, alongside the phone and fax number. "Made in the USA" can be read clearly on the label.

Mustafa al-Arraj, one of the coordinators of the action to decorate Manger Square with these other US "donations," was arrested by Palestinian police later that day for disrupting the otherwise pleasant Christmas scene. Bethlehem police spokesman Loay Zreiqat, for his part, expressed concern that the grenades would "scare tourists."[70] Al-Arraj responded by pointing to the USAID plaques as a provocation: "They help us with schools and hospitals," he explained, "but they also help occupy us. The United States is complicit in the Israeli occupation. They give us $1 for some project and then give Israel $1 million to hit us with tear gas and shoot us."[71]

In this 2013 scene, we see a $400,000 donation from the United States to support Palestinian tourism, a simultaneous Israeli attack on Palestinian youth with US-made weapons only steps away in Aida Refugee Camp, and a protest installation crafted for tourists from the debris of the attack. We see Palestinian police arresting protesters for threatening tourism and disturbing the peace and Palestinian activists attempting to remind tourists of the ways they are deeply implicated in Israel's occupation. Solidarity tourists, too, face constant and repeated reminders of their complicity in the structures of containment and racialized violence that they are ostensibly only witnessing. This is not a tourism defined by efforts, like those of the Ministry of Tourism, to simply increase the number of visitors to Bethlehem. Like the tourists in Manger Square, solidarity tourists are asked to rethink the narrative they are sold about Palestine/Israel. They are asked to reframe the question of what they can do in Palestine to what they are already doing that sustains the occupation, and what they can do back home to end it.

2.2 Tear gas canister art, Aida Refugee Camp. Photo by author (2019).

How much tourists are moved to action, and just how much they do when they get home, is exceedingly difficult to quantify. Many tour agencies and organizations have a difficult time tracking the work that tourists do post-tour and craft advocacy positions to discern more clearly the "outcome" of their tours. This is especially true because some of what tourists "do" post-tour is not always legible or immediately tangible. While some tour alumni participate in demonstrations and advocacy work or report back to community groups, many others put what they witness to work by talking to their friends and families, letter writing, and joining already extant boycotts, divestment, and sanctions campaigns.

Indeed, when I asked tour guides what they saw solidarity tourism doing, they often responded not only by describing what tourists do back home but also by emphasizing what they saw solidarity tourism doing in Palestine. In this regard, they spoke about a different kind of witnessing: not tourists witnessing the daily indignities of the occupation but tour guides witnessing small victories against the ongoing colonization of Palestinian land. Yazan al-Zubaidy, then a fieldworker and guide on olive planting and harvesting initiatives, described the changes he witnessed from taking tourists to Hebron. He explained how the income provided by tourists eating with the same family in Hebron has, for example, allowed the family to stay in their house.[72] He continued, "If they had no income, they would just leave and sell their house to the Israelis."[73] Even more, he adds, "Before, where there was only their shop, now there are four shops around them."[74] Here, al-Zubaidy described how he—and not only the tourists—"witnesses" in Palestine. As a result of solidarity tours, he has witnessed one family keep their shop open and four other families open shops next door. "This is resistance," he concludes. "Just to stay where you are. And to live."[75] He also detailed the effect this witnessing has on him, as a Palestinian living in Bethlehem. He defined his continual, repeated, and daily descriptions of the occupation as an inoculation against complacency in the occupation itself. The consistent narration of occupation, he argued, resists just accepting, for example, that the Wall is there. "Israel wants us to forget," he explained, positioning his work with tourists as a refusal of that erasure.[76] In this way, it is repetition—the recitation of colonial fact—that intervenes, for the host, organizer, or tour guide, in positioning the occupation as inevitable and, for the tourist, in the narrative that Israel circulates ad infinitum that there is no occupation and, if there is, it is wholly justified.

At the same time, solidarity tourism is deliberately *tourism*. It is, by design, a truncated visit, a tour, with the tourists positioned as distinct from the Palestinians facilitating their movement: differently situated, differently privileged, and differently contributing to the occupation they are ostensibly in Palestine to help upend. It is, in many ways, like tourism writ large: voyeuristic, reductive, and incomplete. Solidarity tourists come to Palestine with a host of assumptions and desires that tour guides routinely have to recalibrate in the space of less than a week and, sometimes, less than two hours. Solidarity tours are crafted—like the tree decorated with stun grenades—to produce a spectacle of occupation that tourists cannot continue to deny; they provide evidentiary weight of an occupation in which tourists are implicated and may wish they could ignore. Tourist desire for this evidentiary weight, as first intifada tours have shown us, congeals into a demand in spite of the volumes of literature Palestinians have produced on their own condition. Solidarity tours are thus also deliberately asymmetrical. Tourists require Palestinians to produce evidence that is otherwise freely available to them, they walk in spaces their Palestinian tour guides cannot, they get waved through checkpoints while Palestinians next to them get turned back, and they stand on Jerusalem ground or Tel Aviv beaches that West Bank Palestinians can often only imagine.

In this post-Oslo context of shrinking access to their land—what Julien Bousac illustrated in 2009 as an increasingly archipelagic terrain—Palestinian tour guides are using solidarity tourism, in all its fraught asymmetries, to expose the fragmented terrain they have inherited and attempt to stay rooted on the land that remains. Via studied exercises in repetition, they confront the fiction that heralds the United States as an "honest broker" in a "two-sided conflict" or, even more, as aiding Palestine, and the deception of a tourism that positions Bethlehem as Israel and Israel as a beacon of progress and modernity in a hostile and dangerous Middle East.[77] They expose the United States' role in sedimenting Israel's settler-colonial violence that began not in 1967 but with the foundational violence of the establishment of the state, and that continues apace with expanding settlements, the constriction of Palestinian movement, and the daily violence that threatens Palestinian land and lives. Like Manger Square's grenade ornaments, solidarity tour guiding is a performance of transforming the detritus of war into ornamental reminders of complicity. These performances, their organizers hope, help Palestinians stay on land that has become a set of islands, help fashion four shops out of one, and help hosts stay in their homes under the constant threat of exile. When we imagine what it means to "tour occupation," then, it is worth asking what solidarity tourism does and for whom, from those who craft its itineraries to those who traverse its routes, to those who witness, feel, and reenact its effects.

THREE

RECITATION AGAINST ERASURE
PLANTING, HARVESTING, AND NARRATING
THE CONTINUITIES OF DISPLACEMENT

Solidarity tours in Palestine function as ritual—and this is particularly true of those that follow the seasons. Repeating annually in winter and fall, respectively, olive tree planting and harvesting initiatives in the West Bank are tours of this sort. They are a rehearsal, a repetition, a recitation of fact and itinerary, and an embodied practice of planting or harvesting taken up by farmers, tour guides, and tourists who often return every year as ritual. Edward Said wrote in 1978 that Orientalism functions via the repetition of colonial logics and a citational practice that bolsters conquest; here, solidarity tour guides press repetition and citation into the service of *anti*colonial work. As they guide tourists through the fragmentation of their land, they repeat instructions for hands in the soil, or hands pulling olives off branches, and construct scripts that tether tourists' vision to the histories the landscape may or may not reveal. Framing the land as a palimpsest, where tourists see the contemporary landscape alongside the traces of what came before, tour guides direct tourists' focus toward what used to be, what is, and what could be. As tourists travel by bus past detritus from house demolitions to sprawling terraced vineyards, the past, the present, and the alternative futures of a decolonized Palestine are laid bare.

Trees—olive, almond, and fig—are central to these rituals of telling, and olive trees become the narrative nucleus around which these stories are told. The history of uprooting Palestinian olive trees, alongside fig and almond trees native to the land, predates the establishment of the State of Israel and stretches back as far as 1908. These early Zionist claims to the land came in the form of uprooting native trees and planting forests in their stead that commemorated early Zionist leaders like first Prime Minister David Ben-Gurion who sought to fashion Israel after Europe in the form of a "Switzerland of the Middle East." Olive harvesting and olive tree planting tours walk tourists through this history, using the olive tree as an object that tourists can grasp that can bear the narrative weight of generations of dispossession.[1] Through the truncated recitation of Zionist uprooting practices that have persisted over the past century, tours of this sort anchor contemporary theft and destruction of Palestinian olive groves within the history of Israeli afforestation in Palestine. Tracing a long history of Zionist displacement and the state's attempted erasure of Palestinian agricultural presence, tour guides employ the ritual of repetition—reciting these histories, repeating planting and harvesting instructions, and connecting these rituals to the past, present, and future. In doing so, they showcase erasure in Palestine, frame contemporary settler violence and settlement expansion as part of a long and ongoing history of displacement in Palestine, and keep Palestinian farmers on their land that is under constant threat of annexation. In this sense, their own rituals of repetition intervene in the repetition of the Zionist slogan "making the desert bloom" to reveal it as an invocation that gains legitimacy not through facts on the ground but precisely through its narrative form: repetition. Through rituals of tying the landscape to its many pasts and potential futures, guides thus use the ritual of tour guiding, planting, and harvesting to render visible the Zionist narratives that attempt—and fail—to reify erasure.[2]

"We Inherit the Loss": Generational Grieving and Planting as Pedagogy

Within the context of historical and contemporary state razing of Palestinian olive groves and state-sanctioned settler violence, Palestinian organizers, farmers, activists, and tour guides have independently and collectively sought avenues for supporting Palestinian farmers economically and politically. A number of organizations—including Canaan Fair Trade, the Joint Advocacy Initiative, the

Alternative Tourism Group, the Freedom Bus, and To Be There—have worked to turn the growing international interest in Palestine solidarity into direct support for Palestinian farmers. I will turn to one of these efforts in detail—the Joint Advocacy Initiative (JAI) and Alternative Tourism Group (ATG)'s Olive Tree Campaign—and trace the ritualized work of planting they teach and the history of Zionist afforestation they simultaneously narrate. The planting and harvesting programs I participated in during my research included a mix of participants from the United States, Britain, France, Ireland, Germany, Hungary, Norway, the Netherlands, and Jordan. The groups included husbands and wives, parents whose children were involved in Palestine solidarity activism, high school teachers, stay-at-home moms, grandparents, self-identified activists, churchgoers, interfaith collective participants, Christian youth pastors, young people working in the fashion and beauty industries, researchers, and diaspora Palestinians who had never been on an organized trip to Palestine.

The Olive Tree Campaign's itinerary follows a pattern of guided walking tours, lectures delivered on hillsides overlooking panoramas of fragmented landscapes, presentations in research offices, and, every other day, planting olive trees. On the first planting day of the program in 2012, the group planted four hundred olive trees in al-Khader, on land that has been bisected by a bypass road and is under threat of annexation by the settlement of Navi Daniel. One of the farmers, Nabhan Mousa, wandered through the rows of olive saplings as the tourists planted and told his story to those who asked. He carried his papers, pink, filmy, and worn through from having to routinely produce them for soldiers (and, in this case, tourists) to access his land since 1997. Israeli soldiers hovered on the hill above, guns slung across their shoulders. He explained that the Israelis offered him money when they annexed part of his field for the Israeli-controlled bypass road they are staring down from, but he refused. "Once you accept their money," he said, "it's all over." This refusal parallels other refusals tourists hear, for example in Hebron, when they have lunch with a man who has received multiple offers from the Israelis to leave his home but refuses to, instead remaining sandwiched between settlements, earning his income from tourists having lunch above his storefront and shopping at his store. Within the program's itinerary, these refusals also structurally parallel the process of planting on land threatened by settlement expansion and settler destruction: staying despite being forced, compelled, and/or otherwise bribed to leave. As then fieldworker and now cofounder of To Be There, an organization founded to educate tourists on Palestine in spite of and in response to the excess of coverage on Palestine in the mainstream media, Baha Hilo describes the work of the campaign in the village of al-Walaja: "The Israelis destroyed one hundred trees. We came back with three hundred."[3]

On this program and others like it, half days of planting are combined with lectures, like those from the BADIL Resource Center for Palestinian Residency and Refugee Rights and the Applied Research Institute of Jerusalem (ARIJ). In these lectures, ARIJ researchers introduce tourists to other constellations of statistics: 738 checkpoints, seventy-eight of them in Hebron, splitting neighborhoods and segregating Palestinians from Palestinians, Israeli-controlled bypass roads and Israeli-only highways, the Wall, annexing Palestinian land as it backtracks on itself. Lecturers will speak of the ways the Wall annexes water: sixty-eight million cubic meters of water resources isolated within the western segregation zone of Jerusalem.

On the Olive Tree Campaign's planting program in 2012, tourists learned about Mandate Palestine, the Balfour Declaration, the initial agreement that allotted 56 percent of the land to Jews and 43 percent to Palestinians with Jerusalem the 1 percent *corpus separatum*. They learned how Israelis, after the establishment of the state, overshot the 56 percent by a landslide, claiming 78 percent of Mandate Palestine, leaving 22 percent on which the future state of Palestine was to be built. They learned how the 1993 and 1995 Oslo Accords were ostensibly an interim agreement meant to usher in the establishment of a Palestinian state but in fact divided the land into Areas A, B, and C, with varying levels of nominal Palestinian autonomy, and strategically facilitated the proliferation of settlements and land grabs since 1967.

They learned of violations of international law, escalating settlements, the extant settlements and their planned expansion, the absurdity of the claim that settlements have anything to do with security. They also learned of house demolitions—how most Palestinians are not allowed to get building permits (for example, only 105 permits out of 1,900 applications were granted between 2000 and 2007), and then their houses are subsequently demolished for not having permits: 408 demolitions in 2012 alone. They learned of changing demography, manufacturing demography, the route of the Wall, the intifadas, and Gaza. They learned about what will become of Palestine "without intervention from the international community," reminding tourists why they were there. On tours like these, this constant and deliberate recitation—the ritual of repetition—of statistics, facts, and figures is paired with tourists' movement through the West Bank (itself, as I detailed in chapter 2, more expansive than Palestinian movement). The repetition of movement and narrative coalesces in an overarching chronicle of multiple, repeated displacements, again disrupting the notion that the "Palestine Question" can be limited to the events and aftermath of 1948 or that the uprooting of Palestinian lives and land is either a closed or an aberrant chapter.

In one lecture in particular, the researcher meeting with tourists interrupted his statistics with his own story. Pausing his scripted recitation, he added, "In Jerusalem, my great-grandfather's initials are still carved on the building he owned." He then quickly transitioned to speak about planting and how cypress and fir were used only to quickly hold the land and were then removed once Israel compiled all the necessary paperwork to take it over. The process of planting to hold the land is as evidenced in contemporary state practice as it is in the beginnings of Israeli afforestation. The settlement Har Homa, for example, was classified as a green area, full of cypress and fir, until 1997. Once Israel had all the paperwork it needed, state officials cut down all the trees to rezone the area for settlement. In Beit Sahour, where these solidarity tourists spend much of their time, Har Homa overlooks everything. It hovers, well lit, neatly organized, thoroughly maintained. One tourist from Scotland marveled that the settlement houses that checkered the landscape looked like honeycomb. Another guide, on a different tour, would point to Har Homa and describe how, when it was a forest, he used to hike there with his father, bird-watch, and hunt. The suturing of narratives of loss to the politics of trees—deployed by tour guides, lecturers, and organizers to describe both metaphorical and literal displacement in the occupied West Bank—again reveals the centrality of uprooting to Israel's past and present expansion and the necessity of varied and multiple responses to these sustained processes of erasure.

Tour guides' narrative attempts to expose erasure during the Olive Tree Campaign's programs are almost always anchored to the landscape. When not in a lecture, walking tour, or planting, the tour group traveled between each site via bus. The group routinely passed fields of olive trees, some planted by previous Olive Tree Campaign groups. In 2012, for example, when the group drove past Beit Ummar, a village with a heavy settler and soldier presence, Ayman Abu Zulof, director of media outreach and French and English tour guide for the Alternative Tourism Group, pointed to vineyards and terraces, explaining, "These terraces are very old. This proves that there was always a people here taking care of the land." Terraces in Palestine, meanwhile, form an elaborate watering system that nourishes the trees without flooding the soil, protects against soil erosion, irrigates crops, and allows for water runoff. Abu Zulof's narration, repeated on several other tours—with repetition in fact functioning as strategy—accompanied the Olive Tree Campaign's itinerary of guided movement through a fractured landscape. This deliberate and strategic pairing anchors the view from the bus of cultivated, curated, and cared-for terraces, not (yet) destroyed by Israeli state and settler violence, to not only the history of expulsion but also the settler-colonial justification for that expulsion. It provides evidentiary weight, repeated to rotating groups of tourists, that functions as a response to the colonial narratives that animate Zionist settlement and claim that either there were no trees or, if there were, Palestinians didn't know how to care for them in the first place. Tourists are provided with constant—deliberately repetitious—narration describing a people very much *with* a land and a land very much *with* a people. The tours, then, provide a running and mobile corrective narration to the justificatory colonial narrative that holds that Zionist settlers were the first to care for the land.

Tourists on the Olive Tree Campaign are taken to multiple places that are fraught contact zones between international (and sometimes Palestinian) tourists, Palestinian hosts, Palestinians either uninvolved or unofficially involved in the tours, Israeli antioccupation activists, and sometimes settlers. Between lectures with West Bank organizations like BADIL and ARIJ and planting days, for example, tourists were led through Aida Refugee Camp in Bethlehem, always a voyeuristic portion of solidarity tour itineraries, with tourists walking behind and around people's homes, children running underfoot, and women attempting to go about their daily routine without tripping over the tourists blocking entrances to their homes. On the Olive Tree Campaign's tour through Aida, the guide leading the group, a resident of Bethlehem who was not from a family of refugees, argued—perhaps surprisingly—that Palestinians in refugee camps need to accept the fact that they likely will never return. Baha Hilo, a fellow guide, in an act of corrective narration, refuted the tour guide's pragmatism with his own narrative of what it means to be a refugee: "My grandfather was in a refugee camp. Just because they can't go home doesn't mean they shouldn't be here. Fighting back." Refusing to "move on," he explained, "*We inherit the loss.*" Hilo's narrative of inheriting loss would become central to the rest of the program and central to the way he interprets and envisions his work. Understanding loss as an inheritance not only defines the Nakba as ongoing, the afterlife of which is deeply felt in the present and compounded by continuities of displacement: it also makes clear why the Olive Tree Campaign places such a sustained emphasis on helping farmers stay on their land, in light of how leaving can be either incentivized or compulsory.

The central goal of the program, Hilo explains, is to help farmers stay on land that is increasingly threatened by Israeli settlement expansion. Volunteers plant

3.1 Olive tree saplings, Joint Advocacy Initiative-Alternative Tourism Group Olive Planting Program. Photo by JAI-ATG (February 2019).

olive saplings, like those pictured in figure 3.1, on land threatened by settlement expansion. On the fifth day of the 2012 program, the group planted their seven hundredth olive tree with Palestinian farmers in Beit Ummar on land that continues to be annexed by an illegal Israeli settlement. As the group planted, Israeli military vehicles circled the settlement, parked for extended lengths of time, and then circled again. A small disagreement took place between one of the solidarity tourists—a trained arborist from the UK—and the farmers' sons, with the farmers' sons rushing to plant the land before the IDF (Israel Defense Forces) intervened and the tourist/arborist wanting to loosen the roots, shift the top soil to garner the best nutrients, and face the sapling away from the wind, wanting to take more time, explaining in exasperated tones, "We don't need to rush—we have all day."

Beit Ummar's farmers' planting, in contrast, had everything to do with exigency, planting against time, with three hundred olive trees and a handful of tourists who were positioned as a protective presence for Palestinians who would otherwise not be left alone to plant on their own land. The nearby settlement had already expanded down the hill, pushing its fence outward, farther onto the family's land. The difference between the trees on Beit Ummar's side of the fence and the settlement's was stark: a cultivated and cared-for grove with grapes, spring flowers, and olive trees in neat rows in the spaces that Palestinian farmers could still access and an overgrown underbrush with dying groves within the colony's ever-expanding fence. Every time the settlers annexed more of their land, farmers in Beit Ummar were forced to watch their own trees die. These farmers, then, didn't "have all day"; they had exactly one afternoon with one group of international tourists to get all the donated trees into the ground before their planting could be interrupted and their saplings uprooted.

On the ninth day of the program, the group planted four hundred more trees in Jab'a on a field shared by four farmers now isolated from one another, with "the Wall" in the form of a highway cutting across their villages and closing the road that previously connected them. Tall, foreign, out-of-place pine trees lined the right side of the highway on the way to the land. "The trees look really nice," Hilo explained to the tourists, "but Palestinians look on these groves as a place of danger because settlers hide in them and are armed." Here, Hilo shed light on a shifting and malleable continuity in Israeli policy, with the Haganah first using the forest as a hiding place for snipers and with armed settlers policing the forest now. Here, the Wall is a bypass road that the farmers, whose land was annexed to build it, are not allowed to drive on, which abruptly ends because the Israelis haven't yet decided where they want to go with it, which land and resources they want to annex next.

A blue-and-white water pump is stationed at the edge of the field. Palestinians are not allowed to use the water expropriated from their own fields that comes from this pump, but if there is a leak, the Palestinian will be held responsible for the damage, a subjecthood not deemed worthy of water but fully recognized in terms of his capacity to be punished.[4] As tourists planted on the field, the farmer explained that all of the trees on the other side—the pine and cypress visible beyond the fence—used to be his land and that, if you got too close to the fence, they'd shoot you. The contemporary landscape of the West Bank is an extension of the Zionist afforestation that accompanied the establishment of the state, with forests of pine and cypress serving as their own forms of "protective presence" for Israeli settlers, with forests acting as placeholders for future settlements, and with the threat of violence and expulsion haunting each act of narration.

"If You Plant a Tree, That's Your Land":
Planting as a Technology of Erasure

Solidarity tour programs centered on olive harvesting and planting show how trees serve as both a technology of erasure and evidence of presence. Zionist planting—of cypress, fir, and pine—has long been part of the state project to "make the desert bloom" in Palestine, a call that, following colonial logics, erased as it named. In 1991, anthropologist Susan Slyomovics published a study of Ein Houd, the Palestinian village that became the Israeli Dada artists' colony Ein Hod in 1953 after the establishment of the State of Israel.[5] A decade later, in the documentary *500 Dunam on the Moon*, filmmaker Rachel Jones documented the "unrecognized village" of the new Ein Houd, home to the displaced Palestinian villagers who were not exiled to refugee camps in Jordan or the West Bank but who fashioned an adjacent makeshift village 1.5 kilometers away from their stolen land and homes. In naming villages "unrecognized," Israel abdicates responsibility to connect them to basic municipal amenities like water and electricity. Ein Houd did not receive official recognition—or subsequent connection to the Israeli electric grid—until 2005. Ein Hod and Ein Houd remain stops on contemporary solidarity tours (olive tree campaigns and otherwise) because of the stark disparity between Ein Hod, the affluent bohemian Israeli artist colony, with shops and cafés and art and used bookstores, nestled in a Jewish National Fund (JNF) forest with trees overlaid atop Palestinian village ruins, and Ein Houd, the nearby Palestinian village with homes in close quarters, a paucity of municipal services, dirt roads, and no manicured, beautified landscapes or art installations of the sort that pepper Ein Hod.

In her study, Slyomovics quotes Israeli Ein Hod resident Sofia Hillel, who recounted her father Isaiah Hillel's assessment of the land: "The weeds were taller than a human being. No roads, no electricity, no water. Snakes three meters long, five meters long. Scorpions. The only trees that were here were wild fig trees and the wild kind of oak, and that's all. Nothing. Not a single tree."[6] This assessment that there were no trees accumulated meaning and legitimacy as it was retold throughout the artists' colony's origin story. Slyomovics calls specific attention to the studied unwillingness among the many residents she interviewed to read the olive, fig, almond, and wild oak trees that characterize the Palestinian landscape as trees. Repeating well-worn colonial tropes, they instead characterize the carefully cultivated trees as uncultivated wilderness, virgin land, and—more often than not—"nothing." Slyomovics writes, "Every artist define[d] 'trees' as pine or cypress and never mention[ed] the local olive orchards clearly visible" in photographs from before 1953, when the artists' colony was established.[7]

The repudiation of the carefully curated Palestinian landscape is the guiding logic of the Zionist project of "making the desert bloom." With this formulation, Zionist settlers sought to, in the words of political scientist Joseph Massad, "transform . . . a 'desolate' and 'neglected' Asiatic desert into a blooming, green European terrain full of forests and trees."[8] Through this colonial logic, Palestinians, who just happened to then inhabit the land, unlike Jews to whom the land was gifted by God, did not deserve the land because they could not adequately care for it. Like other colonial settlers, Zionist settlers sought to own the landscape, expel its people, and make it their own, gaining legitimacy through the claim that the native inhabitants did not properly care for their land. Ella Shohat emphasizes how the Zionist project was a specifically Western imperial one. She writes, "Theodore Herzl called for a Western-style capitalist-democratic miniature state, to be made possible by the grace of imperial patrons such as England or Germany, while David Ben-Gurion formulated his visionary utopia of Israel as that of a 'Switzerland of the Middle East.'"[9] Like other states built via colonial settlement, Israel sought to be *in but not of* the Middle East.[10] This "Switzerland of the Middle East" would have to be marked by *trees*, that is, fast-growing pine and cypress to hold the land and quickly approximate European landscapes, and not the sprawling fig, oak, or olive groves that then characterized the land—trees that were considered "nothing" by Israeli settlers like Isaiah Hillel.

In addition to "making the desert bloom," Zionist settlement in Palestine was also predicated on the second tenet of Zionism: "a land without a people for a people without a land." Zionism was founded on an image of a "perceptually depopulated" Palestine—what Lawrence Davidson defines as a systematic discursive erasure of "the demographic and cultural/religious realities of contemporary Palestine" in the name of Judeo-Christian, and specifically American/European/Western, God-ordained investment in the land.[11] This "land without a people" was structured in opposition to the "Diaspora Jew," or "a people without a land." Shohat identifies how "Zionism viewed Europe both as ideal ego and as the signifier of ghettos, persecution, and Holocaust. Within this perspective, the 'Diaspora Jew' was an extraterritorial, rootless wanderer, someone living 'outside of history.'"[12]

This negation of the diaspora and the desire to become rooted, both in the wake of Jewish persecution in Europe and in the spirit of European (and US) settler colonialism, fueled the Zionist project and, by extension, the project of afforestation in Palestine. Simon Schama describes what tree planting in Israel meant to Jews in the diaspora who grew up putting coins in Jewish National Fund boxes in classrooms to contribute to the cause of turning Israel into a forest: "The trees were our proxy immigrants, the forests our implantation. . . . The diaspora was sand. So what should Israel be, if not a forest, fixed and tall?"[13] A "forest, fixed and tall," with cypress and fir as stand-ins for both Israelis and diaspora Jews who will not or have not yet immigrated, and no mention of the extant groves of fig and olive across the landscape, epitomizes the guiding logic behind the process of displacement that inhered and inheres in Zionist afforestation. Even more, the trees served as "proxy immigrants" for those who did not/could not immigrate *and* stood in opposition to the "sand" of the diaspora and the "sand" of the desert they were ostensibly making bloom with their daily/weekly/monthly contributions to the Jewish National Fund.[14]

While accounts of Israeli afforestation as part of the Zionist project of "making the desert bloom" have received vast scholarly attention, much of this literature remains contained to the intersection of environmental studies and Middle East studies.[15] Yet fields like American studies, ethnic studies, feminist studies, and queer studies have much to add to and learn from this place-based conversation about erasure, displacement, and greenwashing, especially since there are so many resonances with other sites, underscored by scholars in these fields, where the colonial logics of deforestation and defoliation have shaped the landscape, from North America to Vietnam to South Africa.[16] The project of afforestation in Palestine, initiated and maintained by the Jewish National Fund, preceded and then accompanied the establishment of the State of Israel and has since seen over 240 million trees planted across Palestine/Israel.[17] The project began, in 1908, with a donor-funded initiative to plant an olive grove to be named the Herzl Forest. In 1902, Herzl published the foundational utopian Zionist novel *Altneuland*, a constituent element of which was the narration (from the future) of the transformation of the landscape from Arab villages, barren nothingness, and "clay hovels . . . unfit for stables" to thriving eucalyptus forests to drain the swamps and "vines, pomegranate and fig trees as in the ancient days of Solomon."[18] Paired with, and in part narrating, this rendering of the landscape was the synecdochic Palestinian character Reschid (studiously referred to throughout as Arab and not Palestinian), who testified to Arabs' inability to care for the land and extolled the merits of the project of "making the desert bloom."

The Herzl Forest was first planted by hired Palestinian workers, which incited so much anger among members of the Jewish community, who advocated exclusively "Hebrew labor," that they arrived at the site, uprooted the olive saplings, and planted their own along with pine and cypress trees to show that the site was "more than just a commercial olive grove."[19] Endemic to this beginning is the sentiment that has shaped the Zionist project of afforestation since its inception: first, the deeply settler-colonial logic that maintains that Indigenous people neglect the land on which they happen to live, and thus need not be granted any rights to its stewardship; second, the notion that the project of Zionist afforestation is a natural extension of biblical times, which characterizes all that came in between biblical times and the establishment of the (then-potential) state as aberrant and indicative of the land not living up to its biblical potential; and third, the disparagement of the "commercial olive grove," an important source of economic sustenance for Palestinians, in favor of a European pine and cypress forest.[20] This hierarchical ordering places cypress and pine, as symbolic manifestations of European allegiances, above income-generating olive groves, which were already conceptualized in the proto-Israeli imaginary as "not trees" as the land was repeatedly described as barren notwithstanding the expansive fig and olive groves that covered the landscape and provided livelihoods for Palestinians. In this way, the Zionist repudiation of Palestinian trees was a negation of Palestinian presence on the land that also paved the way for the destruction of extant Palestinian economies of production.

While the Herzl Forest initiated the project, Israeli afforestation did not begin in earnest until after the massacre at Dayr Yasin in 1948, which was carried out by the Jewish terrorist groups the Stern Gang and the Irgun and also sanctioned by the Haganah's Operation Nachshon.[21] According to Palestinian historian Walid Khalidi, it was "the best-known and perhaps bloodiest atrocity of the war."[22] The Dayr Yasin Massacre took the lives of 245 people, half of whom were women and children, after parading them through Jerusalem in a "victory convoy," notwithstanding the fact that Dayr Yasin had signed a nonaggression pact with the Haganah.[23] The village was left "empty," and afforestation then provided the sole means of employment for the Jewish settlers who occupied the village and renamed it Givat Shaul.[24] In the wake of the massacre, the settlers built a huge forest, which burned down entirely four years later.[25] In 1956, partially in response to the destruction of the forest at Givat Shaul, the JNF expanded its reach and drew up plans for afforestation on a far larger scale.[26] The massacre at Dayr Yasin thus marked the beginning of afforestation in Israel, first after the village's depopulation to employ new Jewish settlers, and again with a renewed vehemence after the cypress and pine forest that the settlers had planted burned down. Today, the eastern part of Dayr Yasin is covered by Givat Shaul; the western sector of the village is surrounded by the urban sprawl of Israeli West Jerusalem.[27] Yad Vashem, Israel's Holocaust museum and remembrance center in Jerusalem, routes tourists and visitors to a final viewpoint from which they take in a view of the Holy Land that, unbeknownst to most visitors, includes the former village lands and massacre site of Dayr Yasin.

After the destruction of the forest, the JNF, under the jurisdiction of Yosef Wietz, director of afforestation and staunch advocate of "transferring" the Palestinian population out of Israel, embarked on planting a "green belt" around Jerusalem. Under Weitz's authority, the JNF planted 130,000 seedlings in its first planting season alone (1956–1957).[28] JNF trees were often planted during periods when the state was violently asserting itself through war, as they were in the aftermath of the massacre at Dayr Yasin. Periods of intense afforestation occurred in the wake of the creation of the state in 1948, during the Suez War in 1956, and accompanying the 1967 occupation of the West Bank, Gaza, East Jerusalem, the Sinai Peninsula, and Golan Heights. Trees were planted to cover up the existence of Palestinian villages and remnants of Israeli violence and to serve strategic purposes that facilitated military action and surveillance. They were marshaled in the service of war as they secured the land, foreclosed Palestinian use, and acted as "security groves" to conceal Israeli soldiers and protect them from sniper fire.[29]

In the wake of 1967, the JNF began planting even more aggressively in the West Bank, adding to the roughly forty-two million trees it planted in the ten years following the massacre at Dayr Yasin. By 1968, it had planted ninety million trees, over seventy million of which were fast-growing evergreens.[30] Since the 1967 War also displaced thousands of refugees, many of whom took their land documents with them, the majority of the land in the West Bank was not registered and thus was immediately named "Abandoned Property" and considered Israeli state land.[31] This appropriation of so-called abandoned property, coupled with land confiscation in the form of military installations, nature reserves, and recreational sites, marked the process of post-1967 afforestation and settlement in the newly occupied territories.[32] The JNF planted quick-growing pine, cypress, and eucalyptus trees to serve as security groves, boundary markers, indicators of ownership, signs of presence, and foreclosures of Palestinian use of the land. The JNF described its trees as "the best guards of the land"; they ascertained that "walls and fences can be cut down. A tree says, 'we are here.' If you plant a tree, that's your land."[33]

Journalist David Bloom, for example, narrates the story of Jayyous, a town in the West Bank of three thousand people, who lost 20 percent of their lands in 1948. Their lands were immediately redistributed to Israeli farmers. After 1948, one villager used to "lead his donkey at night to what was once his family's apricot orchards, across the Green Line, and helped himself to the fruit. He called himself and his donkey 'the Apricot Liberation Front.'"[34] Geographer Shaul Cohen similarly narrates the history of the village of Katannah, where, after 1948, a majority of its land, including its olive grove, remained on the Israeli side of the Green Line and was thus expropriated by the government, which sold the grove to a nearby kibbutz.[35] Following 1967, "the villagers . . . gradually . . . resumed harvesting from [the trees], generally under the cover of darkness."[36] In retaliation, the Israel Land Administration uprooted three thousand trees.[37]

In the years following 1967, Palestinian olive planting in the West Bank became illegal via both civil and military orders. The 1989 Civil Administration prevented Palestinians from planting fruit trees and vegetables in the West Bank without a special permit, and the 1982 Military Order 1015 maintained that no one could plant, transplant, or sow fruit trees in an orchard without a written permit from a certified authority.[38] Israeli authorities punished Palestinian planting with the destruction of the trees in question, one year's imprisonment, and/or a fine that escalated with each day the plant remained in the ground.[39] Israel's attempt to preclude the viability of Palestinian agriculture belies the settler-colonial narrative woven throughout Israeli afforestation projects that claimed Israelis were the first "in seventy generations" to cultivate the land.[40]

Twinning militarization with the strangulation of self-sustaining Palestinian agricultural labor, the state used its forests to provide vantage points and shelter for the Israeli Army, cultivate national sentiment in terms of the production of European sameness, and make the Palestinian agricultural sector untenable, which in turn provided rhetorical justification for the narrative that there were no trees to begin with, and if there were, Palestinians couldn't and didn't deserve to properly care for them anyway. The trees—both the uprooting of Palestinian olive, almond, and fig trees and the planting of cypress and fir— served Israeli land expropriation and military occupation not only by erecting "security groves" and securing the land for the prevention of Palestinian use but also by covering up the debris of the Palestinian villages upon which the Israeli state was built. These newly created national parks, state land, and "facts on the ground" on the ruins of Palestinian olive, fig, almond, and apricot groves served as evidence of Israeli, and not Palestinian, presence and attempted to facilitate the erasure and papering over of all that had come before.

Planting and Harvesting as Evidence of Presence

In his 1974 novel *The Secret Life of Saeed: The Pessoptimist*, a canonical text in Palestinian literary studies, Emile Habiby described the tension between planting as a technology of occupation and planting as a reminder of presence by way of Tawfiq Zayyad's poem "The Olive Tree":

> I shall carve the name of every stolen pot
> And where my village boundaries lay;
> What homes exploded,
> What trees were uprooted, what tiny wild flowers crushed.
> All this to remember. And I'll keep on carving
> Each act of this my tragedy, each phase of the catastrophe,
> All things, minor and major,
> On an olive tree in the courtyard of my home.[41]

The protagonist, Saeed, reflects on the poem to ask, "How long must he continue carving? How soon will these years of oblivion pass, effacing all our memories? When will the words carved on the olive tree be read? And are there any olives left in courtyards still?"[42] This dual reference to the olive tree uprooted and the olive tree in exile is only one of many narrative examples wherein the uprooting of the olive tree mirrors the uprooting of Palestinian people from their land, while the durability of the olive tree simultaneously signals the sumud, or steadfastness, of Palestinian people.

Olive tree program tour guides—ritually and seasonally—teach tourists how to plant or harvest olive trees; they also teach tourists that these histories of uprooting and planting cannot be consigned to the past. With each tour, they not only position Palestinian olive trees as evidence of presence but also show how this uprooting marks a colonial present and not only a colonial past: an ongoing Nakba. One researcher and political tour organizer, who has long arranged and curated harvesting and planting trips to Palestine, described a family with whom he worked who had ever-receding access to the olive trees on their own land:

> In the olive harvest, we help a certain family near Bethlehem. When we started helping them in 2006, their field was accessible. In 2007, there was a gate between us and their [field] that we could open. The following year, there was a wall and a fence and we, the local staff, could not reach the land, but the participants of the olive harvest could go. In just one more year, it

was completely inaccessible, so the participants had to go from a different route, to Jerusalem, which is inaccessible by Palestinians and local staff, and go there and come to the field from a completely different site.[43]

He concluded, "Every year there is a new challenge imposed on you that you will have to deal with."[44] Detailing an expanding regime of Israeli control in the West Bank that determines if and when Palestinians can access their fields, the number of days per year they can plant and/or harvest, and who is allowed to access them, he described a seemingly arbitrary system where one year access is granted and the next year it is taken away, one year Palestinian families can harvest their own land and the next they need to solicit the help of internationals who have access they are not granted.

"What happened in 1948 continues to happen today, but instead of happening in Israel, it's happening in the Occupied West Bank," he surmised.[45] He detailed the Olive Tree Campaign's work in Beit Sahour, for example, where so many tourists reside during their time in Palestine. He explained that there are many families who look at their property without having access to it: "They can see it, they can see their olive trees, they can see their fields, but they can't have access to them because now it's illegal for them."[46] "So," he continued, "just like it was illegal for Palestinians in 1948 to return to their property, Palestinians today are not allowed . . . to have access to their property. It's the same kind of attitude, the same kind of policy, that has been in place and empowered ever since 1948."[47] The history of Israeli afforestation—the uprooting of Palestinian olive trees, the planting of cypress and fir to manufacture a "Switzerland of the Middle East," the use of Israeli groves as boundary markers and "security groves," the foreclosure of Palestinian use of the land, and the erasure of the evidence of Palestinian presence and cultivation—can neither be relegated to a distant past nor circumscribed to the tangible (yet ever shifting) borders of Israel.

The state, the military, and the Jewish National Fund continue to traffic in a sustained process of uprooting Palestinian olive trees in the interest of "security," punishment, and erasure. Since 1967, Israeli authorities have uprooted 800,000 Palestinian olive trees, and 80,000 Palestinian families who rely economically on the olive harvest have lost a total of US$12.3 million from these attacks on their livelihoods.[48] Over 80 percent of olive farmers own orchards of approximately 250 trees, and olive production provides key employment for Palestinian workers, resulting in three million seasonal workdays for agricultural laborers per year.[49] The olive oil sector contributes $100 million to families in Palestine, and olive trees, many of which are between one hundred and one thousand years old, are stolen from the occupied Palestinian territories and sold in Israel, 50 percent without legal permits, for tens of thousands of dollars.[50] Restrictions on farmers' access to their fields—which are manifold in the West Bank—are thus direct attacks on Palestinian farmers' livelihoods and concrete attempts to expel them from their land.

When Palestinian olive trees are uprooted, they are often sold not only within Israel's 1948 borders but also in Israeli settlements.[51] For example, a giant, ancient olive tree can be seen "welcoming" settlers and their guests into the settlement of Ma'ale Adummim. Jeff Halper, director of the Israeli Committee Against House Demolitions (ICAHD), explains to tourists on ICAHD tours that "it's becoming very fashionable among the nouveau riche in northern Tel Aviv to have an olive tree."[52] Here, the olive tree is a mobile and shifting sign—when mobilized for the purposes of the state and its settlements, it can come to signify uninterrupted Israeli claims to the land, irrespective of Palestinian presence, like the "vines, pomegranate and fig trees as in the ancient days of Solomon" from Herzl's *Altneuland*. When olive trees that were cultivated for generations by Palestinians are stolen and replanted for aesthetic purposes in Israeli spaces like northern Tel Aviv, the olive tree can come to signify taste, culture, and status for the nouveau riche. In the case of Ma'ale Adummim, the olive tree also reads as proof of ownership; an ancient olive tree adorning the entrance to a settlement makes it clear to Palestinians that while they may be in close proximity to what was once theirs, they can no longer access it.

The justifications Israel levels for uprooting Palestinian olive trees in the West Bank mark a continuity, not a rupture, with past Zionist afforestation across Palestine/Israel. The state marshals explanations grounded in "national security," especially in terms of the routine uprooting to make way for the ever-expanding Separation Wall. Tens of thousands of trees have been uprooted to facilitate the construction of the Wall.[53] Oxfam noted in 2011 that "once the Wall is completed, some one million trees will be caught in the Seam Zone," where farmers are not allowed access to their land. In the village of Qafeen, for example, 12,600 trees were uprooted for the Wall, and an additional 100,000 remained on land in Seam Zones, inaccessible to the farmers.[54] The villager from Jayyous, who named his and his donkey's post-1948 midnight harvesting the "Apricot Liberation Front," later saw 70 percent of the village's remaining farmland and all its irrigated land caught in the Seam Zone after the Wall was built.[55] Like the three hundred farmers who no longer have access to their lands in Jayyous, all the Palestinian farmers in Qafeen can do is "gaze on the neglect from afar."[56]

As Palestinian lawyer and author Raja Shehadeh noted in 2012, "More than 40 percent of the West Bank is now effectively off limits to Palestinians or very difficult for them to access because of settlements and other outposts, military bases, bypass roads and areas that Israel has declared as nature reserves."[57]

Like trees demarcating settlement perimeters and decorating Israeli landscapes, trees in the form of nature reserves are also deployed to sever Palestinians from their groves and livelihoods. There are seventy-three barriers in the West Bank preventing Palestinians from accessing their olive groves, fifty-two of which are closed during the entire year with the exception of limited hours during harvest season.[58] In 2011 alone, Israeli authorities rejected 42 percent of Palestinian applications to access their fields.[59] This continuity of the destruction of Palestinian livelihood persists also in terms of the JNF's active role in destroying the homes of Palestinians in the West Bank, Palestinian citizens in Israel, and Bedouins inside Israel to make way for Israeli forests. As one example of many, since July 2010, Israel has tried to expel the Bedouin villagers of al-Araqib—an "unrecognized village," like Ein Houd was, in the Negev Desert inside Israel's 1948 borders, with no electricity, water, or infrastructure—186 times via a combination of demolitions, rubber bullets, and tear gas. At the time of this writing, the most recent attempted expulsion occurred on March 11, 2021.[60] It will undoubtedly be more by the time of publication.

This attempted expulsion was meant to make way for a JNF "peace forest" funded by GOD TV, an evangelical TV station based in the United States, the UK, and Israel.[61] That a forest is planned for a site that has seen the repeated demolition of Bedouin villagers' homes reveals the deliberate and sustained settler logic of supplanting the native population and attempting to pave over the extant village with Israeli markers of presence. Even more, that this forest is to be a "peace forest" exposes the twinning of settler logic with liberal political rhetoric, detailing how "peace" and settler colonialism can function in concert. Still more, that this forest is funded by an evangelical Christian Zionist TV station speaks to the long, entangled history of Christian Zionist rhetorical and material support for Israeli settler-colonial state practice.[62] From the punitive destruction of olive trees and rapid planting of cypress and fir in the wake of Dayr Yasin, to the post-1948 apricot smuggling, to the consistent post-1967 restrictions on Palestinian agricultural production, to the contemporary theft of trees and their replanting in settlements, to the "peace forests" planned for Palestinian land, the history of Israel's attempts to make Palestinian sustenance impossible is one of continuity: a settler colonial structure that, in the words of Ann Laura Stoler, rejects "colonial appellations" and travels by other names.[63]

This violence is enacted, without consequence, not only by the Israeli state and through its military orders but also by Israeli settlers. During the annual olive harvest of 2013 alone, field researchers for B'Tselem documented twenty-seven incidents of settler violence against Palestinians and their property.[64] Settlers attacked harvesters with stones, assaulted harvesters physically, and in six cases threatened them with weapons; in another twenty-one cases, settlers burned or chopped down olive trees, destroyed or sawed off branches, stole olives and agricultural equipment, or poisoned olive groves.[65]

These attacks are not only—as is most often reported—the burning down of trees and destruction of olive tree branches. These attacks also often include the theft of the olives themselves. In 2013, Ibrahim Salah, a farmer from the village of Far'ata, described how nearby settlers had vandalized his crops, chopped down his trees, and reduced his crop from 180 to 130 trees; how the Israeli military had regulated his access to his crops, allowing him to plow only one month per year; and then how settlers picked all the olives off his remaining 130 trees. Describing that season's harvest, which was limited to two days, he said, "We got less than one full sack of olives. Before the vandalism began, when I could go to my land and work all year round, we used to get forty to fifty sacks of olives a year."[66] In detailing a system in which the occupying military "allows" him to access his own land only via coordinated visits and only for *two days* during the entire harvest season, Salah describes what anthropologist Irus Braverman calls the "regulatory regime" of Israeli military control over Palestinian agriculture.[67]

In another testimony, collected from field researchers for B'Tselem, Salah Radwan of 'Azzun, who did have regular access to his field and was there almost every day, said he came to his field on October 13, 2013, to prepare to irrigate. "At first," he said, "I thought the wind had broken the trees, but when I got closer, I saw that about sixty trees had been chopped down with a saw."[68] He reflected, echoing the sentiment in Tawfiq Zayyad's poem about the palimpsest of inscriptions on the courtyard olive tree, "When I saw our strong, flowering branches chopped off and lying on the ground, I was in shock. It pained me. I know every single tree there, because I take care of them and I planted and cultivated them with my brothers."[69] Radwan continued, "I dreamt of those trees being a source of income for me and my brothers, but that dream was shattered on Thursday morning."[70] Like the "tiny wildflowers crushed," Salah Radwan's description of severed flowering branches scattered across the ground underscores the violence of Israeli state and settler destruction of Palestinian cultivation. At the same time, his narration underscores the effects of this violence on his family's sustenance: the dream, now rendered impossible, of the olive trees providing income for his family. Here again, as with the destruction at Dayr Yasin, settlers traffic in yet another decimation of a commercial olive grove, a violent circumscription of Palestinian income-generating and self-sustaining agricultural production.

These are only two testimonies from one year. The majority of cases of documented settler violence are closed without indictment. Of ninety-seven cases specifically documenting olive tree destruction between 2005 and 2012, for example, not one case resulted in an indictment.[71] The collusion of the state and its settlers in the destruction of income-generating Palestinian agricultural production renders inadequate and incomplete any condemnation of settler violence that is not sutured to a condemnation of state violence. Further, a condemnation of *only* settler violence and destruction of Palestinian olive trees obscures the multiple ways the state has been destroying Palestinian trees since before its inception—from the 1908 Herzl Forest to the sustained project of "making the desert bloom"—by destroying that which was already blossoming.

Whether uprooted by military orders, uprooted to make way for the Wall, or destroyed because of settler violence condoned by the Israeli state, the 800,000 olive trees that have been uprooted since 1967, with a loss of $55 million to the Palestinian economy per year, are attacks against Palestinian viability that are sanctioned by the State of Israel and part of the continuity of Israeli colonial occupation. Further, whether uprooted to clear the way for planting Israeli exports or decimated through Palestinian Authority policies of indifference and redirected funds, the agricultural fields that have historically provided sustenance for Palestinians and enabled them to stay on their land have been destroyed, rendered inaccessible, or deemed accessible only for Israeli profit.[72] It is in this political and territorial climate that Palestinian organizers have sought, via the fraught vehicle of tourism paired with the ritual acts of planting and harvesting, to negotiate and circumvent both the borders and mandates of the Israeli settler-colonial regulatory regime and the nominal and limited control of the Palestinian Authority and its donor-driven priorities to craft tourist itineraries with the expressed goal of helping Palestinians stay on their land.

Permission to Narrate, Refusal to Leave

From Nabhan Mousa's refusal to sell his land in al-Khader, to tour guides reminding tourists (and other tour guides) that refugees inherit the loss into which they were born, to organizers asking international tourists to help plant trees on land that is increasingly inaccessible to the Palestinian farmers who own it, the Olive Tree Campaign's central purpose is to keep Palestinians on their land. "We know," Hilo emphasized, "the situation gets worse by the year in order to force Palestinians to leave."[73] Here, Hilo described not an inevitable process of land expropriation but a systematic, deliberate process of land theft orchestrated to make Palestinian life so impossible that they will choose exile and diaspora over the fragments of sustenance available to them in the West Bank.

Hilo described a fragmentation of Palestinian land meant to provide Israel with "the land without its native people,"[74] in Ilan Pappé's corrective rephrasing of the Zionist tenet, a "land without a people for a people without a land." Like Pappé, Hilo simultaneously tethered this fragmentation and land expropriation to a long history of uprooting endemic to Israeli state practice since the inception of the state. The itineraries of the Olive Tree Campaign are meant, then, to bring scores of tourists to help Palestinian farmers plant against the clock and harvest fields in an afternoon in a quantity and at a pace they and their families could not otherwise accomplish or on fields they and their families could not otherwise access.

Bisan Kassis, advocacy officer at the Joint Advocacy Initiative at the time of my research, also described her work with the Olive Tree Campaign as buoying her faith in Palestinian resistance. Echoing her colleague Yazan al-Zubaidy, who half joked that Palestinians need a "mass therapist," she explained, "We really need psychological counseling or debriefing. It's very frustrating to be met with these atrocities, but one small thing will recalibrate you. It's 99 percent negative, but this 1 percent positive that happens once in a blue moon."[75] When the University of Johannesburg broke ties with Ben-Gurion University, for example, Kassis recalled how the Campaign rejoiced for a month. As another example, she explained the Campaign's celebration in 2011 when a farmer won a lawsuit against a settler after fighting for ten years. Lingering on these victories within and outside the Campaign, allows Kassis, al-Zubaidy, and Hilo to narrate the effects of occupation in a seemingly endless ritual of recitation while simultaneously finding a way to be sustained by the incremental positive change they witness through their work—change they define as staying in a situation that is attempting to force them to leave.

Kassis, for her part, reframed the touring and witnessing that solidarity tourists do as an act of being *invited* and *allowed* to partake in the harvest. Speaking of the farmers, she explained, "You understand that these people are doing resistance every day. Just by going to their field they are resisting. You going with them during their hottest season for them, which is the season with the most percentage of attacks, you understand that you are partaking in the culture of resistance."[76] Here, Kassis positions generosity not as a gift the tourists are giving Palestinians but as a gift Palestinians are giving tourists—a generosity in sharing their culture of resistance, for a brief moment, with international tourists in Palestine.

Another organizer with the Campaign described the work as restructuring international expectations by disrupting their understandings that they are in Palestine to do charity. She described how internationals come to Palestine, feeling like they have to "do" something and come with an "idea of charity." Shaking her head and rolling her eyes, she explained that Westerners come to Palestine with the mindset, "We will help these poor people who don't know how to do anything themselves."[77] Farmers, she clarified, "could also harvest the trees themselves, but they actually—in their hospitality—*allow you* to take part in this cultural yearly event."[78]

This restructuring of tourists helping farmers into farmers generously allowing tourists to partake in their harvest and their culture of resistance attempts to intervene in tourists approaching Palestine—whether during the first intifada or today—as a site for pity and charity. She continued, "The Palestinians can deal with themselves. You have to go back home and put your efforts into changing your community, your church, your leaders. 'Cause it's a very strange. . . . mentality of the Western people, you know, we have to go and bring the gospel, we have to go and bring democracy, or something. You know, they don't need it."[79] Thus, although Palestinian farmers may use international mobility to access their fields, they don't need it—they could find, and have long found, other ways to work around the restrictions that confine them. Instead, they are allowing internationals to partake in the planting or harvest in order that internationals will join or build movements at their home bases that enable them to continue the work they began in Palestine, the work of keeping Palestinians on their land under a settler-colonial occupation that views them as a demographic threat.

Kassis further emphasized that her work with the Olive Tree Campaign is meant to help tourists understand that solidarity with Palestine is not a humanitarian cause. It is not, she emphasized, for tourists to come to Palestine, plant some trees, and then feel good about themselves. She wanted tourists to feel not pity but "sympathy mixed with anger," to say to themselves, "We are witnessing a new kind of apartheid and not doing anything about it."[80] Kassis's descriptions of her work reflect a disciplined shift away from allowing tourists to feel comfortable and complacent in their "voluntourism." She instead structures her work with the Campaign around making sure tourists understand that they are meant to "participate in a culture of resistance" not just in Palestine but specifically at home.

As the advocacy officer for the JAI, she explained that she tells tourists how well the boycott and divestment campaigns are going and how what she needs from them is to go home, lobby their governments, and work toward sanctions. "The B is going brilliantly, the D is going brilliantly, and we need you for the S," she routinely and ritually says. Central to guides' and organizers' work, then, is restructuring tourists' approach to Palestine in an attempt to divert them away from voluntourism (while still inviting them to volunteer), to get them to understand that they are not the ones doing the gift-giving; to encourage them to see that while they are invited to Palestine for a moment, they are not invited to stay; and to learn that their work is not in helping in Palestine but in boycotting, divesting, and pushing sanctions from home.

These interviews with Campaign fieldworkers and guides evidence an approach to solidarity tourism in Palestine that utilizes the mobility of internationals and the strategy of repetition as ritual to keep Palestinians rooted in their land. Their work, and olive tree harvesting and planting initiatives like it, seeks to intervene in narratives that Israelis were the first to care for the land and instead traces a history of Israel laboring to make Palestinian agricultural production impossible. In this, they aim to shift international perceptions about what their presence in Palestine is and means. In their descriptions of their labor and how they understand it, Hilo, al-Zubaidy, and Kassis explained why they do this work, notwithstanding its incremental rewards and the assumptions they repeatedly have to upend. They describe the moments—from new shops opened to boycott initiatives passed to farmer's settlements won— that make their work meaningful at the same time that they describe their sense of hopelessness at witnessing the things they narrate to tourists and their sense of frustration at tourists' misunderstandings of what they are in Palestine to do.

In this way, they describe a process that is grounded in the precarious, and sometimes impossible, task of keeping Palestinians anchored to the land at the same time that it relies on the precarious, and sometimes impossible, task of repeatedly asking internationals to rethink their role in Israeli occupation, from their purchases and investments at home to their presence and assumptions in Palestine. The work of Palestinian solidarity tour guides—and particularly those who labor to help Palestinians stay on their land—is thus largely about negotiating this precarity and impossibility on a daily basis while also consistently imparting the long and layered history of both displacement and resistance that they have inherited.

"What Trees Were Uprooted, What Tiny Wildflowers Crushed": Stolen Olives and the Continuity of Rupture

The history of displacement that these tours narrate cannot be contained to a single year (1948 or 1967) or a single act (the Nakba or the Naksa, Arabic for setback), or a single process (Israeli afforestation). That displacement spills out beyond the limits of the 1948 invasion of Dayr Yasin, beyond the post-1948 need for the Apricot Liberation Front, beyond the post-1967 harvesting under the cover of darkness in Katannah, beyond Ibrahim Salah's stolen olives in 2013, beyond al-Khader, where farmers like Nabhan Mousa use the protective presence of international tourists to help plant their groves under the surveillance of IDF soldiers pacing on the hill above. That displacement is written into the Zionist project of fashioning a landscape marked by trees of a certain sort, a landscape that necessitates sustained erasure.

The fieldworkers and guides described here are attempting to combat those multiple and daily processes of erasure by helping farmers stay on their land, intervening in Israeli narratives of "making the desert bloom" by exposing histories of expulsion and thwarted cultivation and restructuring international desire. Without requiring displaced Palestinians to repeat and rehearse their own stories of displacement, fieldworkers and guides collect research, gather resources, compile statistics, and narrate histories of erasure. Guides' own stories—from "We inherit the loss" to "In Jerusalem, my great grandfathers' initials are still carved on the building he owned"—appear as a tangential, yet central, piece of the narration of presence in the face of erasure. These tour guides remind tourists that they are in Palestine to help in whatever limited and truncated ways they can (planting on threatened land, harvesting by way of their unrestricted mobility in fields West Bank Palestinians can no longer access); to take note of what they see (remembering who they meet and what kinds of destruction and rebuilding they witness); and to learn (and not to teach, training as an arborist notwithstanding). The Olive Tree Campaign, then, is organized around exposing the continuity of strategic Zionist displacement in Palestine: a collection of similar technologies of uprooting with a set of similar justifications, from "security" to "protection," and a set of similar purposes of foreclosing Palestinian use of the land to hasten the possibility that they will not remain. Their narrations lay bare the cyclical and repeated tactics of state violence and the justifications that bolster it. The narration of a singular, contained event called the Nakba obfuscates the underlying consistency that these tours make clear: a slow and incremental expulsion in the wake of a series of less subtle ones.

Through the fraught, unwieldy, and inherently repetitive vehicle of tourism, where tour guides can script a narrative but can't predict what it will look like to teach fifty tourists to quickly plant and harvest olive trees before the IDF intervenes, the Olive Tree Campaign has crafted a program that is nonetheless a small but significant pedagogical and material intervention in the erasure that makes unchecked Israeli settler colonial expansion possible. This chapter has taken as its subject the histories of expulsion, erasure, and continuity in Palestine, specifically through analyzing sustained practices of uprooting in the contemporary West Bank alongside past and present displacement inside Israel's 1948 borders. Further, this chapter has sought to highlight the work of tour guides attempting to teach this history, with repetition as both ritual and strategy, and attempting to help Palestinian famers stay where they are, from their grove in al-Khader to their terrace in al-Walaja. Through their narrative labor, predicated on repetition, the guides and organizers introduced here draw these connections for tourists and trace these histories of afforestation and expulsion, with the olive tree at the center of the narration. In this way, the continuity between olive trees razed in 2013, the "tiny wildflowers crushed" in 1948, and the saplings uprooted in 1908 demonstrates, for tourists, the need for an end to an endless Nakba. The Olive Tree Campaign thus works within a deliberately historical tenor to ask tourists to reconsider what they thought they knew about the Nakba, displacement, and the ruptures and continuities between past and present Israeli occupation. Like repeatedly describing the Wall to tourists to resist normalizing its looming presence, here, too, guides and organizers mobilize recitation against erasure, intervening in the colonial refrains that they were never there to begin with.

FOUR

ITINERARIES UNDER DURESS
TOURS ACROSS THREE
OCCUPATIONS OF ONE CITY

Halfway through a ten-day delegation in the summer of 2019, solidarity tourists spent the day in Dheisheh Refugee Camp. By this point in the program, delegates had learned about the partition in 1948; afforestation across Historic Palestine; the ravaging of Palestinian communities from Jerusalem to Hebron to Bethlehem to Ramallah to Jaffa; the plight of internally displaced Palestinians inside Israel's 1948 borders; and the theft of Palestinian resources to make Israeli communities thrive. While some delegates worked on a mural, danced dabke with youth from the camp, and made music with local artists, one delegate, a white woman from California, after chatting with a local Palestinian man on his property, began walking around his yard picking up trash for nearly an hour. She had collected two plastic bags full of garbage by the time she neared a group of other delegates. "There's just trash everywhere," she sighed. A Palestinian volunteer with the camp drew from his cigarette and laughed uncomfortably. "Yup, it's everywhere," he offered. She looked mournful and shook her head: "Just no connection to the earth." The volunteer said nothing. This delegate had spent five days hearing about how Palestinians are both exiled from their land and not granted the municipal services to take care of the land they still have. She had learned of how deeply connected generations of

Palestinians are to the land and the trees that have routinely been stolen from them. Yet, "no connection to the earth" was how she explained the prevalence of trash in the West Bank: a damning and wildly inaccurate presupposition that assumes that those who live in beautifully manicured spaces are (1) the ones who do the manicuring and (2) the ones who care for the environment, while those who are forced to live alongside their trash—because authorities refuse to collect it—do not value either cleanliness or the environment.[1]

Similarly, one Jerusalem solidarity tour guide, when taking tourists through the eastern part of Occupied Jerusalem,[2] often labors to point out, as tourists take in scenes of piles of trash, rubble, and debris from their bus windows, "The Palestinians who live here in East Jerusalem who pay taxes and work for the city have to wake up every morning and go clean neighborhoods in the western part of Jerusalem." In an interview with me, she sipped her coffee and rolled her eyes: "If one more tourist asks me about the trash . . ." This willingness to blame Palestinians for the conditions in which they live is not limited to trash and is also not limited to the colonial present; as the preceding chapters have shown, Zionists have long made the case that Palestinians do not deserve to live on their land because they cannot adequately care for it. In this context, tour guides struggle to tether the tourist gaze of what they are witnessing to the concrete material conditions that have produced what they are witnessing. This labor, in a city like Jerusalem, which is teeming with tourists, is an intervention in the narrative sold to tourists—a narrative that both justifies and perpetuates displacement across and beyond the city itself.

This chapter takes Jerusalem as its subject and asks what it means to stage meaningful and incremental interventions in multiple forms across one occupied city. Focusing on Jerusalem as a city under manifold forms of military occupation, and positioning decolonial tourism as a form of creative, albeit fraught, intervention in the narrative Israel sells about Jerusalem, I ask, How are Palestinian tour guides organizing across the different forms of occupation that animate their lives and work? I draw from participant observations on different solidarity tours in Jerusalem and from interviews with tour guides and organizers to show how Israel has consistently sought to isolate Palestinians in Jerusalem and hasten their departure from the city and to study the work tour guides are doing to anchor Palestinian businesses in the city and wrest back the narrative of the city from Israeli control.

Israel's occupation of Jerusalem takes divergent forms, from its attempts to sever Jerusalem from the broader West Bank to its attempts to divide Palestinians in Jerusalem from Palestinians across Historic Palestine. While East Jerusalem

has become a shorthand for "Occupied Jerusalem," all of Jerusalem is occupied. West Jerusalem is home to sprawling mansions that belonged to Palestinians who were exiled in 1948—homes that are currently occupied by affluent
Israelis, settlers by another name. The Old City witnesses Israeli settlers taking
over one apartment floor at a time and Israeli archaeological and tourist projects excavating the tunnels beneath Palestinian homes, forcing the evacuation
of Palestinian families and the shuttering of Palestinian-owned businesses.
The eastern part of Occupied Jerusalem is a site where both the Wall and expanding settlements—treated by the state as "suburbs" of Jerusalem—extract
land and resources from neighboring Palestinian towns that are not granted
municipal services. As with the Old City, East Jerusalem is also marked by the
sustained and repeated violence of forced evictions in the name of Israeli tourist initiatives, seen most recently in the siege on the neighborhoods of Silwan
and Sheikh Jarrah in May 2021 by Israeli settlers and the police who protect
them to make way for Israel's biblically inspired King David Park tourist site.[3]

Palestinian guides labor to organize differentiated tours across these three
sites: bus and walking tours of former Palestinian mansions in West Jerusalem, walking tours of settlement expansion inside the Old City, and bus tours
of a plundered and neglected East Jerusalem. The narratives provided on these
tours intervene in the tourist narrative Israel sells about the city, a narrative
predicated on renewal and return, a narrative that hinges on the erasure of
Palestinian presence in the city. Culling from extensive research and producing
cogent analyses of colonial military occupation, these tour guides and organizers create itineraries under duress through a city they deeply love. This chapter
centralizes this labor of tour guiding under colonial military occupation, both
when it does and doesn't "look like an occupation" and when it travels by other
names. Taken together, these itineraries reveal three different and intersecting
occupations across the same city, resulting in the isolation, fragmentation, and
expulsion of the Palestinians who live there, and the myriad ways organizers
refuse the conditions they are routinely expected to cosign.

Jerusalem as a City Multiply Occupied

Jerusalem is an epicenter of tourism to Israel, attracting four million tourists
per year. Most tourists are carefully routed to Israeli shops, businesses, restaurants, and sites—part of the state's strategy to both Judaicize the city and foreclose
the opportunity for Palestinian businesses, shops, and restaurants to thrive.
Israeli tourist agencies do not want tourists to learn about how Palestinians

experience Jerusalem. They do not want tourists to know how the state does all it can to encourage them to leave the city and thus have their access to Jerusalem, and Historic Palestine more broadly, revoked. They do not want tourists to know how the Israeli army polices Palestinian people's daily lives, routinely stopping and frisking Palestinian youth at Damascus Gate, invading homes and businesses, and otherwise making living conditions unbearable. They do not want tourists to know how Israeli archaeology teams excavate the tunnels beneath Palestinian homes, shaking their foundations as the state works—via academics and other experts—to stake its claim to Jerusalem. They do not want tourists to know how the state reduces the demographic population of Palestinians by expanding settlements and redrawing municipal borders to label them Jerusalem while revoking Jerusalem residency from Palestinians who cannot prove that their "center of life" is in Jerusalem. They do not want tourists to know how the state punishes those it criminalizes by either temporarily or permanently exiling them from Jerusalem or how house demolitions in Jerusalem render Palestinians homeless on a recurring basis. They do not want tourists to know how Palestinians are denied the municipal services to which they would otherwise be entitled as tax-paying residents or how even the nomenclature of Palestinians in Jerusalem—"permanent residents"—is meant to signal a permanence that is not inherited and can be revoked.[4]

Palestinians in the eastern part of Occupied Jerusalem pay taxes to Israeli authorities yet receive minimal, if any, municipal services. Only 10 percent of Jerusalem's city budget is earmarked for Palestinian neighborhoods, although these neighborhoods are home to 37 percent of the Palestinian population of Jerusalem.[5] House demolitions routinely animate Palestinian life in Jerusalem—between 2004 and 2019, 978 housing units were demolished, leaving 3,177 homeless. These frequent demolitions change the demographic and geospatial makeup of Jerusalem and, in the words of the grassroots collective Visualizing Palestine, "privileg[e] Jewish settlers over the indigenous Palestinian population."[6] The Israeli-issued ID cards across Palestine minoritize the Palestinian population and increase the Jewish Israeli demographic, and Jerusalem is no exception to this process. Ten thousand Palestinian children in Jerusalem have no legal status because their parents hold different types of ID cards; unregistered children cannot access either health care or social services.[7] Love Under Apartheid, an educational campaign founded by Tanya Keilani, a New York–based Palestinian American researcher and communications manager at the Institute for Middle East Understanding, documents Israel's labor to separate Palestinian families from one another. Examples include Israel's denying permits for West Bank Palestinians to live with Jerusalemite partners or refusing access for Palestinians from Gaza or the West Bank to visit ill family members or pregnant partners in hospitals in Jerusalem.[8] Stories like these abound across checkpoints, across the Wall, across the West Bank, across Historic Palestine.

Further, while Israelis who live in Jerusalem can travel, study abroad, and come and go from the city as they please, Palestinian "permanent residents" of Jerusalem, even when their partners or other family members in the West Bank or Gaza cannot join them, are in constant danger of having their residency revoked. Between 1967 and 1995, Palestinians could lose their residency status if they left the city for seven years or received residency or citizenship in another country.[9] After 1995, this criterion was expanded to include revocation if Palestinians moved their "center of life" outside of East Jerusalem (including anywhere in the West Bank or Gaza), even if they were abroad for less than seven years or never received residency or citizenship elsewhere.[10] Since 1995, Israel has revoked the Jerusalem residency of 11,500 Jerusalemite Palestinians.[11] In 2006, moreover, the Israeli Ministry of the Interior began punitively revoking the residency status of Palestinians on the basis of "breach of allegiance," which includes revocation for Palestinians who have never left Jerusalem on account of whatever Israel deems a breach of allegiance to the state that militarily occupies them.[12] For any of these "missteps"—in actuality, solely the decision to stay with family in the West Bank, to travel, to study or work abroad, or to criticize the regime under which one lives—Palestinians from Jerusalem can lose access to the city and thus to broader Historic Palestine/Israel and Israeli social benefits altogether. This practice, called by many a "silent transfer" out of the city and, in turn, the country, is, like many other Israeli state practices, a violation of international humanitarian law and international human rights law, as it amounts to forcible transfer, a war crime and breach of the Fourth Geneva Convention.[13]

This sketch of Palestinian life in Occupied Jerusalem does not even include encroaching and expanding Israeli settlements, also illegal under international law, where 200,000 Israelis live with unfettered access to state resources and municipal and social services.[14] Neither does this breakdown touch on the occupation of Jerusalem in (and before) 1948, when Zionist militias forced Palestinians out of their homes and took them over, designating the homes "abandoned" and their owners and residents "absentees." Against this backdrop of historical revisionism and contemporary policing, multiple Palestinian actors and anti-Zionist Israeli allies are working across the city to refashion tourism into a pedagogical endeavor, intervening in the narratives Israel produces about Jerusalem and then sells to tourists, and inviting tourists—international, sometimes Israeli, and sometimes Palestinian—to witness the occupation they have long been asked not to call an occupation.

"The Family Never Lived Here": On the Colonial Weaponization of Denial

In late September 2012, I joined a tour of West Jerusalem that was organized by the Israeli NGO Zochrot. The day-to-day labor of Zochrot (Hebrew for remembering) is predicated on research on, and tours to, Palestinian cities and villages inside Israel that were depopulated in 1948.[15] Against an Israeli civic and political sphere marked by indifference and apathy, or worse, racist vitriol, Zochrot works to turn the tide of Israeli public opinion. The tour was organized to coincide with the publication of Zochrot's guidebook *Omrim Yeshna Eretz* (*Once Upon a Land: A Tour Guide*), published in both Arabic and Hebrew, and the tour navigated through the pages of the guidebook. After the group assembled into its languages for simultaneous translation (Hebrew into Arabic or English), the tour guide, Tamar Avraham, began by pointing to her left: "There used to be vineyards here," she said, asking tourists to imagine what once was. She then gestured toward a construction site atop the Mamilla Cemetery, where the Simon Wiesenthal Institute was (and still is) attempting to paper over Muslim graves to build a Museum of Tolerance, documenting and working to prevent global antisemitism.[16] Moments later, Avraham pointed toward Gaza Street, Jaffa Gate, and al-Khalil (Hebron in Arabic) Gate, indicating that at one time, these gates and streets actually led to their named designation without obstruction. With the exception of Jaffa, checkpoints, borders, and warnings against entry render impossible any attempt to follow each road to its end. Narratives like these, provided in spaces where their content is difficult to imagine, ask tourists to consider what freedom of mobility could—and once did—look like in Palestine.

Echoing what tour guides also do in other parts of Occupied Jerusalem, Avraham encouraged tourists to examine the built environment, asking, "How can we tell this was a Palestinian neighborhood?" She responded with answers referencing architectural cues, stories of whose house belonged to whom, and narratives of when they were forced to leave. She detailed a brief history of the Absentee Property Law, wherein anyone not living in their home, even temporarily, in 1948 lost it permanently. As the tour group moved through

Jerusalem neighborhoods, Umar al-Ghubari, a Palestinian researcher who has long worked with Zochrot, translated Avraham's words into Arabic for other Palestinian tour guides and organizers, young and old, whom I recognized from the solidarity tours they offer elsewhere in Palestine. On this tour, Palestinian tour guides, along with Israeli and international tourists, learn from each other how best to correct the narrative Israel advances that Palestine was a land without a people.

Avraham pointed to Jewish philosopher Martin Buber's home as we passed it and described his discomfort with the circumstances in which he found himself, how he moved all the Palestinian furniture in his new home to preserve it in case the Palestinian family came back, how he held onto it until he died.[17] She pointed to the Jalat family's home with the elaborate facades and explained how the family left in 1948 after the Haganah sent a Jew to the neighborhood who announced, in Arabic, that residents should leave for their own security.[18] The tour began in fits and starts, with the guides—one a Palestinian citizen in Israel and one an Ashkenazi Jewish Israeli—disagreeing over what it meant to "leave by force" in 1948 Jerusalem. Avraham described one family as taken out of their home by force; al-Ghubari corrected her, reminding her that no one left their homes voluntarily. Here, he pointed to the history of this neighborhood: how, regardless of whether the family was exiled from their home at gunpoint or not, it constituted "force" because we know that the Haganah, or a messenger, arrived, telling the residents about the violence one neighborhood or village over; that the messenger warned residents that they should leave lest they subject their family to this danger; and that then Zionist settlers took over their homes in their "absence" via the Absentee Property Law.

The tour continued after this brief upset. We walked through the Talbiya neighborhood of Jerusalem, passing home after home. We stopped at one house, where Avraham explained that this was the first house a Jew came to rent in 1943, how he moved here with his library, and how at that time Jews were renters (and not yet settlers) in Palestine. We soon arrived at Villa Harun ar-Rashid, the home of Hanna Ibrahim Bisharat, the facade of Armenian tile visible from the street. The tour guides explained that Bisharat, falling on hard economic times, had leased his home to the British, who turned it into the headquarters of the British Air Force. The Haganah worked to acquire this house, and it soon became the home of Zionist stateswoman and later prime minister Golda Meir.[19]

To tell this history, the guides turned to the narrative provided by Bisharat's grandson, law professor George Bisharat, in his 2003 essay "Rite of Return to a Palestinian Home." The piece charts Bisharat's 1977 visit to the home his grandfather built in 1926. Bisharat writes, "Although he was a Christian, Papa named the home 'Villa Harun ar-Rashid,' in honor of the Muslim Abbasid Caliph renowned for his eloquence, passion for learning, and generosity. Painted tiles with this name were inset above the second-floor balcony and over a side entrance."[20] Bisharat describes how his father had consistently regaled him with stories about running through the surrounding orchards and fields, of his uncles' births in the home, and of how the children all went to the Catholic school up the road.

He describes how his father's twin, an architect named Victor, had designed the wall enclosing the front yard and how his grandfather had moved to a modest house on the Bethlehem road, with no knowledge that he and his family would never return. George Bisharat's father and uncles were not in Palestine in 1948, and as he describes, Villa Harun ar-Rashid was "picked by Zionist armed groups for the commanding view it offered from its roof."[21] Via the Absentee Property Law, "No blood was shed in taking it, as the British officers simply handed over the keys to the Haganah."[22] Bisharat narrates how the house became divided, with Golda Meir—"author of the famous quip that 'the Palestinian people did not exist,'" he reminds the reader—occupying the upstairs flat when she was Israel's foreign minister.[23]

Zochrot's tour guide explains, and Bisharat's 2003 essay reiterates, that Meir gave the orders to remove the home's name from the facade. In Bisharat's words, "Anticipating a visit from UN Secretary General Dag Hammarskjold, it is said, she ordered the sandblasting of the tiles on the front of the house to obliterate the 'Villa Harun ar-Rashid' and thereby conceal the fact that she was living in an Arab home."[24] The passage from Bisharat's essay that Zochrot's guides read out loud that day was this one (although with a slightly different translation, as the volunteer translator explained that he was going from English to Hebrew back to English):

> When I went to Jerusalem in 1977, I had only a photograph of the home, and a general description of its location from my grandmother. It was summer, hot and dusty, and I paced back and forth through the neighborhood inspecting each of the houses, occasionally asking for directions. All the street names had been changed to those of Zionist leaders and figures from Jewish history, and the hospital that my grandmother had described as a landmark apparently no longer existed. As I was resting against a wall in the shade, I saw a home that resembled Papa's. As I hurried across the street, I could just make out the name in the tile: Villa Harun ar-Rashid. I guess Golda's sandblasters had been a little rushed.[25]

Here, Bisharat points to the palimpsest of settler colonialism in Palestine: Arabic names replaced and obscured, yet sometimes with the original claims to the space still discernible.

Zochrot's tour guides explained how George Bisharat, sad and scared, knocked on the door, showed his American passport to the Eastern European woman who opened the door, and explained to her who he was. She responded, "Your family never lived here."[26] In his essay, Bisharat writes, "Later I would understand this as part of a way of rationalizing the seizure of our property—easier to swallow, in moral terms, the expropriation of a speculative business investment by some rich absentee landlord than to contemplate the taking of a family's home."[27]

Zochrot's guides walked tourists through Bisharat's essay, describing how he was humiliated at having to plead with this Eastern European woman to enter his own family's home. Her husband joined her at the front door and let Bisharat into the foyer. Bisharat stood there, Zochrot's guides explained, sensing everything: feeling the atmosphere, smelling the air, trying to hear the sounds of his father's and sibling's voices. He left five minutes later. Bisharat's essay further reveals that the woman's husband was Zvi Berenson, the now-retired justice of the Israeli Supreme Court; that some ten thousand Arab homes in West Jerusalem were looted and seized in the months before 1948; and that Berenson himself, as a Supreme Court justice, had "upheld laws facilitating Israel's acquisition of Palestinian lands through what amounted to legalized theft."[28]

Zochrot explained that when Bisharat returned much later (his essay specifies in 2000), the owners had changed, but he and his family were greeted with the same sentiment. Bisharat describes the interchange in detail:

> The front door swung open and a man smilingly offered, "May I help you?" Somewhat startled, I thanked him for his kindness, and he explained, "Many tourists come to see this house. It's included in walking tours of the city." The man, an American from New York, permitted us to enter, and venture through more of the first floor than I had seen before. But when I said that my father's family had lived in the home, he was incredulous. This time, I was not surprised as he protested, still congenially: "But the family never lived here." He had gleaned this from a newspaper article, he maintained. Repeatedly, he insisted, it seemed a half dozen times, "The family never lived here."[29]

This reflection—describing only one "return" to only one of the ten thousand homes taken over—reveals much about colonial settlement in Palestine/Israel by Eastern European, and then American, inhabitants, the pillage endemic to this settlement, and the refusal to acknowledge complicity in this dispossession, from erasing the name on the facade to the repeated insistence that "the family never lived here."

This reflection simultaneously reveals the politics of Israeli tourism and how tourism in Palestine is also occupied by Israel. That "many tourists come to see this house," that "it's included in walking tours of the city," and that the narrative circulates that "the family never lived here" all serve as a microcosm for Zionist colonial settlement and its relationship to tourism writ large. Tourism in this context functions to bolster and uphold the justificatory colonial narrative that Israel took over what was already an empty, abandoned space: a "land without a people." That "the family never lived here" is circulated through a touristic citational practice, which consistently returns to this explanatory framework, evidences the inner workings of the colonial project that justified expulsion via recourse to the Absentee Property Law, and that continues to justify the rescinding of any claim to that space, if only for a fleeting moment. Bisharat, we remember, was never let in past the first floor.

In 2019, on a walking tour of the tile work of David Ohanessian, an Armenian ceramicist in Palestine and survivor of the Armenian genocide, several tourists, myself included, slipped into the compound of Villa Harun ar-Rashid for a closer look. While the front facade still reveals where Golda Meir attempted to erase the villa's name, a side entrance still states it clearly: Villa Harun ar-Rashid (1926) (figure 4.1). Now, a giant Israeli flag is planted atop its roof in a bold and injurious claim to ownership (figure 4.2). An Israeli settler emerged to yell at two women in hijab to get off "his" property (figure 4.3).

George Bisharat's story is only one of many from the scores of people who came after 1967 to see their houses. Echoing Baha Hilo's formulation that refugees inherit loss, Bisharat adds that his children are "heirs of the truth about Villa Harun ar-Rashid."[30] Zochrot, basing this section of the tour on Bisharat's narrative as an example of the kinds of dispossession Palestinian refugees have repeatedly experienced, attempts to reveal the truths obfuscated in the repetition of the refrain that "the family never lived here," a repetition that raises the question of who, exactly, those repeating this utterance are trying to convince. As Zochrot's tour is directed to a Hebrew-speaking, predominantly Jewish Israeli audience, with international eavesdroppers hearing the tour in translation, they attempt to intervene in the narrative Israel sells and Israelis (as well as Americans and Eastern Europeans) repeatedly tell to convince

4.1 Villa Harun ar-Rashid. Photo by author (2019).

themselves that the homes they inherited were rendered available via absence and negligence on the part of Palestinians.

"Live in Peace, My Library": Theft and Return in and beyond Jerusalem

The tour group traveled from the site of George Bisharat's family home, past a Greek Orthodox church in a neighborhood that was once mostly Christian except for one Muslim family, past the Greek consulate, past the street Zochrot was trying to get renamed Nakba Street ("No Nakba Street yet, but *inshallah*," one guide explained), to the home of Palestinian author, poet, and scholar Khalil Sakakini. Zochrot explained how Sakakini built his house with enthusiasm, time, and energy in the years before 1936, how he saw it as a personal

4.2 Villa Harun ar-Rashid. Photo by author (2019).

project and a national project, and how, when the house was finished, the family walked room by room, taking it in. "Our house was a world in itself," the tour guide read from Khalil Sakakini's daughter Hala's edited volume of her father's journals and her own published memoirs.

Zochrot explained how Sakakini's home became a strategic place for Zionists and how this neighborhood, Qatamon—translated from Greek to mean "under the monastery"—became a site of constant gunfire in 1948, before Sakakini fled to Cairo. After the UN General Assembly adopted the resolution to partition Palestine in 1947, and although the resolution named Jerusalem a separate international zone, Zionist militias began to target both Palestinian civilians and armed members of neighborhoods like Qatamon.[31] On January 5, 1948, the Haganah blew up the Semiramis hotel, a family establishment

4.3 Villa Harun ar-Rashid. Photo by author (2019).

in Qatamon, claiming, based on mistaken intelligence reports, that the hotel was the headquarters of the Qatamon guard.[32] Eighteen people died, dozens were wounded, and many went into shock.[33] The next day, many families left Qatamon, but the Sakakini family stayed to defend their home.

Khalil Sakakini wrote in his journals, sarcastically, "We have turned our neighborhood, which is encircled by a road and is a kind of island, into an entrenched fortress, compared to which the fortresses of Sebastopol, Verdun, Gibraltar and Malta are as nothing."[34] After a night of constant shooting, Hala Sakakini wrote in her own journal, "If strong security measures are not taken immediately, our turn of leaving our home will come soon. We cannot be expected to wait empty handed for the Jews to come blow us up."[35] Zochrot recounted Hala Sakakini's descriptions of how she lay on the ground, night after night, waiting for the bullets to stop, and how after the San Simon battle, when the Zionists conquered the San Simon Greek Orthodox Monastery, she and her family finally fled. "Only when we passed the last Jewish town did we feel like we were in a free zone," she wrote, and Zochrot narrated.[36]

Spaces like Qatamon and Talbiya are not the villages that were attacked and emptied by Zionist militias in 1948, which are those most often privileged in the retelling of the violent establishment of the state. They are, rather, the middle- and upper-class homes and urban centers. In the introduction of Walid Khalidi's canonical volume on the aftermath of the Nakba on the landscape of Palestine, *All That Remains: The Palestinian Villages Occupied and Depopulated by Israel in 1948* (1992), he wrote that he was focusing deliberately on villages, since urban centers had received at least scant international attention at his time of writing. Khalidi explained how most of these urban centers (with the notable exception of Nazareth) were emptied of their Palestinian residents, while "their immovable assets—commercial centers, residential quarters, schools, banks, hospitals, clinics, mosques, churches, and other public buildings, parks and utilities, all passed en bloc into the possession of the citizens of the nascent state of Israel."[37] "Also appropriated intact by Israelis," Khalidi wrote, "were the moveable assets: furniture, silver, pictures, carpets, libraries, and heirlooms— all accruements of middle-class life of the erstwhile Palestinian residents."[38] Khalidi's description here calls to mind famed Palestinian author Ghassan Kanafani in his novella "Returning to Haifa," when he describes a Palestinian family seeing their peacock feathers still in the vase on the kitchen table, their frames still on the wall, recounting the psychological violence of witnessing their family home and belongings in someone else's hands.[39] Taking up only one object on Khalidi's list—libraries—Zochrot's tour described the theft of Khalil Sakakini's books as his family was forced to leave Qatamon.

Zochrot's tour guide explained how, in the months after April 30, 1948, the day the Sakakini family—the last Palestinian family in Qatamon—fled to Cairo, Sakakini lamented the theft of his books. Zochrot read his words, standing on the street near his home:

Farewell, my library! Farewell, the house of wisdom, the abode of philoso-phers, a house and witness for literature! How many sleepless nights I spent there, reading and writing, the night is silent and the people asleep . . . goodbye, my books! I know not what has become of you after we left: Were you looted? Burnt? Have you been ceremonially transferred to a private or public library? Did you end up on the shelves of grocery stores with your pages used to wrap onions?"[40]

These fragments of Sakakini's narrative, narrated by Zochrot, are meant to, in Zochrot's words, "capture the moment" of exodus, exile, and dispossession. Reading the words of loss in the aftermath of theft, Zochrot compels its audience to imagine that loss. Reading the words at the site of expulsion, while witnessing its contemporary calm and affluence, Zochrot also attempts to remind its audience of what is too easily forgotten at a scene of upper-middle-class neighborhoods in West Jerusalem, not a site, at first glance, of "occupation."[41]

Zochrot's tour lingers with the moment—excerpted from Hala Sakakini's memoir—when Hala and her sister Domiya returned to West Jerusalem from Ramallah after 1967, when Israel occupied the West Bank and the Jordanian-Israeli border no longer prohibited them from traveling to Qatamon: a temporary and fleeting "return" to their childhood home. The tour guides read from the memoir: "We could barely wait. All we could see was a new building and, now, second floors." They came to the street, turned right, and walked toward the house; the shade of the trees was familiar. They saw their house—and that of the Uwwad family, the Budeiri family, and a third house belonging to their neighbors—and finally they were there. The house looked dark, the paint was peeling, the road was dirty and dusty. The beautiful garden with the jasmine tree was not there; instead, the yard was filled with abandoned furniture. The daughters reflected on the loss and disjuncture between what they remembered and what they saw, reflecting that it is the people who create a neighborhood and, though their neighbors' houses were there, their neighbors were not.

Hearing rumors that their father's books were housed at the Hebrew University National Library, Domiya and Hala introduced themselves and were taken to a senior librarian, who told them, "You have no right to claim anything because each volume, individually, and all of them together, are abandoned property."[42] Like the American homeowners at Villa Harun Ar-Rashid, the librarian repeated several times that, since 1948, all Palestinian property, books, buildings, fields, villages, and towns have become the property of the state of Israel. Domiya and Hala asked to touch the books or page through them, but the librarian declined, agreeing to bring them just one book whose title they could remember. The guide explained that the daughters knew their father didn't write his name in the books but would make notes on the page margins. In Hala Sakakini's words, "We selected *The Beggars*, by Al-Jahdh, a ninth century encyclopedist. And, in fact, after some time the librarian returned, holding the book. He let us page through it in front of him, as if we were dangerous culture robbers, and waited for us to return it."[43]

In Zochrot's descriptions of Hala and Domiya's visit to the library, tour guides dwell on the descriptions of Sakakini's books—the moveable assets, in the words of Walid Khalidi—and the trappings of Palestinian middle-class life in Jerusalem. Their focus on books and libraries asks their (mostly Israeli) tourists—in their direct complicity—to imagine what kinds of beloved objects made up the lives of those who lived in their own homes before they did. As Zochrot moved slowly through this narrative of theft, taking the time to ground the tour in literary descriptions of displacement, its focus on books—as a microcosm for displacement writ large—was both sustained and deliberate.[44]

As it weaves through wealthy neighborhoods, talking about the theft of wealth and property, Zochrot's tour intervenes in Israel's narrative about Palestine as a land without a people. At the same time, perhaps in its effort to pitch to an Israeli audience skeptical of the claim that Palestinians are deserving of anything, it depicts "people" as *those who have*, both in terms of things and homes and the trappings of modernity. This depiction can thus flatten class differences between Palestinians before 1948, privileging a narrative of loss that pivots on the loss of mansions rather than thinking through a loss that is less sutured to wealth.[45] Palestinians in and also beyond Jerusalem in 1948 were a deeply heterogeneous group with their own pronounced class divisions that subaltern Palestinians consistently resisted: some were farmers, some were bankers, some were intellectuals, some had land, some didn't, some worked for others, some were *fellahin*—or agricultural laborers—who, as Rana Barakat notes, were central to the political, economic, and social life of Jerusalem during Mandate-era Palestine.[46] Sophia Azeb writes:

> Who have we become, as Palestinians, in the wake of the enduring catastrophe? I am a *fellaha*, the daughter and granddaughter of Palestinian farmers. My relatives are not refugees, though they endured—with many scars (and some dead eyes)—the conditions of the forever disaster. These Palestinians, my Palestinians—illiterate, undereducated, impoverished, though still in possession of our land, our olives, ourselves—chose to leave exile under Occupation to settle in exile, as settlers, in Turtle Island. But exile is a jealous state. We make more exiles. We reproduce the conditions of exile everywhere we land. We do this with one another, too. "Where is your family from" is a question frequently asked by Palestinians of other Palestinians. It is

a familiar question, a demonstration of our mutual understanding and community. But we do not always understand one another, and we are not always in community, and the question also reveals our wariness of one another.[47]

Azeb's words here are a reminder that a cohesive narrative about past displacement that flattens differences between Palestinians before their diaspora, in Walid Khalidi's words, has deeply felt repercussions for how to imagine Palestinian futurity. While these Jerusalem tours center on these spaces of wealth and robbery in West Jerusalem, inviting tourists to recall what was and to imagine what could be returned, other organizations and collectives take tourists to the rest of Occupied Jerusalem—the Old City and the eastern part of Occupied Jerusalem—spaces where the occupation may make itself more visible and felt, spaces where, in Azeb's words, Palestinians continue to endure "the conditions of the forever-disaster." In this way, while tour guides do not necessarily or always emphasize this—since it disrupts the cohesion of the narrative—taken together these tours trace a heterogeneous and disparately positioned people experiencing a continuity of dispossession across multiple, layered temporal frames.

The Colonial Present in the Old City

The eastern part of Occupied Jerusalem, as part of the West Bank, remained under Jordanian control until June 5, 1967, when, during the Naksa, Israel occupied the rest of Palestine, taking the West Bank from Jordan and the Gaza Strip from Egypt along with the Syrian Golan Heights. As soon as Israel controlled Jerusalem, it demolished the Moroccan Quarter (Al-Magharbeh) of the Old City. As the Palestinian community organization in Jerusalem Grassroots Al-Quds writes in their guidebook, *Wujood* (Arabic for existence or presence), which seizes the narrative of Jerusalem (and beyond) from Israeli control: "If during your visit to the Old City you find your way to Al-Buraq Wall (or the Western Wall) and see the Jewish worshippers in the yard, remember that prior to 1967 dozens of Palestinian homes once stood here. The quarter had been a Muslim Waqf since 1193 and was home to one thousand Palestinian residents, who were then displaced to Shufat Refugee Camp and elsewhere in Jerusalem."[48] The Western Wall complex is currently an open area thronged with tourists, tour guides, worshippers, and soldiers. Tour guides assemble different groups, telling different narratives. Only those on alternative or solidarity tours will hear that the site on which they are standing was the Moroccan Quarter, the inhabitants of which have been exiled to refugee camps outside of the Old City.

At the same time, when tourists to Israel now experience the Jewish Quarter, they are touring a space where four thousand Palestinians were evicted and their homes were also occupied by Zionist settlers.[49] At the end of the 1967 War, 66,000 Palestinians remained in Jerusalem; as of 2018, there are 330,000 within the municipal boundaries who consider Jerusalem home.[50] As solidarity tourists walk through the Old City, they learn these histories in cafés in the Muslim Quarter, walking down Via Dolorosa, or standing at lookouts facing the Mount of Olives. They traverse some of the same spaces as other tourists, yet walking though the Old City, you can hear Israeli tour guides route tourists away from the Muslim Quarter and Palestinian-owned business with "concerns about safety" that are nothing more than racist colonial stereotypes about Arabs. The Old City of Jerusalem is a microcosm for how Israel weaponizes tourism to further displace Palestinians. Over three hundred Palestinian shops have shuttered their doors because of the suffocation of the Palestinian tourism industry in the Old City.[51] Israel's tourism practices in and around the Old City, moreover, have altered the landscape, materially displacing Palestinians who have long lived in Jerusalem. As one example of several, in Silwan, outside the Old City and across from Al-Aqsa Mosque, Israeli authorities have granted Elad, a settler organization, the authority to manage an archaeological park that both dispossesses and evicts Palestinian homeowners *and* hosts 300,000 tourists per year.[52] This use of archaeology to sediment Jewish claims to the land and justify the expulsion of Palestinians has long been state practice and is now being mapped onto places across East Jerusalem, including Silwan, Ras al-Amud, Wadi Joz, Al-Suwana, Sheikh Jarrah, and Al-Tur. In a cyclical and cynical pattern, Israel displaces Palestinians in these spaces while expanding the archaeological parks that justify the displacement.[53] King David Park, or City of David National Park, is the same biblically themed archaeological park that provided the justificatory logic for the police violence and expulsions in Silwan and Sheikh Jarrah during the spring 2021 uprisings.

In this way, like anti-Zionist tourism elsewhere in Jerusalem, solidarity tourists' presence in the Old City is a pedagogical exercise, where tourists are learning about displacement that has either predated their arrival or is happening in front of them in ways that are difficult to discern without accompanying narration that explains the contours of that displacement. At the same time, as in Hebron or Bethlehem, it is a tourism that includes poring over maps in Palestinian cafés and restaurants, routing tourists through Palestinian neighborhoods, and inviting tourists to shop at Palestinian businesses. This is neither inconsequential nor crass commercialism. It is a strategic effort on the part of Palestinian organizers and guides across the eastern part of Occupied Jerusalem to contribute to the suffocated Palestinian economy and work toward keeping Palestinians in their homes and businesses against an occupation set on displacing them.

Tourism plays a central role in this displacement. In the Old City alone, only part of the city has been built up for tourists: Jaffa Road and the corridor called Mamilla. These spaces have seen high-end shops connecting the Old City with the main shopping thoroughfare and record numbers of tourists.[54] But, in the words of Grassroots Al-Quds, "The Old City's historical main entrance—Damascus Gate—lies neglected."[55] The authors continue: "Today, Damascus Gate looks more like an imposing military outpost with its three watchpoints," intimidating tourists away from the Palestinian markets in the Muslim Quarter behind Damascus Gate, "which have seen a sharp decline of visitors in recent years."[56] Indeed, three watchtowers surround the Damascus Gate entrance; heavily armed Israeli soldiers stationed there glower at passersby and "randomly" check and search Palestinian youth, check their IDs, and interrogate them while their friends wait nervously for them around the corner. Throughout the Muslim Quarter, Israeli soldiers are stationed on corner after corner, either harassing Palestinians or idly chatting with one another. Tourists to Israel stop them and ask for "selfies with the IDF."[57] They happily oblige. It is a grotesque scene of the celebration of militarism and conquest from within a sustained and decades-long military occupation that Palestinians—tour guides included—witness on a daily basis.

Navigating this landscape, Palestinian solidarity tour guides typically have one day—or a few hours—in Jerusalem to introduce tourists to displacement across the Old City and the eastern part of Occupied Jerusalem. In the Old City, alongside walking tours from Damascus Gate, through the Muslim Quarter, to the Western Wall Plaza and site of the demolished Moroccan Quarter, tourists also meet with Palestinians who call the Old City home as settlers attempt to take it over. They sometimes meet with organizers and guides in the Afro-Palestinian community of the Old City. Ali Jiddah, an elder Afro-Palestinian activist and freelance alternative tour guide, began giving tours for internationals shortly after he was released from an Israeli prison in a 1985 prisoner exchange.[58] On his tours, he guides tourists through the Old City, pointing out settlements and the grates above Palestinian marketplaces to catch settlers' debris, passing armed Israeli soldiers and armed settlers wandering through narrow streets, and describing the contours of occupation in the city. Like other tour guides, he uses humor to cut through the despair of recitation. Passing the apartment in the middle of Palestinian homes that Ariel Sharon took over in 1987, with its menorah on the roof and giant Israeli flag cascading down the side of the building in the middle of Palestinian homes and businesses, he would ask, "Why is Ariel Sharon still in a coma?" The answer: "Because even hell doesn't want him."[59]

At the end of his tours, like other tour guides across Palestine, Ali Jiddah invites tourists to go home. He explains, "Your presence here is very important for my people. It shows them someone is listening. But your work is not here." Ali Jiddah validates the tourists' presence in Palestine, confirming that they are "doing important work" solely through their presence. He simultaneously gestures toward the indifference Palestinians encounter from the international community, reminding the tourists that their presence indexes that they are listening—in contradistinction to the many who do not. Last, he asks the tourists not to stay in Palestine but to do their work at home, writing letters to their representatives and joining and building movements to boycott, divest from, and sanction Israel's occupation.

Ali Jiddah's three-part appeal encapsulates much of what inheres in solidarity tourism in Palestine, an invitation that both meets and subverts tourists' expectations. First, it is a cursory and perfunctory appeal to the benevolence and commitment of solidarity tourists, then an emphasis on international complicity in Israeli occupation, and finally, a reminder to tourists that, yes, they have been invited to Palestine, and now they are being invited to go home. This daily labor on the part of Palestinian tour guides is a project of restructuring international desire from the impulse to do volunteer work in Palestine, join in demonstrations in the West Bank, or otherwise participate in labor that can be visibly read as either for or on behalf of Palestinians, directing them homeward instead.

On other tours of the Old City, tourists may meet with Armenian Palestinians and learn about the experience of the Armenian Palestinian community in the Old City, whose family members were made refugees twice over: once from the Armenian genocide and again from Israeli displacement practices in the Old City and across Jerusalem.[60] Their narratives make clear the fragmentation Israel has sought to make permanent and the state's attempts to make it impossible to imagine a multifaceted, heterogeneous people of Palestine— from the Armenian quarter, to greater Jerusalem, to the West Bank, to Gaza, to 1948, to refugees, to those in exile in the diaspora—who share deeply dissimilar but inevitably linked histories of subjugation and struggle.

"Where the Sidewalk Ends"

On an Israeli Committee Against Housing Demolitions (ICAHD) solidarity tour in the summer of 2012, nearing the perimeter of a settlement in East Jerusalem that has only since expanded, the tour guide explained where the municipal services ended. He showed tourists the well-manicured areas surrounding settlement apartments, the very clear evidence of trash pickup, and the working bus line. He alerted the bus full of tourists to the "edge" of the settlement, where the road and its sidewalk abruptly became a dirt path littered with cigarette butts and candy wrappers. He half joked in a nod to Shel Silverstein, clearly a bit at this moment of his tours, "This is where the sidewalk ends."[61]

Like Ali Jiddah's use of humor to ridicule Sharon while pointing to his apartment in the Old City, here too the ICAHD tour guide uses humor to introduce levity into the witnessing of rotating scenes of destitution, impoverishment, and subjection but also to expose the absurdity of Israeli state practice, the fabrications of Israeli claims, and the impossibility of the two-state solution. Here, in the heart of the eastern part of Occupied Jerusalem, tourists see a settlement sprawling through Palestinian spaces, a clear allocation of resources only to the settlement, and a world in which Israel is happy to sever Palestinian spaces from one another with the Wall and hilltop settlements on both sides of it that obstruct contiguity and maintain Israeli dominance. With one spectacle of "where the sidewalk ends," claims that Palestinians do not care for their own space, claims that Israel stays on its side of whatever malleable borders are being discussed, and claims that Israel "takes care" of Palestinian communities are all revealed to be farcical.

Yet, like the tourist who wandered around a Palestinian man's property, sighed, and explained, "Just no connection to the earth," tourists do not always assimilate this information. They see trash and still see culpability. Many tour guides confided to me that this "trash question" is a thing they are consistently asked about. Tourists—solidarity tourists included—come to Palestine and, aghast at seeing trash in the streets, think something akin to, Why do they not clean their streets? The subtext here is, Why do they choose to live like this? Reproducing this colonial logic Palestinians have long witnessed and been subject to, which maintains that they are intrinsically unwilling to care for the space in which they live, tourists forget what they bring to Palestine: their comfort, their context, their own streets, their own adopted narratives about Palestine. The tourists expressing this shock/disdain are also usually tourists who do not clean their own streets back home, who live in places where the municipality picks up their trash bins and cleans their streets, paves their roads, makes sure there are sidewalks. On her tours, Fayrouz Sharqawi of Grassroots Al-Quds takes tourists to this same settlement, pointing out its uniform and expansive apartments lined with Israeli flags, gesturing toward the stationed Israeli guards drinking coffee in the shade. On one 2019 tour, she too pointed to "where the sidewalk ends." Yet she narrated, sarcastically, "The sidewalk is gone. Because Palestinians don't need sidewalks." Here, Sharqawi lays bare for tourists the deliberate unevenness in infrastructure that makes up only part of Israel's occupation. She reveals both the colonial and tautological nature of the logic that justifies that unevenness: we don't build sidewalks for Palestinians because Palestinians are primitive people who don't need modern things like sidewalks and trash pickup, and simultaneously, Palestinians don't care about trash and sidewalks because they live with and without them, respectively, so why should we build them? Both logics not only blame Palestinians for their condition but also position the trappings of modernity as a barometer for deservingness of freedom.

Later, stopping at the Wall running through the eastern part of Occupied Jerusalem, severing the two-thousand-year-old Jericho Road, Sharqawi again draws tourists' attention to the infrastructure. Other tour guides will stop at this very spot and explain how they and their families used to pack up picnics and drive on this road to spend the day in Jericho, a contiguity between Palestinian space now rendered impossible by the Wall and its accompanying checkpoints. Here on the "Jerusalem" side of the Wall (though the Wall of course cuts through Jerusalem), Sharqawi points to new construction, a rare sight in the eastern part of Occupied Jerusalem. At other moments on this tour, she goes to a lookout that spans eastern and western Jerusalem and asks tourists to point out how many cranes they see in each part of Occupied Jerusalem. Invariably, the ratio is always zero in the eastern part and ten to twenty on the western part. "They are building a roundabout," she explains. Workers were paving a traffic circle—one that was never "necessary" for the Palestinian community here—because new settlement construction was happening up the hill. "Now that the settlements and their visitors need a traffic circle," she explained, "we can have infrastructure." Walking down this road toward a nearby gas station for a bathroom break, one white tourist passed a brown-skinned Palestinian construction worker and said, "*Hola*," with a broad, liberal smile. I think it was lost on her that she mixed up the Latinx workers in her communities with the Palestinian workers here, but I don't think it was lost on the Palestinian worker on the other end of her smile.

On Sharqawi's tour, she connects the colonial present tourists are witnessing *to* tourism. On Temple Mount, she explains, Israelis are building a guest house within a settlement. Tourists will ride a cable car from the German Colony in Jerusalem to Silwan, the site of the settler-run City of David archaeological park, to settlements along the Mount of Olives, and to the settlement inside Ar-Tur, where tourists will end up. "They will not see the occupation and they will not spend money in our shops," she explained. "Now Israel wins twice over." Similarly, Grassroots Al-Quds' guidebook *Wujood* devotes a whole section to Israel's use of tourism as a colonial tool, specifically in Jerusalem. They write, "The Israeli tourism industry and propaganda outfits use the Jewish history in Palestine to justify the Zionization of Jerusalem."[62] By this, the authors refer in part to Israel's monopoly on the tourist narrative by way of the Israeli Ministry of Tourism's tour guide licensing courses that emphasize only Jewish ties to the land.[63] They also refer to how tourists to Israel are routed only to religious sites in the eastern part of Jerusalem and then quickly back to the western part to eat, drink, and shop.[64] Finally, they mean the tourist projects, routed directly through settlements, that Sharqawi outlines on her tours. Beginning in Silwan, where the settler organization Elad evicts Palestinians from their homes to give them to settlers and the City of David project lays exclusively Jewish claim to the land to justify ethnic cleansing, and continuing via cable car to Dung Gate, this nearly seventy million dollar project, which will bring even more visitors to the City of David Center, was defined in 2017 as a "national priority."[65] To this, the authors add the many local and international festivals Israel hosts in Jerusalem to "strengthen Jerusalem's place on the world's cultural stage and to counter the stereotype of Jerusalem as a conservative city where there is little happening," and also to bolster the positioning of Jerusalem as "the capital of Israel."[66]

For Grassroots Al-Quds in *Wujood*, and for many other Palestinian tourism initiatives, it is necessary to provide tourists with the history not only of Israel's monopoly over the tourist industry but also its strategic use of tourism to deny Palestinian claims to the land. For this reason, in *Wujood*, and on myriad solidarity tours across Palestine, the discussion of tourism is followed by a discussion of international complicity and ends with a discussion of the Boycott, Divestment, and Sanctions (BDS) movement. The BDS call, issued by Palestinian civil society in 2005, demands a withdrawal of financial support for companies involved in the violations of Palestinian human rights, including Israeli sporting, cultural, and academic institutions, which are directly complicit in the ruination of Palestinian lives and livelihoods. It also urges banks, churches, pension funds, and universities to divest from Israeli companies and from international companies engaged in violating Palestinian rights. Last, it pressures governments to hold Israel accountable by ending military trade and free-trade agreements and expelling Israel from international forums like the United Nations.[67] These demands remain in place until Israel dismantles the Wall and ends the occupation of Palestinian land, grants equal rights to Palestinian citizens in Israel, and allows Palestinian refugees to return to their homes. With so much of this call centering on disrupting the narrative Israel sells to the world about itself—all while it demolishes houses, evicts Palestinian families, builds a wall severing Palestinian communities from one another, reserves infrastructure for itself, and refuses to allow refugees to return to their homes—solidarity tour guides labor to uncover, for tourists, the colonial infrastructure in places like Jerusalem while inviting tourists to intervene. In this way, in Jerusalem and in other places across the West Bank like Hebron, Bethlehem, Ramallah, Nablus, and as we will see in chapter 5, places across Historic Palestine like Haifa, Jaffa, and Nazareth, Palestinian tour guides invite tourists to witness, to do the work of understanding what they are witnessing, to consider their role in that spectacle, and to work, sometimes via BDS but not always or only via BDS, toward decolonization.

To end with the beginning, when Fayrouz Sharqawi begins her tours in the eastern part of Occupied Jerusalem, she, like Tamar Avraham of Zochrot, asks, How do you know these are Palestinian homes? She points to the arched windows evidencing Palestinian architecture. On one tour in July 2019, she asked tourists to take note of the Israeli flags peppering the neighborhood. Reminiscent of George Bisharat's occupied family home in West Jerusalem, an Israeli flag towering over its roof, she said, "Imagine how painful it is for me to see flags on those windows and those doors." Too often, critics equate solidarity tourism to slum tourism, insinuating that these are tours through impoverished neighborhoods for tourists to suck their teeth and sigh in pity. Here, a Palestinian community organizer who is the granddaughter of two refugees is speaking about how painful the Nakba is, what stolen homes look like, and how it feels and what it is like to do this work in and from the neighborhoods and communities Israel has sought to either destroy or replace. Her narration is, in fact, a refusal of the voyeurism of slum tourism by anchoring what tourists are invited to witness to not only the pain of its narration but also the necessity of reparation and return in the wake of that narration.

An Invitation to Consider Love and Care under Occupation

While perhaps not palpably so, this chapter has been about love. The love of things, the love of books, the love of land, the love of olives, the love of that which is stolen, the remembrance of—and struggle for—a beloved heterogeneous city. This chapter has also been about invitation, about how tour guides invite tourists to rethink their understanding of Jerusalem, to reject the narrative of Jerusalem they have been sold. Traversing through neighborhoods the international community understands as occupied and neighborhoods the international community holds as uncomplicatedly Israeli, the tour guides and organizers introduced in this chapter, taken together, tell a story that refuses the fragmentation Israel has sought to sediment. Instead, they weave together histories of displacement that began well before 1948, which cannot be circumscribed to 1967 with "the occupation of Jerusalem" and its aftermath. Instead, like those in olive harvest season, these tours tell a story of continuity in displacement. They tell a story of the strategic deployment of both tourism *and* the law through which Israel has worked to divide Jerusalem, minoritize its multiple Palestinian populations, including Afro-Palestinians and Armenian Palestinians, including wealthy Palestinians and impoverished Palestinians, and expel the people who cared for and shaped this city for generations.

In this way, these tours also tell a story about care. They tell a story of how Israel has worked to sell a narrative that Palestinians do not and cannot care for this city. These tours tell a story where trash does not mean disinvestment on the part of Palestinians in care for the land, but where trash means disinvestment on the part of the Israeli state in Palestinian communities, neighborhoods, and corners of the Old City. These tours evidence colonization through infrastructure, through investment in Jewish Israeli space, quarters, neighborhoods, and claims to the land at the expense of Palestinian ones. They tell a story of colonization through legalized theft, the takeover of Palestinian homes, the beautification of once-Palestinian neighborhoods for only Israelis to live in, and the labor of Palestinians in East Jerusalem who have to wake up, go to work, and clean West Jerusalem, often the part of the city stolen from their own families. These tours interrupt the refrain, "no connection to the earth," at the same time that they interrupt the refrain, "the family never lived here." They in fact show the elaborate manufacturing of these twinned narratives that bolster the Zionist state-building project, both in 1948 and today: the manufacturing of the narrative that Palestinians were never there and that, even if they were, they do not know how to care for the space and thus are not deserving of it. Instead, tour guides across the multiply occupied city of Jerusalem, from Palestinian citizens in Israel to Jerusalemites, from anti-Zionist Jewish Israelis to Palestinian children of refugees, refuse the narratives that fuel Zionist displacement in Jerusalem *through* tourism: narratives that maintain there is only one part of Jerusalem worth going to, one part of the city worth investing in, one part of the Old City worth shopping in, one Jerusalem to see. In doing so, they gesture toward a Jerusalem where everyone moves freely, across the city and beyond, taking roads without obstruction from Jerusalem to Jaffa, Gaza, Hebron, or Jericho, where everyone can care for and receive care from the city equally: a Jerusalem only possible in the wake of decolonization.

FIVE

COLONIAL RUINS AND
A DECOLONIZED FUTURE
WITNESSING AND RETURN
IN HISTORIC PALESTINE

Traversing landscapes of rubble from razed Palestinian homes amid donor-funded Israeli forests of cypress and fir, cityscapes of segregation inside Israel's borders, and appropriated Palestinian villages as Israeli spaces of culture and recreation, this chapter turns to walking tours in Historic Palestine of spaces too often understood as uncomplicatedly and unequivocally Israeli. By Historic Palestine, I mean the lands across *all* of Palestine, the lands Palestinians were expelled from before, during, and after 1948, lands not limited to just Palestinian "territories": the West Bank and Gaza. Significantly—and not to be relegated to an endnote—during the uprisings in spring 2021, amid and after the Israeli expulsions in Sheikh Jarrah, attacks on Al-Aqsa, mob violence in cities inside Israel, and bombing campaigns on Gaza, Palestinians in Lydda, Haifa, Akka, and Nazareth raised Palestinian flags in protest, signaling their collectivity against the Palestinian fragmentation Israel has sought to impose.[1] This led Palestinians across social media to declare: Historic Palestine is no longer historic.[2]

For this reason, rather than position this chapter as one that takes as its subject solidarity tours "inside Israel's 1948 borders," I instead position it as one that uncovers Israel's malleable and shifting borders across different, though consistent, colonial military occupations of Palestinian land since—and before—1948. From Lifta, a Palestinian village on the outskirts of Jerusalem depopulated in 1948, to Emwas, a Palestinian village sixteen miles west of Jerusalem depopulated in 1967, to 'Ayn Hawd, a Palestinian village near Haifa depopulated in 1948, this chapter follows walking tours of Israeli parks, cultural centers, and picnic areas built atop the ruins of Palestinian villages or among their still standing edifices. Further, from Haifa to Jaffa to Nazareth, this chapter follows Palestinian, Israeli, and international guides who disrupt the notion of happily "mixed cities" inside Israel and instead unearth the multiple ways occupation makes itself felt here too. In the words of one Palestinian citizen in Israel introducing a tour of this sort, "Here you will not see checkpoints, but if you know the layers, you will see occupation." In this way, I refuse to use "solidarity tourism in Palestine" as a shorthand for "solidarity tourism in the West Bank" and instead look at how these tours take shape, and what work they do, across Historic Palestine.

This chapter also maps out the work these tours do to imagine, blueprint, and implement the Palestinian Right of Return. These itineraries, across multiple spaces in Historic Palestine, expose the strategies through which Israel has sought to enact the erasure of Palestine; at the same time, they either gesture toward or, in some cases, practically design a future of reparation and redress that would accommodate the return of Palestinian refugees. The villages and city centers narrated on these tours, from before their occupation in 1948 or 1967 to what tourists witness today, challenge the exclusions that characterize the contemporary sites of depopulated Palestinian villages inside Israel at the same time that they refuse a nostalgic rendering of a pre-1948 Palestine. In this way, these guides, through their labor, ask what role tourism can play in both archiving displacement and imagining return.

Walking Tours of Depopulated Villages: All That Remains in a Place for the Future

Palestinian villages are no longer a neglected site of literature and scholarship on Palestine, as they were when Walid Khalidi turned his attention to them in his canonical archival works, *Before Their Diaspora: A Photographic History of the Palestinians 1876–1948* (1984) and *All That Remains: The Palestinian Villages Occupied and Depopulated by Israel in 1948* (1992). In *Before Their Diaspora* and *All That Remains*, Khalidi includes images like the one (figure 5.1), where an ostensibly benign eucalyptus park, equipped with monkey bars for children and shade for picnics, is also the ruins of a Palestinian cemetery.[3]

5.1 "The Cemetery of Salama (Jaffa), now a park (May 1987)." From Walid Khalidi, *All That Remains: The Palestinian Villages Occupied and Depopulated by Israel in 1948* (1992). Photo by Rafi Safieh (1987).

Since this work—which he defined as a "call, on the threshold of the second century of the Zionist-Arab conflict, for a pause, for a moment of introspection by the contemporary engineers of Zionism and their sympathizers"—a comparatively robust literature on Palestinian villages has emerged alongside archiving work done by NGOs, fieldworkers, tour guides, activists, refugees, internally displaced Palestinians, and Palestinian citizens in Israel (and the many who occupy multiple categories in this list).[4]

Several groups, individuals, and organizations coordinate walking tours in spaces like these in Historic Palestine that were depopulated in 1948 and 1967. As with tours of Jerusalem, one of these organizations is Zochrot. In September 2012, in an air-conditioned office above parking garages and cafés in central Tel Aviv, a short cab ride away from the beach where West Bank Palestinians—and certainly Palestinians in Gaza—cannot go, I interviewed Umar al-Ghubari, a Palestinian citizen in Israel and coordinator of tours for Zochrot. He emphasized, from the onset of the interview, that although he helped from the outside, Zochrot began in 2002 with Jewish Israelis who were certain that if they were to talk about the future of Palestine, they would necessarily have to go to the sources of the conflict in 1948 and 1967.[5] Zochrot's audience, then, has always been Jewish Israelis. Zochrot's work is grounded in consistently remembering—and forcing other Israeli Jews to remember—both the Nakba and the Naksa. This remembering, al-Ghubari explains, is critical and urgent in a context in which the Israeli education system fails to teach Israelis "what happened in 1948."[6]

In Israeli scholar Nurit Peled-Elhanan's assessment, the content and curriculum of Israeli education has everything to do with priming Israeli youth for their compulsory military service by first erasing the Nakba and then rationalizing the occupation. "One of the aims of the Israeli-Zionist narrative, as of every phase of the Zionist project," she writes as she begins her textual analysis of Israeli textbooks in history, geography, and civic studies, "is to create a homogenous identity to all the Jewish ethnicities in Israel . . . while attempting to erase—both physically and spiritually—traces of a continuous Palestinian life on the land, so that both Israeli and Palestinian memory of it would die."[7] In response to the erasure of Palestinian narratives, coupled with a militarized education system that justifies and legitimizes colonial occupation, Zochrot attempts to archive the Nakba via testimonies of displaced refugees from 1948 and tours to depopulated villages, remind Jewish Israeli audiences of what has happened on the ground on which they walk, and imagine a future of reparation in Palestine/Israel.

Al-Ghubari described Zochrot's work as a mobile pedagogical narrative intervention: "Zochrot tries to tell the story through walking, on the ground, visiting the places, seeing the ruins, taking testimonies from the refugees of the villages, establishing the booklets and material about the village, and inviting people to see the place and hear the story from the former residents of the village."[8] Although similar in form to the itinerant narration and testimony gathering of West Bank solidarity tours like the Olive Tree Campaign, Zochrot tours differ in that they are (typically) free, designed for Israeli Jews, and based on refugee testimony and archival research collected to produce pedagogical booklets that archive 1948 and its afterlife.[9] Al-Ghubari explained the process through which Zochrot finds expelled residents of the villages, who are often internally displaced Palestinians inside Israel's 1948 borders, residents of Jerusalem, or living in the West Bank. If they are living in the West Bank, Zochrot gets permission for them to enter Israel to see their former village: a fleeting and incomplete return.

Organizationally, Zochrot will record the refugees' testimony and structure their tours based on the refugees' memory of the village. Al-Ghubari also explained that the degree of participation in the tours is entirely contingent on the desire of the refugee; there is no expectation that the village refugees will continually narrate their painful history of dislocation to rotating groups of Israelis. Instead, the refugees will accompany the tour once, if they choose, and al-Ghubari will do the work of translating the content of their narrative for future tours to the same space. There is no tacit or contractual agreement that the refugee will be expected to lead tours, repeat their story, speak to tourists, or otherwise perform their refugee status, unless they choose to take an active role in shaping and participating in Zochrot's itineraries through their village site. Reflecting on this process, al-Ghubari explained, "You can imagine if you have fifty or seventy people, most of them Israelis, just watching and listening to the refugee telling the story of what happened to himself and his village in 1948 . . ."[10] As he trailed off, his laden pause here asks for recognition, for a moment, of the way these tours demand that Israelis reckon with the acts of violence and displacement that have been carried out in their name. It's clear he also wanted to emphasize the gravity and unevenness of this moment, this contact zone between colonized and colonizer, a "highly asymmetrical" relationship that requires the colonizer to listen carefully and not speak.

Al-Ghubari, moreover, stressed that this work of touring, even while documenting and archiving displacement, is not about the past. It's about looking, politically, at this place "as a place for the future."[11] Each time Zochrot meets with a refugee, he explained, they ask how he or she envisions the future of their village, what they think return should look like. This assessment depends on the reality of the conditions of each village site: "Sometimes you will find a place empty, with the village destroyed; instead of the village you would see only a forest, or land."[12] This description recalls the vast history of Israeli afforestation detailed in chapter 3, where a nature reserve or a forest can mark the site of a raided and depopulated Palestinian village.

Zochrot's project of archiving takes up Khalidi's call for Israeli accountability and, even more, reparations. Published in 1992 and reprinted in 2006, Khalidi's work documents what depopulated villages looked like three decades ago; Zochrot seeks to document what they look like today and what they could potentially look like tomorrow. Zochrot's project, like Khalidi's, is chiefly concerned with what Khalidi calls an Israeli "aversion to scrutiny, with all its moral implications, of Zionism's historical record in Palestine since the 1880s"—an aversion so debilitating and pervasive that it has allowed Israelis and their supporters to convince themselves that "the Palestinians did not exist at all before 1948."[13] But, unlike Khalidi's work, Zochrot's is born from the endeavor to document a colonial project in which one is deeply complicit. Zochrot's tours ask (largely Israeli) tourists to stand in spaces with histories (sometimes no longer visible) of violence and displacement and imagine alternative futures. Pressing their privilege into the service of anticolonial work, Zochrot asks tourists to reckon with what they've ignored and imagine not only what this park/neighborhood/parking lot/coffee shop looked like when it was once a Palestinian home or village but what it could look like after return, what it would look like as a shared space characterized by actual, and not nominal, decolonization.

"I Am Not a Tour Guide": Histories of the Present to Chart a Different Future

In mid-September 2019, I joined a Zochrot tour, led by al-Ghubari, called the Jewish National Fund (JNF) Erasure of Palestine Tour. The tour, beginning in Levinksy Garden in Tel Aviv, would traverse the ruins of the hundreds of Palestinian villages beneath JNF forests and parks across Israel. Taking tourists, largely but not only Israeli, to Ben Shemen Forest, Rabin Park, Britannia Park, Begin Park, and USA Independence Park, Zochrot would recite the names of the destroyed villages, leave signs detailing the village information, and otherwise resist the erasure of Palestinians in Historic Palestine. The bus arrived at its first stop: Ben Shemen Forest, thirty thousand dunams of land (a little over 7,400 acres) planted with JNF trees to cover up the ruins of the Palestinian villages of Jimzu, Dayr Abu Salama, Khirbat Zakariyya, Haditha, and Khirbat al-Duhayriyya. Al-Ghubari began the conversation: "I am not a tour guide. I am a history teller." Situating his work as distinctly not that of a tour guide and instead that of a historian underscores the archival nature of his work, the way these itineraries through these colonial ruins are walking tours of histories of the present. It also, I think, signals a refusal of what constitutes being an official "tour guide" in Israel, where one is expected to parrot state-sanctioned narratives and actively participate in the erasure of Palestine.

Marking another project of this sort, Zochrot also replaced the signs in Israel's national parks in 2014. For Ben Shemen Park, Zochrot's sign read, "Haditha had 880 inhabitants when it was captured. Ben-Gurion ordered it demolished; moshav Hadid was established on its land. Jimzu had 1,750 inhabitants.

Ben-Gurion ordered it demolished; moshav Gamzu was established on its land. Dayr Abu Salama had seventy inhabitants. Khirbat al-Duhayriyya had 116 inhabitants. The number of inhabitants in Khirbat Zakariyya is unknown. These villages were captured in July, 1948."[14] Zochrot's 2019 tour emphasized that 80 percent of the signs marking the recreational sites of these villages ignore the village histories altogether, erasing Palestinian presence. Tours like these, then, work to make this history visible. Tourists learn that the JNF in fact purchased 70 percent of the land *before* 1948, a strategy meant to hold the land for Jewish and not Palestinian use. Like the Zionist planting initiatives detailed on olive planting and harvesting programs in the West Bank, the razing of villages, too, was a state strategy to both eradicate village remains, and thus deny Palestinian presence, and also foreclose the possibility for Palestinians to return to their former homes and villages. This state policy to conceal, Zochrot explained, exists in all the national parks.

On tours like these, Zochrot or otherwise, group leaders, organizers, historians, and tour guides will point to the cacti peppering the landscape as signs of Indigenous Palestinian presence, boundary markers for Palestinian villages, and plants that long produced fruit for Palestinian sustenance (see figure 5.2).

5.2 Haditha, Zochrot JNF Erasure of Palestine Tour. Photo by author (2019).

Like Palestinian guides and organizers on olive tree campaigns in the West Bank, Palestinian and anti-Zionist Israeli guides and organizers on these tours flag signs of Indigenous presence as a refutation of the claim that Palestinians were either "never there" or were ill equipped or otherwise uninterested in cultivating the land.

As the group moved through Haditha, partially covered by Ben Shemen Forest, they searched for the rubble of Palestinian homes, demolished so refugees would have nowhere to return to. Their guides explain, "This used to be a cemetery." Leaning toward me, and my furious note-taking, another tourist asked, "Are you writing a report?" "Sort of. I'm writing a book." She sighed, and explained, "Oh, I wanted to send it to a friend." As she watched, another participant began posting the tour live to Facebook. After a brief pause, she took in the rubble from the demolished home, turned back to me, and said, "If only there was Facebook Live when this shit happened." The temporal logic encapsulated in her reflection signals outrage, resignation, and horror at the crime scene she is witnessing. At the same time, it disappears the home demolitions that continue apace—daily—fifty kilometers away in Jerusalem, across the West Bank, and every time there is an Israeli bombing campaign on Gaza. These are house demolitions that *are* broadcasted on Facebook Live, that are widely publicized, that are reported as they happen. In this way, the work of commemoration, of *remembering*, can sometimes foreclose the capacity to see simultaneity and continuity across different historical moments and different contemporary landscapes.

A 2018 issue of *Comparative Studies of South Asia, Africa, and the Middle East* included a forum titled "Palestine: Doing Things with Archives." The forum, as Lila Abu-Lughod underscores in its introduction, pivoted on questions like "what archives are or should be in this case of a dispersed people with no state archive, no less a state, a majority of whom live in exile or under occupation and have had their 'proper' archive destroyed, seized, or sealed in inaccessible colonial archives belonging to those who dispossessed them and still rule over them with force."[15] Sherene Seikaly, in particular, reflects on paging through familial—not state—archives about her great-grandfather Naim Coltran and tracing familial interventions in those archives. She writes about how, with his orchards expropriated and his bank accounts expropriated as a result of the Absentee Property Law meant to facilitate Zionist expulsion, Coltran was dispossessed of everything through the bureaucratic structures he continued to have faith in, petitioning until his death for remuneration. "Even with all of his fluency and status," she writes, "Naim faltered in the face of a bureaucratic structure that intended to exclude and deprive him at every turn."[16] Grappling also with moments when he had sold property to the JNF, and, significantly, the *conditions* that led him to do so, she outlines what she calls an epistemology of shame that "determines what stories we erase."[17] "At the base of this epistemology of shame," she continues, "is the directive that Palestinians must repeatedly evidence their worthiness."[18] While her essay doesn't speak directly to futurity, it demands a nuance that not only refuses to relegate displacement to the past or imagine that past as unarchived but unpacks the machinations of how that displacement took/takes place and, as Timothy Mitchell and Anupama Rao write in their editor's note to the forum, names "the power of writing, writing against (state) power, and the archive's relation to a future for Palestine."[19] This future of Palestine is one, Seikaly insists, in which Palestinians do not have to repeatedly evidence their worthiness for the state and its various technologies of rule—or for archivists, readers, and scholars alike. Tours, even in their committed anticolonialism, can flatten this kind of nuance in the outrage they engender—even while they detail the expansive theft that occurred not just through straightforward force but also through bureaucracy.

In each of these sites in donor-funded forests across Palestine/Israel, the groups huddle around aerial photos of where they are standing, pre-1948 (figure 5.3). They discuss the site, learn the village names, hear about the village's depopulation in 1948, and learn about what structures were razed, which remain standing, which belonged to a school, which belonged to a mosque, which refugee camps the villagers were sent to. On the third site of that day's tour, the group walked through Britannia Park, a forest funded by British donors after the paving over of nearby Dayr al-Dubban (Luzit was established on its land), Kudna (Beit Nir was established on its land), and 'Aijur (Agur, Tirosh, Li-On, Tzafririm, and Giv'at Yeshayahu were established on its land).[20] An elderly Israeli man began to speak in Hebrew, translated to English for the non-Hebrew-speaking tourists, in sentences broken by emotion. He explained that he came to Israel with his family as a child. In 1949, he was eleven years old and went hiking in a park near where he lived. He came across a house and, as a curious child, he went inside. "Everything was *exactly the same* as the family had left it," he recounted. There were plates on the table and, on the living room floor, a spinning toy from a child's game, stopped in the middle. He explained, "I wanted to take it, but I left it there in case they came back."

Tours of this sort are a reckoning. They demand that Israelis contend with the foundational violence of the Israeli state, not only—and not always on a

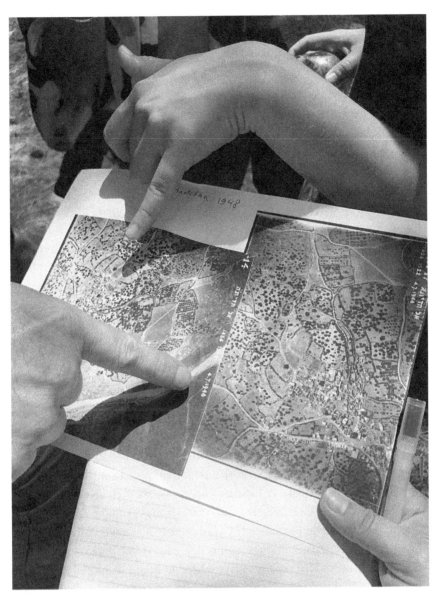

5.3 Haditha, Zochrot JNF Erasure of Palestine Tour. Photo by author (2019).

continuum—with the "Occupation" when it is used only to describe what's happening in the West Bank and Gaza. They demand that Israelis think about being forced out of their home midgame as a child, forced to leave all their belongings in place, the way they would leave a house if they imagined, and were told, they'd be allowed to come back to it after the dust settled. They demand that international tourists eavesdropping on this tour think about what it means that they are stumbling through a forest funded by their fellow citizens in the United Kingdom, in the United States, and in Canada. These tours initiate a reckoning not, however, as a land acknowledgment, not only to state whose land we are walking on. Zochrot tours end with a demand for the Right of Return, which they describe as "just, necessary, and possible," refuting the claim that what's done is done. Standing atop the palimpsest of settler colonialism, in Palestinian spaces that go by Israeli names, the organizers issue calls for a multicultural society in Palestine/Israel that sees itself as part of the Orient, of the East, and not apart from it. They call for an end to segregated space and segregated educational systems, where no one is expelled, Israelis included, and where freedom and equality thrive: in other words, a reckoning with the past that demands a different future.

Walking Tours of Repurposed Villages: Recreation at the Expense of Return

Tours like these are not only led by Zochrot, they are not only tours of forests, and the structures that are toured are not always reduced to rubble. In other spaces in Historic Palestine, Palestinian structures remain and are repurposed into exclusively Israeli sites of leisure and living. Near Haifa, Ein Hod, itself nestled inside a JNF forest planted with funds from US donors, is one of these spaces. On a delegation organized by US-based Eyewitness Palestine (formerly Interfaith Peacebuilders) in August 2019, delegates visited both the Israeli artist colony Ein Hod and the nearby village where internally displaced Palestinians from 'Ayn Hawd had to make their home. Their alternative guide for the day, Bilal Dirbas, of Bil'aaks Alternative Tours (Bil'aaks translates roughly to on the contrary), is, like al-Ghubari, a Palestinian citizen in Israel invested in providing listeners with a history of Israeli settler colonialism in Palestine. He began his tour by explaining, in fact, "Today, we'll be talking about settler colonialism, the same history as you have back home with Native Americans." In doing so, he reminded tourists that what they are invited to witness is not so much of an anomaly, and not as far from home, as they might think.

Before entering Ein Hod, by way of the JNF park planted in the name of US citizens supportive of Israel, Dirbas detailed the occupation of 'Ayn Hawd in 1948.[21] The Palestinian villagers, who numbered 650 in 1945 and 800 in 1948, had held their village through two previous Zionist attacks but were forced out by the Israeli army and navy on July 15, 1948.[22] The villagers who were not exiled to refugee camps in Jenin and Irbid like the rest of the village created a new village nearby, which was unrecognized by the Israeli state until 1994 and did not begin to be connected to the electrical grid or receive municipal services until official recognition in 2005.[23] Dirbas described the transformation of the village: "The village mosque is now used as a bar and restaurant. The minaret is gone." He described the new demographic of the colony, established in 1953: "They are the bohemian, radical left Israelis, but they are Zionists and their mindset is settler colonial." Like other Palestinian guides and organizers in the West Bank and Jerusalem, Dirbas anchored his analysis of tourism in Israel to settler colonialism. He spoke about Marcel Janco, cofounder of the Dada movement, who emigrated to Mandate Palestine in 1941 and cofounded Ein Hod in 1954 in the wake of the depopulation of 'Ayn Hawd: "He brought tourism to this village and gave legitimacy to the new project of Zionism." Tourists come to understand, as they traverse alternative tours of Palestine, that even in its earliest iterations during and after state formation, tourism has been tied to Zionism and settler-colonial displacement in Palestine.

Dirbas first walked tourists through the JNF forest at the base of the village, funded by US donors in the wake of the Mount Carmel forest fires in 2010 (figure 5.4)—fires that thrived, as they do in California, because Indigenous knowledge on how to prevent forest fires is ignored and because nonnative trees, planted to foreclose refugees' return, cover up demolished villages, and fashion Israel into a "Switzerland of the Middle East," not only make the soil acidic and thereby decimate native foliage, but also make the forests susceptible to uncontainable fires in Palestine's climate.[24] He then guided the group through the Ein Hod, the Dada artist colony, an ostensibly aesthetically "charming" village, with Dada art sculptures, standing stone structures from stolen Palestinian homes, the 'Ayn Hawd mosque repurposed into a bar and restaurant, bookstores, coffee shops, and outdoor cafés—meeting tourists' desires for the exotic and the quaint as well as the ancient and the modern. Tourists to Ein Hod, unless they are on a tour of the ruins of 'Ayn Hawd, neither hear this history nor sense its significance but are invited to celebrate the beauty of the erasure of Palestine (figures 5.5 and 5.6). The Ein Hod Artists Village website boasts local charm, ancient ruins, art galleries, a place that has—unlike other

5.4 Ein Hod
Eyewitness
Palestine dele-
gation. Photo
by author
(August 2019).

places in Israel—been able to "retain the authentic quality of the Mediterranean."[25] With "Mediterranean" doing the work of distancing Israel from the
Middle East while simultaneously laying claim to the landscape of the Levant,
the invitation is structured through erasure:

> One can still discern in the old structures the many textures and architec-
> tural forms of earlier occupants—from the Christian Crusades to the Turkish
> Empire. The roads and byways, a mixture of ancient and modern, all add to
> a very special atmosphere. Yet perhaps it is the landscape, the vegetation,
> and the view that make this place so unique and exciting—natural Mediter-
> ranean gardens of olive, pomegranate, almond, and carob trees, grape vines
> and figs. Ein Hod has remained a nature reserve, preserving the biblical flora
> of ancient Israel—a perfect environment for the creative muse.[26]

5.5 Ein Hod, Eyewitness Palestine delegation. Photo by author (August 2019).

5.6 Ein Hod, Eyewitness Palestine delegation. Photo by author (August 2019).

Here, in this invitation to a potential tourist, a creative thinker, and lefty bohemian traveler, the authors carry out the discursive erasure of Palestine on top of the material one they describe. The "earlier occupants" conveniently become not Palestinians or Arabs but time periods: the Christian Crusades and Turkish Empire. Mandate Palestine, let alone contemporary Palestine, fails to exist in this timeline. And, predictably, like Herzl's foundational *Altneuland*, the leap from biblical foliage to still-extant Palestinian almond, carob, and olive trees crafts a through line between the biblical Holy Land and today, which sutures only Jewish people to the land and positions Palestinians as an inconvenient, misplaced anomaly on land that never belonged to them in the first place. Here we see the erasure of Palestine in the name of tourism, another moment when tourism and settler colonialism share the same state-sanctioned goal.

Even more, in a ubiquitously circulated claim, Ein Hod's promotional litera-ture describes the village as resurrected from abandonment, and not a militar-ily occupied one whose residents were forced out, not allowed to return, and compelled to set up camp within eyesight of their former village:

> After the War of Independence the area was abandoned and left in ruin. In the fifties, a group of artists led by the acclaimed Dada artist Marcel Janco decided that Ein Hod would be a place where they could work, build studios and workshops, and form a creative environment for art and art education. The founders' dream ran into the harsh reality of those days. [But] perse-verance and vision gradually transformed Ein Hod into the only artists' village in Israel, one of the few in the world, where artists live and create in every artistic media from the visual arts, to theater, music and literature.[27]

Painting Ein Hod as a utopian vision of an artists' dream created on top of an "abandoned" village that had been "left in ruin" positions it as a miracle born out of the hard work and perseverance of artists who recognized beauty where nameless and faceless Palestinians did not, rather than a settlement born out of war and military occupation and compulsory exile. It forecloses even the possibility of imagining that villagers from 'Ayn Hawd, two kilometers away in a village unrecognized by the state for decades, produce archives, village maps, and memory books commemorating their village and long for their eventual return.

The Bil'aaks Alternative Tour of Ein Hod ends in the new 'Ayn Hawd. Dirbas describes the village's struggle to be recognized by the state, how this recognition— and with it the construction of the road to the village, the connection of (some of) the houses to the electrical grid, water, and sewage—was not fully realized until 2006. Even still, the road is dangerous, the deed to the land precarious for the three hundred villagers who live there, the work unstable as it is contingent on rural tourism or private contractors in surrounding settlements.

In this, as with Zochrot's tours, solidarity tourists come to understand that settlements are not only circumscribed to the West Bank, that the root of the "conflict" is in the Nakba and the displacement of 750,000 Palestinians—whether they were exiled to refugee camps in neighboring countries like Jordan, Lebanon, and Syria; exiled to cities, towns, or other refugee camps in the West Bank or Gaza; exiled from the region altogether; or internally displaced inside Israel in villages like 'Ayn Hawd. Tourists, then, are invited to witness continuities in displacement, in geographies across Historic Palestine, even when they are called other—albeit deceptively similar—names.

Jerusalem, Revisited: Ruins and Return

To give tourists a fuller understanding of what becomes of villages depopulated by Israel in both 1948 and 1967, organizers often turn to spaces like Lifta and Emwas, with Lifta's structures still standing and its springs used by settlers as a site of restoration and recreation, and Emwas's structures mostly reduced to rubble and its grounds mostly covered by Canada Park. Lifta, occupied by Zionist forces in 1948, was a village that functioned as a "suburb of the city of Jerusalem"—which is, not coincidentally, how Israel refers to settlements off Jerusalem in the West Bank now.[28] Lifta had 2,550 Palestinian residents in the mid-1940s; the village had a mosque, shops, elementary schools, two coffeehouses, a social club, and a thriving agricultural presence.[29] After a Stern Gang attack on one of the coffeehouses, which left five patrons dead and more wounded, along with repeated Haganah and Stern Gang raids on the village and a series of home demolitions in Lifta and nearby villages, villagers of Lifta were forced to leave.[30] David Ben-Gurion celebrated their military prowess, stating to his constituents: "From your entry into Jerusalem through Lifta—Romema, through Mahane Yehuda, King George Street and Mea Sharim—there are no strangers. One hundred percent Jews."[31]

In July 2019, one villager, Yacoub Odeh, gave an international student group a walking tour of his village, not, he explained, as a tour guide but as a villager. Odeh, an elder, was forced out of the village with his family as a child. His narration was full of pauses where, in sorrow, he took in the state of the village: the neglect of its agriculture, the damage done by settlers in the shape of fires and graffiti, the use of the still-standing stone structures—some of them mosques—by Israeli youth as places to party. He paused many times, apologizing. "I'm so sorry," he would say. "Everything has changed." He spoke of how he had only been gone a few weeks, yet entire terraces had been burned in that time. "This was all plants," he gestured mournfully toward the charred slope. His narration makes evident why Zochrot refuses to ask refugees to narrate the histories of their villages to strangers, unless they want to as part of their work. It is clear that this is painful work for Odeh, work that asks him to dwell, in front of an audience, on the violence that shaped his childhood and continues to define his relationship to this place in his old age (figure 5.7).

Odeh described the life of the village: the weather, the six olive oil presses, the olive groves—long since uprooted—the village well, now appropriated by Israelis swimming in its waters along with the water pumped from beneath the ground in endless supply to settlements. "They say they need more water than us," he explained. "Why? Because they are cleaner than us? They drink more than us? They need flowers more than us? It is a racist mentality." Suturing cleanliness to sustenance to beauty, Odeh describes things people need to survive and thrive. He pointed to the spring, where settlers bathed and stared

5.7 Lifta, FFIP tour. Photo by author (July 2019).

at the group of foreigners gathered around their narrator. "My childhood was between here and here," he gestured to the spring and what remained of his family home. "I was like a fish, always in the water." A group of elementary-aged Israeli schoolchildren and their teachers approached the spring. The children readied themselves to go in the water as Odeh led the group out of their way, into a different section of the village, displaced midstory about his own childhood by a scene of Israeli children's unfettered access to what was once his, before his family's displacement from Lifta.

He led us to his family home. "This is my mother's *tabun* [clay oven]." The tour group leaders, eager to not miss the next lecture on their itinerary, began rushing Odeh. He ignored them. Echoing Yazan Al-Zubaidy's narration that he tells tourists about the Wall so he doesn't just forget it's there, "We tell this story so we don't forget." He continued: "I was small. I didn't forget. This is our village. We should return. We will never forget. I have a right to go back to my home. We can build a democratic state together." Suturing the Right of Return to the capacity to remake the state as a democratic one, and not in name only, he turned to what the tourists could do. The group leaders interrupted him again, reiterating that they were late for their next meeting. He ignored them again, centering his own pain and the purpose of his retelling, making sure his listeners understood what they were being invited to do. This interchange speaks to the pace of solidarity tours—what one Palestinian American artist and activist calls "Occupation Bootcamp" to signal the itinerary of cycling through rotating scenes of devastation with no breaks to pause or process—and how much it precludes sitting with stories, honoring the teller, fully listening to what you are being asked to do.

He ended his tour with an appeal. "These buildings"—he gestured to the homes, half demolished but still standing, surrounding the group—"are witnesses to what happened in the Nakba. Do not let them be destroyed." He asked the group to write to UNESCO to make sure Lifta is registered as a World Heritage Site so that Israel cannot destroy it. The Jerusalem Municipality and the Israel Land Authority remain hard at work planning Construction Plan 6036, which intends to demolish Lifta and build in its place an elite villa neighborhood—parking structures, retaining walls, roads, rock cutting into the mountainside.[32] The group leaders impatiently wait for him to finish. It is difficult to hear his final words over the construction and drilling atop the mountain overlooking the village. In UNESCO's own description of the village, submitted by the Permanent Delegation of Israel to UNESCO, the authors advocate for its preservation, but refer to it as "abandoned" three times and laud the fact that—unlike places like Ein Hod—it has been untouched by modernization. "No new infrastructure," the document concludes. "No added construction and no traces of modern life."[33] Heir to a village that was never abandoned, Yacoub Odeh, with this narrative, reclaims his dignity, even to a group of international youths attempting to hurry him, even in spite of settlers eavesdropping and bathing in his village's spring, even among ruins tagged with graffiti and covered with debris, and even among charred terraces. He demands, with his presence, his rightful return and sees, in his family's future, the restoration of Lifta in one democratic state.[34]

Rana Barakat, in her piece "Lifta, the Nakba, and the Museumification of Palestine's History," cautions against the settler logics entrenched in efforts to solely preserve Lifta—including those of UNESCO—without any emphasis on restoration and return. She writes:

> In this settler narrative, the uniqueness of the story of Lifta begins with how [the] particular exodus [of Palestinian refugees in Lifta in 1948] is memorialized as a "beginning" to an "end" of the Palestinian history in Lifta. That is, as the "only remaining abandoned Arab village," the settler narrative of the place becomes one framed as a story of preservation. Lifta's story of preservation is a drama full of all kinds of actors—from settlers who want to be natives, settlers who want to make their own style of native chic, natives who were metamorphosed (and who in some ways and instances metamorphosed themselves) into folk stories, and, off this stage framed by the settler and imperial powers, Indigenous Palestinians who work to return.[35]

Barakat takes issue particularly with the positioning, as in the UNESCO appeal, of Lifta as the "only abandoned Arab village in Israel not to have been destroyed or repopulated since 1948."[36] She shows that not only was Lifta *not* abandoned but it is also not the only remaining Palestinian village. Moreover, she argues, this insistence on uniqueness is precisely what results in the museumification of Lifta: the desire for Lifta to be preserved, as is, with structures and without life, rather than as a place of vitality, restoration, and return. In her words, "Preservation . . . is incommensurate with restoration (or deruination). If preservation serves settlers' interests, then restoration serves Indigenous interests."[37] "As such," she continues, "restoration means Palestinians will return to their village—repatriated as a lived space, not as a symbolic museum space of a former past. What lies at the heart of this is the distinction between conceptualizing Lifta as a symbol of a dead past rather than as a living village thriving beyond museumification and preservation."[38] In this way, Yacoub Odeh's rushed yet insistent appeal to preserve Lifta, fraught as it is and contingent as it is on collaborating with settler desires to preserve Lifta as an act of *refusing* return, still ends with a restructuring of that appeal: a demand for preservation of Lifta from destruction but a simultaneous demand for its restoration as a site of life and return for his family.

Elsewhere on the outskirts of Jerusalem, during that same summer, another group of tourists witnessed a different landscape of Israeli state violence, this time a village razed in 1967, not 1948. After taking a bus from their hotel in Jerusalem to Canada Park, ostensibly inside Israel, Eyewitness Palestine delegates arrived in Emwas. Zochrot's al-Ghubari introduced himself to this group, again reiterating that he is a historian, not a tour guide, and explained that they are, in fact, on occupied West Bank land and would be learning about three villages—Yalo, Beit Nuba, and Emwas—occupied by Israel in 1967 because it couldn't occupy them in 1948. "This is the West Bank," he explained. "We are *outside* the Green Line." Disrupting tourists' sense of where they are, al-Ghubari explained that, though they were hiking in an Israeli park, planted by the JNF and funded by Canadian donors, they are in fact in the Latrun salient of the West Bank. Here is another moment, then, that resonates with tourists in visualizing how far into the West Bank—an ostensibly Palestinian territory—Israel reaches.

He gestured to the forest around the tourists. "This area was full of houses only fifty years ago," during the June 1967 War when Israel took Jerusalem, the West Bank, Gaza, and Sinai. "How many people were killed here?" one macabre question arose from the group. "Not many," al-Ghubari answered. "The ethnic cleansing was planned in advance. Six people were killed in their homes." He explained that there was no war; ten to twenty Egyptian and Jordanian soldiers left after ten minutes of clashes. The group walked farther into the forest, where they stopped at the site of the village cemetery, partially destroyed. Al-Ghubari explained, "Two thousand people lived here until 1967." The villagers who were expelled became refugees in Ramallah and Jordan. The group settled around the stones, poring over maps provided by al-Ghubari. "Bulldozers razed the village over the following weeks," al-Ghubari continued. "People were killed inside their houses." One diaspora Palestinian participant turned away from the group and cried silently; later, during a processing session, she detailed the pain of listening to the displacement of her ancestors while watching a bunch of tourists lean against, sit on, and otherwise disrespect their tombstones.

The group continued walking, with al-Ghubari again pointing out the cacti, the village boundary markers. "Refugees from Emwas, Yalo, and Beit Nuba are waiting for their right to return," he explained as the group prepared to get back on the bus. "That is the whole mission of these tours: to not only know the history but to support the Right of Return." This one tour reveals the multiple workings of solidarity delegations in Historic Palestine: the suturing of the site of the tour to the demand for return, the fraught spectacle of tourists misunderstanding the land on which they walk, the pain of the "walking tour of Palestine" for Palestinian participants whose families have long been exiled and who are only allowed to return—if allowed at all—as tourists, the reminders to tourists that while it may feel like they are in Canada Park, Israel, they are in fact in the Occupied West Bank, Palestine.

A few days later, the group would meet in Ramallah with refugees from Emwas. They would hear from refugees who have laboriously archived the destruction of their village and articulated—in multiple forms—their demand for return. Delegates met with Dima Abu Ghoush, the director of *Emwas: Restoring Memories*, a documentary, premiered at the 2019 Boston Palestine Film Festival, on the labor Abu Ghoush and her family have done to reconstruct their village in the form of a model. Abu Ghoush, forced to leave at two years old, decided in 2009 to rebuild the village with the help of memories from village elders and with the assistance of her sons, a labor of documenting the past and reconstructing the future. Looking over the village model and meeting with the villagers, a tourist asked a village elder if he remembered anything, even though he was only thirteen years old when he was forced to walk in the road, under threat of getting shot, away from his village. "I remember every road and every stone," he answered.

Abu Ghoush anchored the conversation in decolonization, modeling Barakat's restoration with life instead of museumification: "We made a model village as a plan for return." She distributed booklets detailing the history of the demolition of the village and outlining the refugees' demands:

1   What happened in Emwas and Yalu and Beit Nuba is a crime of war.
2   The residents of the three villages have the right to return back to their villages and rebuild them regardless of any political solution.
3   We refuse compensation that is not linked with the right to return.
4   We refuse resettlement anywhere except in our hometowns.
5   We refuse any border modification that abuses the status of our land occupied in the year 1967 and that must be treated as the whole occupied territories.[39]

Strewn on the table at the entrance to where the model was displayed were a series of postcards. Turning the postcard—a staple of tourism—on its head, the image across the faces of the postcards include bulldozers razing village houses (figure 5.8), village ruins (figure 5.9), and before-and-after shots of the demolition in 1967 (figure 5.10). The ephemera to mark this tourist experience—the brochures and the postcards—remind tourists that what they have been invited to witness on their walk in "Canada Park," as they study the carefully constructed village model and as they listen to village elders, is not only the destruction of Palestinian lives and livelihoods across the West Bank, Jerusalem, and Israel but also the unequivocal demand for return. In this way, through and not in spite of the tropes of tourism, refugees are asking tourists to join that call—not solely for an end to the occupation but for a return of Palestinian refugees to their former homes and villages across Historic Palestine.

Blueprinting Return

In my interview with Umar al-Ghubari about his work at Zochrot, he described how Zochrot's tours—mostly to villages depopulated in 1948—focus not only on imagining what once was but on imagining the potentiality of what

5.8 Postcards from Emwas. Photo by author (2020).

مقام معاذ ابن جبل " سيدي الشيخ معلّا "

5.9 Postcards from Emwas. Photo by author (2020).

could be if Palestinian refugees were given back what was once theirs. Israeli audiences, while sympathetic to the plight of Palestinian refugees, often cannot take this extra, even imaginary, step toward reparations. "Most of the Israelis still have the ability to listen, maybe also to remember, if they saw, and even to express how they understand the pain of the refugees," he explained. "But they don't want to talk about return or see the place with Palestinians again. Many of them politically see that as a destruction of the Jewish state and they want, they insist, to see the state with a Jewish majority and that's it. So, for this reason, they do not want to allow or accept the return of the refugees."[40] He further qualified that this is not about the right or left of the Israeli state, but that this is the stance held by the majority of Jewish Israelis, including many who go on his tours.

Al-Ghubari described an impasse wherein Israeli audiences are willing to be moved by narratives about the past yet are unwilling to move toward a different future. He enumerated sentiments that approximate an embrace of an empathetic—and even complicit—look backward but an unwillingness to consider redress. The tourists' attitudes approximate a refusal to imagine otherwise.[41]

عواس سنة ١٩٥٨

عواس سنة 1968 بعد قهم

5.10 Postcards from Emwas. Photo by author (2020).

Al-Ghubari described a situation wherein Israelis acknowledge how painful this history is but reject return because they believe it means there would be no place for them in the country. He described tourists who fear the refugees killing them, or the destruction of the fabric of the society, or another Holocaust—fears that foreclose even the possibility of talking about "a common future." Needless to say, he continued, this fear is grounded in racism that necessitates that Jewish Israelis be stronger, be the majority, keep themselves protected, be superior— sentiments that make the destruction of Palestinian lives inevitable. He

جمعية أهالي عمواس الخيرية
www.imwas.org

رام الله - بيتونيا

5.11 Postcards from Emwas. Photo by author (2020).

characterized this impasse as a "border," still in place, "between the past and the future": a willingness to have feelings about the past but not to move toward the future. "We want the tour," he continued, "to put the question there."[42] In other words, Zochrot makes these multiple histories of displacement impossible to ignore—at least during the duration of the tour—and at the very least, raises the question of return. Moreover, he emphasized how refugees have to routinely explain to Israelis, "I'm not kicking you out. I want us to build the village. I want to be your neighbor."[43] Starting from there is very important, he explained, because Jewish Israeli fears are so sedimented that, when they hear this answer, it opens a space for them to think through the question.

Zochrot's most sustained collaboration on the question of return is with the BADIL Resource Center for Palestinian Residency and Refugee Rights, a West Bank organization dedicated to protecting the rights of Palestinian refugees and internally displaced Palestinians. At the time of my interview with Umar al-Ghubari in 2012, Zochrot and BADIL had been collaborating for three years on a project titled "The Practicalities of Return." This project takes the question of return seriously and demarcates the failures and impossibilities of peace and justice without return.[44] Their work up to that point had centered on touring, workshopping, and mapping. The Zochrot-BADIL collaboration began in 2009 with a workshop on Miska, a Palestinian village in the Tulkarem subdistrict of Mandatory Palestine, now inside Israel's 1948 borders, approximately twenty-seven kilometers north of Tel Aviv. (Miska was, in fact, the site of Zochrot's first tour on Land Day in 2002.[45])

After the workshop on Miska, attended by internally displaced refugees and organizers from Zochrot, BADIL and Zochrot began planning return, practically. Together—since organizers at BADIL in the West Bank cannot enter Israel—members of Zochrot and BADIL traveled to several international sites for seminars, field tours, and workshops, including South Africa and the former Yugoslavia for field tours and Istanbul for workshops. After each study tour, composed of lectures, site visits, and workshops, Zochrot and BADIL jointly produced documents, each of which, as al-Ghubari explained, updated and augmented the previous one, creating an archive of "accumulated knowledge."[46] Al-Ghubari explained this process as trying to learn from others' experiences with return and restitution.

He spoke of his tour to Cape Town, South Africa, in January and February 2012. Ten people from Zochrot and ten people from BADIL traveled to Cape Town to meet with organizations dealing with truth and reconciliation after the apartheid era, to hear lectures from experts on restitution and compensation, and to study housing in Cape Town and the many problems that remained post-apartheid. Zochrot and BADIL, in their partnership, he explained, study both what has succeeded in these spaces and what has failed. Zochrot learned from the field tours in Cape Town that organizers there had decided to begin with one point in the conflict—1913, when the apartheid regime confiscated large swaths of land and expelled Black South Africans from their cities and villages—and start conversations about compensation, return, and restitution from that point.

From field tours in Serbia, Zochrot learned that there are sometimes multiple directions of refugees and returns, that different moments in the conflict produced different refugee experiences. In Serbia, they also learned that, even after return became a viable option, many refugees did not return or sold the property returned to them, because they didn't feel comfortable living alongside the enemy. "This is why," al-Ghubari explained, "we would not call for refugees to come back to the Israeli regime."[47] Refugees, he maintained, would not agree to come live in a Jewish state under a Jewish government. "The regime, or the political system, would need to be changed in order for the refugees to feel like they are coming to their homeland and to their state."[48] What Zochrot works toward, then, is not a piecemeal return of a handful of Palestinian refugees as a symbolic overture; what they advocate is a wholesale overturning of Zionism, a "fundamental change in the regime."

Al-Ghubari explained this touring, workshopping, and mapping as a long and complex process. First, he described the production of the document: "We had a field tour and then a workshop and divided ourselves into three subgroups and each group took one title or one subject and drafted a document on how we see the future of this place, or this country, and the question of restitution."[49] After Cape Town, Zochrot and BADIL produced the twenty-five-page "Study Visit to Cape Town," a report-back of sorts that is full of observations; preliminary plans; actions and proposals; outlines of lessons learned from South Africa; shared principles and visions between the two organizations; and pages and pages of lingering concerns, disagreements, and unanswered questions.

The document's introduction, written by Hazim Jamjum, begins by outlining the work around the imperative of return that Zochrot and BADIL had been conceptualizing long before they embarked on the study tour together:

> For both BADIL and Zochrot, it is this aspect of the liberation of Palestine to which we have dedicated our efforts for over a decade since our organizations' establishment. Through the course of our work, however, we have found that conceptions of "return" have remained somewhat superficial. This is true among the settler community that sees it as a calamity to be avoided at any cost as well as among the indigenous community that equates return to a reversal of six decades of settler-colonialism; the return to a paradise lost.[50]

Here, Jamjum outlines some of the central difficulties of this work that al-Ghubari also reiterated in his interview: first, the fear on the part of Jewish Israelis that return will result in a dissolution of their lives and livelihoods and the fabric of their society as they know it; and second, the desire on the part of Palestinian refugees to return to Palestine before 1948, a Palestine that no longer exists in that form.

Al-Ghubari, in his interview, detailed some of the fraught questions that have arisen out of workshops to plan return. Paralleling some of the necessary questions about class that Sophia Azeb asks in her piece, "Who Will We Be When We Are Free?," he explained, "In our case, there are internal Palestinian discussions—very interesting ones—regarding the relationship between families inside the Palestinian society . . . before 1948 . . . between the rich people and poor people, rich families and poor families."[51] He elaborated, "Some of the refugees, when the Nakba started in 1948, they lost thousands of dunams of land. But some of the refugees didn't have anything except their small house. So what does the return mean for this family and the return for this family?"[52] Jamjum raises a similar question in the introductory words of the report-back:

"Are the descendants of large landowners to return to bountiful properties, while the many more descendants of workers, sharecroppers, and tenant farmers to return to no property at all? Is what remains of Palestine's terraced hillsides to be turned into concrete jungles of parceled out houses over which present and future heirs can differ? What will be the fate of a productive factory that lies on the land of Palestinian returnees?"[53] Or, as al-Ghubari said, "This family, in 1948, was just a couple and two sons. Today they are about fifty people—if they don't have land, what does the return mean? Where are they supposed to come back? And is it just if the rich families come back and are rich families again?"[54] For his part, Jamjum asks, "How, for instance, is return to materialize to a village whose inhabitants numbered less than two thousand before the Nakba, and who now number in the tens of thousands?"[55] Zochrot and BADIL clarify, in their section on principles, that "the purpose of return and reparations is not to return the descendants of landlords and peasants to the socioeconomic positions of poverty that they were in before the Nakba."[56] These fraught questions detailing, outlining, and mapping the contingencies of return in the context of Palestine animate Zochrot and BADIL's collaborative workshops, mapping sessions, and study tours. The report-backs they produce are less definitive solutions than open-ended uncertainties, raising questions now for fear that they may never be raised if return were in fact implemented.

These questions arise, further, based on the particularity of Zochrot and BADIL's experience of touring sites of reconciliation where questions about implementation were not asked and thus not carefully mapped out. In their report-back, they explain that their work needs to be sustainable: it "needs to take place continuously, not only before the return itself, but also during and after the return process."[57] They continue: "The point is to avoid what happened in South Africa, where all the struggle of civil society against Apartheid was focused on bringing about the formal regime change, and when this happened in 1994, civil society lost its orientation in the new reality while many aspects of Apartheid persisted in different forms."[58] Zochrot and BADIL thus learn whatever amount of truncated knowledge they can while on the ten-day tour (much like those seeking to learn whatever they can on their own ten-day solidarity tours in Palestine), and then use this accumulation of collective knowledge to begin workshopping, planning, and blueprinting what return would look like.

In this way, both organizations work against exceptionalizing Palestine. They do not position Palestine as uniquely evidencing forced displacement and expulsion; they want to learn from other sites with similar—but not the same—histories. On the first page of their report-back, they write that the case of Palestine is "not the only one in which mass forced displacement has been carried out, nor will it be the only one in which return will constitute part of a just solution."[59] They explain that there is "much for us to learn from cases of expulsion and return stretching from East Timor, the former Yugoslavia and Cyprus, to Rwanda, Zimbabwe and South Africa. The idea is not to replicate models but rather to try and learn their lessons and incorporate them into our thinking of Palestinian return."[60] Modeling their work on the successes and failures of other contexts, they envision their goal as practical redistribution rather than a return to a static and idyllic pre-1948 Palestine. They define the justice they seek as restorative rather than retributive. Further, they maintain that their approach must be flexible; in the context of Palestine/Israel, where the facts on the ground—on both sides of the Green Line—change daily and where one village's remains might exist today but not tomorrow, the mapping must be able to account for sudden changes in geopolitical circumstances. In this way, through their work of touring, they craft a flexible, sustainable, and cumulative approach toward return.

Part of this collective work, too, is characterized by the profound disparities in citizenship and in freedom of movement between the participants from BADIL and Zochrot. These disparities take the form of settler and colonized, citizen and stateless subject, those free to move and those confined to the West Bank, those, in fact, with the leisure to imagine return and those without. As one participant from BADIL put it on the study tour in South Africa, "How am I to imagine a postliberation future when I am still under occupation?"[61] Umar al-Ghubari also fleshed out his assessment that Palestinian refugees in the West Bank or Jordan are not as able to talk about the issue of return as he is as a Palestinian living inside Israel:

> I interviewed Palestinian refugees in the West Bank, even in Jordan, and this question is very far away from them. They are in difficult situations, and they are just running after the daily difficulties: how are they going to live tomorrow or have citizenship in Jordan, or not going to have citizenship, do they have a job, do they have bread, do they have money, what donations are UNRWA bringing tomorrow, [who is] staying with them, not staying? They are busy with very basic issues, and they don't have time or ability to imagine or to plan or to act toward return.[62]

With this, both the anonymous participant in BADIL-Zochrot's report and Umar al-Ghubari, in his reflections on Palestinian refugee responses to the question of return, underscore the time and space that planning return necessitates.

This too, al-Ghubari added, results from decades of occupation and the way that it not only restricts movement but also restricts imagination. "It's amazing what this Wall is doing," he surmised. "It's not only a Wall blocking their movement. It's also blocking their ideas, their imagination. They can't see beyond the Wall."[63] This sentiment was echoed in interviews I conducted with organizers in the West Bank in 2012 as they reflected on the difficulties of coordinating and organizing tours with activists inside the Wall in the context of such stark separation, though the breadth and capacity for West Bank tours to include itineraries inside Israel changed dramatically over the course of my research. While in 2012, it was rare for a West Bank tour to include, for example, a day in Haifa in its itinerary, in 2019 many did. This sea change speaks to the on-the-ground organizing work of tour guides refusing the circumscription of "Palestine" to strictly the West Bank, Gaza, and East Jerusalem. Now, organizers across Historic Palestine coordinate schedules to give tourists a vision of displacement in Palestine that is as temporally and geographically extensive as the occupation itself has been. It takes time and space and the capacity to connect to lay concrete plans for an imagined future, let alone concrete plans for possibilities that are both contingent and hypothetical. Still, planning—hypothetical and contingent as it is—is urgent for Zochrot and BADIL's organizers because they are afraid that return without a plan would perpetuate the inequities that thrive under Zionism.

Flowers Instead of Fences

Next, al-Ghubari began to tell me about Zochrot's return tours to specific village sites after study tours, when they go with architects, Israelis who live at or near the contemporary village sites, and internally displaced refugees from the depopulated villages who work with them to imagine and implement return. He asked if I had seen the mapping blueprints for some of the return workshops. He shuffled through the bookcases behind him to produce stacks of maps from the planning workshops, looking for the one in English. His phone buzzed on the table, but he ignored it, intent on finding the maps from the field tours. He produced a map of Miska, a draft with a green space cutting through the page, blue sketches emanating outward, scattered housing structures, and a town center. The map, reproduced in Zochrot's digital archives, is overlaid atop aerial photos of the landscape (figure 5.10).[64] The palimpsest of planning visible in the photo underscores the labor undertaken at the workshop after Zochrot's tours to the village ruins. The photo archives the collaborative labor

5.12 Zochrot, "Countermapping Miska." Photo by Einat Manof (July 30, 2010).

between internally displaced Palestinians from the village and Israelis who live near it now, working to imagine a future of shared space on and around that same site.

Al-Ghubari traced the village site on the paper and explained that this was a case study of Miska, a village very close to Kfar Saba, a big city near Tel Aviv. The workshop, he explained, was for refugees from the village and Israelis who live nearby. Using aerial photos from 1948 and from the contemporary moment, the villagers and Israelis drew how they wanted to see the village. Al-Ghubari pointed to the map: "So this is the valley and this is the college and this is the swimming pool and this is the neighboring kibbutz from Ramat HaKovesh, and instead of fences they want to open the fence and plant some flowers."[65] In reference to the flowers, he paused and added, "You know, people can fantasize things."[66]

He continued, "This is the center of the village; they want to make that a public cultural center and the neighborhoods should be here. So they ask the questions of really how to plan, how to live, is it possible to live there and, if so, how."[67] The language of al-Ghubari's description here reflects the same kind of self-reflexivity that went into the Cape Town delegation, the difficult and messy labor of collaboration, the fragmented consensus that emerges out of discussions. Drafting atop aerial photos from both 1948 and today, the workshop participants, after touring the site, begin the labor of imagination: a pool here, a college here, the kibbutz in its extant space, flowers instead of fences. With his interjection, "You know, people can fantasize things," al-Ghubari acknowledged the way thinking about flowers in the context of occupation can be understood as lofty or frivolous while he simultaneously defended that work of imagination. This work of fantasy is grounded in historical context yet mapped onto an unscripted future, so why not propose hypothetical borders of flowers? The center of the village—perhaps eventually a public cultural center—and the homes that surround it all chart out the materialities of what return to this space would and could potentially look like.

Cataloging the discussions between Israelis and Palestinians about where to place which set of houses, the school, and the community pool, al-Ghubari also described the tensions felt by Palestinian architects and organizers displaced from the village itself but still living inside Israel. "It's not easy for them either," al-Ghubari explained. "They ask, what is my mandate to plan the village when I didn't talk with the other refugees on the outside?"[68] This question highlights the profound differences in access and mobility experienced by Palestinians inside Israel's 1948 borders and those in exile in the West Bank or beyond. It further indexes the impossibilities of including Palestinian refugees "on the outside" in tours of the village sites, as they are not allowed to return—even temporarily. Because of these proliferating tensions and difficulties, like the posed but not answered questions in the Cape Town report-back, al-Ghubari explained that the workshops always set out to propose not the only perfect solution but ideas people can react to, improve, and augment.

Lingering with Miska as a case study, he explained, "For example, with Miska, this village, they offered different cases or different ways of return. Sometimes they took the center of the village for a cultural place, sometimes they took it for the old people of the village, or the refugees who are still alive and deserve to live inside the village."[69] Still, he emphasized, "They have different ideas, but *all* the ideas are based on the acceptance of the right of return."[70] Taking return as the starting point, Zochrot facilitates these tours and workshops with village architects, Israeli architects, planners, organizers, Palestinian refugees, and Israeli nearby residents, and then meets with BADIL to exchange research, collaborate further, and continue to brainstorm return. This mapping—contentious but coterminous on the question of return—and the simultaneous and multiple uses and sites of touring written into the process are reflected not only in al-Ghubari's descriptions but also in the (many) documents produced about each mapping project.

In the Zochrot publication *Sedek: A Journal on the Ongoing Nakba*, architect and environmental designer Ahmad Barclay describes a project that developed out of the Decolonizing Architecture Art Residency (DAAR) in Beit Sahour. DAAR's work—through art; architectural intervention in the present; projected urban-planning blueprints for the future; and collaborations with artists, architects, scholars, researchers, writers, and activists—proposes a "subversion, reuse, profanation, and recycling of the existing infrastructure of colonial occupation."[71] Barclay's piece in *Sedek* documents four stages of "re-emergence" specifically in the village of Miska: symbolic interventions on the site of the village, a token return to Miska by Palestinians living in Israel, an actual return by a handful of families "who begin to recreate the urban fabric," and a "solidification of the urban fabric" as remaining families return.[72]

Barclay begins with an account Umar al-Ghubari published on Miska in 2009. In it, al-Ghubari writes that, in 2005, on the fifty-seventh anniversary commemoration of the Nakba, internally displaced Palestinians from Miska established the Committee of Miska's Uprooted. The committee's first act was to visit the village with dozens from the village, their supporters, and members of Zochrot. Al-Ghubari writes, "The participants planted olive and fig saplings. A few days later the authorities uprooted the saplings and blocked the roads leading to the village school, barring its door."[73] Israeli authorities proceeded to shut down cultural events at the village site: they surrounded the school with barbed wire after it hosted *Memory*, a play by Salman Natour, and after a cultural event with Iraqi-Jewish writer Sami Michael and then a protest display with artists, activists, and villagers, the authorities tore down the artworks in response.[74]

Then, a year later, actor Luft Nuweser presented "Uncle Matta," a story of the Nakba for children, at the site of the village remains; Israeli authorities bulldozed the school building in response and planted orange trees to hide the ruins. "Our response was to mark on the ground the location where the school had stood before the Nakba," al-Ghubari explains.[75] He continues, "In May, 2007, we held the first commemoration of the Nakba without the school building. But we nevertheless planned a special children's activity—drawing a huge wall mural. This time, after the regime finally understood that the destruction failed to stop us, it didn't respond."[76] This anecdote details the history of Israeli afforestation, the punitive uprooting, and the deliberate planting to cover up the state destruction that has accompanied Israeli statecraft. This anecdote also reflects collective labor that is contingent on repurposing and restoring life to colonial ruins, the construction of a new relationship to "all that remains" of Palestinian life and livelihoods from before 1948.

Since their first tour in Miska, and as with the JNF Erasure of Palestine Tour in 2019, when Zochrot tours a depopulated village, they signpost the presence of the village, marking the ground with plaques and posters, reminding passersby of the history of the sites they refuse to see. Barclay's piece maps out the possibility of return to Miska, beginning with this signposting: "laying markers to reappropriate the site of the village."[77] The second phase represents the symbolic return of Palestinian citizens in Israel who have physical access to the site but are denied any rights to it, a process he calls "planting catalysts." Next, returning villagers from outside Israel, postreturn, will begin to "'densify' the original grain of the village as the original family plots start to expand vertically and consolidate into dense urban blocks."[78] The image that accompanies this phase is of the returned refugees beginning to build overlaid on black-and-white shots of the village site as it stands (figure 5.13).[79] Again, the method employed to index expulsion, erasure, and return is a palimpsestic layering that does not disappear that which currently exists but leaves it visible to show both history and process. Barclay further explains that the "densified architecture of presence juxtaposed with the landscape of erasure continues to mark the families whose futures are undecided or who are still unable to return."[80]

In this way, he wants to leave some of the "colonial debris" evident as a reminder of what came before and as an homage to those who have yet to return or whose futures are uncertain.[81] In the fourth phase, every exiled family that wants to return will return, and the "voids of absence become protected communal spaces within the fabric of the village."[82] His concluding words explain that these absences in the urban fabric become "public spaces with an architecture composed of a dialogue between the layers of memory, erasure, and presence."[83] Here, Barclay writes history into his urban planning. Refusing the kinds of erasure that has accompanied Zionist settlement in Palestine and sustained Israeli occupation, Barclay proposes a vision of Miska that is predicated on remembering.

This vision is also predicated on a right to the city. In an abstract accompanying a 2014 DAAR exhibit at the Delfina Foundation in London, participants Alessandro Petti, Sandi Hilal, Eyal Weizman, Ismail Shek Hassan, Muhammed

5.13 Ahmad Barclay, "Exile and Return to Miska" (2011). © Ahmad Barclay.

Jabali, Shourideh Molavi, Gautam Bhan, Ruba Saleh, and Umar al-Ghubari penned a statement outlining return as a political act that is both practiced in the present and projected into an uncertain future. In it, they ascertain, "The right of return is the right to the urban, to a condition of heterogeneity and multiplicity that may already distinguish the sites of origin."[84] In this way, participants of Zochrot and DAAR, in addition to and in collaboration with individual artists and urban planners, assert a Palestinian right to return broadly, but specifically a right to a return that is marked by a right to the urban, the city that is marked by heterogeneity and multiplicity.

At Zochrot's September 2013 conference, "From Truth to Redress: Realizing the Return of the Palestinian Refugees," participants screened short videos of sites postreturn, amalgamations of the old and new, superimposed with images of a profound multiplicity and heterogeneity: animated students strolling across university sites, some women in hijab, some in tank tops; aerial views of bustling social spaces of Muslims, Christians, and Jews; families peppering the landscape; multiculturalism evident in each setting.[85] The multiculturalism proposed (even demanded) here is not one that functions, as Hazel Carby wrote in 1992 in the context of the United States, as an alibi or "convenient substitute" for actual structural change and desegregation; instead, it is a multiculturalism—and an urbanism—that is entirely contingent on reparation, restitution, desegregation, and return.[86] Multiculturalism would ring hollow here without concrete, material decolonization characterized by a return to an urban, decolonized, genuinely shared heterogeneous space, not a static pre-1948 Palestine. This mapping proposes a heterogenous future, perhaps even one that replaces barbed-wire fences and bulldozers with flower beds and open universities.

Solidarity tours to densely populated cities like Haifa, Nazareth, and Jaffa also do the work of documenting displacement and laying claim to the city. Rather than imagining a pastoral, idyllic village life, these tours—like those of West Jerusalem neighborhoods—trace military occupations of the city and imagine a return characterized by a real and not nominal multiplicity. Sites like Haifa and Jaffa, in particular, are touted by Israel as "mixed cities," held up as proof that Israel is neither segregated nor racist. Tours of Jaffa, like those taken by Eyewitness Palestine delegations, instead show city centers marked by past and present displacement, thriving Israeli cultural tourism sites, high-end stores like Ahava selling stolen Dead Sea products from settlements housed in formerly Palestinian businesses and political headquarters, rampant gentrification of Arab neighborhoods, and a city animated by Palestinian and Jewish Israeli presence but not equality. Tours of Haifa, like Bil'aaks Alternative Tours, showcase a coastal city militarily occupied in 1948, its residents forced outward to Jenin and Nablus, a city that is "mixed" in the sense of having Palestinian residents but where Jewish Israelis have long fought to quiet the sound of the *adhan*, the Muslim call to prayer, where Arab Orthodox Christian churches are preserved but surrounded by commercial buildings so as not to serve as a constant reminder of Palestinian presence in the city, where gentrification forces Palestinians out of neighborhoods and communities, and where Palestinian citizens in Israel do not learn their own histories in school. And, in Nazareth, tours like British journalist Jonathon Cook's end at Liwan Café, a Palestinian cultural space, bookstore, coffee shop, and community center working to revive and restore the Old City of Nazareth, anchor it to its Palestinian roots, and remind tourists that there is more to see in Nazareth than the religious tourist sites of mass consumerism, showing passersby that there is a long Palestinian history here in spite of the many ways it has been repressed. In this way, these tours of Palestinian city centers inside Israel force a reckoning with what it means to be a "mixed city" in name only, and what the city could look like in the wake of a just return. Indeed, the General Strike on Tuesday, May 19, 2021, in response to the evictions in Sheikh Jarrah, the attacks on worshippers at Al-Aqsa, the bombing of Gaza, and the police-protected Israeli mob attacks on Palestinians in Israel's mixed cities, was the first that united Palestinians across Historic Palestine since 1936; it revealed, as Jonathon Cook wrote, that "the coexistence model in the 'mixed cities' was always an illusion, one that the protests finally served to smash. Coexistence worked for one ethnic group only, Jews. It was built on the continuing Judaization of these historic Palestinian communities to erase their Palestinian heritage and drive out their Palestinian populations."[87] In this way, the return imagined through tours like these is one that hinges on naming the violence of coexistence models in the absence of decolonization.

Digital Signposting, Demanding Return

In 2014, Zochrot created an app called iNakba for individual tourists to navigate depopulated villages on their own and learn about the sites under their feet. This product/project is a digital signposting that, in its description in the iTunes store, both promotes Israeli Jewish society's acknowledgment and accountability for the Nakba and positions return as the "imperative redress of the Nakba" and as a central condition for shared life in the country.[88] The app itself, with its title meant to conjure images of iPhones, iTunes, and iMessages spliced with remembering the Nakba, is free and works by enabling tourists to enter the GPS coordinates of village sites and city centers and then pull up descriptions of the depopulation of the space on which they stand.

Like some of Zochrot's tours, the app is trilingual, in Arabic, Hebrew, and English. It provides coordinates and maps of Palestinian localities that were demolished or partially demolished, or those that remained standing but were depopulated during the Nakba or as a result of it. For each site, the app provides the district, population before occupation, occupation date, occupying unit (for example, the Irgun), the Jewish settlements, if any, that were on the land before occupation, and the Jewish settlements built up on the area of the village after occupation (figures 5.14–5.16). Navigating the app reveals archival images, videos, and historical information on each locality. The pictures and information come from Zochrot's archive, which is largely indebted to Walid Khalidi's research, and also from users, who can add to the historical picture given with family archives of their own. Built into the interface on each village site are tabs to access photos, videos, directions to the village, and

5.14 Screenshots from iNakba (September 15, 2014).

profiles of app users who follow the fate of said village. The photos include images of Zochrot tours to the site, preoccupation and postoccupation maps, photos of the village remains, and pre-1948 (for example, in Haifa) or pre-1967 (for example, in Emwas) Palestine. Videos include footage of Zochrot tours, interviews with village refugees, and news footage of the site's history. Each of the location bubbles indexes a Palestinian locality that came before. A screenshot of those localities alone reveals the volume and breadth of the Nakba, in that each location on the map contains within it a history of depopulation, theft, and ruination. Zochrot's app does what most of their tours also attempt to do: it provides free and easy access to the history of Israeli colonization, supplies evidence of that ruination in a form that can be circulated and shared, and makes this information readily available, first, to Israelis who would rather ignore it, and, second, to both Palestinians who want to learn more about the spaces from which their families were expelled and internationals who want to understand the historical context of the sites they are touring.

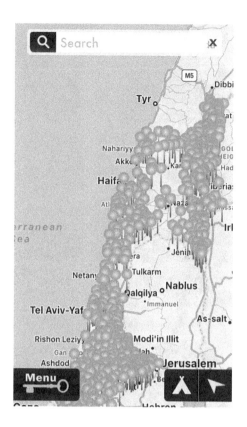

5.15 Screenshots from iNakba (September 15, 2014).

In a May 2014 article on the app's development, journalist Ian Black described how the app—like Zochrot's work more broadly—puts Palestine back on the map but also connects Palestinian refugees with the contemporary status of the villages from which they were expelled. Zochrot's media director, Raneen Jeries, tells Black, "There is an app for everything these days, and this one will show all the places that have been wiped off the map. It means that Palestinians in Ein Hilweh refugee camp in Lebanon, say, can follow what happened to the village in Galilee that their family came from—and they will get a notification every time there's an update."[89] Again, while Zochrot's work aims to force a confrontation between Jewish Israelis and the histories they choose to ignore, with iNakba they also create a space for interactive archival work to connect Palestinians, especially those who cannot (yet) return, to the spaces that were stolen from them.

Other digital projects have taken up this work, most recently Palestine VR, a virtual reality app launched to give users—and specifically Palestinians in exile—access to everyday life in Palestine. Developed by the Palestine Institute

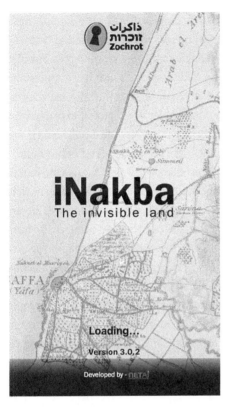

5.16 Screenshots from iNakba
(September 15, 2014).

for Public Diplomacy (PIPD), the app was released in the wake of Israel's denial
of entry to US Congresswomen Rashida Tlaib and Ilhan Omar in August 2019,
an entry denial requested by Donald Trump in yet another joint US and Israeli
move. In a press release, the PIPD explained that Palestine VR would allow
users to see highlights from the trip Tlaib and Omar were not allowed to
take.[90] One news brief on the project stated the following:

> Through the app, users can see historic and sacred sites like the Dome of
> the Rock in Jerusalem, and how Israeli settlers are pushing Palestinians out
> of their homes in Jerusalem's Old City; take in how massive the separation
> wall surrounding Aida Refugee Camp in Bethlehem is; walk the streets
> of the old town of Hebron with a former Israeli soldier and Palestinian
> human rights advocate who share how violent attacks by Israeli settlers
> on Palestinians living in Hebron turned the business center into a ghost
> town; or get to know members of the Bedouin community of Khan al
> Ahmar, who are protecting their homes and schools from being demol-
> ished by the Israeli government.[91]

Palestine VR emerges in the context of Israeli denials of entry, the deportation of Palestinians (and allies) seeking entry, and racialized harassment and threats of refusal at whatever border crossing is available to those who can enter. For diaspora Palestinians in exile, like Tlaib, who had planned to visit her grandmother in Beit Ur in the West Bank, something like Palestine VR is the only way they can see their homeland. Salem Barahmeh, PIPD's executive director, explained that Palestine VR "aims to give viewers a glimpse of life in Palestine despite Israel's routine entry denial and attempts to cut Palestinians off from the rest of the world."[92]

In this way, Palestine VR brings to those diaspora Palestinians who cannot enter a Palestine denied to them. Unable to take walking tours of Jerusalem, Hebron, Bethlehem, or villages and city centers inside Israel's malleable and shifting borders, Palestinians outside Palestine can traverse some of the landscapes they have only heard about. This chapter, which has brought together a constellation of different types of tours in different spaces across Palestine/Israel, shows that Palestine cannot be defined by the West Bank, Gaza, or even Jerusalem. Palestine is Palestinian citizens in Haifa with family exiled in Jenin, Palestinian residents of Jerusalem collecting evidence of the city as their center of life, Palestinian tour guides giving tours of Canada Park trees covering village sites, Palestinian filmmakers in Ramallah fighting for return to Emwas, Palestinian villagers in exile uploading archival photos to the iNakba app, and Palestinians in the diaspora touring Hebron on Palestine VR. Palestinian space remains Palestinian even when it travels by other names, and it remains occupied, even when, in the words of one guide who introduced tourists to Haifa, "you do not see checkpoints."

Tours of the sort charted here, then, either implicitly or explicitly demand a wholesale end to occupation *across* Historic Palestine, an end to occupation that only is possible via freedom of movement and the Right of Return for Palestinian refugees. In this way, these artists, guides, organizers, and historians are doing the work to reshape tourism—including its tropes, conventions, and rituals—into a decolonial act. Through their labor, they use tourism to archive exile, from the village to the city, and imagine return to both. Through their work, they envision a Palestine that a Palestinian in exile does not have to visit as a tourist, if they are allowed entry, or virtually, if they are not: a Palestine marked by futurity and vitality that they can return to if they so choose.

SIX

"WELCOME TO GAZA"
ON THE POLITICS OF INVITATION
AND THE RIGHT TO TOURISM

In August 2017, US Campaign for Palestinian Rights and Interfaith Peace Builders (now Eyewitness Palestine) hosted a virtual delegation to Gaza.[1] As the organizers began to introduce their speaker, Raji Sourani from Palestinians for Human Rights in Gaza, they warned of potential technical difficulties. After several minutes of failed attempts to connect with Sourani, one organizer explained, "This shows us how hard it is for folks in Palestine to connect with anyone in Palestine or elsewhere in the world." She continued, "If he is not able to connect today, because of the arbitrariness of siege and because of the limitations of electricity in Gaza, we will reschedule the webinar."

Of sixty minutes of the scheduled webinar, it took twenty-seven minutes for Sourani to finally connect. When his voice rang through on the speakers, the joy at connecting, on his and the organizers' parts, was palpable. He explained the many ways he, and other Palestinians, do not give up in a context structured to force them to. He explained how Israel has strategically separated Gaza from the rest of Palestine, with no access for Palestinians in Gaza to reach the West Bank or Jerusalem except for those few Palestinians with permits to allow them exit and entry. He described the contours of the siege on Gaza, the three hours of electricity a day and no fresh water, the inability for Palestinians in Gaza to treat their sewage, their resultant incapacity to swim in the ocean. He closed his now-truncated talk by reiterating that Israel delimits Palestinian life in Gaza so that Palestinians will leave. The organizers thanked him for his time, closing the virtual delegation with the following words: "Thank you for joining us, thank you for your patience with our technical difficulties. Raji, from the bottom of hearts, thank you, and we will keep working until Palestine is liberated and we will take our lead from you, from Palestinians on the ground in Palestine."

With the siege on Gaza in its fifteenth year, at the time of writing, Palestinians in Gaza have described their colonial condition and navigated their cleavage from the rest of Palestine through virtual collaborative projects—like this virtual delegation—that rehearse, satirize, and reimagine tourism. Through virtual tours that simultaneously describe suffering and create joy, Palestinians in Gaza are combating not only the siege but also the representations of themselves as under siege and nothing more. In this chapter, I trace how, since Israel has foreclosed even the possibility of "occupation tourism" in Gaza, Palestinians there have worked to connect to the rest of Palestine and the international world at large in forms that resemble tourism. I move chronologically through some of the myriad forms of virtual tourism that Palestinians in Gaza have crafted during and in between the Israeli military incursions into Gaza of "Operation Cast Lead" (2008–2009), "Operation Pillar of Defense" (2012), and "Operation Protective Edge" (2014). I discuss projects as disparate as *Gaza Mom* blogger and journalist Laila El-Haddad's collaborative digital tourism project "You Are Not Here" in 2007–2009; celebrity chef Anthony Bourdain's widely publicized 2013 trip to Gaza; photographer Tanya Habjouqa's 2013 images of Gaza that show joy under contexts of siege; Palestinian responses to guerrilla artist Banksy's installations in Gaza in 2015; and, finally, a 2014–2015 virtual and transnational student project at Gaza University that imagined another world in which tourism played a key role in a thriving Gaza 2050. I show how, since before the siege began, Palestinians in Gaza have used forms of digital connection to resist the fragmentation Israel has sought to impose on their lives.

This chapter thus shows how Palestinian guides, organizers, and activists in Gaza are intervening in narratives that circumscribe Palestine to the geographical borders of the West Bank. At the same time, they are intervening in narratives that position Gaza as solely a site of suffering, a site where tourism could never flourish; they are asking, instead, what it would mean if Palestinians in Gaza could actually invite tourists, host their own tours, control their own borders, live freely. Unlike elsewhere in Palestine, the politics of invitation in Gaza are not performative in the sense that they do not produce the effects they seek to name; except in rare cases, invitations to Gaza do not result in the physical presence of tourists in Gaza.[2] However, the politics of invitation in Gaza are performative in the sense that they are performances that seek to underscore the right to freedom of movement, the right to tourism, and the right to invitation in Palestine.

"You Are Not Here"

In 2007, designer Mushon Zer-Aviv and Laila El-Haddad, proprietor of the blog *Gaza Mom* and coauthor of *Gaza Kitchen: A Palestinian Culinary Journey*, launched a Gaza–Tel Aviv virtual tourism platform called You Are Not Here (YANH). The virtual tour, which originated with a New York–Baghdad version conceptualized by Zer-Aviv, allows people in one city to take a walking tour of another city that they cannot physically reach. The Gaza–Tel Aviv version, hosted by El-Haddad, was directed at a Tel Aviv audience—of either Israelis or tourists visiting Tel Aviv—and forced the "tourist" to reckon with the long-standing effects of Israel's colonial occupation of Palestine and the then-recent Israeli assault on Gaza, Operation Cast Lead in 2008–2009. While YANH's Gaza–Tel Aviv virtual tour was launched in 2007, it ceased being active in 2009, as Operation Cast Lead made an initiative like this impossible to sustain. However, the tour's maps and several recordings on its itinerary are archived as ephemera of the now-defunct initiative, what Zer-Aviv and El-Haddad call an "urban tourism mash-up."[3] Through the mash-up, tourists are invited to download a PDF of a double-sided map with Gaza on one side and Tel Aviv on the other (figure 6.1). Each "stop" on the tour is marked by a "You Are Not Here" symbol to parody the "You Are Here" symbols on so many tourist maps; at each stop, the tourist is instructed to call the Tourist Hotline (03–915–0880) to hear a recorded guided tour by El-Haddad. In an orchestrated reversal of Israel's history of mapping Israeli sites and names onto Palestinian spaces, this tour functions by mapping the streets of Gaza onto Tel Aviv.

In this way, rather than the palimpsestic covering up of Palestinian villages enumerated in chapter 5, here we see the ephemeral and temporary papering over of Tel Aviv streets to reveal tourist destinations in Gaza. This (literal) papering over does not leave destruction in its wake, as has Israeli state formation; instead, like Zochrot and BADIL's mapping projects, it reminds the viewer what the well-maintained city streets of Tel Aviv eclipse: the devastation of

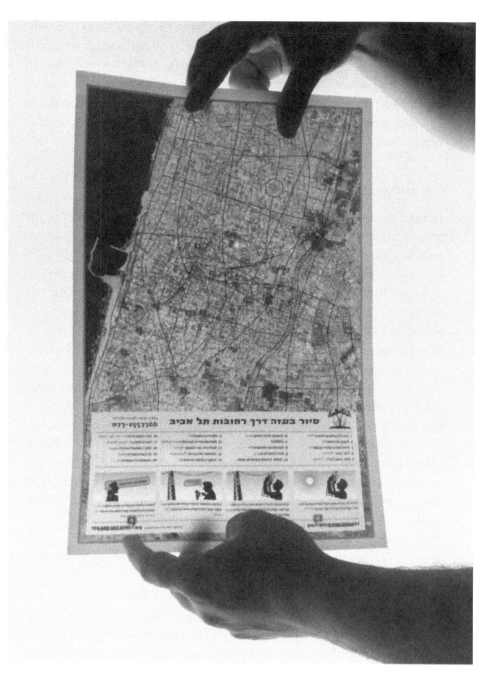

6.1 Printable maps from the virtual tour "You Are Not Here: Gaza/Tel Aviv (2009)."

Palestinian lives and homes just outside the perimeter. In a way that is comparable to yet subtler than these mapping projects, Zer-Aviv and El-Haddad also ask their listeners to imagine return. Yet they do so by disorienting their listeners: asking them to walk along a well-paved Tel Aviv street and pretend they are standing in Gaza—a mobility foreclosed to them and far more so foreclosed to the Palestinians they are imagining meeting. This impossible "meeting," in turn, asks the virtual tourist to consider what open borders might look like in this space, what it might look like if this tour were real.

The destination sites on the tour include not only universities and stadiums and sites of commemoration but also ice-cream shops and restaurants. The sites included are Arts and Crafts Village, Islamic University, United Nations Relief and Works Agency (UNRWA), Rashad Shawa Cultural Center, Palestinian Parliament, Park of the Unknown Soldier, Palestine Stadium, Kazem's Ice-Cream Parlor, Akeela's Restaurant, The Shifa Taxi Station, Qattan Center for the Child, Hammam al-Samara, Souk al-Zawya, Al-Qissariya Market, Qassr Al-Basha (Napoleon's Castle), the Great Omari Mosque, and Beach Camp.[4] El-Haddad walks us through Beach Camp, where the Alternative Museum's first intifada delegation encountered the woman, furious with the voyeuristic and seemingly futile visits of rotating scores of delegates, who exclaimed, "What is this roadshow all about? This isn't a picnic here." Pushing back against voyeurism but also insisting on joy, El-Haddad walks the listener/virtual tourist through restaurants and ice-cream shops, describing the flavors and inviting her listener to try them. Each recording is full of impossible interpellations like these, inviting the tourist to "sample" Gaza.

In this way, the virtual tour is animated by impossibility. Each recording describes what used to be possible in these spaces in Gaza and what is no longer possible in the wake of Israel's violent, and frequent, incursions into the Strip. The temporality reflected in each of the two-minute recordings shifts, in seconds, from nostalgia for a lost, and comparatively more stable, past, to a present of relative calm amid intermittent shelling, to an uncertain future. At Barcelona Peace Park, for example, El-Haddad describes the donation of the park in "more hopeful times," in 1998, during a triple sister cities declaration between Barcelona, Tel Aviv, and Gaza City. She reflects, "I remember my own son frolicking around a green patch of field, just over there, near a group of shebab [youth] playing football one spring day. He attempted to climb the monkey bars on the playground but was a little too young, and stuck to the slide instead."[5] Immediately, she changes course: "But all of that was destroyed by Israeli tanks in January 2009. Now more than anything hopeful, the park's ruins represent the shattered dreams of peace and prosperity and the malicious nature of occupation, which has led to some disenchanted demands for the twinning of cities to be canceled."[6]

In this recording, the first available of the eight You Are Not Here chose to archive, El-Haddad transports her (ostensibly Israeli) listener to a nostalgic moment of reprieve for her own son, whose fear in that instant was merely a set of daunting monkey bars. She then reminds her listener of all that has been rendered impossible since Israel's (then) most recent assault on Gaza. For a listener strolling down the streets of Tel Aviv, this reminder is meant to be an interruption, a disorienting reminder of their own complicity in the destruction of Gaza and the Palestinians who live there.

El-Haddad's narrative includes discussions of attacks on UNRWA (which Trump worked diligently to defund, withholding $350 million in annual aid from the agency in 2018, of which Biden restored less than half in 2021); Palestinian demands for the Right of Return; and the history of Saraya Prison in Gaza and the (then) nine thousand Palestinian prisoners in Israeli prisons, a third without sentencing, many of them children her own son's age.[7] As they near Saraya Prison, she reminds the listener, "In January 2009, UNRWA had to temporarily suspend its activities because of the continual attacks on its institutions and employees. This bloody relationship reflects the tension around the international communities' refused demands for Israel to settle the Palestinian refugees' Right of Return."[8] Here she reminds her listener, safe on their stroll, that Palestinians still await return; they still nurture a longing for return, they still petition international bodies for return, and they still anticipate return. In her narration, there is as much a longing for return in the future as there is nostalgia for a past not uninterrupted—but less interrupted—by Israeli assaults on Palestinian space.

Once actually at Saraya Prison, El-Haddad explains the long history of the prison, from when it was established by the ruling British in 1929 as both administrative quarters and sitting jail. She then catalogs how it has since "been used by the Egyptians who jailed the Palestinians, by the Israelis who jailed the Palestinians, by the Palestinian Authority and its then-ruling Fatah party who jailed and tortured Hamas members here, and most recently by the Hamas government who jailed many of their Fatah opponents in the recent infighting between the two factions."[9] She explains how Hamas Prime Minister Ismail Hanieyh had planned to turn Saraya into a shopping mall, "citing tainted history as a symbol of torture and occupation," but Israeli forces destroyed the prison in January 2009 to undermine Hamas's power in the Strip.[10]

The rubble, she explains, holds in it histories of the present that include not only Gilad Shalit, an Israeli prisoner held in changing locations all over the Strip, but also the "nearly nine thousand Palestinian prisoners being held in Israeli prisons, nearly a third of them being detained without a jail sentence, denied family visits, and some of them only twelve years old when they are jailed."[11] In another disorienting move, El-Haddad asks her (again, ostensibly Israeli) listener to think about imprisonment not only in terms of the name they know—Gilad Shalit—but also in terms of the nameless (to them) Palestinian prisoners, some of whom are children isolated in Israeli prisons. In this way, El-Haddad labors to remind her listener of all that they too often ignore; she asks them to imagine the families of those in Israeli prisons, and the Palestinian youth who, like the listener, walk their own streets in their own cities, yet in cities that have been decimated by Israeli weaponry.

At the same time, El-Haddad includes moments of pleasure in Palestine. On her tour of Roots restaurant, she announces, "I hope you're hungry and ready to empty your pockets!"[12] before walking her listener through detailed descriptions of the best courses on the menu. She then describes resentment directed at the establishment for its catering to a largely middle- and upper-class clientele but, in the same breath, explains: "Yet to many Gazans, Roots provides a temporary refuge from the poverty and sorrow that dominate the Strip's daily life. It's also a great place to bring kids because of the playground in the outdoor café. My own son spent many a sticky long summer evening playing there as I dined with friends."[13] Evoking the summer humidity and the refuge from poverty and sorrow available to those who can afford it, El-Haddad evidences a Gaza that is multifaceted in class and perspectives and defined by more than solely siege.

Similarly, she goes into great detail at Kazem's Ice-Cream Parlor, not only about each flavor and their potential combinations but also about tips and tricks to help negotiate the crowd. "Check your shyness at the door," she advises, "and jostle your way through the throngs of thirsty customers."[14] Like imagining her son frolicking on a playground, here she asks her listener to imagine elbowing their way through a crowded room to get their share of ice cream. This, too, functions as disorienting for a listener expecting to hear and imagine only scenes of subjection.[15] El-Haddad dwells on these moments of pleasure. She does not rush through them, or interrupt them, to reroute her listener away from thinking through the possibilities of Palestinian joy.

As a final stop on the tour of the Gaza Strip, El-Haddad introduces her listener to the famous PLO Flag Shop. She again invites them to imagine another impossibility: "It's tourism shopping time! As you can see by the sign on the door, we've now reached the self-proclaimed first tourist shop in Palestine: the PLO Flag Shop. If you'd like to grab some cheap souvenirs for your family back in Tel Aviv, this is the place to do it."[16] Here, I would argue, El-Haddad mobilizes tourist conventions to point to not only their impossibility but also their possibility, to ask her listeners to consider what it would look like if Palestinians in Gaza could host tourists, if they could exercise the kind of pride in place that stokes tourist initiatives. Citing Abu Daya, the owner of the PLO Flag Shop, she explains, "Conflict is good business for Abu Daya, but, as he often says, *I want to run a tourist shop and I want to sell souvenirs, not politics.*"[17] Reckoning with the kinds of tourism available to him, Abu Daya echoes tour guides I interviewed in the West Bank who wished for the obsolescence of their own profession: rather than solidarity tour guides, they would love to *just be tour guides.*

In a November 17, 2009, post on *Gaza Mom*, El-Haddad described the project and stressed, clearly in response to critiques and misunderstandings of the project, "As we made clear to all media outlets we spoke with, this is NOT a normalization initiative."[18] By this, she meant it is not a project meant to "bring Palestinians and Israelis together," to have "dialogue," as though Palestine/Israel is a conflict that needs to be smoothed out via conversation rather than a colonial military occupation that requires decolonization and reparation. She asked her readers to reflect for a moment on the logo, crafted by Dan Phiffer, for You Are Not Here: a broken beach umbrella and a crossed-out "You Are Here" symbol (figure 6.2). She continued, "As one of the journalists covering the project put it, the tour serves to 'create an association in the mind of the listener—to momentarily disorient the tourist and then reorient them with a new perspective—one that includes Gaza as part of their consciousness.'"[19] For El-Haddad, the key to this project is disorientation. Invoking both the impossibilities and possibilities of tourism in Gaza, El-Haddad and You Are Not Here play with the politics of invitation. They "invite" tourists—"Welcome to Gaza"—in a context in which they cannot actually extend invitations to tourists. In their satirical logo, they boast of a beach, but in the content of the tour, they remind the listener of its contamination by the assaults on Gaza's sewage system. They offer an image of a beach and a beach umbrella, but a broken one. They offer tours, but the tours are both impossible and imaginary: a crossed-out "You Are Here" marker replaced with the reminder that "you" are not.

The politics of invitation are further complicated for El-Haddad herself. El-Haddad lives in Baltimore, Maryland, and has been repeatedly denied reentry

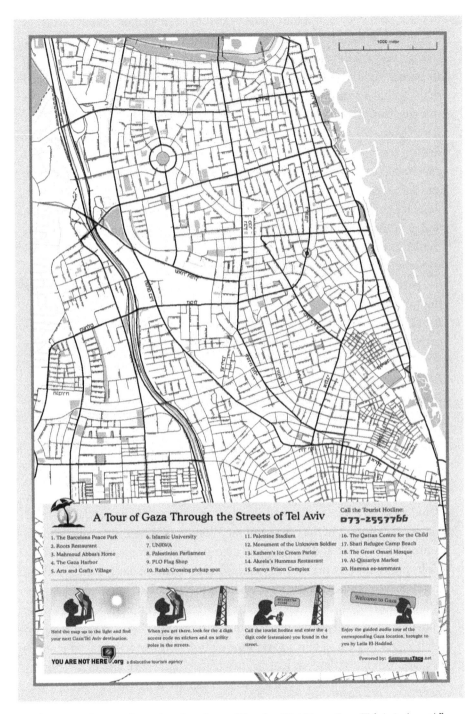

6.2 Printable maps from the virtual tour "You Are Not Here: Gaza/Tel Aviv (2009)."

to Gaza, so her work as a tour guide extending an invitation, if only virtual, is a project of piecing together. She writes: "Rerecording the locations was a very strange, very emotional experience, something that is mirrored in the tour itself. It's been a while since I've been able to return to Gaza, and so much has changed that I feel like a stranger—one that is nevertheless intimately familiar—with this city, this place I call home."[20] The crafting of the tour itself is also a stitching together of an alternative horizon. She describes the collaborative effort of making the "tour" come to life: "So relying on my own personal knowledge and experience, and filling in the details with the help of my parents, Wikimapia, and some research of our own, we pieced together the most accurate descriptions we could."[21] She continues, "I tried to make the recordings as intimate and as colorful as possible—I really wanted to disorient the listener/walker, challenge their commonly held perceptions and their relationship to Gaza, all while reflecting the current reality."[22] El-Haddad's piecing together, reliant on her parents, her memories, Wikimapia, and other forms of research, reflects the work Palestinians in exile have to do to remember in a context wherein Israel consistently fragments their land, shatters and/or papers over the physical embodiments of those memories, and then continues to deny them entry. You Are Not Here is, in this way, both a memory project and a project for the future, evoking the kind of Palestinian waiting in exile that Brooklyn-based Palestinian filmmaker Nadia Awad has called a nostalgia for the future.[23]

"My Boy Anthony Brought Gaza to Me"

On September 15, 2013, CNN aired an episode of Anthony Bourdain's television show *Parts Unknown* where Bourdain traveled to Jerusalem, the West Bank, and Gaza. Bourdain's visit is not, at first glance, an episode of "virtual tourism." However, in the context of the West Bank, where entry and exit are controlled by Israel, and Gaza, where international visits are often only possible by proxy, his visit in many ways served as a virtual solidarity trip. Bourdain travels first to Jerusalem's Old City, where he meets with Israeli chef and author Yotam Ottolenghi. Upon their meeting, Ottolenghi immediately raises the much-anticipated question of to whom falafel belongs: "We just have to go for a falafel because it's so much part of the culture here. And again, contentious because, you know, Jews or Israelis make falafel their own and everybody in the world thinks falafel is—you know, an Israeli food. The actual fact is [that] it's been done for generations here."[24] With this admission opening the episode, it quickly becomes evident that Bourdain is not going to present a typical Zionist story about food to his viewers.

Soon after his time in Jerusalem, Bourdain takes a tour with the all-women racing team, the Speed Sisters in Ramallah. He meets with Betty Saadeh, a member of the racing team. In her second sentence, she says, "When I drive, I speed. I feel free."[25] In these two scenes alone, Bourdain's Palestine is not one that can be defined by one representative actor in one representative space; instead, he aims to show multiplicity across all of Palestine. In the wake of this episode, multiple Palestinian authors published op-eds outlining their support for *Parts Unknown*'s atypical portrayal of Palestinians as leading full lives, not just looking mournfully at the camera. For her part, comedian, actress, and writer Maysoon Zayid wrote in the *Daily Beast*: "With Bourdain in the passenger's seat, [Saadeh] sped through the Ramallah bubble, sporting a fantastic hot pink Bebe tank top, bursting negative Arab female stereotypes, and showing everyone that there is more to Palestine than slingshots."[26] In her description of Betty Saadeh and Anthony Bourdain's ride around Ramallah, Zayid reminds the reader that Arab women are too often portrayed as both demure and lacking agency, and she pushes back against the portrayal of Palestinians as slingshot-slinging youth—and nothing more. Zayid continues, "Betty also reminded viewers that Palestinians are trapped like rats in a cage with little open space to race or even breathe."[27] In this way, as Zayid makes clear, Bourdain makes space on his show not for a "variety of views," as is so often marshaled as an excuse to include Zionist perspectives in discussions about Palestine, but for a glimpse of Palestinian life that is not limited to suffering but also does not ignore suffering or evade assigning culpability for that suffering.

Returning from a commercial break, *Parts Unknown* then shows Anthony Bourdain traveling along the Wall. He looks out the window and explains, "It's right there for all to see. And it feels like something out of a science fiction film. This is the Wall. From the other side, from inside this place, for instance, the Aida Refugee Camp in the district of Bethlehem, it doesn't feel like anything other than what it is. A prison."[28] Likening Aida Refugee Camp to a prison, Bourdain shows viewers what tour guides labor to show solidarity tourists: the foreclosure of Palestinian movement throughout the West Bank, how Palestinians, like prisoners, do not have the freedom to travel, move, leave, or return. There are many ways this analogy fails to account for literal Palestinian prisoners in Israeli jails, on whose bodies torture techniques are perfected, and fails to consider the differences between a nine-by-five-foot cell and life in an occupied homeland.[29] However, this analogy functions to remind those who either don't know or refuse to see that Palestinians are subject to Israeli control over every aspect of their lives.

In his recounting of Bourdain's episode, Palestinian comedian, writer, and academic Amer Zahr wrote, "Something amazing happened on CNN last night. Palestinians were portrayed as human beings."[30] Here, he refers to how Palestinians were shown not as a nameless mass identified by suffering and stone throwing. They were instead individuals—with disparate aspirations, hardships, loves, and losses—meeting one curious celebrity tourist with a love of food. About Aida Refugee Camp in particular, Zahr writes, "The honest portrayal of the residents of the camp, from their squalor to their own struggle to find productive channels of resistance, was something I had never seen on American TV."[31] He continued, "Bourdain noted that these Palestinian children do not have the luxury of idolizing pop stars and athletes. They turn to politics early, sometimes idolizing martyrs and politicians. And he's right, there's something wrong with that. We Palestinians are normal in so many ways. And we're so not normal in so many others."[32] Zahr, like Zayid, expresses surprise, respect, and even admiration for Bourdain's choice to portray Palestinians as full, multifaceted people with joy and trauma. This, he adds near the end of his piece, is ultimately dismal: "Part of being Palestinian in America is getting really excited whenever someone tells the truth about us on American TV. Kind of depressing, right?"[33] What both Zahr and Zayid underscore is that Bourdain in fact did something so ordinary, what he did on all other episodes of *Parts Unknown*: meeting people and talking to them about the food they love, the generations that nurtured it, and the geopolitical climate that produces it. Yet, in Palestine, this portrayal is deeply atypical. In Palestine, and particularly for Palestinians in the diaspora who watch the stories of their families twisted beyond recognition in the US news media, Bourdain's *Parts Unknown* episode was an anomaly.

As with Jerusalem and the West Bank, Bourdain begins the segment on Gaza by discussing his entry into the region. He foregrounds the Israeli closure of Gaza's borders that regulates all entry to and exit from Gaza, including his own. He explains, "Getting in and out of Gaza from Israel is truly one of the most surreal travel experiences you could have on Earth."[34] He continues, "Over 1.5 million people live in Gaza, most of them considered refugees, meaning they are not from the place they are compelled to live now. In most cases, they are either prohibited from or unable to leave. Israel decides who comes and goes, what gets in and what stays out."[35] Indeed, Maysoon Zayid echoes Bourdain's description of this foreclosure of Palestinian mobility through an appreciation of the way Anthony Bourdain was able to bring Gaza *to her*. She explains how she, as a Palestinian in the diaspora with cerebral palsy, has long dreamed of going to Gaza and seeing the disability center A. M. Qattan Foundation's Centre for the Child:

> I have been traveling to the Holy Land since the day I was born and I have seen pretty much everything between the river and the sea I am allowed to see. Bourdain showed me parts of Palestine I have been denied access to by Israel. I have always wanted to visit Gaza because it houses a state-of-the-art disability center, the A. M. Qattan Foundation's Centre for the Child, located in Gaza City. Try as I may, I have not been able to get permission to cross the Erez checkpoint that separates the Palestinians in Gaza from those in the West Bank. The only other way in is through Rafah, but as a person living with a disability I am unable to handle traveling through the Egyptian/Palestinian border, which is treacherous and more often closed than not. My boy Anthony brought Gaza to me.[36]

In this way, Bourdain's trip is not only a virtual tour for internationals curious about what too many call the "Israeli-Palestinian conflict." His trip is also a virtual tour for the *many* Palestinians who have not and cannot enter Gaza. Palestinians in the diaspora often cannot even enter Israel and the West Bank—let alone Gaza—as their denial of entry is contingent on the surveillance of their activist presence, their research, their online profile, and/or the whims of racist Israeli officers at customs trained to detain Palestinians and those in solidarity with them. For these Palestinians, Bourdain's episode is both a welcome vision of that which they love but cannot see and a painful reminder of his expansive mobility—as a famous, international, Jewish, and non-Palestinian traveler—in their homeland.

Mirroring her own virtual tourism project of 2013, Laila El-Haddad also acts as Anthony Bourdain's tour guide upon his entrance into Gaza. In journalist Alex Kane's retelling, he notes that El-Haddad speaks for herself on Bourdain's show: a perspective not often seen on American TV.[37] Over meals, she reminds Bourdain of the limitations of cooking under siege:

> The catches are not as big as they used to be, and that's primarily because the fishermen can't go beyond three to six nautical miles," says Haddad, explaining the Israeli Navy's enforcement of the blockade. "They'll shoot at the fishermen, they'll spray cold water at them, they'll destroy their boats, they'll cut their fishing nets, they'll detain them. So it's obviously really

risky business. Nine nautical miles, that's where that deep sea channel is where you're going to get the really good catches.[38]

Here, El-Haddad underscores how Israel limits not only how Palestinians can move but also what they can eat. She does not even mention the ways Israel used a "calorie count" to limit Gaza food during the blockade between 2007 and 2010.[39] Yet she shows unequivocally the restrictions on movement and life-sustaining practice that characterize life under the Israeli blockade and shape the content and (im)possibilities of Palestinian culinary practice. Indeed, as Yasmin Khan, author of the cookbook *Zaitoun: Recipes and Stories from the Palestinian Kitchen* (2019), was told by her interviewee Essa Ghrayeb as they lunched in the courtyard of the Zahra hotel in the eastern part of Occupied Jerusalem: "I understand that you want to share our culture, but you can't discuss Palestinian food without talking about the Occupation. About the water restrictions, about the inability to move freely, about the checkpoints, about the house demolitions. This isn't me being political, this is me explaining that the Occupation affects how we eat. You can't escape it."[40] Anthony Bourdain, too, sought to show how both the joys of Palestinian cooking and the occupation affect how Palestinians eat. In Alex Kane's words, Bourdain's episode—while not without problems—provided American viewers with "a window into how ordinary Palestinians live—and eat."[41]

In reflecting on his time in Palestine, Anthony Bourdain described how excited the Palestinians he met were to simply be portrayed living their daily lives. Recalling the outrage by the woman in Gaza during the first intifada who demanded to know why yet another delegation in Gaza was necessary, Bourdain said, "[Palestinians] are so used to camera crews coming in to just get the usual shots of rock throwing kids and crying women."[42] Here, Bourdain touches on the tropes ubiquitously employed by photographers, journalists, activists, and researchers to represent Palestinians. Whether mobilized to generate outrage about Israel's occupation or to paint all Palestinians with the same brush, these tropes obscure the fact that, as Maysoon Zayid described, there is more to Palestine than slingshots. Bourdain elaborated, folding this critique of the representation of Palestinians into a description of the pushback he was likely to receive in the wake of this episode's airing. He explained, "For some, unfortunately, depicting Palestinians as anything other than terrorists is proof positive that you have an agenda, that you have bought into some sinister propaganda guidelines issuing from some evil central command in charge of interfacing with Western com/symp dupes. A photo of a Palestinian washing their car or playing with their child is, therefore automatically 'propaganda.'"[43] In his reflection on the episode, and its inevitable backlash, Anthony Bourdain thus accomplishes a twofold task that many visitors to Gaza do not attempt: first, he works against the trope of representing Palestinians as solely despondent victims by refusing to center his story on their subjection, and second, he brings Gaza to the outside world and the outside world to Gaza in a context in which Gaza is sequestered not only from the rest of Palestine but also from the international world at large. As Maysoon Zayid wrote, her boy Anthony brought Gaza to her.

"What, You Don't Have Babies in Your Country?": On the Visual Economy of Palestine and the Foreclosure of Palestinian Joy

Palestinian life beyond subjection is rarely—if ever—the subject of report-backs in the wake of solidarity tours and delegations. Palestinian social life, in particular, is eclipsed by representations of Palestinians subjected to Israel's punitive whims. Palestinians hanging out and living life does not incite the kind of outrage and impetus for movement building that thick descriptions of the Wall and settlers in Hebron do. This preoccupation with images of downtrodden, oppressed Palestinians that circulate so frequently in media outlets is precisely what led photographer Tanya Habjouqa to embark on the photography project *Occupied Pleasures* (2015). Habjouqa, a Texas-born Circassian and Jordanian feminist photographer, seeks to capture Palestinian pleasure and the humor Palestinians use to make visible and manageable the daily indignities of occupation.[44]

She works against the "visual narrative of Palestinians" that has been circumscribed to images of "stone-throwing teenagers confronting Israeli soldiers, refugee camps, mothers mourning children killed in conflicts, and long lines at border crossing points."[45] Here, Habjouqa echoes Maysoon Zayid's words in praise of Bourdain's capacity to show that there is more to Palestine than slingshots. In a *New York Times* piece about Habjouqa's project, journalist James Estrin adds, "Particularly dramatic variations on these visual tropes make the front pages and win awards."[46] In this assessment, Estrin points not only to the ubiquity of these images and tropes but also to their international demand. Estrin's words recollect what one international tour guide in the West Bank described to me as the tendency for artists, like photographers, to come to Palestine to make their own work more meaningful by taking pictures of stone-throwing youth or despondent children. Yet another tour guide I interviewed rolled his eyes as he told me about watching scores of tourists snap nonconsensual photographs of poor Palestinian children in refugee camps. Out of sheer puzzlement about the visual tropes that so many tourists find compelling, he told me that he wanted to (but didn't) ask them, "What, you don't have babies in your country?"

Habjouqa wanted to "find another way to tell the story."[47] In *Occupied Pleasures*, the reader/viewer happens upon photographs of women practicing yoga on a nature walk. These yogis "go to nature spots Jewish settlers try to intimidate Palestinians from accessing" (figure 6.3). In other images, Al Quds University students participate in javelin practice near the Wall (figure 6.4). In still others, teenagers in Ramallah get ready for a school dance (figure 6.5).[48] In each of these photos, Habjouqa presents something that is, in fact, quotidian but is rendered unusual and surprising given the visual economy of images of Palestine. The ubiquity of black-and-white photos of children with searching eyes in refugee camps, women with searing gazes or looking toward the camera through tears, young men with covered faces swinging slingshots, men of all ages navigating the cages of checkpoints, and older men holding their weeping or injured babies makes these images of Palestinian women practicing yoga and teenage girls playing sports and getting ready for dances seem atypical and extraordinary.

6.3 Tanya Habjouqa, *Occupied Pleasures* (2013). © Tanya Habjouqa/NOOR.

6.4 Tanya Habjouqa, *Occupied Pleasures* (2013). © Tanya Habjouqa/NOOR.

6.5 Tanya Habjouqa, *Occupied Pleasures* (2013). © Tanya Habjouqa / NOOR.

Like Anthony Bourdain's interview with Betty Saadeh, through Habjouqa's work we meet Palestinians who are resisting the ways Israel wants to delimit their opportunities, foreclose their movement, and eclipse their joy. In her own words, Habjouqa is "telling the same story"—one of dispossession, land theft, settler colonialism, occupation, militarism, and siege—yet she has found "another way," one not so tethered to the impulse to generate sympathy and outrage. Her images instead ask her viewer to consider how they had hitherto allowed Palestine and Palestinians to become so abstract—as we saw with so many delegate report-backs during the first intifada—that seeing these kinds of images now renders them not only concrete but also whole.

In Gaza, conventional tourism is rendered impossible, and the visual economy is structured by international photographers and journalists who can get press passes and who, in turn, produce and circulate almost exclusively images of a suffering, war-torn population. Habjouqa, instead, brings the world of pleasure under siege to the fore. Habjouqa includes, for example, an image of a parkour troupe in Gaza as they propel off buildings damaged from Israeli incursions. In the image, two youth are airborne, a third is preparing to leap backward into the sky, and a fourth waits for his turn to vault off of the shelled building (figure 6.6). Another image shows a van driving along the coast with streamers and cartoons affixed to its sides and balloons careening off its roof. The caption reads, "Gaza: A toy store van drives along Gaza's beach highway (2013)" (figure 6.7). In a third image, Habjouqa shows a woman on a picnic bench cuddling a lion cub while another cub looks off the edge of the picnic table at which she sits. The caption reads: "Gaza: A woman plays with two baby lion cubs born in the Rafah Zoo. Gaza once had six zoos, but two were closed due to financial losses and the deaths of large animals. Gazan zoo keepers are renowned for creativity in limited options, having famously painted a donkey as a zebra, smuggling in animals in the tunnels, and stuffing them once they are dead as animals are not easy to replace (2013)" (figure 6.8).

Finally, a fourth image shows a woman walking the length of an underground tunnel, most of her body obscured by a large bouquet of flowers. In this caption, Habjouqa writes, "A woman in Gaza without a travel permit, marches through the silent dark of an underground tunnel on her way to a party in Egypt, clutching a bouquet of flowers (2013)" (figure 6.9). Habjouqa adds an addendum to this one: "Recently, the Egyptian army has restricted movement of goods and people through the tunnels, which are an essential lifeline for the 1.7m population of the coastal enclave under Israeli control. For a vast majority of Gazans, the tunnels remain the main passage in or out—

6.6 Tanya Habjouqa, *Occupied Pleasures* (2013). © Tanya Habjouqa/NOOR.

6.7 Tanya Habjouqa, *Occupied Pleasures* (2013). © Tanya Habjouqa/NOOR.

6.8 Tanya Habjouqa, *Occupied Pleasures* (2013). © Tanya Habjouqa/NOOR.

6.9 Tanya Habjouqa, *Occupied Pleasures* (2013). © Tanya Habjouqa/NOOR.

including for weddings that would not occur if not for smuggling the bride through the tunnel after denial of permission from the Egyptian authorities."[49] Habjouqa's images document the in-between of the party: the toys on their way to the toy store, the partygoer on her clandestine way to the party. They show the creativity that characterizes life-making in Gaza: the painted donkey for the zebra, the taxidermy, the proximity to lion cubs to bring joy to a place that, of course, experiences joy but is never associated with it.

When poet and activist Rafeef Ziadah responds to the ubiquity of narratives that construct Palestinians as teaching their children to hate, she explains, in the now-famous line from one of her spoken word poems, "We teach life, Sir."[50] Here, Habjouqa shows Palestinians teaching life. Her work resists the narrative of a Palestine that is defined solely by occupation, a narrative that can be understood only through the visual cues of checkpoints and the Wall and crying children. Yet her work simultaneously resists the narrative that life equals joy and all else is not living. She, like Betty Saadeh and Laila El-Haddad, shows a Palestine where Palestinians simultaneously break bread, laugh, speed, play, cook, eat, jump, dance, scream, cry, go to parties, and struggle. This Palestine is one marked by pleasure under occupation. For some audiences, this imagery renders Palestinians human, as Amer Zahr described Anthony Bourdain's *Parts Unknown* episode. Yet these images, I would argue, more importantly ask their reader to ask themselves what narratives they have assimilated to need to be reminded that Palestinians are human.

"So Meet Your Tour Guides": On the Palestinian Right to Tourism

In February 2015, guerrilla graffiti artist Banksy went to Gaza to create three pieces to indict Israel's then most recent assault on Palestinians in the coastal enclave. Upon his return, he released a satirical touristic promotional video, naming Gaza as a hot, new tourist destination.[51] The minidocumentary, at just under two minutes, begins with a shot of clouds from a plane window, interpellating the viewer to "Make this the year YOU discover a new destination," followed by the words "Welcome to Gaza" (figure 6.10).[52] Alongside the words "Well away from the tourist track," we see a figure who we are led to believe is Banksy crawling through tunnels. New words appear in parentheses: "(Access is via a network of illegal tunnels)."[53] A door opens and we see Gaza: cement blocks and destroyed buildings alongside children playing. The captions read, "The locals like it so much they never leave," and then, in parentheses, "(Because they're not allowed to)."[54]

6.10 Banksy, *Welcome to Gaza* (2015).

Strangely, we then see a shot of Qalandia checkpoint in Ramallah and Israeli soldiers gathering there, ostensibly for an incursion. It is unclear why the West Bank is included in this Gaza montage, perhaps to show the Wall, perhaps to show soldiers in repose, perhaps because, for Banksy's viewers, Gaza can be easily collapsed with the West Bank, perhaps the videos' creators (or Banksy himself?) didn't recognize the differences between Ramallah and, for example, Rafah. The images return to Gaza, with the words "Nestled in an exclusive set-ting."[55] In parentheses, we read, "(Surrounded by a Wall on three sides and a line of gunboats on the other)."[56] The producers pair the words "Watched over by friendly neighbours" with, in parentheses, "(In 2014, Operation Protective Edge destroyed 18,000 homes)."[57] More lines from the mock advertisement include "Development opportunities are everywhere," followed by "(No ce-ment has been allowed into Gaza since the bombing)" and "Plenty of scope for refurbishment."[58]

We see no words as the camera pans over Banksy's art pieces: an image of the Greek goddess Niobe weeping on the still-standing wall of a demolished building, ostensibly symbolizing the bereaved mother; an image on the side of another building of a military surveillance tower transformed into an amuse-ment park swing; and an image of a cat with a paw extended to play with what looks like a ball of yarn but is actually coiled-up debris (figures 6.11–6.13).[59] A Palestinian man interviewed in the minidocumentary comments, "The cat found something to play with. But what about our children?"[60] Children play in the street as he speaks. Banksy later explained the inclusion of the cat as a

6.11 Banksy, *Welcome to Gaza* (2015). Photo by Suhaib Salem.

6.12 Banksy, *Welcome to Gaza* (2015). Photo by Suhaib Salem.

6.13 Banksy, *Welcome to Gaza* (2015). Photo by Suhaib Salem.

commentary on how he wanted to show the destruction of Gaza on his website, but on the Internet people only look at pictures of kittens.[61] The final shot shows writing on a wall, red and in all caps: "If we wash our hands of the conflict between the powerful and the powerless we side with the powerful—we don't remain neutral."[62] Chickens roam among shrubbery and piles of trash under the words.

Immediately after the release of Banksy's promotional mock tourist invitation, the Gaza Parkour Team responded with a video of their own: *After Banksy: The Parkour Guide to Gaza*. In it, they show that there is more to Gaza than falling bombs and destroyed buildings. Instead of taking Banksy's mockery of the possibility of tourism in Gaza as the joke he tries to make it, they treat tourism seriously and use his video as a provocation to instead detail *why* tourism in Gaza has been rendered so impossible. The video begins with the words, overlaid on top of Banksy's kitten, "Banksy says make Gaza your destination" (figure 6.14).[63] British Palestinian hip-hop artist Shadia Mansour's music begins, and a Palestinian youth does backflips in an open space with Israeli bombs exploding in the background.[64] The words "so meet your tour guides" appear over his backflips (figure 6.15).[65]

As the parkour team walks through Gaza, we see close-ups of their sneakers, true to hip-hop genre form. The camera eventually settles on the team as member Abdallah AlQassab takes up where Banksy leaves off, explaining, "Nearly 50 percent of us are unemployed and we are very available to show you

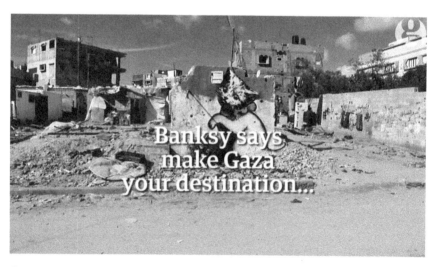

6.14 Gaza Parkour Team, *After Banksy: The Parkour Guide to Gaza* (2015).

so meet your tour guides

6.15 Gaza Parkour Team, *After Banksy: The Parkour Guide to Gaza* (2015).

around."[66] The camera pans to multiple shots of the parkour team scaling walls, jumping off partially demolished buildings, doing backflips and front flips off exposed pipes, and scaling Banksy's own art pieces (figure 6.16). In this scene, the team's critique of Banksy emerges: while Banksy wants to foreground the inconceivability of *play* in Gaza, the teenagers training off the wall where he left this piece belie that claim. The team's performance and choice of venue disrupt the notion that Palestine can be defined solely and entirely by its status as stateless and occupied. Projecting images of what "occupied pleasure" looks like, the parkour team intervenes in both Israeli state-sanctioned narratives that erase the past and present of Palestinians *living* in Palestine and "disaster tourist" narratives that position Palestinians as besieged and nothing more.

This parkour montage is followed by a chorus of "Welcome to Gaza" on the part of the team. The team transforms the landscape from the detritus of military incursion to a parkour training course as they extend multiple invitations to a hypothetical tourist. Over panning scenes of bread, olive oil, and tomatoes, AlQassab explains that while Israel refuses to allow them construction materials and twelve thousand people are homeless, they could find a place to host a guest; that while Israel limits their electricity and shut down Gaza's single power plant, they could find a way to offer the tourist meals; that while water in Gaza is undrinkable, they are happy to share their expensive bottled water.[67] As the camera pans to the team as they walk along the sea, AlQassab explains that many in Gaza come to the sea because "they want to go out; they

6.16 Gaza Parkour Team, *After Banksy: The Parkour Guide to Gaza* (2015).

want to see the world."[68] He transitions back to the team: "We want to go out, we want to see the parkour teams, we want to see everything. We want to do a lot of things and we dream a lot."[69] A parenthetical interruption explains: "Seeing the world will remain a dream until the borders open."[70] Here, the parkour team positions what the viewer is witnessing not merely as evidence of Israeli state violence but, significantly, as the scene of occupation before return and open borders. The video closes with what reads as an earnest plea: "But with all of this happening in Gaza, we are here, and alive, and our spirit is very strong. So come, and discover us, and make Gaza your destination."[71] The final shots show the team again, performing in the open space that began the minifilm and doing back handsprings and aerial twists as bombs explode in the distance.[72]

In *After Banksy: The Parkour Guide to Gaza*, the parkour team plays with/in the landscape of loss they have inherited. They also play with the impossibilities of tourism in Gaza, taking up the role of informal tour guides, correcting the singular lens of unfathomable devastation that animated Banksy's video, and detailing the multiple ways they would be happy to host, happy for the employment, and happy to share their culture, their sense of place, their food, and, if they could, their water. The Gaza Parkour Team makes it clear that Banksy's installation pieces, like his art on the Wall in the West Bank (and most of the art on the Wall in the West Bank) and his hotel, The Walled Off Hotel, in Bethlehem, are by internationals and for internationals even though they are in Palestine. That is not the parkour team's critique, however. Their video, too, is in English, a direct address to a very specific and particular audience—the same audience as Banksy's. Their critique, instead, is that his is an incomplete narrative, one that pivots solely on devastation and evacuates the question of hope, and one that positions tourism as a joke instead of a potentiality under different conditions. Walking by the sea, they explain that they spend their time there because they want to go out, see the world, meet other parkour teams. In this way, their critique theorizes their own conditions of isolation, expressing not only a desire to host tourists but also a desire to *be* tourists. Here, I am reminded of the words of an international tour guide I interviewed as we sat in a café in Beit Sahour: "You know, Palestinians," she explained, *"they have a right to tourism."*

The Gaza Strip 2050

A "nostalgia for the future," as described by Palestinian filmmaker Nadia Awad, takes work; it is equal parts the labor of remembering, the labor of preserving, and the labor of projecting. During the 2014–2015 academic school year, students at Gaza University did precisely that. In a collaboration with Indiana University in Indianapolis and under the joint guidance of Director of International Partnerships at Indiana Ian McIntosh and Director of International Affairs at Gaza University Jamil Alfaleet, students in Gaza were asked to chart a vision for Gaza in 2050. Through a process that included research, interviews, field trips, video conference calls, and meetings with archivists and archaeologists, students in Gaza identified tourism as the "key to a renewed and thriving economy."[73] Together, students in Gaza and students in Indianapolis crafted a virtual museum, where they identified 252 sites of touristic potential alongside an imagined overland pilgrimage route connecting Gaza City and Jerusalem. Like the imagined cities of futurity crafted by organizers and architects from Zochrot and BADIL, these imagined tourist stops also hinge on mobility. When asked to envision Gaza 2050, the students placed connection at the center of their vision, bypassing the fragmentation and circumscription that occupied their lives and severed them from family, friends, and strangers in the West Bank and Jerusalem, Israel, and in the diaspora. Gaza, the students explained, would return to its former status as the "jewel of the Mediterranean," yet—as with Zochrot and BADIL's collaborations on return—not in its pre-1948 version but in a contemporary, thriving, bustling iteration.

The students' visioning exercise, which they had just begun to put into practice, came to an abrupt halt with Operation Protective Edge, the brutal assault on Gaza that Israel launched on July 7, 2014. Operation Protective Edge lasted fifty days. Between the 7th of July and the 26th of August, 2,131 Palestinians were murdered and 18,000 housing units were destroyed, rendering 108,000

Palestinians in Gaza homeless.[74] Civilian infrastructure was decimated: the assault caused vast damage to Gaza's already precarious electrical power grid, especially with Israel's bombing of Gaza's only power plant on July 29.[75] This bombing, in turn, caused the shutdown of water treatment plants, while other attacks destroyed Gaza's largest sewage treatment plant.[76] Students saw twenty-two of their schools destroyed and six of their teachers killed.[77] Industry and commerce suffered immensely, with 419 businesses damaged and 128 destroyed entirely.[78] Agricultural and fishing sectors suffered, with access to the sea prohibited and 42,000 acres of cropland destroyed.[79]

The imagining work students had done before July 7 was thus performed against a backdrop of precarity. Much like Laila El-Haddad's work of imagined border crossing, with tourists envisioning themselves in places they cannot access, here too students envisioned a world in which they could get to Jerusalem by an open-access overpass. And, much as the work of You Are Not Here came to an abrupt halt with Operation Cast Lead, the 2008–2009 assault on Gaza, here too the students' work of imaging alternative futures for Gaza was foreclosed by the destruction they and their communities faced immediately after they had finished blueprinting Gaza 2050. These works of imagining otherwise, between and around Israeli assaults on Gaza, demonstrate not only the sumud, or steadfastness, of the Palestinian people in the midst and in the wake of Israeli destruction. They also foreground the role that tourism can play in imagining otherwise. Echoing the international tour guide's claim that Palestinians have a right to tourism, contrary to assumptions that would render tourism always-already exploitative, these students articulated their own right to tourism, their own right to see Gaza as, once again, the jewel of the Mediterranean. They articulated a pride in place, an affirmation of the beauty and significance of the place they live despite the images that circulate about it. In this, they articulated a tourism predicated on research, preservation, connection, and mobility: a tourism born out of interviews, archival work, restoration, and the capacity to move freely.

The students choose 2050 to give enough time and distance from the contemporary blockade, the unemployment and poverty, the sewage and water crisis, and the destruction caused by each assault on the Strip.[80] The scene they painted, through images and descriptions, looked like this: vibrant seaports and airports, bustling high-tech and high-rise shopping and residential facilities, sports centers, thriving transportation networks, vast green spaces, and water parks.[81] Fishing and strawberry and citrus production thrived.[82] Yet, after brainstorming all of this for the full fall semester, the students chose to dedicate the spring semester solely to tourism, the sector where they felt Gaza had the most to build, offer, and create. Students visited and identified over 250 sites of archaeological and touristic merit, including churches; mosques; bazaars; the ruins from the Silk Route; sites associated with Cleopatra's Egypt; garrisoned fortresses; and Cypriot, Mycenaean, and Minoan artifacts.[83] Students also envisioned the *return* of artifacts stolen from Gaza and placed in art museums in Israel and elsewhere.[84]

Like the organizers, architects, and artists blueprinting the return of Palestinian refugees, students faced questions of logistics. They asked: "If three million tourists or pilgrims were to pass through the Gaza Strip and on to Haram al-Sharif, how would the people of Gaza feed them? Where would they be housed? What forms of entertainment would be available to them, like museums, parks, and cultural activities?"[85] Professors McIntosh and Alfaleet guided the students through a process of "back casting," where each step forward needed to be both brainstormed and mapped.[86] The students were then asked to conduct a survey of major archaeological and historical treasures in the Gaza Strip, and then imagine where these sites and objects would feature in Gaza 2050.

They visited antique shops to ascertain what would belong in new museums; they met with government agencies and those who had worked in the tourism sector. Each student had to upload their work to a site that they envisioned and collectively crafted as a Virtual Museum of Gaza, both a blueprint for the type of museum they saw as possible in Gaza 2050 and a guidebook for potential tourists who might want to visit the (new) Gaza Strip. Here, they would upload footage of interviews, visits to sites, analyses of artifacts, and expert talking heads.[87] One entry, for example, charted the discovery in 2013 of a statue of Apollo by Jawdat Abu Ghurab, a Gaza fisherman. It described its age (2,100 years), weight (450 kilograms), height (1.75 meters), estimated value (US$340 million), and the circumstances of its find.[88] The students and their professors had begun to solicit expert advice to catalog each artifact and construct a virtual museum as a placeholder until the real Gaza museum could become a possibility when Israel further decimated the Gaza Strip with Operation Protective Edge (2014), which came on the heels of Operation Pillar of Defense (2012) and Operation Cast Lead (2008–2009).

In an article on their collaboration and the course, McIntosh and Alfaleet describe in great detail how they tried to hold the course and the vision together as bombs rained down on the Strip. They write about the fifty-one days of destruction and massacre, how Israel targeted the "entire infrastructure of life in the Gaza Strip." Alfaleet used his car battery to power Skype calls with McIntosh and describe the scenes he was witnessing. In this, Alfaleet became a tour guide of the macabre, guiding students and McIntosh through Gaza's destruction in real time. The coauthors describe McIntosh's failed efforts to comfort Alfaleet with descriptions of US gestures of solidarity; Alfaleet was "tired of words."[89] At the end of the 2014–2015 academic school year, at the time of McIntosh and Alfaleet's piece, it remained unknown how many of the 252 tourist sites in Gaza that students identified still existed.[90] While there are other virtual museums of Gaza and digital mapping projects of the Strip, like You Are Not Here, and various virtual tours, ranging from Laila El-Haddad's to Banksy's, this particular virtual museum of Gaza has not (yet) come to fruition other than its commemoration in Alfaleet's and McIntosh's writing about the project. However, the ephemera identified, the labor undertaken, and the collaboration crafted reveal much about the im/possibilities of tourism in Gaza. Students in Gaza, with interlocutors in Indianapolis, researched, conducted interviews, and went on tours of their own to learn histories denied to them and papered over by a present of imminent and intermittent destruction. They paused to reflect on what tourism could do, what its potentialities could be. In doing so, they positioned tourism as both an anticolonial project and a project ultimately possible in the wake of decolonization. Their vision resisted the foreclosure of movement that cleaved them from Jerusalem, negated the erasure of their histories, named the colonial looting of Palestinian art and artifacts, allowed for a thriving Palestinian agricultural sector that Israeli colonial state practice had worked so hard to destroy, and restored the beauty and pride in place that Israeli devaluations of Palestinian personhood and land had sought to entrench. In this way, Gaza 2050 positioned tourism as key—not only key as synonym for central but also, I would argue, in reference to the key as the symbol for Palestinian return, with Palestinians displaced in 1948 still holding on to the keys to their homes and passing them down generationally. If tourism has the potential to be key in this way, for these students, it has the potential to name and demand the right of a Palestinian return to a life undefined by colonial rule.

Imagining a Future Beyond Incursions

As part of +972 *Magazine*'s New Futures project in 2020, where contributors were asked to imagine radical postpandemic futures for Palestine/Israel, anthropologist and filmmaker Hadeel Assali crafted a piece titled "Postcard from a Liberated Gaza" (December 25, 2020).[91] Dated July 20, 2024, and addressed simply to "E," this postcard narrates a future Gaza, liberated from colonial rule and teeming with vitality (figure 6.17). Assali writes that, every day, she meets friends on the beach "just like we do in Luquillo"—a deliberate reference to another beach under colonial rule, in Puerto Rico, that too will see its day of liberation. She writes that she listens to elders who, "like stand-up comedians," regale her with tales of throwing off the occupiers—and how, soon, they will liberate the rest of Palestine.

"Since liberation," she writes, in tones that feel rushed and exhilarating, "people have been coming to Gaza from all over."[92] "The elders," she continues, "say it is just like the old days when everyone from the surrounding regions would descend on Gaza, in part for the beaches and the fresh seafood—grilled grouper, clay pot shrimp, and fried sardines are the favorites. But people especially come for the shopping. You should see the markets!"[93] She writes about how the landscape is transformed because of the return of refugees, the tunnels metamorphosed into educational tourist sites where people can learn about the resistance. She analogizes these tour guides, telling tales of the resistance, to the way "E" speaks of Puerto Rican resistance: "I see your eyes when you tell me about the Macheteros in Puerto Rico."[94] She too ends with an invitation: "What do you say? Come to Gaza. I will wait for you here."[95] The addressee, "E," is hailed here as a potential tourist, invited to witness not just Gaza but a Gaza after liberation, a Gaza that is the first place in Palestine to

6.17 Illustration by Nerian Keywan, in "Postcard from a Liberated Gaza," by Hadeel Assali (2020). © Nerian Keywan.

throw off its occupiers, a Gaza that has resonance for a Puerto Rican solidarity tourist who also knows what it means to inherit loss.

In the fifteen years since the most recent siege on Gaza began, and both in spite of and because of the United Nations' declarations, recirculated everywhere, that Gaza would be unlivable by 2020, Palestinians have labored to imagine otherwise. Tourism has figured centrally in these imaginings. Through collaborative, creative, transnational, and virtual tourism projects, Palestinians in Gaza—activists, professors, students, chefs, shop owners, performers, anthropologists, filmmakers, and science fiction writers alike—have asked what it would mean if they could exercise their right to both host and be tourists in Gaza and beyond. In this, they have intervened in Israel's attempts to sever them from the rest of Palestine and the international world. At the same time, Palestinians in Gaza have sought to intervene in the internationally circulated images of Gaza as solely a site of destruction. Subverting conventional imagery of the region, they have demanded an understanding of Gaza beyond subjection, a Gaza of comedy clubs and tunnel tours and museums and beach cafés and mobility and vitality.

In between the immeasurable losses they experienced in the wake of Operation Cast Lead, Operation Pillar of Defense, and Operation Protective Edge, among other untitled bombing campaigns such as the eleven-day Israeli assault on Gaza in May 2021, Palestinians in Gaza have attempted to "teach life" through tourism. They have attempted to teach life by reminding tourists that while they are "not there," they can still disorient themselves and disrupt their complacency. They have attempted to teach life by celebrating the Palestinian food and lifeways that Israel repeatedly attempts to destroy. They have attempted to teach life by foregrounding their own pleasure in a context imagined to foreclose it. They have attempted to teach life by asking viewers what it would be like if they were allowed to be both tourists in and tour guides of their own homeland. And they have attempted to teach life by crafting their own Gaza, either in 2024 or 2050: a world in which they can take tourists from Gaza City to Jerusalem, introduce them to the rich history of the land in which they were born, tell stories of resistance that ended colonial rule, and move freely—with tourists and like tourists—from one site of significance to another across Palestine. In this way, Palestinians in Gaza and in the diaspora have imagined otherwise in between the military incursions that seek to decimate their communities. Through virtual tours across time and space, they have described and resisted the containment of Palestinians in Gaza, foregrounded pleasure and joy under—and beyond—occupation, and insisted on their own futures.

SEVEN

WITNESSES IN PALESTINE
IMPERFECT ANALOGIES, ACTS OF
TRANSLATION, AND REFUSALS TO PERFORM

As a Palestinian tour guide led a group of twenty solidarity tourists around the city center of Nablus in the northern West Bank in 2012, a curious US tourist stopped to marvel at a blackened section of a nearby wall. "What happened here?" she asked, pointing to the unidentifiable black matter next to where a shop door was coming off its hinges. The other tourists followed her gaze eagerly, in search of evidence. "Oh, that?" The tour guide shrugged. "Someone was just spray-painting their bedframe against the wall." The tourist, visibly disenchanted, resumed the walking tour, mumbling, "Oh . . . I thought it was from, like, a bomb or something."

In another moment, walking through Aida Refugee Camp in 2019, a returning tourist to Palestine asked the guide what happened to the United Nations school next to the Wall in Bethlehem. The school, which was riddled with bullet holes, had recently been shuttered and moved to a new location. The guide explained that he was glad it was moving farther away from the Wall, less a monument to Israeli assaults. The tourist expressed palpable disappointment, explaining, "But it would have been so good to show tourists!" "Why?" the guide asked. "For evidence!" she answered. "Look around you," he said, gesturing to the narrow streets of the camp, the Wall, the murals. "There is evidence everywhere."

As with the first intifada delegations that began this book, these scenes raise the following questions: What does it mean for solidarity tourists to come to Palestine in search of evidence of Israeli occupation despite the voluminous archive of Palestinian scholarship that has named and documented Palestinian displacement? How do tourists reconcile their expectations of what they will see in Palestine with what they actually witness? And how do Palestinian tour guides use moments like these to resist performing subjection for the tourist gaze? In particular, how do they do so within a profession that, in fact, relies on their willingness to provide evidence of their own dispossession and perform their own subjection for the tourist? In this chapter, I return to tourists and to encounters like these, yet I also trouble the categories that animate solidarity tourism. This chapter acknowledges but also refuses a good tour guide/bad tourist framework. While the stories of badly behaved tourists are many and the temptation to recount them all is great, this chapter instead unearths what assumptions and investments underlie the questions tourists ask and explores who even counts as a "solidarity tourist." From diaspora Palestinians who can only return to their homeland as tourists to backpackers to Israel who stumble across a solidarity tour, this chapter looks at the composition of the tour, the investments and preoccupation of its varied participants, and how tour guides negotiate the space in between.[1]

Solidarity tourism and the relationships forged in its itineraries reveal the burden placed on Palestinians to provide evidence of their own already extremely well-documented dispossession. As the preceding pages have shown, the English-language Palestinian archive of displacement—in other words, the archive available to most tourists—is vast and varied. Palestinian scholars have detailed, to merely scratch the surface of the literature, Israel's use of archaeology to solidify its claims to the land; the many befores and afters of the Nakba; the disruption of the myth of the United States as an honest broker in Palestine/Israel; the contours of the occupation of the West Bank; the racialized and gendered violence of Zionism; Palestinian women and reproduction under occupation; the cultural and intellectual work of Palestinian citizens in Israel; and the promise and perils of international law in relation to Palestine.[2] Memoirs on displacement, state violence in Gaza, and returns to Palestine from exile abound.[3] Works of fiction have detailed the displacement of Palestinians inside and outside of Israel's 1948 borders, and widely circulated Palestinian poets from Mahmoud Darwish to Rafeef Ziadah have described the longing for Palestinian freedom, not to mention the corpus of Palestinian filmmakers and artists who have produced work on the Nakba, on exile and the Right of Return, and on life under occupation.[4]

Yet because state-sanctioned narratives from Israel and the United States have constructed Palestinians as unreliable narrators, Palestinian organizers are compelled to strategically use solidarity tourists as "witnesses in Palestine" to furnish their accounts of settler-colonial violence with evidentiary weight.[5] In this context, as evidenced in first intifada report-backs, and as Sherna Gluck reflected on in her retrospective analysis of her time in Palestine, solidarity tour alumni's words, and particularly their translation of what they witness in Palestine, often carry a legitimacy not granted to Palestinian narrators. Thus, while solidarity tourism puts settler colonialism on display and intervenes in histories of displacement, it is also wholly rendered necessary by settler-colonial logics that construct Palestinian narrators as suspect and indelibly shape what counts as evidence.

At the same time that I detail tour guides' marshaling of evidence for tourists, I also theorize tour guides' studied refusal to perform subjection for tourists. I trace the ways Palestinian tour guides design tours that not only allow tourists to witness displacement in Palestine but also enable them to temporarily take part in moments of Palestinian joy by joining the annual olive harvest, sharing in Palestinian meals, hanging out in the off-moments of the tour. The inclusion of moments like these in each tour, I argue, cannot be understood solely as colonial examples of "Native hospitality" performed for scores of tourist consumers; instead, in a context wherein Israel polices every entry to and exit and from Palestine, and in a context wherein tourists expect Palestinian evidence of dispossession and performances of subjection, these moments foreground a Palestine that refuses to be defined solely by the restrictions on living that Israel attempts to impose.

In crafting these connections, tour guides attempt to reveal, for tourists, a social life in Palestine that resists what Lila Sharif calls the vanishment of Palestine.[6] In what follows, I show how solidarity tourists and Palestinian organizers foster connections with one another, outside of a strictly witness/witnessed relationship and despite the epistemic violence and settler logics that structure their encounter. I further document how and when tourist efforts to understand what they witness in Palestine can either strengthen their relational and comparative analysis of the United States and Israel as settler states or enable them to position Palestine's "present" as the United States' "past" and thus absolve the United States of the critique of settler-colonial violence.[7]

In this way, in addition to documenting the moments when tourists seek out both evidence and performance of displacement in Palestine, in ways that exonerate the United States and otherwise, I also document the moments when Palestinian tour guides correct tourist misconceptions and reject performing subjection for the tourist gaze, notwithstanding their employment in an industry that treats the performance of subjection as a prerequisite.

"You Almost Can't Believe It until You See the Tears in Their Eyes"

Echoing many of the first intifada tourists report-backs detailed in chapter 1, contemporary solidarity tourists describe what they saw in Palestine as so egregious that they could not believe it until they saw it. Some tourists will anchor their witnessing in the books that they read, asserting that no amount of research could have prepared them for what they saw on the ground. Others will blame the incapacity of the US media to accurately represent Palestine in advance of their visit. Still other tourists will position their disbelief as something reconciled only by seeing another's suffering. As one tourist bluntly put it, "You almost can't believe it until you see the tears in their eyes." This statement epitomizes the asymmetry in power and privilege that inheres in what many call "occupation tourism." Grounded in both skepticism and spectatorship, it demands a performance of suffering that is deemed necessary to demonstrate veracity. The statement contains within it a caveat—an almost—which, in part, rhetorically absolves the tourist of guilt for her disbelief. Simultaneously, however, she affirms her disbelief by centering witnessing, and, specifically witnessing suffering, as proof for what she would otherwise not believe.

Many solidarity tourists I interviewed punctuated the narratives of their time in Palestine with descriptions of nearly irreconcilable disbelief. In this shared and repeated recitation, it is clear that as Palestinian guides and organizers navigate the demand for evidence they are in fact confronting problems of epistemology.[8] In spite of the volumes of work produced by and about Palestinians, despite the many times Palestinians have narrated and renarrated their stories of displacement and dispossession, and notwithstanding the extensive historical work and cultural production centered on the Nakba and its aftermath, tourists still *cannot believe it until they see it*. This simultaneous incapacity and refusal to believe Palestinian narratives of displacement cannot only be reduced to stubborn ignorance on the part of the tourist; instead, it speaks to the many reasons tourists are unprepared for what they witness. They come to Palestine in a context wherein the more broadly circulated knowledge produced about Palestine/Israel, which positions Israel as a beacon of democracy in the Middle East, invalidates a Palestinian perspective before it is even uttered. They travel to Palestine against a backdrop where the mainstream US media demands an Israeli perspective to "balance" a Palestinian one, where Palestinians are presumed to be unable to accurately diagnose their own condition. For this reason, the feminist analytics that have spelled out the contours of epistemic violence, or violence at the site of knowledge production, are crucial for understanding solidarity tourism as a site, if only aspirational, of anticolonial praxis in Palestine. It is only through understanding the violence at the site of knowledge production about Palestine, which has predetermined the "imagined geographies" through which tourists understand Palestine, that we can begin to understand the deeply imbricated relationship between colonial rule and the calculus of veracity that structures why Palestinian narrators have had to make their case through tourism in the first place.[9]

In this way, while an evaluative analysis of solidarity tourism as simply occupation voyeurism would cast tourists as hopelessly ignorant, their sustained disbelief in fact points to a much larger historical context in which Palestinians have not been cast as truth-telling subjects or reliable narrators of their own histories. Against this backdrop, Palestinian solidarity tour organizing is a refusal to ask "permission to narrate."[10] It is a refusal to parrot the narrative advanced through the shared settler logics of the United States and Israel, a narrative that celebrates Israeli progress while hastening the erasure of Palestine. For guides, solidarity tour organizing becomes a tool with which to confront tourists' incredulity while reckoning with the roots of their disbelief. Further, this refusal to ask permission to narrate is also confronting the transactional buying and selling of knowledge about Palestine/Israel wherein the state-sanctioned story Israel (and the United States) sells is a story about Palestinians as a dangerous demographic threat. This violence at the site of knowledge production is precisely what enables tourists to describe their time in Palestine as eye-opening in a way they "couldn't possibly have imagined."

Tourists' incredulity, this incapacity to believe Palestinian voices until they are corroborated by the tourists' "own eyes," is a theme that appears not only in the interviews I conducted over the course of my research but also in interviews and other report-back literature solidarity tour alumni produce. Alice Walker, for instance, visited Palestine in the aftermath of Operation Cast Lead, Israel's bombing campaign against the Gaza Strip in the winter of 2008–2009. She explained as she walked the demolished streets of Gaza, "It's shocking beyond anything I have ever experienced, and it's actually so horrible that it's basically unbelievable even as I am standing here and I've been walking here and looking at things here."[11]

For some tourists, this incapacity to understand displacement in Palestine until they see it is predicated on dissonance with the narratives they bring with them, for example, when tourists come to Palestine with an imagined geography at odds with what they see when they arrive. On learning she would be traveling to Palestine, one tourist I interviewed exclaimed, "I didn't even know where Palestine was!" and recalled asking her friends and colleagues if she would have to wear a headscarf everywhere.[12] She described the dissonance between her expectations of Palestine and Palestine itself in a hushed, near-embarrassed tone, "I was literally expecting *tents*."[13] A landscape of tents and compulsory headscarves, animated by both historical black-and-white images of a Palestine unchanged since 1948 and the Orientalist and Islamophobic assumptions of what Muslim spaces are like, haunts this tourist's retelling.

For some, this incapacity to believe is based on decades of internalizing media representations of Palestine and Palestinians; as one interlocutor put it, "When I thought of Palestine, I thought of hijacking airplanes and the *Achille Lauro*; I thought of the Palestinians murdering an old Jewish man in a wheelchair."[14] Here, a tourist who came of age during the 1970s describes the suturing of Palestinians to violence and the memory of media coverage that made this suturing make sense to her. She also describes the confusion she experienced in Palestine as she reconciled what she thought she knew with what she saw.

Still other interlocutors, including Palestinian American tourists who came on diaspora-oriented tours or solidarity tours more broadly, knew about the brutality of Israeli occupation, but still found it "one hundred times worse" than they expected. Solidarity tour alumni who are academics often referenced the research they had done that could not prepare them for what they witnessed. Other scholars have argued that they experienced a shock at the similarities between the colonial situations they studied and what they saw in Palestine. Anthropologist Ann Laura Stoler described what she saw in Palestine, as a scholar of colonialism, as a "shock of recognition" that she could no longer ignore or deny.[15] This collection of adjectives describing a state of shock—astonishment and disbelief, recognition and misrecognition, expectations and their disjunctures—demonstrates the multiple ways working on behalf of Palestine has become tethered to witnessing its effects. Seeing Palestine, for many activists and would-be activists, has become a central means by which tourists reconcile the Palestine of their imagination with Palestine on the ground and confront the narratives that have allowed them to ignore or deny Palestinian displacement.

Tour guides' narratives are often pitched to an audience that is already skeptical and doubtful of the veracity of their claims at worst, or unfamiliar with them at best. Moreover, this narration is material that will, in turn, be translated for other skeptical audiences. This narration, then, on the part of tour guide and tourist, is also about the work of translation—the process of assimilating the raw material, so to speak, of witnessing and making it "believable" for US audiences. Alice Walker illustrates this point, when, following her statement about the unbelievable nature of Gaza's destruction, she says:

> It still feels like, you know, you could never convince anyone that this is actually happening and what has happened to these people and what the Israeli government has done. It will be a very difficult thing for anyone to actually believe in, so it's totally important that people come to visit and to see for themselves because the world community that cares about peace and that cares about truth and that cares about justice will have to find a way to deal with this. We cannot let this go as if it's just ok, especially those of us in the United States who pay for this. You know, I have come here, in part, to see what I'm buying with my tax money.[16]

Walker's words, like those of other delegates and solidarity tourists, point to a pattern that is endemic to many forms of reporting back: first, a declaration of astonishment ("basically unbelievable even as I am standing here"); second, a discussion of translating this witnessing into storytelling for US audiences ("you could never convince anyone that this is actually happening"); third, an endorsement of solidarity tourism ("it's totally important that people come to visit and to see for themselves"); and fourth, a call to action based on complicity as a member of the US body politic ("I have come here, in part, to see what I'm buying with my tax money").[17]

This series of ways through which solidarity tourists assimilate the information they confront in Palestine is repeated so often it is almost a formula: disbelief, reconciliation of shock, strategizing on how to share this information, endorsements of witnessing in Palestine, and outrage as a US citizen. To highlight this formula is not to dismiss its political importance but rather to discern what resonates with solidarity tourists and why, to call attention to the stages through which solidarity tourists attempt to understand what they are witnessing, and to convey how they interpret and articulate their work in, and after, their time in Palestine. To call attention to this formula is also an act of naming that recognizes the colonial knowledge production that has rendered Palestinian narratives so illegible that tourists must not only see it to believe it but also spend much of their time in Palestine calculating how to best translate their witnessing to a recalcitrant audience back home, an audience who, out of convenience or conviction, would prefer to ignore the human rights violations bought and paid for, as Alice Walker reminds her audience, with their tax dollars.[18]

"What Hits Home": Evidentiary Weight and Its Translation(s)

As tourists grapple with how to believe Palestinians in Palestine and how to be believed once they return home, a steady pattern emerges wherein Palestinians are compelled to repeatedly construct themselves as truth-telling subjects for tourists. Further, they labor to do so to an audience that itself needs convincing. In turn, tourists translate what they witnessed in Palestine to yet another doubtful audience that remains skeptical until convinced. I asked each tourist I interviewed to reflect on the work of translating what they witnessed into the narratives they share when they report back, whether to family and friends in their social circles, in churches, in university settings, or in community spaces. More often than not, they pulled out meaningful moments that they believed would resonate, or "hit home," with US audiences.

One US tourist, Maggie Goff, shared stories of Palestinians they met who lived near the Wall, which had separated them from their relatives and strangled their businesses.[19] These stories, Goff explained, resonated in ways that the lectures and the narratives provided on the tour did not. Another US tourist, Addis Green, shared stories of spending time communicating with children through gestures and fragments of English and Arabic. Green explained that these moments of stilted yet expansive dialogue with kids in Jenin allowed for Green to do something in a context where they otherwise felt helpless.[20] Sarah Alzanoon, a Palestinian American tourist who was the first in her family to visit Palestine since they were expelled in 1948, shared stories about the Israeli state-sanctioned theft of West Bank water—something tangible that people in California, where she was from, could wrap their minds around as people who know the fallout of drought.[21] Olga Negrón, a New Yorker visiting Palestine for the first time, explained that it was her pictures from her trip that most affected those with whom she spoke.[22] Marietta Macy, originally from rural Indiana, shared stories about the farming communities she worked with, and the land she saw destroyed, confident in the knowledge that a shared understanding of agriculture would help her community better understand displacement in Palestine.[23] In each of these moments, tourists narrated the reasons for the choices they made in curating the content of their report-backs. They described how they carefully worked to craft a narrative they believed would help in overcoming the ignorance, skepticism, indifference, and/or hostility of US audiences.

Marietta Macy, in particular, narrated the varied approaches she takes with audiences of disparate spatial and economic demographics. As a Presbyterian youth minister living in Louisville, Kentucky, but from rural Indiana, she explained how the stories she shared differed dramatically depending on her audience. She described how she grew up on a farm in Indiana and began doing Palestine solidarity work while still living there. Her audience in Indiana, in her assessment, had an experiential understanding of what it means to be a farmer, with their land routinely threatened by corporations and crop mandates. They knew what it meant to have their land and livelihood in danger. For her Indiana audience, Macy drew from her experience on the Olive Tree Campaign.

She described planting olive trees in Jab'a and watching Palestinian kids play on the tractors as their parents drove through and around the fields. "City folk [on the tour]," she said with a laugh, "were super worried about the kids, but I knew they were fine because that's what my childhood looked like."[24] She described telling vignettes like these, alongside stories of displacement and land theft, in her report-backs to rural Indiana farmers. She also emphasized the role her own positionality played in her legitimacy to speak and the political purchase it carried in making sure her audience believed her. "I had a personal attachment to them," she explained. "Me—a white girl they know and trust—is talking to them about people they've been told are terrorists and deserve everything that is happening to them."[25] In this statement, relatively tangential to the larger narrative of her time in Palestine, Macy raises questions about white privilege, rural America, the politics of youth, the proliferating narratives that construct Palestinians as terrorists, and the layered issues of translation and legibility. As a white, rural, young woman from an Indiana farming family, she reads as trustworthy to her audience. Specifically, she reads as *able* to tell them about a people whom they otherwise already have contempt for at worst, and indifference toward at best, in terms that are deeply racially coded. Macy's retelling highlights how she is imbued with expertise against an Islamophobic and racialized rendering of who counts as trustworthy. In this alchemy, which turns her from tourist to expert because of the knowledge granted by her whiteness, Macy's reception by her audience(s) is a textbook example of what Arab American feminist scholarship has long theorized as the coalescence of sexism, Orientalism, Islamophobia, and Zionism in widely circulated knowledge production about Palestine.[26] It is her position as a white woman that renders her a verifiable source for her audience—and specifically her position as a white woman against not only her West Bank tour guide interlocutors but also against the undifferentiated Palestinian mass of which they are a part. For her audience, that she is not Arab—and thus biased, and thus also presumed Muslim, and thus suspect, and thus tethered to antiquated antifeminist social norms—renders her a reliable narrator of the Palestinian condition (as if, additionally, there is only one Palestinian condition).[27]

Macy further described how these strategies of narration differ vastly from those she employs in her church in Louisville, Kentucky, where she currently lives and works, and where church members are wealthy, white, and Republican. In Indiana, she explains, people had more of a "Fox News mentality."[28] They were less likely to know a Jewish person at all and felt that, as Christians, by default they should support Israelis. In Louisville, on the other hand, her audience was far more likely to be connected to the Republican Party and support Israel for nontheological reasons. For her Louisville audiences, she explained, she relies more on examples rooted in the Bible, connecting church members back to scripture and explaining the multiple ways that, if Jesus tried to ride a donkey from Nazareth to Bethlehem, checkpoints would obstruct his path at every turn. Macy thus describes the task of translating the "raw material" of tours to different US audiences, asking what will resonate for rural Indiana farmers versus elite Kentucky Presbyterians. In both instances, she describes building her own legitimacy and legibility, as a youth minister in Kentucky and as a white farmer's daughter in rural Indiana, against a skeptical and indifferent audience. The labor on the part of solidarity tourists thus centers on how to assimilate the knowledge imparted on their tour and how to translate it in a way that will read as true to varied audiences in the United States.

The labor of solidarity tourism, as a profession, business, and organizing strategy, is thus predicated, as Baha Hilo described, on Palestinians "correcting the story the state of Israel sells." It is labor defined by debunking the racist, dehumanizing stereotypes tourists bring with them to Palestine and replacing them—tour guides hope—with a vision of a multifaceted people subject to generations of displacement and who are living their lives in spite of repeated attempts to subject them to premature death.[29] It is a labor defined, too, by enabling tourists with the tools to "correct the story" for audiences in their home countries. That, for some, believing Palestinians necessitates traveling to Palestine, or listening to those who have traveled to (but are not from)

Palestine, is what makes solidarity tourism a project wholly limited by its own starting point. It is a project rendered necessary by colonial logics that force Palestinians to provide evidence of histories of displacement that have long been in the historical record but have been disappeared by the knowledge produced about Palestinians that position them as incapable of truthfully telling their own histories.

Translating Palestine

To reconcile what they are witnessing with what they know, many solidarity tourists turn to analogy to understand the racial taxonomies that characterize Israeli settlement in Palestine. When Palestinian American tourist Sarah Alzanoon, for example, described being compelled to stay on the bus when the Palestinians around her were ordered off to be searched at the checkpoints, detailed in chapter 2, she explained:

> So I kind of felt like there was Black and white people on the bus, and the Black people have to leave the bus to get searched, and the white person . . . you know? Like I kind of felt like it was a situation like that, where you have people with more rights than others, who are first class and second class. That's something that really . . . I was crying on the bus behind my sunglasses, because I was just like, this is so wrong.[30]

She explained how she uses this moment and the analogy of the Jim Crow South when she translates what she saw in Palestine to the report-backs she gives for both Palestinian audiences at cultural events back home and mixed audiences on college campuses.

In an effort to help audiences better understand the racialized, uneven distribution of rights and resources in Palestine, she gives them a contextual grounding that might read as more familiar. Yvonne Lory, for her part, spoke about gauging audience responses in her own process of translating the materials of the tours. In her experience, she explained, she found that "only the people who have done civil rights work in the United States or somewhere else, like if they've been to South Africa or somewhere like that, those are the only people who kind of understand without having been there."[31] For Lory, only the people who have done civil rights work or "been to South Africa" can understand Palestine without having been there, people whose own experience, in her estimation, renders racialized segregation legible without further explanation. Otherwise, she surmises, Palestine is illegible. For many tourists, then, the only touchstones to get people to understand Palestine are to draw upon the analogies of the Jim Crow South and apartheid South Africa.

Both Alzanoon and Lory used the analogy of the Jim Crow South as a shorthand descriptor of life in Palestine: in Lory's case, as a way to describe the everyday violence of segregation to US audiences; in Alzanoon's case, as a way to understand and assimilate what she was witnessing—and embodying—on the bus. This shorthand is common to solidarity tour report-back texts, speeches, and interviews, from activists to curious tourists to public intellectuals and scholars upon return from solidarity delegations or fact-finding missions to Palestine. These analogies typically center on (1) comparisons between the contemporary West Bank and the Jim Crow South and, in the wake of Ferguson and the Black Lives Matter movement, contemporaneous comparisons around militarized racialized policing; (2) comparisons between apartheid South Africa and contemporary Palestine; and (3) less frequently, comparisons between Native American genocide across Turtle Island and settler colonialism in Palestine.[32] These almost-scripted turns to analogy raise many questions: What are the limitations and the political expediency of these analogies? Why do solidarity tour alumni repeatedly invoke them? How do solidarity tourists invoke them differently? What political purchase do these analogies provide in the act of translating the material of the tour, and what gets lost in translation?

The Jim Crow and South Africa analogies, as well as analogies to early settler colonialism across Turtle Island, on the one hand resist exceptionalizing Palestine, drawing connections between different sites of colonial rule. On the other hand, these analogies can also serve to relegate racialized violence outside of Palestine/Israel to the past and position Israel's occupation as a last colonial outpost or a space where—shockingly—racist vitriol still exists. In a moment when racialized violence against Black people across the United States makes it impossible to consign anti-Black racism to the past and struggles against pipelines and state-sponsored environmental degradation animate the daily Indigenous struggle against land theft in North America, it is worth examining how these comparisons might give historical texture to solidarity tour alumni's speech acts but also inadvertently position the struggle for freedom and decolonization in the United States as a "finished project."[33]

In Lory's words, the only people who could understand Palestine without having seen it are those who have done civil rights work in the United States or been to South Africa. Her nebulous reference to time (when might they have done civil rights work?) and space (wherein and when might they have gone to South Africa?) positions both pre–civil rights segregation and apartheid South Africa as touchstone references that both allow for an explanation without witnessing and need no further explanation. Without this experiential reference, Lory maintains, one needs to witness. Both Lory and Alzanoon also describe these acts of witnessing as participatory ones, in which the "witness" is enacting segregation rather than merely observing it. Lory describes walking down Shuhada Street in Hebron without the Palestinian participants and guides she had come to understand as friends. In the United States, she had explained, "your friends would just come along," but in Hebron "they literally could not leave an area to join you, or to join me."[34] The shock of this experience is palpable in her retelling, even almost two years after her tour. Further, her correction at the end of her sentence from the collective "you" of a wide audience to the circumscribed "me" of her memory also indexes her complicity in the acts of segregation she witnessed, particularly with her repeated descriptions of feeling horrible. Similarly, but in a different register, when Alzanoon describes staying on a bus while West Bank Palestinians get searched on the street outside, she turns to an equally nebulous civil rights–era segregated transit system to understand what she was not only witnessing but embodying. She analogizes her privilege to whiteness even though moments before she explained being just as Palestinian as everyone surrounding her.

While these are the references of young tourists and organizers, renowned scholars, writers, musicians, and activists echo many of these sentiments. Writer Alice Walker, for example, described the situation in Palestine as "more brutal" than the Jim Crow South.[35] Similarly, historian Robin D. G. Kelley, after a tour organized by the US Campaign for the Academic and Cultural Boycott of Israel (USACBI), described witnessing in Palestine as "a level of racist violence [he] had never seen growing up as a Black person in the States," even after having experienced police brutality.[36] Achille Mbembe describes Palestine as worse than the South African Bantustans, far more lethal than apartheid South Africa, and approximating a "high-tech Jim Crow cum Apartheid."[37] More than determining the historical accuracy of these analogies or tallying up their veracity, I am interested in asking the following questions: In a time of egregious human rights violations within and outside the United States, mass incarceration in the United States and in Israel, state-sanctioned torture in both countries, escalating deportations in both countries, accelerated United States and Israeli drone attacks, and both countries' military occupations, what do we gain from positioning the occupation of Palestine as the "biggest moral scandal of our times"?[38] What are the implications of imagining a Palestine whose violence is so egregious, it is worse than Jim Crow and apartheid? What is communicated through these analogies, what is gained and lost in this positioning, and why is it that solidarity tourism so frequently traffics in these comparative and hierarchical analogies?

The blog and collective Africa Is a Country published an e-book devoted entirely to the question of the South Africa/Israel analogy.[39] Troubled by what has too often been a comparison used for purposes of efficacy and not an actual engagement with the history of apartheid in South Africa, the editors sought to probe the politics of the analogy itself. In their introduction to the edited volume, Jon Soske and Sean Jacobs argue that the analogy between South Africa and Israel is, in many ways, apt: both sites of conquest and settlement are predicated on religion and ethnic nationalism; both instituted discriminatory laws based on racial and ethnic grounds; both displaced previous inhabitants from their land and homes.[40] They continue to flag how leading members of the antiapartheid struggle, like Archbishop Tutu, have stated that the "conditions in the West Bank and Gaza are 'worse than apartheid.'"[41] While some of the volume's authors look toward South Africa to glean lessons from the antiapartheid movement for anti-Zionist movement building, others caution against using South Africa as an example for what liberation looks like.

Much like how the collaboration between Zochrot and BADIL, detailed in chapter 5, looked to Cape Town not to provide a model but to reflect on potential limitations of that model, Soske and Jacobs conclude, "In pursuing the comparison, there may be as much to learn from the questions of liberation that the South African struggle failed to answer fully."[42] The essays include analyses of South Africa's role in Israel's arms trade; cautions against the sectarianism of the antiapartheid struggle; comparisons of neoliberal postapartheid South Africa and the neoliberalization of the West Bank, focusing on post-1990 transitions in both spaces; analyses of the power of the analogy and the ways it flattens historic differences; discussions of what complexities the analogy doesn't sustain and what settler logics it illuminates; and arguments in hopes that BDS will shake Israeli universities to the extent that it shook the Afrikaner elite and university administrations in South Africa.[43] In his essay, Robin D. G. Kelley uses his USACBI solidarity tour of the West Bank as a refutation of the claim that the South Africa/Israel analogy doesn't hold, citing how he witnessed the path of the Apartheid Wall carving up the landscape; how he witnessed house demolitions and checkpoints, uprooted olive trees, segregated pristine Israeli settlements and dilapidated refugee camps; and how he heard stories of state-sanctioned theft through the Absentee Property Law and narratives of generations of dispossession.[44] Kelley's choice to foreground his essay with his experience as part of a delegation speaks to the affective resonance of these trips, as well as how solidarity tour alumni and public intellectuals alike use analogy to both understand their own experiences and render what they witnessed legible for US audiences.

In the wake of yet another delegation, Palestinian Youth Movement (PYM) organizer and ethnic studies scholar Loubna Qutami wrote about the April 2019 PYM delegation to Johannesburg, South Africa, and the lessons learned from their trip. Describing the political uneasiness some PYM organizers had with the analogy—particularly its focus on racial desegregation over decolonization—and its embrace by other PYM members as a means to work toward boycott, divestment, and sanctions, Qutami underscored the fraught and difficult conversations that go into determining the political uses of an analogy. In the wake of their meetings, lectures, and walking tours in South Africa, PYM delegates understood, as had the Zochrot and BADIL collaboration, not that South Africa is a model of success for Palestine, a figuratively temporal yet actually coeval future to which Palestine should aspire. Instead, they found in South Africa an "incomplete decolonization," an unfinished project that requires joint-struggle analyses of the differences between racialized labor exploitation, gendered liberation struggles, land and resource confiscation, the danger of negotiated settlements and, in total, the renewed commitment to global—and full—decolonization.[45]

Another analogy that often undergirds the genre of solidarity tour alumni report-backs compares the experiences of Palestinians with the experiences of First Nations peoples across Turtle Island. T. J. Tallie's essay complicates the analogy between South Africa and Israel by pointing to Israel's settler logic, which positions Palestinian death as lamentable but necessary for Israeli safety, as neither new nor unique to either South Africa or Israel. Tallie argues, "As Chickasaw scholar Jodi Byrd has addressed, my own country, the United States, is built upon a history of the ungrievable Indian, a necropolitics that decides that while unfortunate, the death and clearing of Indigenous peoples is a necessity for securing the settler state."[46] Tallie continues, reflecting not only on shared settler logics but also on the naturalization of settler violence in the United States, which is often either disappeared or relegated to a distant past. An African American scholar of South African history, Tallie first identifies the parallels between colonial South Africa and its apartheid regime and Israel's settler logics. At the same time, Tallie underscores the normalization of settler violence in the United States:

> As a non-native person of color, I understand very well the constant and disproportionate violence meted out to nonwhite peoples within the United States. And these moments of repression are still shaped by a complicated relationship to a settler nation-state: the very claims I make to belong to a body politic, to push against oppression, are often done through recourse to an American identity that exists only through the oppression and marginalization of indigenous North Americans.[47]

Tallie wants to trouble the distance not between past oppression of Indigenous people in North America and Palestine but between contemporary marginalization of Native Americans in rights appeals to the US state by US citizens, including people of color. More than solely a factual comparison between settler logics in North America, South Africa, and Palestine/Israel, Tallie wants to raise questions about a present, not a past, of oppression of Indigenous people and US scholar/activist/citizen complicity in it.

Focusing on the question of settler colonialism, scholars, activists, and organizers will often draw comparisons between the United States and Palestine/Israel. However, much of this comparative work inadvertently functions to position the United States as a colonialism that is "settled," while Palestine is positioned as a colonialism "we" can still do something about. This logic is frequently at work in analogies that position Palestine as a last colonial outpost and caution that, if we don't act, what happened to the Native Americans will happen to Palestinians. This formulation assumes that colonialism elsewhere, outside of Palestine, is over, that Native peoples and their land no longer exist, and that Palestine is in danger of becoming settled in the way that the United States ostensibly is. These kinds of shorthands and signposts for displacement traffic in erasure and exceptionalize Palestine in the same way that declarations of Palestine as the worst colonialism and most brutal racism similarly do.

Indeed, in 2019, on a tour in Bethlehem with Baha Hilo of To Be There, an older white woman from Bethesda, Maryland, gawked at the towering Wall in front of her as Hilo explained the history of this place. Describing the conversion of Indigenous names to settler names, he spoke of how Israel renames Palestinian sites—particularly through tourist initiatives—to lay claim to that space. The tourist reflected on how egregious that is. He agreed and asked where she was from. "Bethesda, Maryland," she answered. "Right," he continued, "and what do the Indigenous people of Bethesda, Maryland, call their land?" Flustered, she balked. "They don't, I don't know, no one is alive to ask, they're all dead." The defensiveness with which she immediately and vehemently clung to the idea that "they're all dead," solely to justify her inability to answer this question, is precisely what makes solidarity tourism a fraught exercise in asking tourists not to examine Palestine's "present" as the US's "past" but to reflect on the colonial present in both sites. This tourist was, of course, wrong; the land of Bethesda, Maryland, is that of the Piscataway Conoy Tribe and Piscataway Indian Nation, recognized by the State of Maryland in 2012, with monthly meetings and triannual community events in Pomfret, Maryland—less than an hour's drive from Bethesda.[48] In this case, this tourist's concession of analogy, but only when relegated to the past, allows her to communicate her outrage as a witness in Palestine while positioning settler colonialism where she lives as resolved, with nothing left to witness.

At other times, works circulated by solidarity tour alumni tacitly cosign the disappearance of First Nations people by way of not making the comparison or analogy at all. In a panel on teaching Palestine at the American Studies Association's annual meeting in November 2014, Palestinian American Research Center Faculty Development Seminar Fellows spoke about their own solidarity delegation to the West Bank, East Jerusalem, and inside Israel's 1948 borders. English scholar Katie Kane spoke about her experience in Hebron, the segregation she saw in Jerusalem, and the destruction of olive trees she witnessed. She used an infographic by the collective Visualizing Palestine on the effects of Israel's uprooting of olive trees (figure 7.1) to signal the kinds of destruction she witnessed, although admitting offhandedly that the image itself was reductive and problematic, but still potentially useful.[49]

The image attempts to render Israeli uprooting legible to US citizens by depicting bulldozers uprooting Central Park alongside information about the destruction to Palestinian farming families during harvest and planting seasons in Palestine. In its efficacious analogizing, however, the image—which was also sometimes circulated by the Olive Tree Campaign—enacts its own erasure of Native histories on the island of Manhattan. Audience member J. Kēhaulani Kauanui—herself a delegate, with Robin D. G. Kelley, on USACBI's solidarity tour of Palestine—intervened in this conversation to raise questions about the Lenape people for whom the uprooting of what is now Central Park was not hypothetical but in fact very real and very much still a part of the lived memories of the trauma of settler colonialism in the United States.

7.1 Visualizing Palestine, "Uprooted" (2011).

This conversation, much like the disparities between solidarity tourists Addis Green and Yvonne Lory, or Sarah Alzanoon and Maggie Goff, troubles the coherence of the category "solidarity tourist." Solidarity tourists see Palestine differently, use the materials of their tours in Palestine differently, draw connections differently, and, like tour guides in Palestine/Israel, contradict one another. As has unfolded in this chapter and others, solidarity tourists, like the guides and organizers who facilitate their movement, can enact their own forms of erasure as they organize against the erasure of Palestine; they can critique voyeurism as they tour refugee camps, snapping nonconsensual photos of kids playing in front of their homes; they can rehearse the segregation they are seeking to upend; and they can advance some colonial logics while trying to deconstruct others.

Palestine solidarity organizing more broadly has also been criticized for the same kinds of erasure, particularly in the form of memes and infographics like the "Uprooted" one in figure 7.1, that traffic in violence of their own as they attempt to do anticolonial work. Salient examples often come amid Israel's serial bombardments of Gaza, when images circulate rapidly on social media. In the wake of Israel's 2014 assault on Gaza, images made the rounds on Twitter, Facebook, and elsewhere with Photoshopped shrinking landmasses on maps of Canada, the United States, Australia, and elsewhere under the caption "How would you feel?" In one tweet—among countless others like it—Canadians for Justice and Peace in the Middle East asked, "If #Canada were #Palestine, how would you feel?" accompanied by such an image.[50] Their tweet met with the response "That's pretty much how the Indigenous people of Canada do feel."[51] This eleven-word response encapsulates the sentiments shared by many Indigenous organizers in reaction to maps like these that eclipse other histories of erasure in efforts to shore up Palestine advocacy. These maps have their corrective analogue in maps frequently circulated by Palestinian and Indigenous activists to highlight their shared legacies of past and present settler colonialism, which attempt to highlight land grabs in both contexts while relegating neither to the past.

When the solidarity tour report-back genre functions through a logic that positions Palestine, either tacitly or explicitly, as a last colonial outpost, it positions colonialism elsewhere as over. It positions Indigenous people elsewhere as no longer grieving, relevant, or resisting. And it erases the past and present of Native resistance to US colonial projects, not to mention the vibrant anticolonial movements in both former and contemporary sites of US overseas expansion. Similarly, when solidarity tour alumni position Palestine's racialized state and settler violence as legible only in comparison with a *past* of racialized aggression, police violence, lynching, and racial inequality in the United States or a *past* of race-based segregation in South Africa, they eclipse the structural inequality that characterizes the contemporary moment in those spaces, and they render present racial inequity as both settled and no longer urgent. These kinds of analogies, endemic to the report-back genre, exceptionalize Palestine even as they purport to do the opposite.

In the wake of Ferguson and Black Lives Matter movement building in 2014 and renewed global Black liberation uprisings in the wake of George Floyd's murder in the summer of 2020, much work has been devoted to understanding, historicizing, and contextualizing the contours of Black-Palestine solidarity and its analogies.[52] Indeed, as Black liberation uprisings across the United States continued, changed shape, and grew during the summer of 2020, numerous social media posts and articles indicted the very real alliance between the Israeli military and US police forces. However, many did so in a way that insinuated that the United States was learning how to "do" racist state violence from Israel. United States police forces did not need to learn racist state violence from Israel; they were born in racist violence. In the South, US police forces began as slave patrols; in the North and Midwest, they functioned as a way to control migrant industrial workers; and in the West, they functioned to coerce Native labor and enforce immigration controls.[53] In US colonies and across Indigenous land, police forces have aided land expropriation and worked to quell anticolonial rebellion. As Palestinian scholar-activist Nada Elia immediately noted upon the emergence of articles like these, alongside a proliferation of side-by-side imaging of George Floyd and Palestinians with IDF soldiers kneeling on their necks, the Israeli military and police only began training US police forces after 9/11, while US police forces have been exacting racist state violence against Black, brown, Indigenous, migrant, and refugee communities for centuries, far before Israel even existed.[54] The positioning of Israel as having taught the United States how to enact racialized violence is a genealogical claim that absolves the United States of its own colonial history.

Many delegates and guides, at the same time, refuse these kinds of temporal logics, insisting on nuance and context, often via a reversal of the tropes most tourists use. In a 2019 interview, on the last day of a ten-day solidarity tour across Palestine, RL, a Black artist and organizer with the Dream Defenders, reflected on Palestine not as a relic of the past of United States but as both a reminder of legalized segregation and dangerous prediction of the future. "I'll tell my mom," she said. "Ma, this is happening. They drive on separate roads. They can't *move* without someone telling them, 'This is OK to move.' And she'll think back to when her grandmother told her, 'Oh yeah, you gotta be at home before the sun goes down, because if you get caught out on the streets you're dead.'"[55] She uses this example, she reiterated, to remind people, "We're not the only ones. This is a global struggle that we're in. And if we sit by and just watch it happen, then we're already dead." She emphasized, "I want *my* folks to understand what's happening."[56]

At the same time, RL turned this analogizing on its head. She looked around the café, gesturing to Jerusalem beyond, and Palestine beyond that. "I want to give credence to what this is now. Because it is evolved. And we need to understand what those evolutions and revolutions look like. Because they're going to evolve again. And we need to be right up on that shit as it happens."[57] Tracking the evolution of shared technologies of racialized violence, between the United States and Israel, RL pointed not to Palestine as a *past* but as a *future* neither Palestinians nor Black and brown people across the world can afford. She again reiterated that that is why she came to Palestine, why she does this work, why she continues to plead with people not to "sit idly by and let the world crumble."[58] She paused. "Like, we *live* here. We all live here. Somebody is actively trying to push all the Black and brown folks out of this world. Why is that? Like, who said that only one person can live on this planet? And then, furthermore, who said only one person can benefit from what this planet produces?"[59] This, she concluded, is why she connects the racialized technologies, surveillance, and tactics of state violence shared between the United States to Israel and weaponized upon Black and brown people. It's also why she studies the shared refusal—past and present—to cosign or ignore that violence and the revolutions in addition to the evolutions of those technologies to know what to do when they crop up again. In this way, the point is not to decipher which analogy, temporal or spatial, "works" but to think through what it means to understand Palestine through analogy—what it obfuscates and what it lays bare.

Witnessing, Contextualized

Translating and witnessing, then, are experienced differently by differently positioned participants on solidarity tours. For Palestinians in exile who are "allowed" entry to their homeland, like Sarah Alzanoon, a solidarity tour is the only way back to Palestine. Over mint tea and cigarettes in a café in the eastern part of Occupied Jerusalem in 2019, one interlocutor, Noelle Farasha, explained how she saw this summer's delegation as the only option for her to experience a return, if only temporary and fleeting, to Palestine. Her father was born in a small farming village, Silat ad-Dhahr—"It's either Jenin or Nablus, depending on who you're talking to," she joked.[60] His father was abroad, working construction in Kuwait, in 1967 when the Israelis invaded the village, and his mother, unsure of what trauma would befall her children if she stayed, left via Jordan to meet his father in Kuwait. "There was still a generational memory of the Nakba that was present or may have played a factor in that decision," Farasha explained. "And what she ended up doing [was] deciding to leave, to protect her family."[61] She concluded: "My dad's family is split between three, well, four places, technically. Jordan, Kuwait, the United States, Palestine. And with most of our immediate family being in Kuwait and Jordan."[62] There was thus no real way to visit family in Silat ad-Dhahr. "What the occupation does is force you to not have that connection," Farasha continued, so even finding out where her family is and what their names are was difficult. She described her family ties in Palestine as lost to the "chopping block" not only as a result of forced displacement but also because of her father's own difficulty in communicating. Severed from family in Palestine, she described her potential return to them by saying: "If I just went back by myself, what actually would I be getting out of it? Really? Because they'd be like, Who's this woman showing up?"[63]

"There wasn't really a good way for me to go, especially by myself," she explained.[64] With a partner from Gaza who cannot go back and a father who, in her words, "probably will never go back," she asked herself, "How do I safely go to the homeland? And be able to see it and experience it?"[65] In a context of exile across two families, her own and her partner's, with ties severed by the occupation forces and by time, and to avoid being a random woman showing up on someone's doorstep, Farasha chose the tour that made the most sense for her as a diaspora Palestinian and as a practitioner of Palestinian embroidery: an activist delegation with an emphasis on cultural production and the arts.

Moreover, even with an organized tour, this *only way back* invariably poses hours of questioning, invasive interrogation, racial profiling, derision, detention, potential deportation. As Sarah Alzanoon described being detained at the airport for "somewhere between five and seven hours" before she was eventually allowed entry, kept in a room where they ostensibly "randomly check people" but which was populated, in her words, solely by "brown people like me,"[66] Alzanoon's first moments in Palestine were animated by relentless interrogation, coupled with the weight of being her family's fleeting emissary of return. Farasha, too, experienced a first encounter with Palestine marked by interrogation and the heaviness of withstanding it to be a witness for her family. She was detained and interrogated at the airport for hours—Who is your father? Who do you know in Palestine? No one? Really? Give me your phone. Who is your husband? Where is he from? Sign in to your email. Where are you from? Who are you meeting? No one? Really? She knew this would happen, having already had her campus activism monitored by blacklisting groups in the United States like Canary Mission. "These risks are the reasons why a regular Palestinian wouldn't come," she explained as a side note.[67] She also described her presence in Palestine as a witness—not a witness to the human rights violations Israel routinely commits, the kind of witnessing so many solidarity tourists mean when they describe what they are in Palestine to do, but a witnessing for her father, for her husband. Reflecting on the week, and on being interviewed for a research project on solidarity tourism, she said, "I think this research project made me contextualize a lot of stuff that was happening, like the idea of being a tourist, of being Palestinian, of return in some way. And how all those things are true in specific times, like all at once, and so I think the best way for me as a Palestinian is just the witness part of this. *Witnessing my homeland for other people.* And I think that probably wasn't what [the organizers] were thinking when they [called this witnessing]. It's like something else entirely."[68] Here, Farasha describes the subtle and stark differences between being a witness *to* and being a witness *for*. She rephrases: "A big part of this trip was being in Palestine for other people."[69]

Moreover, Farasha—like many other diaspora Palestinians with whom I spoke—was a witness *for* people who either refused or were refused that witnessing. Her father was deeply opposed to her taking this trip. She described his reluctance as a trauma Black and brown parents have, a trauma particular to having been exiled from Israel in 1967 as a child, a generational trauma that viscerally understands the boundless cruelty of the Israeli state:

> My dad said, "I heard you're going on a culture tour in Palestine." I said it was in August. And then he starts asking all these questions, like: "Who runs the program? It sounds good, but dangerous. How are you going to be safe? Obviously, having your name is a dead giveaway about your identity." And then he proceeds to go, "You're going to this horrible place, where people don't care about people like you," and I said, "You know, I'm aware of that, and I know what's happening, and I understand [your] concerns. But also this org is pretty efficient at helping people go through this process." And this is the highlight that I tell everyone because it's kind of insane, but my dad says, "When it comes to Israel no one can or will help you—trust me. There are many fine examples out there for you to consider. When you're dead, in prison, or seriously injured, there's little to nothing that can be done for you. Do not like the idea."[70]

Humor helped her process his reaction as "kind of insane," but she also framed her "return" as one both for him and against his wishes, one animated by going to a place "where people don't care about people like you," where "no one will help you," but also a place—she knew from other childhood lore—where he harvested olives, where he has grounded memories of his village, where he remembers *kanafeh*, where he remembers everything else stolen from him.

So, with the weight of being a disavowed emissary of return, a reluctant witness for, and having just been subjected to hours of interrogation, Farasha emerged from the airport to be met with a failure of solidarity from the tour itself. Those who had flown with her, other delegates, and the organizers, in an effort to avoid the "risk" of waiting for her at the airport while she was interrogated, had already made their way to the hotel in Jerusalem, an hour away from Ben Gurion. She took a taxi by herself, with her own money, to meet the other tourists at the hotel. She explained, "They were like, 'We're going to wait an hour' (and, of course, it takes longer than an hour). 'The bus will leave and then you have to like figure it out a bit.' If you're a young Palestinian woman, that's kind of like a risky situation; they were like, 'Good luck! We're on WhatsApp!'"[71]

In this cluster of narratives—exile, generational memory, preparation, apprehension, finding the only way back, witnessing for those who refuse it, intrusion, interrogation, and abandonment—we see the multiple ways solidarity tours, for diaspora Palestinians, are manufactured by the state to fail. We see Palestinian mobility, policed by the Israeli state, alongside Palestinian familial ties severed and Palestinian privacy violated. We see how much Israel does not want Palestinians to return, even as tourists. Yet we also see a profound failure of solidarity, an absence of care via a calculation of risk. The narratives of diaspora Palestinians—many of whom have the option of going back only with a tour, with or without their families' blessings, with the knowledge that they might do all of this only to be denied entry—are peppered with moments like these, moments where care on the part of organizers or other tourists could have mitigated the violence of this kind of return and nurtured the bittersweet joy that can come with being in Palestine as a witness for those who can't or don't want to risk coming. If a tour is ostensibly for diaspora Palestinians, or organized with diaspora Palestinians in mind, one would think organizers would be cognizant of the reminders of exile those tourists experience in Palestine and make their time in Palestine—which everyone knows could be their *only* time in Palestine—a potentially healing experience. Instead, many solidarity tourists from the diaspora find their trauma further reproduced through an absence of care on the part of organizers, delegate leaders (who are often but not always US-based and not always Palestinian), and other tourists.

Returning to the narration of witnessing *for*, Farasha described one day of the tour that was organized around a talk with Omar Barghouti in Haifa in the morning, a meeting with Mustafa Sheta at the Freedom Theatre in Jenin in the afternoon, a stop in the outskirts of Nablus for *kanafeh* in the early evening, and an arrival to Nabi Saleh in the evening. Four cities and villages in one day: one inside Israel's 1948 borders and three across the northern West Bank. This is such a discombobulating itinerary, across so many borders manufactured by the State of Israel, that, having met with Barghouti in the morning, one tourist asked Sheta, at the Freedom Theatre in the West Bank in the afternoon, if he was a Palestinian citizen in Israel.

On this day, having driven from Jenin to Nablus, the tour bus drove through Farasha's family's village without stopping. "Throughout this trip," she explained. "like when we were driving through my village, I took a whole video of that. Or when we were in Yafa, where my partner's paternal family is from, I was taking pictures the whole time to send to him later. So part of it is being a witness for them, to share that experience with them, because who knows when/if/ever they want to come back to their village." Her position as witness collided with her position as exiled Palestinian, with the bus of solidarity tourists—among them prison abolitionists, Dream Defenders, feminists, longtime Palestine solidarity activists—so wedded to an itinerary that they can imagine stopping in Nablus for *kanafeh* but can't imagine stopping in Silat ad-Dhahr for one delegate to step foot in her father's village, even for just a moment.

Farasha reflected: "Just the whole disconnect. Like you were always on the move, really." Here, we can recall the reference to the pace of itineraries like these as "Occupation Bootcamp," itineraries that don't allow for any exercise of Palestinian hospitality. Farasha paused, fighting back tears:

> I would have loved to stop in my village, for, you know, just like five minutes. You know? And I wish that had been more of a priority for their Palestinian delegates. Like, this is like a return, in a way. So how are you incorporating that idea into the program? Shouldn't there be at least a free day for the Palestinians to figure out how to get to their village, experience their village, in whatever way they could? If they can, you know? And so that is something I kind of wish had been part of the program, especially if part of their priority is to have Palestinians going on this delegation. . . . Because we were on the go so much that it was hard for a lot of people to even fully digest what had happened. And even for me, I still can't kind of even understand that I even saw my dad's village. Like I still can't even think about it. And if I think about it, I'll cry. And I cried on the bus when I saw it.[72]

The last thing a solidarity tour of Palestine should be for a Palestinian is heartbreaking in more ways that it invariably already will be. It's already heartbreaking. It's already a negotiation with family, with colleagues, with coworkers; it's already a subjection to surveillance and policed mobility; it's already a reminder of your family's exile as only you can or will return; it's already a reminder of how limited that return actually is. In a settler-colonial context of displacement, diaspora, and exile, solidarity tours can—and sometimes do—enact a politics of radical care, a politics that would prioritize the differently positioned Palestinian in exile as tourist, already subjected to a return only possible within the context of a "tour" of their homeland. As with Alzanoon's moments on the bus, where she, as a diaspora Palestinian and tourist in Palestine, was meant to stay on the bus while "Palestinians" had to exit it for further surveillance, for the diaspora Palestinian, a solidarity tour is both the joy of return and the painful reminder of exile.

Solidarity tourism, as this and the preceding chapters have shown, is an incoherent category. Solidarity tourists—like their guides—are never one thing. For Palestinian delegates, the solidarity tour is not just a solidarity tour. It is a calculated risk and a circumscribed return. It is animated by joy and by pain, replete with moments of connection and moments of alienation. Because it is rendered impossible in so many ways—by exile, by racialized policing at the airport, by the Israeli state's refusal of return—it also has a responsibility to slow down and make space for joy amid trauma. Solidarity tourists on delegations like these are rarely encouraged to spend time in places in Palestine in substantive ways, like visiting the sea, getting lost, lingering, wandering around, taking days off from touring, or making space for other kinds of returns. In this way, when the actual markers of tourism—pleasure, leisure, slowness, exploration, food, beauty—are sometimes written *out* of solidarity tours, it can reenact the violence of another narrative: that there is no joy, no pleasure, no slowness in Palestine. For tours that can already be painful for some, tours already foreclosed by a settler state that doesn't want tourists to witness Palestine (either as witnesses *to* human rights violations or witnesses *for* others in exile), the invitation to Palestine—in a context when the Palestinians doing the inviting do not control either their borders or the narrative about Palestine—is one that is an invitation to be a witness, but also a tourist, in Palestine. The organizers' desire to manufacture a semblance of "Occupation Bootcamp," with an itinerary so inflexible that it can't wait for an interrogation to be over, so rigid that it can't stop in a delegate's village, and so wedded to showcasing pain that it can't account for pleasure, misses an opportunity to mitigate harm and make space for Palestinian joy—diaspora and otherwise. The insistence on joy and the slowness of pleasure are radical and necessary acts of care, which are too often absent from both solidarity and tourism.

"Hanging Out in Palestine": Leisure and Rupture in the In-Between of Solidarity Tours

Indeed, marking the imagined geography of a solidarity tour and the incomprehensibility of leisure and pleasure within one, tourist Addis Green once mused in an interview, "I never thought there would be hanging out in Palestine."[73] A Black queer prison abolitionist from Chicago, Green had traveled to Palestine to express solidarity with the Palestinian people and also to counter the disparate challenges to their legitimacy to speak about Palestine: the repeatedly invoked question "Have you been there?" always asked in a combative, and not curious, tenor. Green came to Palestine with the Freedom Bus, a ten-day tour that negotiates the fragmented terrain of the West Bank via bus, stopping in villages and city centers where Palestinian actors from Jenin's Freedom Theatre act out the narratives told to them by the Palestinian residents of the spaces that they are touring. While the playback theater was edifying, Green explained, after ten performances it "lost its charm," and it was the conversations with people—the nonorchestrated moments of the tour, meeting children in Jenin and Bethlehem, and connecting with Palestinians on a one-to-one level—that were far more important. Moments where the schedule was ruptured by laughter and hanging out powerfully figured into many recollections of the solidarity tourists I interviewed, including Green. These moments also served an unanticipated pedagogical purpose, providing valuable lessons about power, solidarity, and recognition for solidarity tourists—while also appealing to tourists' voracious desire for the "authentic."[74] Green explained that "in the fragments between scheduled events," you saw a Palestine that wasn't defined only by its status as being "always under attack," where "everything is fucked up and bad," where the only way one is expected to relate to the place is as an activist.[75] "Hanging out with people" resonated, Green explained, "because I felt like we weren't 'witnessing' them, because it wasn't like a safari adventure through a war zone. It deviated from that."[76] Here, Green positions leisure—a staple of most forms of tourism—as having the potential to disrupt the asymmetrical power relations that inhere within witnessing in Palestine.[77] For Green, leisure was what made solidarity possible on what would otherwise have been a "safari adventure through a war zone."

These moments of hanging out are sometimes defined by sharing recipes, talking about favorite movies or bands, having tea, telling jokes, playing music, making food, singing, laughing. Yazan al-Zubaidy, a former organizer and guide for the Olive Tree Campaign, referenced these post-tour, end-of-day moments as necessary for the functioning of the tour, a needed detox for both tour guides and tourists.[78] For tourists, these moments provide a reprieve from the overload of information or, on the Olive Tree Campaign in particular, a break from the physically draining activity of harvesting and planting; for guides, these moments provide a break from the near-endless recitation of state violence that characterizes their work.

Green, however, stressed that hanging out is complicated, because if people enjoy themselves on a solidarity tour, it weakens their argument about the brutality of Israel's occupation. With solidarity tourism, tourists are expected to be witnesses to state violence while, at the same time, the relationships they are forging with people are not solely defined by those people's subjugation and their responses to it. Green elaborated that they wanted to be in "real time," less concerned with taking notes for later, or, in other words, accumulating evidence, and more concerned with being there. "You have to honor the thing," they concluded, a nod toward being honest about what is taking place, toward calling hanging out hanging out, and toward not wanting or needing the entire tour to be a performance of subjection met with a performance of witnessing. In this way, for Green, solidarity tourism has the potential to offer a *critique* of disaster tourism—the process of witnessing a war-torn site and seeing its people as defined entirely by their subjection.

At the same time, Green described feeling helpless in Palestine, at a loss for knowing what to do. Green's narrative reflects the shared anxiety tourists feel about doing something in Palestine and the palpable limitations tourists sense in their presence in the West Bank. Though tour guides routinely emphasize that tourists' work is *not* in Palestine but in their home countries, solidarity tourists still feel like they are in Palestine to do something *in* Palestine. The Olive Tree Campaign, for example, attempts to resolve this anxiety by both helping Palestinian farmers and giving tourists something to do, something they can feel good about having done. Solidarity tours in Palestine, then, are inextricably wrapped up in the feelings of tourists, from their apolitical ugly feelings of boredom, discomfort, and uselessness, to their sense of "feeling good" at having done something to make a difference.[79] The preoccupation with tourists' feelings is not only endemic to "occupation tourism" but is characteristic of tourism writ large as it correlates the success of the tour in direct relationship to the tourist's feeling of satisfaction. While Green's narrative does not traffic in the language of consumer/consumed, it does reveal the deeply felt affects of solidarity tourism, how the phenomenon itself is characterized by multiple, competing but ultimately unequal, anxieties, preconceptions, and preoccupations on the part of both the tourists and the "toured."

For many solidarity tourists and tour guides alike, hanging out, circulating images and narratives of Palestinian people living—and enjoying—their lives does not weaken Palestinian freedom struggles. As Green explained, "People want to put the most horrific images out there to create the urgency and to vilify the occupation, but there aren't enough images of Palestinian people, framed in a way that doesn't mitigate [critiques of] Israel, images of the hospitality, kindness, images that aren't about witnessing them."[80] Here, Green constructs witnessing as a voyeuristic relationship to images of horror, one in which Green—as a witness in Palestine—is very much implicated. Green then positions hanging out as a partial and inadequate, but necessary, way to work against the violence of witnessing and an endeavor to craft a narrative that is not wholly about subjection and victimhood.

Like hanging out, other tourists positioned the "hospitality" and "friendliness" they experienced in Palestine as beyond the scope of what they had imagined. Olga Negrón, for example, expressed her initial surprise at the hospitality she experienced as a tourist in Palestine. She reflected, "We witnessed the extreme kindness, generosity, and friendliness of the Palestinian people. It was actually quite startling to me that, even though living under years and years of the occupation, people wouldn't be hardened or bitter toward outsiders, especially Americans."[81] With this sentiment, Negrón touches on yet another frequently repeated expectation: that Palestinians would "hate" Americans, even if understandably so. She continued, "I realized that the Palestinians, although portrayed often as not human, were very much in fact one of the most welcoming people I have ever visited."[82] Here, again, Negrón positions Palestinian hospitality as a surprise, not in keeping with her understanding from US media sources—and reflected in US State Department descriptions of the West Bank and Jerusalem—that paint Palestine as a hostile place full of dangerous potential terrorists who especially hate Americans. This also reveals the deeply evaluative relationship tourists often have with Palestine, raising the question, Why do Palestinians have to be welcoming to be free?

This "friendliness" and "hospitality" is in keeping with colonial tourist tropes, as evidenced in feminist and postcolonial critiques of the effects of tourism on colonized spaces. Works by Jamaica Kincaid, Jacqui Alexander, and Derek

Walcott, among many others, remind us of the innumerable ways the "friendliness of the Native" is expected to outdo the friendliness of any space in the United States or Europe.[83] At the same time, solidarity tourism in Palestine occurs in a context in which tourism to Palestine is policed and surveilled. Palestinian guides and organizers are, in this sense, inviting tourists to Palestine when they do not control the borders or the conditions that would allow tourists entry.

In 2012, Palestinian guides and organizers collaborated to call attention to this restriction of visitors, inaugurating the "Welcome to Palestine" campaign, or the Flytilla (referencing the flotillas that have attempted to break the siege on Gaza), wherein international activists flew to Ben Gurion and declared that they were going to Palestine instead of the usual performance of "passing" as a tourist to Israel to get to the West Bank (figure 7.2). These activists were not let in the country and often were not even allowed to board Israel-bound planes in their home countries. Here, restrictions on movement are simultaneously restrictions on movement building. By imposing restrictions on visitors to Palestine, the Israeli state attempts to circumscribe international solidarity efforts in the name of "security." Highlighting the militarized, policed state of surveillance, control, restriction of movement, and bars against being visited, Mazin Qumsiyeh, Palestinian Flytilla campaign organizer and invited guest

7.2 "Welcome to Palestine." Photo by Oren Ziv (2012).

speaker on many solidarity tours in Palestine, emphasizes, "Even prisoners are allowed visits."[84]

In this political landscape, the hospitality of the invitation "Welcome to Palestine" is not meant to mimic colonial tropes and signify the "friendliness of the Native"; rather, this invocation is meant to underscore the isolation, in Qumsiyeh's formulation akin to prison, that Palestinians in the West Bank, and especially in Gaza, experience. Further, this hospitality also occurs in a context in which many solidarity tours are organized as hurried and harried tours through the West Bank, taking tourists through an "Occupation Bootcamp." In this context, friendliness on the part of Palestinian hosts can be understood as endemic to a colonial form of tourism that demands generosity; yet this friendliness is also reflective of an anticolonial praxis that challenges the isolation that the Israeli state has sought to sediment. Leisure, hanging out, and hospitality form a response to a state apparatus that seeks to keep Palestinians isolated. In this way, tour guides' acts of hanging out refuse the subjection Palestinians are expected to perform at the same time that they function as reversals of tropes that typically animate the tourist encounter. These acts bring into focus a Palestine defined not solely by siege and occupation, yet they do so within a profession predicated on meeting tourists' desire for authenticity *and* on providing evidence of the occupation under which Palestinians live.

Embedded in narratives of a Palestine defined solely by its status as under siege is a refusal to consider Palestinian joy. As chapter 6 enumerated, the social life of Palestine is seldom the subject of the report-back genre. Images of Palestinian joy do not catalyze activism as images of Palestinian suffering do. This refusal to prioritize Palestinian joy, a refusal ubiquitous in reporting about Palestine, has led many solidarity tour guides to organize tours that allow space for more than just "Occupation Bootcamp." As guides like Yazan Al-Zubaidy positioned post-tour hangouts as a necessary reprieve, for tourists and tour guides alike, from the constant recitation of occupation statistics, these moments where tourists are not witnessing Palestinians but, in fact, sharing time and space with them are not moments saved for the report-back, for discerning what will hit home. Instead, they are moments when tour guides resist performing subjugation for the tourist gaze and instead spend time relating to the tourists who have come to Palestine—as Baha Hilo once put it, in an assessment marked by generosity, having come across the world to Palestine against all the narratives that tell them not to. Hanging out with tourists, or the leisure usually typified by and promised in tourist initiatives, is not the opportunistic employment of a tourist trope to satisfy tourist expectations of a vacation. Instead, hanging out in Palestine carries with it the defiance of an occupation that attempts to preclude solidarity tourism *and* proscribe the intimacies forged in the space between the tours.

In tour guides' refusal to craft tours organized entirely around witnessing suffering, they refuse to reinforce the narrative, circulated by the Israeli state, that Palestinians have never lived—in all senses of the word—in Palestine. They refuse to construct tours that traffic in a narrative that sees Palestinians as defined only by their subjugation. We can recall, as a telling example, how the Olive Tree Campaign fieldworkers and organizers reframed tourist presence in Palestine not as a gift tourists are giving Palestinians but as a gift Palestinians, in their generosity and hospitality, are giving tourists. Understanding this reversal, within and against the tourist encounter, allows us to think differently about radical hospitality, tourist tropes, and the visual narratives that coalesce in this industry as it attempts to keep Palestinians on their land under a settler-colonial occupation that seeks to displace them.

Placing hanging out, fun, cultures of resistance, tourism, and occupation in the same visual and analytic field not only asks when and if tourists derive pleasure (or a sense of adventure) from touring the occupied but also asks to what extent hanging out in Palestine has the potential to push back against the image of a perennially occupied people. Hanging out in Palestine also works against the accumulation of evidence in a context in which evidence in fact abounds. Focusing on both the content of the tours and also on the reprieve from them makes space for feminist readings of solidarity tourism in Palestine that are prismatic: that see solidarity tourism as both an industry and anticolonial praxis; that do not ask Palestinians to again recount the trauma of dispossession for scores of rotating tourists; that acknowledge the multiple forms of living that take shape under occupation; and that treat the evidence of Israeli settler colonialism as already real—with or without witnessing.[85]

Solidarity Tourists, the Incoherence of a Category, and Joy Reconsidered

Returning to the tourists with whom we began, one registering her disappointment at not having discovered the afterlife of "a bomb or something" in Nablus, the other registering disappointment that a bullet-riddled school had moved, denying other tourists evidence of occupation, it becomes clear that many tourists, sometimes in spite of themselves, come to Palestine in search of *evidence*. Moreover, they come in search of evidence against the histories

Palestinians have been marshaling since before 1948. They then sift through that evidence, looking for resonant pieces that will convince skeptical audiences back home. At the same time, like the tour guide who described witnessing four shops in Hebron where there was once one, differently positioned solidarity tourists have a different relationship to being invited to witness. For Farasha, witnessing is witnessing for one's family, a policed and surveilled return, but a return nonetheless, in the place of those who cannot.

The labor of tour guides and solidarity tour organizers is thus to navigate and refuse tourist expectations, like Lory's, that guides and hosts will rehearse their dispossession and reenact their trauma of exile. At the same time, tour guides enact these microrefusals even while their profession traffics in walking tourists through the evidence of destruction wrought by the Israeli state. Tour guides slowly and deliberately attempt to shift tourists' allegiances, to invite them to rethink their role in Palestinian freedom struggles. At the same time, they must make space for tourists who refuse the spectacle but who, like Farasha, also may be in Palestine to step foot in a village their family cannot return to.

Sometimes tour guides, organizers, and tourists alike succeed, and sometimes they fail spectacularly. Solidarity tourism is not without its discontents; it is a project that is only possible in a context where violence at the site of knowledge production—the epistemic violence Gayatri Spivak outlined in 1988 in "Can the Subaltern Speak?"—has structured the relationship between tour guide and tourist. It is a relationship set against the backdrop of the celebration of Israel as a moral and modern democracy and the celebration of the solidarity tourist as one who is "saving" the subaltern. Solidarity tour guides, in their everyday labor, are trying to intervene in both of these colonial structuring logics. Through employing a form of movement so often pressed into the service of colonial projects, guides and organizers use tourism to intervene in the very structures that make their work necessary.

In a different context, feminist theorist Sara Ahmed calls evidence "what you accumulate when you are not given places to go."[86] In the same piece, she describes how "evidence of walls does not bring the walls down" yet still you accumulate it. In solidarity tour itineraries in Palestine, guides have accumulated evidence against the machinations of a settler-colonial state that has sought to bring about their physical and narrative erasure. They are "not given places to go" in a literal sense in that their movement is foreclosed and their geography circumscribed. At the same time, they are "not given places to go" in terms of narration: their stories are prewritten, the expectations for their narratives predetermined, the narrative evidence they have accumulated too often ignored and dismissed. Even on a solidarity tour, their itineraries are so scripted they sometimes cannot even make space for the exiled whose stories make up the content of the tour.

However, because they are "not allowed visitors" and often not allowed to leave (or, if they do, or leave for too long, they are not often allowed to come back), Palestinians, particularly in Jerusalem and the West Bank, are also not given any place *other* than tourism to go: a fraught strategy they have sought to rework in efforts to confront the epistemic violence that structures their relationship to the tourist.[87] Tour guides know that providing evidence is not enough; tourists' work does not begin in Palestine but is, guides hope, catalyzed there. As a pedagogical endeavor, tour guides, like teachers, describe their work as a success if it reaches a fraction of their audience. As several guides explained, "If I have a tour of twenty, and I reach five people, or one, I consider that a success." In the slow and incremental chipping away at colonial land theft and colonial knowledge regimes, "success" is difficult to quantify. But part of that success is not only evidencing for tourists the displacement put into motion by the establishment of the Israeli state on Palestinian land but also evidencing that Palestinians are living, and crafting pleasure under occupation, in Palestine. Under a settler-colonial regime that refuses to acknowledge Palestinian lives except through the joint processes of calling for and enumerating their displacement, Palestinian tour guides are reworking the tourist encounter in ways that refuse to rehearse the performance of their own suffering and refuse to accept the foreclosure of their own joy.

CONCLUSION
ON FUTURITY, FAILURE,
AND PRECARIOUS HOPE

In one of his many final belligerent—though not anomalous—acts before leaving office, in January 2020 Donald Trump issued a 181-page "Deal of the Century," a continuation of US-backed Israeli state policy intent on annexing as much land as possible. It included within it a bright and cheery note on tourism. "Gifting" Palestine with investments in tourism, the plan, authored by Jared Kushner, who proudly explained that he was expert enough to divide Palestinian land because he had read twenty-five books on "the conflict," extolled the value of tourism to the West Bank and Gaza. In one paragraph lauding the remarkable historical and religious sites across the West Bank and Gaza and likening the future of the Gaza coast to Beirut, Hong Kong, Lisbon, Rio de Janeiro, Singapore, and Tel Aviv, the plan outlined the following: "Unique and exciting characteristics give the West Bank and Gaza the potential to transform into a successful global tourism destination."[1] Even co-opting language that approximates Laila el-Haddad's You Are Not Here, the plan references Palestinian desserts, writing in tourist-brochure form about Ramallah's famous Rukab's Ice Cream and Nablus's kanafeh. Turning the West Bank and Gaza—since, for its authors, these are the only places remotely Palestine—into an investment opportunity, the plan weds tourism to apartheid, explaining how both can function in tandem. Positioning tourism as a "Breakout Venture," the shiny pages of the plan explain the financing it would take—$750 million in concessional financing, $200 million in grant funding, and, of course, $375 million in loans—to allow for the "rehabilitation and development of tourism sites."[2]

This plan produces a vision of Palestine even further segmented—with segregated roads and racialized enclaves of Palestinian presence scattered, severed from one another, and connected only by roads and tunnels all controlled by Israel. In the words of Yara Hawari, the plan is one of "total Palestinian capitulation."[3] This proposed plan—an acceleration, or evolution in the words of Dream Defenders delegate RL, of the dystopian archipelago Julien Bousac envisioned in 2009—contains not just a nod to tourism but specifically one that imagines a thriving tourism sector paired with entrenched colonization. This seamless pairing demonstrates how tourism is so often intrinsic to the colonial project—and the danger of imagining, for example, postcards from Gaza without liberation first. I have traced the work of those who, deeply cognizant of the relationship between tourism and colonialism, press tourism into work it was not made for—the work of those who refuse tourism and its narratives in the absence of decolonization while simultaneously reworking its conventions to imagine a different future.

Tourism matters in Palestine because, as Israel has expropriated land, it has also expropriated Palestinian narratives. And, as my interlocutors were quick to point out, it has expropriated Palestinian land and narratives *through* tourism. Correspondingly, the formula through which (most) tourists understand what they witness—from shock and disbelief to outrage—is almost always coupled with descriptions of how impossible it was to prepare for what they saw. No matter how many books they read, how much news coverage they saw, how knowledgeable they were about Palestine, they could never have prepared for what they witnessed. In this book, I question why that is: why tourists *cannot believe it until they see it*, why working in solidarity with Palestine has become so sutured to witnessing its effects.

This unwillingness to believe is structured by the systematic erasure of Palestinian narratives and the failure to construct Palestinians as truth-telling subjects. In many ways, then, solidarity tourism is about failure: on the part of guides, a last-ditch attempt to "get through" to internationals when other attempts have failed and, on the part of international audiences, a failure to believe Palestinian narratives until they themselves witness them. This witnessing is meant to catalyze, in Ann Laura Stoler's words, a shock of recognition they can no longer deny or ignore. This recognition can also constitute a failure of its own: whether or not tourists recognize the racialized colonial rule they see in Palestine/Israel as something also reflected and refracted in their own country's past and present.

The impulse for tourists to eschew a relational reading of what they witness in Palestine is a strong one; many US tourists can clearly identify the unwavering and exorbitant US financial and political support that sustains Israeli rule in Palestine, but they have a harder time seeing the "settler solidarities," or the settler logics shared between the United States and Israel.[4] This refusal to see is also about having the privilege to ignore. For this reason, for many tourists, solidarity tourism has everything to do with privilege: the privilege to deny, the privilege to decide to learn, the privilege to travel, the privilege to move, and the privilege to leave. It is about the privilege of surveying a scene, evaluating whether to give the "gift of freedom," gawking at disparity, being disappointed when what looks like remnants from a bomb turns out to be traces of someone painting their bed frame.[5] It is about the privilege of not knowing where Palestine is on a map, of expecting to see only tents, of describing Palestine/Israel as one's first encounter with racism. It is also about the privilege of demanding evidentiary weight, the privilege of not believing in the first place and not having to. These stark failures of solidarity make it impossible, and irresponsible, to romanticize solidarity tourism as either an exemplar of resistance or a foolproof model for movement building.

At the same time, solidarity tourism cannot be dismissed as merely, or wholly, "occupation tourism"—an object we already know and can describe, one worthy of our derision. I have resisted the assertion that solidarity tourism is inherently voyeuristic and exploitative, a process doomed to failure because of the medium in which it traffics. To dismiss solidarity tourism not only misses the point of how—and more importantly why—this phenomenon has emerged; it also erases the labor of the tour guides and organizers who have thought carefully about their anticolonial tactics and movement-building strategies under conditions of colonial rule and international indifference. It refuses a generous reading, one often shared by Palestinian and anti-Zionist Israeli tour guides, of tourists who have sought to meaningfully interrogate their own privilege and complicity in Israel's occupation of Palestine. And, finally, like the circumscription of Palestine to, simply, the West Bank and Gaza, assuming we know where solidarity tourism happens erases Palestine within Jerusalem and cities and villages across Israel. Likewise, assuming we know who solidarity tourists are disappears Palestinians in the diaspora, in exile, who are forced to experience their return to Palestine—if they are allowed at all—as tourists. To assume we already know what solidarity tourism is and does is to miss an analysis of the transnational connections both forged and foreclosed in solidarity tourism, the anticolonial possibilities that can inhere in a strategy that is cognizant of its failures, and the decolonized futurity that is imagined in a tourism that ostensibly only tours the colonial past and present.

I have instead asked how and why solidarity tourism emerged as an organizing strategy and an industry that is both embedded in and working against histories of displacement in Palestine/Israel. Rather than treat solidarity tourism as a story about solely the contemporary moment, or as a story about the West Bank alone, I have offered a narrative, woven through tour guides' retellings, that spans over a century and traverses Historic Palestine. I have sought, in my own retelling, not to mirror the fragmentation of Palestine in book form by discursively severing Palestinian communities from one another: in this story, Palestinians in the diaspora visit Palestine; organizers in Gaza strategize via video chat with organizers in the West Bank; Palestinians in the West Bank craft tours with Palestinians inside Israel's 1948 borders even though they can never meet in person in Palestine; and Palestinian organizers from Tel Aviv and Bethlehem meet at workshops in Cape Town. I have also sought not to confine my retelling to the contemporary. The narratives tour guides provide trace histories of displacement, an ongoing Nakba beginning with Zionist afforestation projects that started uprooting native trees in 1908, histories of dispossession and theft in Jerusalem neighborhoods in and before 1948, uprooting and exile in the years before and after occupation in 1967, punitive violence and collective punishment during the first and second intifadas, and still, the cultivation of both resistance and joy at every stage of colonial rule.

This work has taken as its subject uprooted olive trees and stolen books, bus rides and walking tours, gendered colonial readings of the land and feminist demands for return. I have traced blueprints for return and visions of decolonized futures. I have critiqued tourist demand for evidence in contexts where evidence abounds, and I have charted tour guides' negotiations of these demands, which lay bare the epistemic violence and settler logics of the tourist encounter. I have shown how solidarity tourist witnessing can function as an alibi for research, a refusal to read, and also as an absolution for their country's own violence, a refusal to think relationally. I have also charted how Palestinian tour guides and organizers in fact use the asymmetries of the tourist encounter to both reveal and circumvent their own immobility and stay rooted to land that is under the constant threat of expropriation. I have shown how, in contexts of restricted movement and Israeli-enforced isolation, organizers have crafted connections across the borders, boundaries, checkpoints, and blockades that divide them from each other and from the world at large.

In situating solidarity tourism in its historical context, I have shown how tour guides in Palestine have also formulated a tourism that is wholly invested in ending Israeli colonial rule, a tourism that is in essence anticipating its own obsolescence. What was at first envisioned as a short-lived tactic on the way to statehood has, with the escalation of settlements, expansion, and exile, since become a profession. As one guide explained, "I would love to not do this. If the occupation ended tomorrow, I would do something else. But it hasn't, so I am here."[6] In another tour guide's words, "We've tried violent resistance; we've tried negotiations; we've tried peace talks; we've tried complying with what the United States told us to do by working toward a two-state solution. The only thing left is to show the international community what is happening and compel them to do something."[7] He elaborated, contextualizing the malleability of the tactic: "It's part of the struggle now. If the third intifada happened tomorrow, our strategies would change."[8]

In this way, solidarity tourism is not a new, crass, voyeuristic enterprise characterized by investments and "breakout ventures"; it is, in fact, part of a historical trajectory of multiple, shifting, contested iterations of Palestinian struggles for freedom from occupation—a tactic, industry, and profession laced with pessimism and optimism, cynicism and capacious imagination. Anthropologist Lori Allen argues that Palestinian "cynicism can be a form of awareness and a motor of action by which subjection and subjectification are self-consciously resisted or at least creatively engaged."[9] In solidarity tourism's multiple valences, there is cynicism with the positioning of the United States as an impartial broker, cynicism with the futility of solidarity tourism, and cynicism with the empty rhetoric of peace plans. There is also capacious imaginative labor in blueprinting, alongside return, flowerbeds instead of fences in response to and as reparation for the "tiny wildflowers crushed" in and after 1948. Like Emile Habiby's *The Secret Life of Saeed: The Pessoptimist*, in solidarity tourism we see optimism and pessimism functioning in concert, a simultaneous commitment and resignation that animates the positioning of solidarity tourism as both the only thing left and a malleable strategy now, a strategy that would change if the third intifada happened tomorrow.

In many ways, then, the future, in addition to the past, haunts solidarity tourism. These conditional futures—a third intifada and an end to colonial rule—animate the "now" of solidarity tourism. Tour guides' work, while it sustains them and provides them with income, hinges on their hopes that their work will be rendered unnecessary and irrelevant, that the liberation of Palestine will enable them to "do something else." Their capacity to do something else would then also be punctuated by their ability to return to the village their family came from, stare at the sea from the sand, and have the freedom to move. These conditional futures thus render their work necessary in the hopes that it will soon become obsolete.

In the preceding pages, I have traced how guides and organizers have used tourism, in varied forms, to keep Palestinians in their homes and on their land, work that is also anchored to the potentiality of a free Palestine. I have shown how tour guides, by inviting tourists to participate, in Bisan Kassis's words, in the culture of resistance of harvesting and planting, keep Palestinians, even if incrementally, on land that is routinely stolen from them. Tourists planted three hundred, four hundred, or five hundred saplings at a time, to help—to "do something" as they so often want to do—but also to understand that what is happening to Palestinians and their crops in the West Bank is not anomalous. Guides do not describe an occupation circumscribed to a post-1967 and post-1993 terrain but a settler-colonial history of state-sanctioned uprooting that began before 1948. Solidarity tourism, while fraught and inadequate, and with multiple narrators correcting one another's narratives, thus functions as a historically grounded, if contested, anticolonial tactic, confronting histories of uprooting and displacement with narratives of presence and promises of futurity.

Solidarity tour guides' work is also animated by yet another conditional future and potential failure—the unstable assessment of what tourists *do* afterward and what change they can possibly effect. There are tourists in this narrative who had no plan for what they would do upon their return home, who stumbled across fragments of information in Palestine they are still trying to piece together. There are tourists who talked about hanging out, being bored, making friends, feeling guilty. There are tourists who talked about the productivity of their shame, the mobilizing effect it can have, and those who felt immobilized by guilt. Their narratives show that the "solidarity tourist" is not one figure, and "solidarity tourism" is not one thing. Solidarity tourists are motivated by different emotions—among them nostalgia, apathy, curiosity, boredom, guilt, shame, and outrage. They occupy different positions and are differently aged, gendered, classed, and raced. Like the Palestinian and anti-Zionist Israeli guides they are trying to learn from, they sometimes agree and sometimes do not. They are sharing space they probably never would share at home and are tolerating each other with a generosity that perhaps only exists in shared travel. They are in Palestine for substantially different purposes and to significantly different ends. Tour guides know this, and their tours are a gamble, hoping to reach just a portion of their audience. In this way, solidarity tourism in Palestine is a pedagogical endeavor, a long-game strategy, where success is impossible to quantify in the here and now.

At the same time, the daily work of guiding tours, reciting demolitions, narrating dispossessions, and explaining fragmentation is haunted by the possibility of failure. This daily work is haunted by the possibility that tourists will in fact do nothing. Further, that for so many, believing Palestinians necessitates traveling to Palestine, or listening to those who have traveled to (but are not from) Palestine, shows how solidarity tourism is rendered necessary by colonial logics that force Palestinians to provide evidence of histories of displacement that have long been in the historical record but have been disappeared by the knowledge produced about Palestinians that positions them as incapable of truthfully telling their own histories. It is a project with no guaranteed outcome that is wholly limited by its own starting point.

Yet, as Bisan Kassis explained, "one small thing will recalibrate you." For solidarity tour guides, there are many ways solidarity tourism "works," many ways tiny successes recalibrate tour guides and organizers and sustain them in their work. Though some who have been on tours to Palestine will do nothing, others will go home and begin divestment initiatives at their institutions, successfully lobby their organizations to boycott Israeli academic institutions, give report-backs wherein they, too, hope to reach one, or five, people, and bring other people back to Palestine to do the same. They will construct working relationships with Palestinians, using Palestinian farmers' olive oil in their company's products or collaborating with Palestinian scholars and archivists.[10] Or they will make friendships predicated on reciprocal solidarity, on a joint commitment to honor the time spent together and resolve to do the work of conscientious alliance.[11] At other times, they will do nothing other than talk to their friends and families—or students or colleagues—an act many guides and organizers defined as a success in and of itself.

In this way, solidarity tourism matters because it tells us something about pedagogy, knowledge production, and hope in the context of settler colonialism and military occupation. In its exhaustion of narration and seeming futility of repetition, it reminds us of the difficulties of quantifying pedagogical success, the patience required to wait and find out which repeated narratives stick, what stories resonate, what accounts catalyze paradigm shifts. In its endlessness even as it wishes for obsolescence, solidarity tourism tells us something about the productive potential of contradiction, the new forms of organizing that take shape under a politics of pessimism and optimism, hope and despair.[12] And, in its willingness to be recalibrated in the work of movement building by "1 percent positive" in a sea of "99 percent negative," solidarity tourism positions hope, like solidarity itself, as an incomplete and sometimes impossible endeavor, yet one that is altogether necessary.

Like the circumscribed invitation "Welcome to Palestine/Your Work Is Not Here" that began this work and is threaded throughout its pages, solidarity tourism is an invitation that is both introduction and valediction. Its meanings and implications are shifting and contradictory. The work of solidarity tourism resists evaluative assessments of its efficacy at the same time that those who craft its itineraries celebrate their victories and offer their own self-reflexive critiques. At its core, it is not meant to last forever. In fact, its organizers hope that it won't and remain haunted by the fear that it might. It is not meant to accompany, subsidize, or provide an alibi for colonial projects. It is an indictment of colonialism and a labor of decolonization at the same time that it is both constrained and defined by colonial restrictions. As a shifting and transient strategy, a fraught tactic under occupation, it refuses to treat settler colonialism as intractable, and it imagines a future under conditions that are meant to render the colonized futureless.[13] And, in the context of Palestine, where "intractable" peppers the vocabulary as much as "conflict" does, refusing narratives of peace that sediment dispossession, insisting on a tourism that centers decolonization, and demanding the impossible are necessary interventions.

NOTES

Introduction

1. Following José Esteban Muñoz, I use *disidentification* deliberately here, not because tourists are always—or even often—minoritarian subjects but because they are interpellated and repelled by the tourism project and they seek to rework tourism to accommodate the type of travel they do in Palestine. They often see themselves in the tourist yet reject identifying with the tourist, opting instead for the moniker of *organizer, activist,* or *comrade.* I track this ambivalence across interviews with tourists and the report-backs they produce in the wake of their time in Palestine. For more on disidentification as a concept, see Muñoz, *Disidentifications.*

2. Mary Louise Pratt defines the contact zone as "social spaces where cultures meet, clash, and grapple with each other, often in contexts of highly asymmetrical relations of power, such as colonialism, slavery, or their aftermaths as they are lived out in many parts of the world today" (Pratt, "Arts of the Contact Zone," 34).

3. Haunani-Kay Trask has explained, "My advice is, if you're thinking about coming to Hawai'i, don't come. Stay right where you are. If you do come, know that you are contributing to the oppression of a Native people in their home country" (Barsamian, *Louder than Bombs*, 92). On Filipino settlement in Hawai'i, see Saranillio, "Colonial Amnesia."

4. See Aikau and Gonzalez, *Detours.* See also the discussion of Kyle Kajihiro and Terri Keko'olani's work in Gonzalez and Mei-Singh's "DeTours."

5. For early work on Israeli settler colonialism, see Rodinson, *Israel*. For Patrick Wolfe's work on settler colonialism as a structure and not an event, including in Palestine, see Wolfe, *Settler Colonialism and the Transformation of Anthropology*. For a reflection on the study of settler colonialism in a Palestinian context, see Barakat, "Writing/Righting Palestine Studies"; here she argues that while the study of Zionism necessitates a settler-colonial studies analytic, it is Indigenous studies that makes for a more fitting political and intellectual home for the study of Palestine. For theorizations of the gaps and overlaps between Palestine studies and settler-colonial studies, see the 2012 special issue of *Settler Colonial Studies* and particularly the introduction: Salamanca et al., "Past Is Present." See also Bhandar and Ziadah, "Acts and Omissions," for a short primer on how Palestinians have long analyzed Israeli settler colonial practices even when they have not used the term *settler colonialism* to describe them.

6. Said, "Permission to Narrate," 27–48.

7. I am grateful to Rabab Ibrahim Abdulhadi for her insight that international solidarity presence in Palestine has come to constitute a "solidarity industry." She expressed this both in an interview I conducted with her in November 2012 and when she served as chair/discussant for our panel, "Tourism, Solidarity, Intervention, and Management: Negotiating International Presence in the Post-Oslo West Bank," at the Middle East Studies Association's annual meeting in October 2013.

8. By "history of the present," I reference Michel Foucault's *Discipline and Punish*, in which he suggests that a history of the prison needs to be written not because he is simply interested in the past, nor because he is interested in writing a history of the past in terms of the present, but because he is interested in writing a history *of* the present. In my understanding of histories of the present, I also refer to Ann Laura Stoler's reading of colonialism as a history of the present as well as her efforts, with Karen Strassler, to trouble that reading. See Stoler and Strassler, "Casting for the Colonial"; and Stoler, "Memory Work in Java." Gayatri Spivak coined the term "epistemic violence" in "Can the Subaltern Speak?" to index violence at the site of knowledge production, particularly in reference to the colonial logics that circulate in the knowledge white feminists in the Global North produce about women in the Global South.

9. Makdisi, *Palestine Inside Out*, 45.

10. Israeli settlements refer to the housing units, complexes, and neighborhoods that house Israeli citizens. These are built in the occupied West Bank in contravention of Article 49 of the Geneva Convention, which forbids an occupying power from moving its civilian population into Occupied Territories. The metaphor of an archipelago of Palestinian islands surrounded by a sea of Israeli settlements appears in the many explanations Palestinian guides and organizers give those who are touring the West Bank. See Makdisi, *Palestine Inside Out* (particularly the first chapter); and Kadman, "Acting the Landlord." See also Julien Bousac's map that begins chapter 4.

11. Kassis, "Struggle for Justice," 229.

12. During the first intifada tours, solidarity activists traveled to Beit Sahour, where they learned about the tax boycott and alternative farming practices that were making the small town near Bethlehem famous (Abu Zulof, interview by author, August 22, 2012). For more on the tax boycott during the first intifada, see Hiltermann, "Israel's Strategy to Break the Uprising." For more on histories of the tax resistance

and alternative farming in Beit Sahour, see Grace, "Tax Resistance at Bayt Sahur." For work on the specificities of political tourism during the first intifada, see Jean-Klein, "Alternative Modernities"; and Jailer and McAlister, "The Israeli-Palestinian Conflict and the US Peace Movement."

13. For more on how the Oslo Accords also changed the landscape of Israeli tourism to Palestinian spaces, see Stein, *Itineraries in Conflict*.

14. Kassis, "Struggle for Justice," 228.

15. Kassis, "Struggle for Justice," 228.

16. Kassis, "Struggle for Justice," 228.

17. Kassis, "Struggle for Justice," 228.

18. Lisle, "Consuming Danger," 100.

19. The Nakba, or catastrophe, refers to the process by which 750,000–800,000 Palestinians were forcibly displaced from their homes and lands in 1948 with the establishment of the State of Israel. Solidarity tourists often meet with the BADIL Resource Center for Palestinian Residency and Refugee Rights to learn about the ongoing Nakba through BADIL's Ongoing Nakba project.

20. Abu Zulof, interview by author, August 22, 2012.

21. Kassis, "Struggle for Justice," 230.

22. Awad, interview by author, August 16, 2012.

23. For literature on disaster tourism and dark tourism, see Foley and Lennon, *Dark Tourism*; Sharpley and Stone, *The Darker Side of Travel*; and Sion, *Death Tourism*. On adventure tourism, see Taylor, Varley, and Johnston, *Adventure Tourism*.

24. Stamatopoulou-Robbins, "Joys and Dangers of Solidarity in Palestine," 125. For a detailed account of the role of race, power, and privilege in the International Solidarity Movement, see also Mahrouse, *Conflicted Commitments*.

25. During their time in Palestine, tourists struggle with guides' attempts to reorient them, in reactions that range from pushing back against tour guides' expectations to quickly reassessing their own, phenomena I detail throughout this work.

26. I want to thank Jordan Flaherty for pointing this out to me. He spoke of his time in Palestine and a shift in International Solidarity Movement organizing after the realization that even international presence, like that of Rachel Corrie, was not protected.

27. The literature on witnessing, and particularly witnessing racialized, military, and colonial violence, is vast and varied. For studies of photography, see Wexler, *Tender Violence*; Smith, *Photography on the Color Line*; Campt, *Listening to Images*; Azoulay, *Civil Imagination*; Azoulay, *The Civil Contract of Photography*; and Azoulay, *From Palestine to Israel*. For studies on the consumption of scenes of racialized violence, see Johnson, *Soul by Soul*; Wood, *Lynching and Spectacle*; Thomas, *Desire and Disaster in New Orleans*; and Thomas, *Political Life in the Wake of the Plantation*. Studies, like Saidiya Hartman's *Scenes of Subjection*, that are not wholly about witnessing also note the abdication of complicity that witnessing can enable. In thinking about the role of the witness in Palestine, I am guided by this literature and literature on witnessing that centers questions of militarism and warfare. Recent touchstone texts include Kozol, *Distant Wars Visible*; Parks and Kaplan, *Life in the Age of Drone Warfare*; and Kaplan, *Aerial Aftermaths*. Finally, this book is anchored by critical refugee studies texts that deal with witnessing in terms of how refugees are expected

to perform for witnesses, from human rights observers to nongovernmental agencies. These works include Nguyen, *The Gift of Freedom*; Atanasoski, *Humanitarian Violence*; and Feldman, *Life Lived in Relief*. See also Emily Hue's book in progress, *Economies of Vulnerability: Humanitarian Imperialism and Performance in the Burmese Diaspora*. Following Susan Harding in *The Book of Jerry Falwell*, I see witnessing as twofold: *witnessing*, as in taking in the scene to which the tourist has been invited, and *witnessing to*, as in doing the performative work of translating what they witnessed into meaningful messaging for audiences back home. In this performance of *witnessing to*, as Harding describes in reference to evangelism, the actor crafts speech acts that are meant to act on their listener and compel them toward different affective ties—in this case, away from Zionism and toward a free Palestine.

28. Ajanebed Out, "Palestine: For All Your Professional and Academic Career Needs!"

29. Ajanebed Out, "Need a Purpose in Life?"

30. See, for example, Kincaid, *A Small Place*; and Alexander, *Pedagogies of Crossing*. In thinking about the relationships between tourism and colonialism, and especially how tourism has paved the way for colonial projects, I am indebted to Said, *Orientalism*; Mitchell, *Colonising Egypt*; and Walcott, *What the Twilight Says*.

31. Kincaid, *A Small Place*, 4. On the colonial present, see Gregory, *The Colonial Present*.

32. Alexander, *Pedagogies of Crossing*, 59, 81.

33. Teaiwa, "Reading Gauguin's *Noa Noa*," 251. Teaiwa writes about the genealogy, potential, and limitations of the term "militourism"—including its emergence through her conversations with Louis Owens in the History of Consciousness Program at the University of California, Santa Cruz—in "Reflections on Militourism, US Imperialism, and American Studies." On the coalescence and routinization of militarism and tourism in spaces of US imperial reach, see Enloe, *Bananas, Beaches, and Bases* and Gonzalez, *Securing Paradise*. On tourism, militarism, and memory, particularly in regard to the space of the museum, see Laderman, *Tours of Vietnam*.

34. MacCannell, *The Tourist*; Urry, *The Tourist Gaze*; Hutnyk, *The Rumour of Calcutta*; Mostafanezhad, *Volunteer Tourism*; MacCannell, *The Ethics of Sightseeing*.

35. On domestic tourism and race-making, see Thomas, *Desire and Disaster in New Orleans*.

36. Here, I reference the methodological approaches and research questions asked in works like Manalansan, *Global Divas*; Nguyen, *The Gift of Freedom*; and Paik, *Rightlessness*.

37. See, for example, Teves, *Defiant Indigeneity*; Imada, *Aloha America*; and Barraclough, Cheng, and Pulido, *People's Guide to Los Angeles*.

38. On fictional works justifying colonial state practice and serving as an integral part of Orientalism, see Said, *Orientalism*. For analyses of US investments—via travel and otherwise—in Palestine before, during, and after the establishment of the State of Israel, see Obenzinger, *American Palestine*; McAlister, *Epic Encounters*; and Kaplan, *Our American Israel*. For studies of Palestinian politics and institution building inside Israel during and after the establishment of Israel, see Robinson, *Citizen Strangers*; Nassar, *Brothers Apart*; Dallasheh, "Troubled Waters"; and Dallasheh, "Persevering through Colonial Transition." For detailed studies of Mandate Palestine

politics and institution building, some of which included tourism, see Feldman, *Governing Gaza*; Stanton, *This Is Jerusalem Calling*; and Seikaly, *Men of Capital*. For Middle East studies work on tourism during British Mandate Palestine, see Stanton, *This Is Jerusalem Calling*; and Stanton, "Locating Palestine's Summer Residency." For studies of Palestinian institution building, including tourism, during the Ottoman period, see Campos, *Ottoman Brothers*; and Doumani, "Rediscovering Ottoman Palestine." And for work on tourism in and to Ottoman Palestine, see Cohen-Hattab and Katz, "The Attraction of Palestine."

39. See, for example, Cohen-Hattab and Katz, "The Attraction of Palestine"; Cohen-Hattab, "Zionism, Tourism, and the Battle for Palestine"; and Stanton, "Locating Palestine's Summer Residency."

40. See, for example, Alqasis, "Israel's Grip on the Palestinian Tourism Economy"; Saadeh, "Experiential Community-Based Rural Tourism Potential in Palestine"; Isaac et al., "Giving Palestinian Tourism(s) a Voice"; and Ahmad, "Tourism in the Service of Occupation and Annexation."

41. Hazbun, *Beaches, Ruins, Resorts*; Stein, *Itineraries in Conflict*; and Zerubavel, *Recovered Roots*. Other work on tourism in Israel includes books on birthright tourism, like Kelner, *Tours That Bind*.

42. Studies of alternative tours in Palestine include Koensler and Papa, "Political Tourism in the Israeli-Palestinian Space"; Noy, "The Political Ends of Tourism"; and Bel'Hassen, Uriely, and Assor, "The Touristification of a Conflict Zone." See also Eldad Brin's site-specific studies of Jerusalem (Brin, "Politically-Oriented Tourism in Jerusalem") and studies that attempt to illustrate "both sides" of tourism in Palestine/Israel, like Richard Clarke's work on Israeli settler tours and Palestinian alternative tours in Hebron (Clarke, "Self-Presentation in a Contested City"). For studies of Israeli tours to Palestinian space, see Stein, *Itineraries in Conflict*; Stein, "Israeli Routes through Nakba Landscapes; and Amram, "Digesting the Massacre." For thoughtful reflections on the use of tourism in Palestine as a pedagogical endeavor to teach US students about settler colonialism, see Lubin et al., "The Israel/Palestine Field School"; and Klinker and Morrison, "On the Pedagogy of 'Boomerangs.'" For a careful study of the use of tourism to complicate Jewish American allegiance to Israel, and the extent to which these tours in fact do shift allegiances, see Schneider, "It Changed My Sympathy."

43. Ahmed, "Making Feminist Points."

44. Said, *Orientalism*, 31. Indeed, he writes, "Orientalism is after all a system for citing works and authors."

45. In "A Manifesto for Patchwork Ethnography," Gökce Günel, Saiba Varma, and Chika Watanabe theorize what they call patchwork ethnography. My project began in graduate school, was undertaken in American studies and women's and gender studies programs, and was not anchored in an anthropology department. Thus, it was not a legible project for full-year anthropology grants, nor was I willing to affiliate with an Israeli institution to extend my duration in the field. For this reason, alongside the flexibility and capaciousness of my interdisciplinary training, I too stitched together my fieldwork in a way that could only be described as patchwork. For a longer reflection on how I came to this project during graduate school, how I did fieldwork in an underfunded interdisciplinary graduate program, how the

dissertation began, and how I shaped it toward a book manuscript, see Kelly, "Locating Palestine within American Studies."

Chapter One. The Colonial Calculus of Veracity

1. Solidarity delegations to Palestine and to Palestinian refugee camps in the broader region were not inaugurated during the first intifada. Indeed, Black Panther presence in Palestine included Malcolm X's 1964 trip to Gaza, during which he visited mosques and refugee camps and held a press conference; and Huey Newton's 1980 trip, during which he visited Palestinian refugee camps in Lebanon and met with Yasser Arafat. For more on these visits and their political import for global anticolonial and antiracist organizing, see Fischbach, *Black Power and Palestine*; Feldman, *A Shadow over Palestine*; and Lubin, *Geographies of Liberation*. For a sustained discussion of the past and present of Black-Palestine solidarity, including a roundtable with Ahmad Abuznaid, Phillip Agnew, Maytha Alhassen, Kristian Davis Bailey, and Nadya Tannous on past and present delegations to Palestine (Abuznaid et al., "Roundtable"), see the "Black-Palestinian Transnational Solidarity" special issue of *Journal of Palestine Studies* 48, no. 4 (2019). For a history on Palestinian engagement with Black freedom struggles in the United States, see Nassar, "Palestinian Engagement." I focus here on delegations during the first intifada not because they were the first but because they mark a moment when delegations to Palestine began to become more formalized (though not yet legalized)—a moment when visiting Palestine as a tourist became a central way to engage with Palestine as an activist.

2. I specify that Gluck is a white Jewish American to disrupt the assumption that Jewish American, as a category, is synonymous with whiteness. As so many scholars have labored to show, and as Jews of color organizers in the United States have insisted, Jewish American is a category that does not necessarily index race and racialization. Indeed, the literature on how Jews in the United States erroneously became understood as transparently white is extensive, from books like Karen Brodkin's *How Jews Became White Folks and What That Says about Race in America* to articles like Andrea Freud Lowenstein's "Confronting Stereotypes: Reading Maus in Crown Heights." To scratch the surface of this literature in relationship to Palestine/Israel alone, particularly around the Zionist severing of Jew from Arab, see Alcalay, *After Jews and Arabs*; Anidjar, *The Jew, the Arab*; Azoulay, *Potential History*; Bouteldja, *Whites, Jews, and Us*; Raz-Krakotzkin, "On the Right Side of the Barricades"; Shohat, *On the Arab-Jew, Palestine, and Other Displacements*; and Shohat, *Taboo Memories, Diasporic Voices*. See also *Unruly*, home page.

3. Barbara Harlow, as my dissertation cochair in the beginning and my friend and mentor in the end, guided this project since its inception. She was never convinced of the merits of solidarity tourism in Palestine, though she both went on her own solidarity tour during the first intifada and she positively reviewed Gluck's book in 1994. Indeed, at my dissertation defense, she acknowledged her long skepticism of the phenomenon and, as we closed the conversation, said, "Now I'm even more convinced by this project and even less convinced by solidarity tourism!" My intent has never been to either diminish or garner support for solidarity tours. It has been

to trouble the easy evaluative claims we make about them—a commitment shaped, in large part, by conversations with Barbara.

4. See Saliba, "Review."

5. Saliba, "Review," 753.

6. Tamari, "Tourists with Agendas," 24.

7. For more on "womenandchildren" as a singular phenomenon and the presupposition of Palestinian men as always-already criminal, see Mikdashi, "Can Palestinian Men Be Victims?"; and Elia, "Looking Beyond 'Women and Children' in Gaza's Casualties."

8. For more on the struggle to centralize in Palestine in the US Left, see Pennock, *The Rise of the Arab American Left.*

9. I am grateful to A. Naomi Paik for encouraging me to clarify the relationship between evidence and epistemology in solidarity tours.

10. Gluck, *An American Feminist in Palestine*, 62–63.

11. Gluck, *An American Feminist in Palestine*, 63.

12. Gluck, *An American Feminist in Palestine*, 63.

13. Gluck, *An American Feminist in Palestine*, 63.

14. Gluck, *An American Feminist in Palestine*, 11.

15. Gluck, *An American Feminist in Palestine*, 124.

16. Gluck, *An American Feminist in Palestine*, 143.

17. Gluck, *An American Feminist in Palestine*, 172.

18. Gluck, *An American Feminist in Palestine*, 46, emphasis mine.

19. Gluck, *An American Feminist in Palestine*, 46.

20. Gluck, *An American Feminist in Palestine*, 29.

21. Gluck, *An American Feminist in Palestine*, 29.

22. Gluck, *An American Feminist in Palestine*, 34, emphasis mine.

23. Gluck, *An American Feminist in Palestine*, 65.

24. Gluck, *An American Feminist in Palestine*, 143.

25. Gluck, *An American Feminist in Palestine*, 143.

26. Gluck, *An American Feminist in Palestine*, 143.

27. Gluck, *An American Feminist in Palestine*, 143.

28. Pennock, *The Rise of the Arab American Left*, 91.

29. Center for Constitutional Rights, National Lawyers Guild, and ACLU of Southern California, "Charges Dropped."

30. Gluck, interview by author, April 27, 2019.

31. Gluck, interview by author, April 27, 2019.

32. Gluck, interview by author, April 27, 2019.

33. Denson, "Know Thine Enemy," 7.

34. Denson, "Know Thine Enemy," 7.

35. Denson, "Know Thine Enemy," 7, emphasis mine.

36. Rybnicki, "To Gaza and Back," 19.

37. Rybnicki, "To Gaza and Back," 19.

38. Rybnicki, "To Gaza and Back," 19.

39. In thinking about the conversion from statistic to human, I am guided by the literature on how colonial rule has shaped the category of the human, specifically

in the Middle East. Samera Esmeir, for example, details how British colonial rule in Egypt functioned as a "constellation of secular modern powers aiming precisely to humanize Egyptians by declaring them subjects of the rule of law" (Esmeir, *Juridical Humanity*, 4.). Esmeir's research enables us to ask, What does it mean to humanize subjects by declaring them subjects of—and subject to—the law? For the purposes of this study, what does it mean to humanize subjects by positioning them as witnessed, as seen? If, in rendering a subject seen, one names their humanity, it not only positions their humanity as both malleable and mediated; it also, as Esmeir notes, erases the subjugation inherent in that naming—the ways that the jurisdiction to name is an exercise in colonial power.

40. For one of the most instructive and expansive texts on the first intifada, see Lockman and Beinin, *Intifada*. Beginning, too, with the figure of the witness, the edited volume covers multiple aspects of the uprising, including the significance of the timing of the intifada two decades after 1967, the role of children in the intifada, the significance of Palestinian women's organizing, the effects of the intifada on Israel, and the relationship(s) between the United States and Israel. In a multilayered review essay, Erika Alin covers much of the (then extant) literature on the first intifada, pointing to a collection of eight texts, including *Intifada*, that demarcate the "varying dimensions of this major event in the history of the Palestinian national struggle, including its underlying and more immediate causes, its political leadership and social class structure, its impact on Palestinian politics and society, and its consequences for the political future of the Palestinian movement" (Alin, "Dynamics of the Palestinian Uprising"). See also Naser-Najjab and Khatib, "The First Intifada," for a comparative analysis of how engaging with thinkers and leaders who were active in resistance movements during the first intifada allows us to think about contemporary resistance and reflect on how the entrenched fragmentation of Palestinian land and people today necessitates new praxes of anticolonial movement building.

41. Scholarship on shifts in US foreign policy post-1967 is extensive and expansive. For a short reflective primer, see Nassar et al., "Fifty Years of Occupation." This piece covers shifts in Israeli society, 1967's effects on both Palestinian nationalism and Arab states, the lands Israel occupied in 1967, the role of Palestinian citizens in Israel in the Palestinian national cause post-1967, and the effects of the entrenchment of occupation in Gaza.

42. See McAlister, *Epic Encounters*, particularly chapter 4: "The Good Fight: Israel after Vietnam, 1972–1980."

43. Gluck, *An American Feminist in Palestine*, 30.

44. Gluck, *An American Feminist in Palestine*, 30, emphasis mine.

45. Gluck, *An American Feminist in Palestine*, 96.

46. Gluck, *An American Feminist in Palestine*, 182.

47. "Academics Refute Israeli Claims," 4.

48. "Academics Refute Israeli Claims," 4.

49. Hamad and Nuseibeh, "BZU Discusses Uprising," 8–9.

50. Hamad and Nuseibeh, "BZU Discusses Uprising," 8–9.

51. Hamad and Nuseibeh, "BZU Discusses Uprising," 8–9.

52. Hamad and Nuseibeh, "BZU Discusses Uprising," 8–9.

53. Denson, "Know Thine Enemy," 11. The transliteration of al-Am'ari has changed since publication.

54. Denson, "Know Thine Enemy," 11.

55. Denson, "Know Thine Enemy," 11.

56. Denson, "Know Thine Enemy," 11.

57. Denson, "Know Thine Enemy," 15.

58. Denson, "Know Thine Enemy," 15, emphasis mine.

59. Denson, "Know Thine Enemy," 15.

60. Denson, "Know Thine Enemy," 15.

61. Gluck, *An American Feminist in Palestine*, 39.

62. For a work that takes the maiming of Palestinians as one of its central subjects, see Puar, *The Right to Maim*.

63. Gluck, *An American Feminist in Palestine*, 39.

64. Gluck, interview by author, April 27, 2019.

65. Gluck, *An American Feminist in Palestine*, 39. Gluck's text contains many moments like this where she invokes, and then dismisses, comparisons between conditions Palestinians suffer and those some communities in the United States suffer, particularly in Chicago. In these moments, there is an unspoken invocation of Blackness as a comparison that Gluck gestures toward but does not explore in detail, raising the question of what her book would look like if she (and many other US tourists) were to think comparatively about state violence against Black and brown youth in the United States and Palestinian youth in Palestine/Israel. However, as chapter 7 makes clear, over the past decade of doing this research, amidst Black Lives Matter protests during and after 2014 and 2020, I have also watched these comparisons become more pronounced and more thoughtful.

66. Mary, "From the Diary of an American in Occupied Palestine," 4.

67. Mary, "From the Diary of an American in Occupied Palestine," 4.

68. Mary, "From the Diary of an American in Occupied Palestine," 4.

69. Denson, "Know Thine Enemy," 9.

70. Mullen and Wedeman, "They Went to the Beach to Play."

71. Denson, "Know Thine Enemy," 9.

72. Denson, "Know Thine Enemy," 9.

73. Denson, "Know Thine Enemy," 9.

74. Denson, "Know Thine Enemy," 9.

75. For more on mobilizing versus stultifying guilt, see Gilroy, *Postcolonial Melancholia*, 99.

76. Ngai, *Ugly Feelings*.

77. Mary, "From the Diary of an American in Occupied Palestine," 9, emphasis mine.

78. Mary, "From the Diary of an American in Occupied Palestine," 9.

79. In 2014, Israel introduced the Anti-Terror Bill, which sought to recriminalize the Palestinian flag. See Strickland, "Israel Plans to Reintroduce Ban on Palestinian Flag."

80. Mary, "From the Diary of an American in Occupied Palestine," 9.

81. The photo essay is named after a line in Palestinian poet Mahmoud Darwish's poem "The Earth Is Closing on Us," which asks, "Where should birds fly after the last sky?" See Darwish, "The Earth Is Closing on Us."

82. Ziadah, "We Teach Life, Sir."

83. Said, *After the Last Sky*, 3.

84. Said, *After the Last Sky*, 3.

85. Said, *After the Last Sky*, 3, emphasis mine.

86. Said, *After the Last Sky*, 3.

87. Said, *After the Last Sky*, 3.

88. Gluck, *An American Feminist in Palestine*, 120.

89. Gluck, *An American Feminist in Palestine*, 120.

90. Gluck, *An American Feminist in Palestine*, 122.

91. Gluck, *An American Feminist in Palestine*, 122. "The Israelis are not our representatives," the woman explained to Gluck and her tour group, "and we want a solution for us."

92. Gluck, *An American Feminist in Palestine*, 46. The transliteration of the thobe has changed since publication.

93. Gluck, *An American Feminist in Palestine*, 46, emphasis mine.

94. Simpson, *Mohawk Interruptus*, 10.

95. Said, *After the Last Sky*, 4.

96. Denson, "Know Thine Enemy," 6. Denson writes: "Ming Fay was born in Shanghai during the Japanese occupation and fled Mao's Red Army with his family to Hong Kong. René Castro was exiled from Chile after being wounded and imprisoned for two years by the military regime of General Augusto Pinochet Ugarte because he had supported the former president, Salvador Allende. Yong Soon Min was a child in Seoul, Korea who remembers a cityscape brimming with truckloads of soldiers during the 1960 overthrow of the government. Dieter Froese had been a child when his family was forced to leave East Prussia during the Second World War. And the Palestinian family of Magda Dajani's father lost their home and orange groves to the Israelis when they were forced to flee Jaffa at gunpoint and settle in a refugee camp, only to be deported from Israel later on" (7).

97. Murphy, "The Intifada Makes Many Artists," 33.

98. Murphy, "The Intifada Makes Many Artists," 33. Adnan Zobidy is the father of Yazan al-Zubaidy, a former fieldworker for the Olive Tree Campaign, discussed at length in chapter 3.

99. Murphy, "The Intifada Makes Many Artists," 33.

100. Berkowitz, "Somebody's Brother, Somebody's Son," 62.

101. Dajani, "Mona Lisa Minus the Forbidden Colors of the Palestinian Flag," 63.

102. Meibers, "Untitled," 68.

103. Meibers, "Untitled," 68.

104. Morita, "House Demolition II," 70.

105. Willis, "Mothers and the Shebab," 74.

106. Middle East Children's Alliance, "Break the Silence Mural Project," 75.

107. Middle East Children's Alliance, "Break the Silence Mural Project."

108. Middle East Children's Alliance, "Break the Silence Mural Project."

109. See Art Forces, "Vision and History." In June 2021, Susan Greene and Art Forces, along with the Madaa Creative Center and Eyewitness Palestine, cohosted a virtual delegation to Silwan, in part to discuss the mural project "I Witness Silwan,"

which showcases the painted eyes of martyrs witnessing Israel's repeated attempts to force Palestinians out of Silwan. Greene writes about the project in "I Witness Silwan."

110. Middle East Children's Alliance, "History."

111. Middle East Children's Alliance, "Board, Staff, and Advisors."

112. Urry, *The Tourist Gaze.*

Chapter Two. Asymmetrical Itineraries

1. Bousac, "L'archipel de Palestine orientale." See also Mackey, "West Bank Archipelago."

2. Aware of how his map may lend itself to accusations of depicting Israeli Jews being "pushed into the sea," Bousac underscores that his map is distinctly not about "'drowning' or 'flooding' the Israeli population, nor dividing territories along ethnic lines." He explains that it is, rather, "an illustration of the West Bank's ongoing fragmentation based on the (originally temporary) A/B/C zoning which came out of the Oslo process" (Mackey, quoting a *Strange Maps* blog interview, in "West Bank Archipelago"). It should also be noted that this map is not aspirational but diagnostic; it documents the post-Oslo fragmentation that has already marred the West Bank and Gaza.

3. I borrow the phrase "regulatory regime" from Braverman, "Uprooting Identities," 239.

4. An abridged version of this chapter appears as "Asymmetrical Itineraries: Militarism, Tourism, and Solidarity in Occupied Palestine," in the "Tours of Duty/Tours of Leisure" special issue of *American Quarterly* 68, no. 3 (2016): 723–45.

5. Makdisi, *Palestine Inside Out*, 92. See also Peteet, *Space and Mobility in Palestine.*

6. To similarly spell out the post-Oslo archipelagic fragmentation of the West Bank, one lecturer for the Applied Research Institute of Jerusalem, which meets frequently with solidarity tour groups, jokes, "It's like Indonesia, but instead of the sea, we have the C."

7. B'Tselem, "Taking Control of Land." This 2013 data also serves as a reminder of how much land Palestinians in the West Bank have continued to lose, annually, since then.

8. B'Tselem, "Taking Control of Land."

9. B'Tselem, "Taking Control of Land."

10. B'Tselem, "Taking Control of Land."

11. B'Tselem, "Taking Control of Land."

12. Erakat, *Justice for Some*, 213.

13. Pappé, "More Oslos."

14. Pappé, "More Oslos."

15. Makdisi, *Palestine Inside Out*, 85. For a detailed account of the effects of these closures, curfews, and restrictions on mobility in the post-Oslo West Bank, see Peteet, *Space and Mobility in Palestine.* On the anticolonial resistance of fragmented mobility in the West Bank through public transportation, see Griffin, *Vehicles of Decolonization.*

16. Makdisi, *Palestine Inside Out*, 92.

17. Shehadeh, *Palestinian Walks*, 32. Borrowing Eyal Weizman's description of the "politics of verticality" that inhere in settlers claiming hilltops, Derek Gregory also

traces the division of the West Bank into noncontiguous Bantustan-like territories. He describes the "baroque system of underpasses [and] overpasses" that enables Israel to maintain its settlement blocs (Gregory, *The Colonial Present*, 125). See also Segal and Weizman, *A Civilian Occupation*; and Weizman, *Hollow Land*.

18. Shehadeh, *Palestinian Walks*, 33.

19. Shehadeh, *Palestinian Walks*, 87–97, 186–98.

20. Rashid, *Brokers of Deceit*, 49. See also Makdisi, *Palestine Inside Out*, 91. In an unprecedented move, multiple members of Congress immediately challenged this weapons sale. See Reuters, "US House Democrats Offer Resolution Blocking $735 Million Israel Weapons Sale."

21. Hawari, "Radical Futures."

22. Democracy Now!, "Kerry: Settlement Expansion Doesn't Threaten Peace Talks." John Kerry, speaking to an audience in Brazil, said, "The policy of the United States of America with respect to all settlements is that they are illegitimate, and we oppose settlements taking place at any time, not just the time of the peace process. But, here's the 'but,' that said, Prime Minster Netanyahu was completely upfront with me and with President Abbas that he would be announcing some additional building that would take place in places that will not affect the peace map."

23. Said, *Peace and Its Discontents*, 163.

24. Awad, interview by author, August 16, 2012.

25. Siraj Center for Holy Land Studies, home page.

26. For a primer on Brand Israel and Israeli pinkwashing campaigns, see Schulman, "A Documentary Guide to Brand Israel." For Palestinian organizing and scholarship that names and resists Israeli pinkwashing initiatives, see Al Qaws for Gender and Sexual Diversity in Palestinian Society (accessed April 13, 2022, http://alqaws.org/siteEn/index); and Aswat: Palestinian Feminist Center for Gender and Sexual Freedoms (accessed April 13, 2022, https://www.aswatgroup.org). And for my own analysis of how Israeli pinkwashing initiatives in fact celebrate the militarized violence they are understood to obscure, see Kelly, "Israeli Gay Tourist Initiatives."

27. Awad, interview by author, August 16, 2012.

28. Awad, interview by author, August 16, 2012.

29. Said, "Permission to Narrate."

30. Hilo, interview by author, July 23, 2012.

31. Hilo, interview by author, July 23, 2012.

32. Hilo, interview by author, July 23, 2012.

33. Hilo, interview by author, July 23, 2012. See also Said, *Orientalism*.

34. Hilo, interview by author, July 23, 2012.

35. Hilo, interview by author, July 23, 2012.

36. Hilo, interview by author, July 23, 2012.

37. Said writes, "There have been refugees before. There have been new states built on the ruins of old. The unique thing about this situation is Palestine's unusual centrality, which privileges a Western master narrative, highlighting Jewish alienation and redemption—with all of it taking place as a modern spectacle before the world's eyes." He continues: "When Palestinians are told to stop complaining and settle elsewhere like other refugees before them, they are entitled to respond that no

other refugees have been required systematically to watch an unending ceremony of public approbation for the political movement, army, or country that made them refugees and occupied their territory. . . . To top it all, Palestinians are expected to participate in the dismantling of their own history at the same time" (Said, "Permission to Narrate," 258).

38. Awad, interview by author, August 16, 2012.

39. Awad, interview by author, August 16, 2012.

40. For more on strategies of containment and post-Oslo enclosure of Palestinian communities as time-honored Israeli strategies, see Fields, *Enclosure*.

41. Awad, interview by author, August 16, 2012.

42. Said writes, "The divide itself was to redivide and subdivide an already divided Palestinian territory into three subzones, Areas A, B, and C, in ways entirely devised and controlled by the Israeli side since, I have pointed out for several years, the Palestinians until only quite recently had neither maps of their own nor, among the negotiating team, any individuals who were familiar enough with the actual geography to contest decisions or provide alternative plans" (Said, *From Oslo to Iraq and the Road Map*, 12).

43. Awad, interview by author, August 16, 2012.

44. Awad, interview by author, August 16, 2012.

45. Awad, interview by author, August 16, 2012.

46. Awad, interview by author, August 16, 2012.

47. See "Code of Conduct for Tourism in the Holy Land: A Palestinian Initiative." See also Palestinian Campaign for the Academic and Cultural Boycott of Israel (PACBI)'s 2019 "Do No Harm! Palestinian Call for Ethical Tourism/Pilgrimage."

48. Anonymous, interview by author, September 2, 2019.

49. Anonymous, interview by author, September 2, 2019.

50. The literature on the post-Oslo West Bank, the prevalence of NGOs in Palestine, and the racialized neoliberal turn in Palestine/Israel since the mid-1990s is substantial. For examples, see Haddad, *Palestine Ltd.*; and Clarno, *Neoliberal Apartheid*.

51. Gilroy, *Postcolonial Melancholia*, 99.

52. Many solidarity tours employ narratives of sameness between delegates and Palestinians on the basis of solidarities between people subject to different forms of racialized state violence. Delegations of this sort include the 2011 Women of Color and Indigenous Feminist Delegation; the 2011, 2012, and 2014 Interfaith Peace Builder's African Heritage Delegations; and the 2015 delegation of artists, journalists, and organizers from Ferguson, Black Lives Matter, the Black Youth Project 100, and the Dream Defenders. These delegations are instrumental in coalitional movement building, especially around Boycott, Divestment, and Sanctions (BDS) organizing. At the same time, while in Palestine, these delegates often experience a freedom of mobility that is foreclosed to many of the organizers they meet in Palestine. It is this difference that I am flagging here: a difference in mobility, access, and privilege *in Palestine*, which can coexist with delegates' shared experiences of colonization and racism with Palestinians, and the complicated ethics of their presence in Palestine as US tourists (a paradox that is also evident, for example, in Sarah Alzanoon's interview analyzed in this chapter).

53. Stamatopoulou-Robbins, "Joys and Dangers of Solidarity in Palestine," 115.

54. I borrow this notion of rearranging desire from Gayatri Spivak, who argues that education in the humanities attempts to be "an *uncoercive* rearrangement of desires." Spivak, "Righting the Wrongs," 526, emphasis in original. Similarly, I see in solidarity tourism an attempt on the part of tour guides to shift tourists' (read: students') allegiances, to ask them (noncoercively) to rethink their unexamined assumptions, and to encourage them to listen for guidance on precisely what their role in Palestinian freedom struggles should be.

55. For more on these statistics and the fluctuations between them, see Brannon, "Hebron Settlers"; Hatuqa, "Saving the West Bank's Shuhada Street"; and International Middle East Media Center, "Palestinian Popular Resistance in Hebron."

56. B'Tselem, "Hebron City Center."

57. Goff, interview by author, September 14, 2013, emphasis mine.

58. For more on the militarization of Palestinian space, see Shehadeh's descriptions of landscape transformation (*Palestinian Walks*), Weizman's study of the (literal) hierarchies of militarized control in the West Bank (*Hollow Land*), and Gregory's analysis of the spatialized manifestations of military power in Palestine (*The Colonial Present*). For more on the mobility of the tourist (and soldier-as-tourist) and the porousness of the war/tourism divide, see Lisle, "Consuming Danger."

59. Lory, interview by author, October 4, 2013.

60. Lory, interview by author, October 4, 2013.

61. Alzanoon, interview by author, November 22, 2014.

62. Alzanoon, interview by author, November 22, 2014.

63. Alzanoon, interview by author, November 22, 2014.

64. Alzanoon, interview by author, November 22, 2014.

65. Many thanks to A. Naomi Paik for helping me think through the simultaneous displacement and privilege that coalesces in Alzanoon's descriptions of home.

66. I am grateful to Bisan Adnan Salhi for helping me think through the experience of diaspora Palestinians in Palestine and the reminders of exile that they experience on our panel "Spaces Under Construction: Building towards an Anthropology of Contemporary Settler Colonialism in Palestine-Israel," at the American Anthropological Association Annual Meeting in December 2014.

67. For a detailed analysis of colonization, resistance, and tourism in Manger Square, after 1967 and before the signing of the Oslo Accords and the nominal withdrawal of Israeli troops from the center of Bethlehem in 1995, see Barnard, "Colonization and Resistance."

68. Harris, "In Little Town of Bethlehem."

69. Harris, "In Little Town of Bethlehem." Lisa Bhungalia's forthcoming book, *"From the American People": Aid, War, and US Security State in Palestine*, is an ethnographic study of USAID in Palestine. For articles emerging from this careful research, see Bhungalia, "From the American People"; and Bhungalia, "Managing Violence."

70. Beiler, "US-Made Weapons Used on Bethlehemites." See also Beiler and ActiveStills, "PHOTOS: This Tear Gas Brought to You by the USA." See also Harris, "In Little Town of Bethlehem."

71. Beiler, "US-Made Weapons Used on Bethlehemites."

72. Al-Zubaidy, interview by author, September 6, 2012.

73. Al-Zubaidy, interview by author, September 6, 2012.

74. Al-Zubaidy, interview by author, September 6, 2012.

75. Al-Zubaidy, interview by author, September 6, 2012.

76. Al-Zubaidy, interview by author, September 6, 2012.

77. As a recent example, on a 2020 episode of *Jeopardy!*, contestant Katie Needle correctly answered the clue "Built in the 300s A.D., the Church of the Nativity," with the question "What is Palestine?" Her answer, however, was deemed incorrect and the correct answer was her competitor's "What is Israel?" (Siddiqui, "Outrage after Jeopardy Host Rules Bethlehem Not in Palestine").

Chapter Three. Recitation against Erasure

1. For an extended meditation on the olive as a way to understand the selective consumption of Palestinianness alongside Palestinian displacement and the erasure of Palestinian landscapes, see Lila Sharif's forthcoming book and 2014 dissertation, "Savory Politics: Land, Memory, and the Ecological Occupation of Palestine."

2. I developed the initial thoughts for the work in this chapter early in graduate school in Ella Shohat's course Imaging Palestine and Israel at New York University and Ann Laura Stoler's course Anthropology of the Present at the New School, during which Stoler was drafting *Imperial Debris: On Ruins and Ruination*. I credit the way I think about trees in Palestine to the joining of work across these two classes. I include this note both to honor the work we do in graduate school that can shape central parts of our first monographs and to reiterate the value of interdisciplinary work across the humanities and social sciences and the need for scholarship of this sort to be prioritized and funded by universities. For more of my reflections on the fieldwork I did in graduate school, despite a paucity of funding, see Kelly, "Locating Palestine within American Studies." For more on why graduate students, within and outside the humanities, need to be paid enough to work where they live, see the archived posts at https://payusmoreucsc.com/, compiled by graduate students on strike in 2020 at my home institution. See also Evans, Mitchell, and Wondergem. "Scenes from the Wildcat Strike: A Documentary History."

3. Brownsell, "Resistance Is Fertile." For coverage on To Be There's work, see Ibrahim, "Olive Groves in the West Bank Have Become a Battleground."

4. Though not equivalent in content or context, I am reminded here of Saidiya Hartman's description of the subjectivity of the enslaved recognized only as they violate the law or are violated, "considered a subject only insofar as he was criminal(ized), wounded body, or mortified flesh" (Hartman, *Scenes of Subjection*, 94).

5. While Slyomovics used the transliteration Ein Houd, transliterations evolve, and most current accounts of the Palestinian village use the name 'Ayn Hawd.

6. Slyomovics, *The Object of Memory*, 48.

7. Slyomovics, *The Object of Memory*, 49.

8. Massad, "The Persistence of the Palestinian Question," 6.

9. Shohat, *Taboo Memories, Diasporic Voices*, 216.

10. On Israel's self-positioning of "in but not of" the Middle East, see Shohat's essays, particularly "The Invention of the Mizrahim."

11. Davidson, "Christian Zionism as a Representation of American Manifest Destiny," 160.

12. Shohat, *Taboo Memories, Diasporic Voices*, 217. Similarly, Massad notes that Zionism "insisted that only those Jews who answered its transformative call in its settler colony escaped the fate that befell Jews who insisted on their diaspora/Jewish condition" (Massad, "The Persistence of the Palestinian Question," 5).

13. Schama, *Landscape and Memory*, 5–7, quoted in Slyomovics, *The Object of Memory*, 49.

14. Schama, *Landscape and Memory*, 5–7, quoted in Slyomovics, *The Object of Memory*, 49. The Jewish National Fund (JNF) was created in 1901 as a subsidiary of the World Zionist Organization (WZO) to "acquire lands in Palestine and Syria" for the benefit of "persons of Jewish race, religion, or origin" (BADIL, "The Jewish National Fund"). The JNF (with the WZO) funded the Zionist military effort in 1947–1948, and by 1954, 35 percent of the land that belonged to internally displaced peoples and refugees was transferred to the JNF for substantive amounts of money donated (through tax-exempt charity status) from abroad. In 2007, the JNF controlled 13 percent of the land in Israel exclusively for the use and benefit of Jews. After the 2009 Israel Land Authority Law, and the amendment of the 2010 Land Acquisition Law, the JNF continued to have six out of thirteen members represented in the Israel Land Authority, thus "continuing to play a key role in the policies and programs pertaining to 93 percent of the land of Israel" (Mahajneh, "Situating the JNF in Israel's Land Laws"). The JNF has thus been central to the colonization of Palestine and continues to hold huge amounts of Palestinian land for exclusively Jewish use.

15. See Cohen, *The Politics of Planting*; Slyomovics, *The Object of Memory*; Long, "(En)planting Israel"; Braverman, "Uprooting Identities"; Braverman, "Planting the Promised Landscape"; Braverman, *Planted Flags*; Long, "Rooting Diaspora, Reviving Nation"; Lorber, "Keren Kayemet LeYisrael and Environmental Racism in Palestine"; Pappé and Jaber, "Ethnic Cleansing by All Means"; and Fields, *Enclosure*.

16. On deforestation in North America, see Teisch, *Engineering Nature*. On deforestation in Vietnam, see Nguyen, "Coal Mining"; and Aso, *Rubber and the Making of Vietnam*. On afforestation in South Africa, see Brett Bennett's work, particularly on the racial dynamics of white settlers planting Australian trees in South Africa, in "Naturalising Australian Trees in South Africa," and *Plantations and Protected Areas*.

17. For a detailed study of how the JNF drew on other settler-colonial models, transnationally, to institute its agricultural stamp on Palestine, see Teisch, *Engineering Nature*.

18. Herzl, *Altneuland*, 125. Many other Zionist settlers and their advocates made a similar case. One colonist characterized the Valley of Esdraelon as a "desolate plain of five 'small and squalid Arab villages'"; an engineer, who forged agricultural links between California, Australia, Hawai'i, and Palestine, described Palestine as "impaired by centuries of wasteful [Arab] cultivation" (Teisch, *Engineering Nature*, 164). Mark Twain himself, traveling to Palestine in 1867, described it as a "hopeless, dreary, heartbroken land"; the adjectives he used to describe the place and its people

included silent, mournful, nasty, miserable, squalid, filthy, infested, sore-eyed, muti-
lated, and decay[ed] (Twain, *Innocents Abroad*, 457; other adjectives quoted in Press,
"How a Mark Twain Travel Book Turned Palestine into a Desert").

19. Cohen, *The Politics of Planting*, 248.

20. Said, *The Question of Palestine*, 9. Said writes, "Because the land was Palestine
and therefore controlled, in the Western mind, not by its present realities and inhabitants, but by its glorious, portentous past and the seemingly limitless potential of its
(possibly) just as glorious future, Palestine was seen as a place to be possessed *anew*
and reconstructed" (9, emphasis in original).

21. The Haganah became the Israel Defense Forces, the official army of Israel, on
May 26, 1948. The massacre at Dayr Yasin took place on April 9, 1948. Operation
Nachshon was planned by the Jewish Agency chairman David Ben-Gurion and the
Haganah General Staff with "the intention and effort to clear a whole area, perma-
nently, of Arab villages and hostile or potentially hostile villagers" (Khalidi, *All That
Remains*, 278).

22. Khalidi, *All That Remains*, 290.

23. Khalidi, *All That Remains*, 290–91.

24. Cohen, *The Politics of Planting*, 65.

25. Cohen, *The Politics of Planting*, 65. Cohen does not assign blame for the
burning down of the forest, writing largely in passive voice: "The work on the slope
continued for four years, though at the end of this period a fire destroyed nearly all
of the four hundred dunams that had been planted" (65).

26. Cohen, *The Politics of Planting*, 68.

27. For more on contemporary village lands, see Zochrot, "Dayr Yasin."

28. Cohen, *The Politics of Planting*, 69.

29. Cohen, *The Politics of Planting*, 63.

30. Cohen, *The Politics of Planting*, 72.

31. Cohen, *The Politics of Planting*, 97.

32. Cohen, *The Politics of Planting*, 99.

33. Cohen, *The Politics of Planting*, 67. Cohen identifies three purposes for which
the JNF, in conjunction with foreign donors, Israeli citizens, and the Israeli government, planted trees after the 1948 establishment of the state: as "'security groves,'
stands of trees that either sheltered roads from the view of observers and soldiers
in the hostile neighbor states, or provided a marshaling point for Israeli military
forces"; as "memorials to individuals and communities"; and as "planting to hold the
land . . . [and] for the prevention of land use by Arab citizens of Israel who had lost
their lands in the 1948 Arab-Israeli War or its aftermath" (63; quoted in Slyomovics,
The Object of Memory, 48). A fourth reason, evidenced here, is to cover up village
remains and the remnants of the Palestinian lives and livelihoods that predated
the establishment of the Israeli state. For more on the use of trees to cover up village
remains, see Pappé and Jaber, "Ethnic Cleansing by All Means."

34. Bloom, "Letter from Jayyous."

35. Cohen, *The Politics of Planting*, 128.

36. Cohen, *The Politics of Planting*, 128.

37. Cohen, *The Politics of Planting*, 128.

38. Military Order 1015, Order Concerning the Supervision of Fruits and Vegetables, Judea and Samaria" (1982), quoted in Cohen, *The Politics of Planting*, 127n63.

39. Cohen, *The Politics of Planting*, 127. Also cited in Said, *After the Last Sky*, 28. Said does not mention the fine but does mention Law 1039, which also penalizes "illegal planting."

40. Yitzhak Ben-Zvi, the second president of Israel, commemorated renewed planting efforts in 1956 with the words, "For more than seventy generations Jerusalem has been ruined and its surroundings barren. . . . There were in this land large and powerful countries . . . but none of them took care of Jerusalem, to make the city and its surroundings grow, to beautify it with grass and trees. It will be a sign that since the ruin of Jerusalem and the ruin of the nation, she has been waiting for the return of her sons [who will] surround Jerusalem with trees" (Weitz, *Forests and Afforestation in Israel*, 369–70, quoted in Cohen, *The Politics of Planting*, 70).

41. Habiby, *The Secret Life of Saeed*, 22.

42. Habiby, *The Secret Life of Saeed*, 22.

43. Hilo, interview by author, July 23, 2012.

44. Hilo, interview by author, July 23, 2012.

45. Hilo, interview by author, July 23, 2012. Here, Hilo spoke specifically of uprooting in the West Bank and did not reference contemporary parallels inside Israel's 1948 borders. Palestinians in Jaffa, for example, regularly experience displacement, and internally displaced Palestinians across Israel, like those in the new Ein Houd, can see the Israeli iteration of their former village from the spaces in which they live. During my initial research in 2012, I consistently heard organizers in the West Bank, Jerusalem, and inside Israel's 1948 borders lament their inability to build and sustain face-to-face relationships with each other and with activists in Gaza. This fragmentation is a deliberate effort by the Israeli state to fracture Palestinians and weaken their capacity to collectively organize, mobilize, and see similarities among their experiences. When I conducted follow-up research in 2019, there was much more capacity for organizers in the West Bank and inside Israel to collaborate, working toward a Palestine not defined by Israel's policing and ever-shifting borders. This kind of organizing work had its parallel in the uprisings across all of Palestine in May and June 2021 in response to expulsions in Sheikh Jarrah known as the Unity Intifada.

46. Hilo, interview by author, July 23, 2012.

47. Hilo, interview by author, July 23, 2012.

48. Visualizing Palestine, "Uprooted."

49. Oxfam Briefing Paper: On the Road to Olive Farming, 19.

50. Abdelnour, Tartir, and Zurayk, "Farming Palestine for Freedom."

51. Abdelnour, Tartir, and Zurayk, "Farming Palestine for Freedom."

52. Weiss, "Jeff Halper Tours Ma'ale Adummim."

53. "Oxfam Briefing Paper," 19.

54. On Seam Zones, see both "Oxfam Briefing Paper," 19; and Braverman, "Uprooting Identities," 247. The Seam Zone refers to the area between the Green Line and the Wall. Aside from the fifty thousand Palestinians stuck living within the Seam Zone, West Bank Palestinians do not have access to these spaces.

55. Bloom, "Letter from Jayyous."

56. Hass, "It's Not the Olive Trees."

57. Shehadeh, "The Plight of the Palestinian Olive Tree."

58. Shehadeh, "The Plight of the Palestinian Olive Tree."

59. Shehadeh, "The Plight of the Palestinian Olive Tree." Indeed, the olive tree cannot be divorced from other staples of Palestinian agricultural production that have been policed, foreclosed, and confiscated by Israeli authorities. This list includes za'atar, which soldiers have confiscated at checkpoints; thyme, which Palestinian citizens in Israel have been forbidden from collecting in the wild; and cardamom and cumin (along with goats, donkeys, and cattle) that have been prohibited from entering Gaza under the blockade (Abdelnour, Tartir, and Zurayk, "Farming Palestine for Freedom"). As Abdelnour, Tartir, and Zurayk point out, these restrictions harken back to the first intifada when Israeli occupation forces ransacked Beit Sahour, attempting to capture cows to prevent local milk production. "Such actions," they write, "are just examples of Israel's control and devastation of Palestinian food culture and capability as part of the attempt to definitively break the tie to Palestine. As Henry Kissinger allegedly said, 'control food and you control the people'" (Abdelnour, Tartir, and Zurayk, "Farming Palestine for Freedom").

60. Arna'out and Asmar, "Israel Demolishes al-Araqib Village for the 184th Time." Every time I edit this chapter, the Israeli Army has yet again attempted to destroy and eradicate this village. When I filed my dissertation in the spring of 2015, it had "only" been destroyed eighty times; when this manuscript went to press, it had been destroyed 186 times. For more on afforestation in the Negev, see chapter 7, "From Imagination to Redemption: Crafting a Hebrew Landscape on Palestinian Land," in Fields, *Enclosure*.

61. See Gordon, "Uprooting the Bedouins of Israel"; and Zonzsein, "Jewish National Fund Resumes Forestation Project in Al-Arakib."

62. For more on Christian Zionism, see McAlister, "Prophecy, Politics, and the Popular"; Lampman, "Mixing Prophecy and Politics"; Davidson, "Christian Zionism as a Representation of American Manifest Destiny"; Sizer, *Christian Zionism*; and McAlister, *The Kingdom of God Has No Borders*.

63. Stoler, "Intimidations of Empire," 1.

64. B'Tselem, "Olive Harvest 2013."

65. B'Tselem, "Olive Harvest 2013." Of the twenty-one attacks, eight occurred on land near settlements, which Palestinian farmers are forbidden from accessing outside of harvest season. This causes neglect and thus a smaller yield of lesser quality. Further, when they are allowed to visit their groves, they must first coordinate with the military and have a military escort for part of the harvest. In seven of these cases, the farmer saw the destruction when they came to the field; in the eighth case, the farmer learned about the destruction of their groves only via the media (B'Tselem, "Olive Harvest 2013").

66. B'Tselem, "Olive Harvest 2013."

67. Braverman, "Uprooting Identities," 239.

68. B'Tselem, "Olive Harvest 2013."

69. B'Tselem, "Olive Harvest 2013."

70. B'Tselem, "Olive Harvest 2013."

71. "Olive Harvest Fact Sheet." Since 2008, attacks on Palestinian olive trees have escalated in what settlers have named Price Tag Attacks, retaliations for state-ordered evacuations of outposts. The evacuations themselves are a result of international pressure on Israel to adhere to international law.

72. For more on how, in the post-Oslo West Bank, the Palestinian Authority's accelerated pursuit of donor funds has also shifted the PA's attention away from self-sustaining Palestinian agriculture, and for more on how Israel profits from Palestinian agricultural production, see Abdelnour, Tartir, and Zurayk, "Farming Palestine for Freedom."

73. Hilo, interview by author, July 23, 2012.

74. Pappé, "More Oslos."

75. Kassis, interview by author, September 3, 2012.

76. Kassis, interview by author, September 3, 2012.

77. Anonymous, interview by author, August 2, 2012.

78. Anonymous, interview by author, August 2, 2012.

79. Anonymous, interview by author, August 2, 2012.

80. Kassis, interview by author, September 3, 2012.

Chapter Four. Itineraries under Duress

1. For a historical and ethnographic account of waste in the West Bank, see Stamatopoulou-Robbins, *Waste Siege*. She shows how multiple authorities—Israel, municipalities, the Palestinian Authority, international aid organizations, NGOs—have collectively created the conditions that oblige Palestinians to live with waste as an experience of everyday life.

2. Following the work of Grassroots Al-Quds, an organizing collective working—largely through tourism—to resist the occupation and anchor Palestinians in Jerusalem, I use the designations eastern and western part of Occupied Jerusalem as opposed to Occupied East Jerusalem. I do so in an effort to signal that *all* of Jerusalem is occupied. While Israel occupied East Jerusalem in 1967, it also occupied West Jerusalem in 1948, though West Jerusalem has been normalized as "simply" part of Israel. Calling only East Jerusalem occupied reifies the occupation of West Jerusalem as settled, notwithstanding the fact that many of the homes and structures of West Jerusalem are properties stolen from Palestinian families that have never been returned.

3. For more on these violent expulsions, see Essa, "Sheikh Jarrah." On the specific role of the police in these expulsions, see Ziv, "Israeli Police Determined to Escalate the Violence in Jerusalem." For more on organizing against these expulsions that is mindful of Israel's tourist visions for Sheikh Jarrah, see "Stop Israel's Forced Displacement of Palestinians from East Jerusalem!" Like the "Peace Forest" outlined in chapter 3, this, too, is one of many ways Christian Zionism fuels displacement in Palestine through tourism.

4. For more on permanent residency status for native Jerusalemite Palestinians, see Ir'Amim, "Permanent Residency."

5. Visualizing Palestine, "Jerusalem: A City for All?," with statistics from Ir'Amim, "Jerusalem Municipality Budget Analysis for 2013."

6. Statistics from B'Tselem, "Statistics on Demolitions of Houses Built without Permits in East Jerusalem," and analysis from Visualizing Palestine, "Jerusalem: A City for All?"

7. Visualizing Palestine, "Jerusalem: A City for All?," with statistics from BADIL Resource Center for Palestinian Residency and Refugee Rights.

8. For more on the project, see Love Under Apartheid Team, "Love Under Apartheid."

9. Al-Haq, "Residency Revocation."

10. Al-Haq, "Residency Revocation."

11. Al-Haq, "Residency Revocation."

12. Al-Haq, "Residency Revocation."

13. Al-Haq, "Residency Revocation." For more on stories of this sort, see Estrin, "Israel Accused of Revoking Thousands of Jerusalem Residency Permits from Palestinians." For more on international law and the many ways Israel has used it strategically to facilitate the colonial occupation of Palestine, see Erakat, *Justice for Some*.

14. Visualizing Palestine, "Jerusalem: A City for All?"

15. There are other accounts of Zochrot's tours, including those of tours to this particular neighborhood. On ethnography, displacement, and the objects of tourism, see Stein, "Israeli Routes through Nakba Landscapes"; and Stein, "Dispossession Reconsidered." For an account on Zochrot as situated in the context of alternative Jewish tourism in Palestine/Israel, see Aviv, "The Emergence of Alternative Jewish Tourism."

16. In addition to the controversy of papering over a Palestinian Muslim cemetery with a "Museum of Tolerance," the Simon Wiesenthal Institute was also involved in the firing of Steven Salaita by the University of Illinois at Urbana-Champaign in 2014. Robin D. G. Kelley explains that the "decision to summarily fire Professor Salaita had more to do with outside pressure, including a strongly worded letter from the Simon Wiesenthal Center, demanding that the University of Illinois rescind its offer because Salaita held 'aberrational views' and thus 'cannot be trusted to confine his discussions to his area of study'" (Kelley, "Why Did You Fire Steven Salaita?").

17. For Edward Said's writing on how Martin Buber supported a binational state in Palestine, see Said, "One State Solution."

18. For more on the facades across Jerusalem and how the work of Armenian ceramicist David Ohannessian adorned many Palestinian homes, churches, and businesses, see the biography of his life authored by his granddaughter Sato Moughalian, *Feast of Ashes: The Life and Art of David Ohannessian*.

19. For another account of this particular home, see Amiry, *Golda Slept Here*.

20. Bisharat, "Rite of Return to a Palestinian Home." See also Bisharat, "Talbiyeh Days."

21. Bisharat, "Rite of Return to a Palestinian Home."

22. Bisharat, "Rite of Return to a Palestinian Home."

23. Bisharat, "Rite of Return to a Palestinian Home."

24. Bisharat, "Rite of Return to a Palestinian Home."

25. Bisharat, "Rite of Return to a Palestinian Home."

26. Bisharat, "Rite of Return to a Palestinian Home."

27. Bisharat, "Rite of Return to a Palestinian Home."

28. Bisharat, "Rite of Return to a Palestinian Home." For more on how Israel strategically deploys, rather than flouts, the law, see Erakat, *Justice for Some.*

29. Bisharat, "Rite of Return to a Palestinian Home."

30. Bisharat, "Rite of Return to a Palestinian Home."

31. Radai, "Qatamon, 1948," 7.

32. Radai, "Qatamon, 1948," 7.

33. Radai, "Qatamon, 1948," 7.

34. Radai, "Qatamon, 1948," 7.

35. Radai, "Qatamon, 1948," 7.

36. Radai, "Qatamon, 1948," 7.

37. Khalidi, *All That Remains*, xxxii.

38. Radai, "Qatamon, 1948," 7. For more on the wholesale appropriation of Palestinian goods, belongings, and objects, see Shlaim, *The Iron Wall.*

39. Kanafani, "Returning to Haifa."

40. Sakakini, quoted in *The Great Book Robbery.*

41. For an account of the history of these houses, including the Sakakini home, published by Zochrot, see Hanegbi and Ostrovosky, "Palestinian Houses in West Jerusalem."

42. Hanegbi and Ostrovosky, "Palestinian Houses in West Jerusalem," 3.

43. Hanegbi and Ostrovosky, "Palestinian Houses in West Jerusalem," 3.

44. Zochrot's focus on the theft of Palestinian books does not occur in a cultural vacuum. Palestinian artists have narrated this history as refugees who have inherited this loss. Palestinian artist and filmmaker Emily Jacir, for example, spent two years photographing every book in the National Library that was stolen from Palestinian personal libraries. In her installation *Ex Libris* (2010–2012), she documents the thirty thousand books appropriated by the Israeli state in 1948 from Palestinian homes, libraries, and institutions, six thousand of which were labeled "AP: Abandoned Property" (see Jacir, "Ex Libris 2010–2012"; and Cruz, "Silence Is Enough"). Benny Brunner's 2012 documentary, *The Great Book Robbery*, meanwhile, draws on narratives provided by eyewitnesses, librarians, archivists, heirs, authors, and historians to archive the theft described by Hala Sakakini, George Bisharat, and Emily Jacir.

45. I am grateful to the anonymous reviewer at Duke University Press for offering insight both on what transformative work these tours can do and the elisions, particularly around class, that they can reenact.

46. Barakat, "The Jerusalem Fellah." There are volumes of literature on Palestine before 1948. For work on the diversity of Jerusalem during late Ottoman and Mandate-era Palestine, see Tamari, "Jerusalem 1948." For more on dynamic class constructions that made up Palestinian society more broadly under British rule, see Seikaly, *Men of Capital.* And for transformations in Palestinian society during the Ottoman period, see Campos, *Ottoman Brothers.*

47. Azeb, "Who Will We Be When We Are Free?," 24.

48. Abowd, "The Moroccan Quarter," 7, 9, quoted in Grassroots Al-Quds, *Wujood*, 77.

49. Grassroots Al-Quds, *Wujood*, 77.

50. Grassroots Al-Quds, *Wujood*, 77.

51. Said Rabiyeh, Introductory Comments at book launch for Grassroot Al-Quds's *Wujood: The Grassroots Guide to Jerusalem*, Educational Bookshop, Jerusalem, Palestine, August 4, 2019.

52. Palestinian Liberation Organization Negotiation Affairs Department, "The Annexation of Tourism."

53. Palestinian Liberation Organization Negotiation Affairs Department, "The Annexation of Tourism."

54. Grassroots Al-Quds, *Wujood*, 125.

55. Grassroots Al-Quds, *Wujood*, 125.

56. Grassroots Al-Quds, *Wujood*, 125.

57. IDF is the acronym for the formal name of the Israeli military—the Israel Defense Forces—though many anti-Zionist organizers and scholars instead refer to the military as the more aptly named IOF: Israeli Occupation Forces.

58. Ali Jiddah is an Afro-Palestinian Jerusalemite whose family is originally from Chad. He is quick to remind tourists who do not understand the racial politics of the Old City that he is Afro-Palestinian but Palestinian wholly. On tours in 2012, he explained his limited mobility, describing his slow recovery from being attacked in the Jewish Quarter by two teenage settlers while he was leading a French tour group around the Old City. He told me later, in an interview, about how this tour group had stayed with him at the hospital the whole night and how amazed he was at their commitment. His incredulousness at their generosity reveals the commodification of narrative that occurs through tourism, even, or perhaps especially, solidarity tourism: how he can tell a group his story but would not expect them to go with him to the hospital if he was severely beaten in the middle of a tour. For more on Jiddah's particular place in Palestinian liberation struggles, see Hassan, "African-Palestinian Community's Deep Roots in Liberation Struggle." For recent work on Afro-Palestinian communities' role in transnational Black-Palestinian solidarity movements, see Fischback, *Black Power and Palestine*; Erakat and Hill, "Black-Palestinian Transnational Solidarity"; and Erakat, "Geographies of Intimacy."

59. At the time of my initial research, Ariel Sharon was still in a coma, though he subsequently died in 2014. Sharon remained in a coma for eight years, from 2006 to 2014.

60. For more on tours of this sort, see Kelly, "On Being There."

61. See Silverstein, *Where the Sidewalk Ends*.

62. Grassroots Al-Quds, *Wujood*, 129.

63. Grassroots Al-Quds, *Wujood*, 130

64. Grassroots Al-Quds, *Wujood*, 130

65. Grassroots Al-Quds, *Wujood*, 131.

66. Grassroots Al-Quds, *Wujood*, 131.

67. Grassroots Al-Quds, *Wujood*, 129.

Chapter Five. Colonial Ruins and a Decolonized Future

1. Alsaafin, "Palestinian Protests in Israel Showcase Unprecedented Unity."

2. Here, I am reminded of Emile Habiby's protagonist in *The Secret Life of Saeed: The Pessoptimist*, who was imprisoned in Haifa during the 1967 War for displaying a

white sheet above his roof when he heard a radio broadcaster ask Palestinians in the West Bank to display a flag of surrender. Saeed, confused and forgetting his mandate to be an "Israeli Arab" instead of a Palestinian, was punished for reminding his occupiers—who preferred to think of themselves as his "neighbors"—that he has a collectivity in identity and freedom struggles with Palestinians elsewhere in Palestine (Habiby, *The Secret Life of Saeed*, 96–115).

3. Khalidi, *All That Remains*, xxxix. For more on the struggle to protect Jaffa's Palestinian cemeteries, see Nasser, "Fight to Save Jaffa's Last Muslim Cemetery from Israeli Bulldozers." For more on Salama's history, see Zochrot, "Salama."

4. Khalidi, *All That Remains*, xxxix. In 2010, anthropologist Rochelle Davis published *Palestinian Village Histories: Geographies of the Displaced*, a comprehensive account of how displaced Palestinians have archived and memorialized the over four hundred villages depopulated by Israel in 1948 in village memory books. And, in 2015, Noga Kadman, researcher and licensed Israeli tour guide who coedited the Zochrot guidebook *Once Upon a Land: A Tour Guide to Depopulated Palestinian Villages and Towns*, published *Erased from Space and Consciousness: Israel and the Depopulated Palestinian Villages of 1948*. This text chronicles the contemporary landscape of the 418 villages depopulated by Israel in 1948 and underscores the state's efforts to paper over, erase, rename, and otherwise repurpose Palestinian space.

5. Al-Ghubari, interview by author, September 12, 2012.

6. Al-Ghubari, interview by author, September 12, 2012.

7. Peled-Elhannan, *Palestine in Israeli Schoolbooks*, 15.

8. Al-Ghubari, interview by author, September 12, 2012.

9. Zochrot's regularly scheduled tours are free, but they charge a fee for tours they design for other organizations, for example, when they offer Zochrot tours as part of West Bank organizations' itineraries that cross the Green Line.

10. Al-Ghubari, interview by author, September 12, 2012.

11. Al-Ghubari, interview by author, September 12, 2012.

12. Al-Ghubari, interview by author, September 12, 2012.

13. Khalidi, *Before Their Diaspora*, 14, 15.

14. Aparicio, "Most JNF-KKL Forests and Sites Are Located on the Ruins of Palestinian Villages."

15. Abu-Lughod, "Palestine," 3.

16. Seikaly, "How I Met My Great-Grandfather," 16.

17. Seikaly, "How I Met My Great-Grandfather," 18.

18. Seikaly, "How I Met My Great-Grandfather," 18.

19. Mitchell and Rao, "Editor's Note," 1.

20. Aparicio, "Most JNF-KKL Forests and Sites Are Located on the Ruins of Palestinian Villages."

21. For a comprehensive ethnographic study of Ein Hod, see Slyomovics, *The Object of Memory*.

22. For more, see Zochrot, "'Ayn Hawd."

23. Zochrot, "'Ayn Hawd."

24. For more on California wildfires and Indigenous knowledge, see Robins and Lopez, "A Conversation on Wildfire Ecologies."

25. Ein Hod Artists' Village, home page.

26. Ein Hod Artists' Village, home page.

27. Ein Hod Artists' Village, home page.

28. Zochrot, "Lifta," citing Khalidi, *All That Remains*.

29. Zochrot, "Lifta."

30. Zochrot, "Lifta."

31. Zochrot, "Lifta."

32. Save Lifta, "About Lifta."

33. UNESCO, "Lifta (Mey Naftoah)."

34. UNESCO, "Lifta (Mey Naftoah)."

35. Barakat, "Lifta, the Nakba, and the Museumification of Palestine's History," 2.

36. Barakat, "Lifta, the Nakba, and the Museumification of Palestine's History," 4.

37. Barakat, "Lifta, the Nakba, and the Museumification of Palestine's History," 9.

38. Barakat, "Lifta, the Nakba, and the Museumification of Palestine's History," 9.

39. Imwas Human Society, *Emwas Will Never Go into Oblivion*.

40. Al-Ghubari, interview by author, September 12, 2012.

41. In tracing failures of imagination, I am indebted to queer theorizing that has outlined the coalescence of liberalism and empire as well as the limits of color-blind multiculturalism at the expense of redress. As two examples, see Somerville, *Queering the Color Line*; and Eng, *Feeling of Kinship*.

42. Al-Ghubari, interview by author, September 12, 2012.

43. Al-Ghubari, interview by author, September 12, 2012.

44. For a more recent publication on the initiative, see International Middle East Media Center, "The Practicalities of the Palestinian Right of Return."

45. For more on Zochrot's work on Miska, see Zochrot, "Miska."

46. Al-Ghubari, interview by author, September 12, 2012.

47. Al-Ghubari, interview by author, September 12, 2012.

48. Al-Ghubari, interview by author, September 12, 2012.

49. Al-Ghubari, interview by author, September 12, 2012.

50. BADIL-Zochrot, "Study Visit to Cape Town."

51. Azeb, "Who Will We Be When We Are Free?"; al-Ghubari, interview by author, September 12, 2012.

52. Al-Ghubari, interview by author, September 12, 2012.

53. BADIL-Zochrot, "Study Visit to Cape Town."

54. al-Ghubari, interview by author, September 12, 2012.

55. BADIL-Zochrot, "Study Visit to Cape Town."

56. BADIL-Zochrot, "Study Visit to Cape Town."

57. BADIL-Zochrot, "Study Visit to Cape Town."

58. BADIL-Zochrot, "Study Visit to Cape Town." For a recent meditation on the limits of the apartheid analogy, the argument for which was also formed in the wake of a delegation to South Africa, see Qutami, "Moving Beyond the Apartheid Analogy in Palestine and South Africa."

59. BADIL-Zochrot, "Study Visit to Cape Town."

60. BADIL-Zochrot, "Study Visit to Cape Town."

61. BADIL-Zochrot, "Study Visit to Cape Town."

62. Al-Ghubari, interview by author, September 12, 2012.

63. Al-Ghubari, interview by author, September 12, 2012.

64. The image of the map Umar al-Ghubari showed me in our interview is reproduced digitally on Zochrot's website, where it is overlaid on an aerial map of the landscape. Manof, "Countermapping Return."

65. Al-Ghubari, interview by author, September 12, 2012.

66. Al-Ghubari, interview by author, September 12, 2012.

67. Al-Ghubari, interview by author, September 12, 2012.

68. Al-Ghubari, interview by author, September 12, 2012.

69. Al-Ghubari, interview by author, September 12, 2012.

70. Al-Ghubari, interview by author, September 12, 2012.

71. Decolonizing Architecture Art Research (DAAR), "About."

72. Barclay, "Exile and Return to Miska," 2.

73. Barclay, "Exile and Return to Miska," 2.

74. Barclay, "Exile and Return to Miska," 2.

75. Barclay, "Exile and Return to Miska," 2.

76. Barclay, "Exile and Return to Miska," 2.

77. Barclay, "Exile and Return to Miska," 5.

78. Barclay, "Exile and Return to Miska," 7.

79. Barclay, "Exile and Return to Miska," 8.

80. Barclay, "Exile and Return to Miska," 8.

81. For more on imperial debris and processes of ruination, see Stoler, *Imperial Debris*; and Stoler, "Imperial Debris."

82. Barclay, "Exile and Return to Miska," 8.

83. Barclay, "Exile and Return to Miska," 10.

84. Decolonizing Architecture Art Research (DAAR), "DAAR/Studio in Exile."

85. For the archived conference, see Zochrot, "Truth and Redress."

86. Carby, "The Multicultural Wars," 13.

87. Cook, "Coexistence in Israel's 'Mixed Cities' Was Always an Illusion."

88. Remembering, "iNakba."

89. Black, "Remembering the Nakba."

90. Palestinian News and Information Agency (WAFA), "Virtual Reality App Gives Users Access to Everyday Life in Palestine."

91. Palestinian News and Information Agency (WAFA), "Virtual Reality App Gives Users Access to Everyday Life in Palestine."

92. Palestinian News and Information Agency (WAFA), "Virtual Reality App Gives Users Access to Everyday Life in Palestine."

Chapter Six. "Welcome to Gaza"

1. Interfaith Peace Builders and US Campaign for Palestinian Rights, Virtual Delegation to Palestine, August 17, 2017, https://uscpr.org/virtualdelegation/, last accessed March 18, 2018.

2. For more on the performative as producing what it names, see Butler, *Gender Trouble*; and Butler, *Bodies that Matter*. Butler draws on Austin, *How to Do Things with Words*.

3. You Are Not Here, home page.

4. You Are Not Here, home page. Of these sites, the Arts and Crafts Village was damaged by Israeli strikes in July 2018 and Kazem's Ice Cream Parlor's factory was destroyed by Israeli shelling in May 2021. In May 2021, Israel also murdered ten members of the Abu Hatab family, eight of them children, at the Al-Shati Refugee Camp, known as Beach Camp. This timeline reveals the cyclical nature of Israeli state violence in Gaza that El-Haddad describes in the 2009 recordings.

5. You Are Not Here, home page.

6. You Are Not Here, home page.

7. You Are Not Here, home page.

8. You Are Not Here, home page.

9. You Are Not Here, home page.

10. You Are Not Here, home page.

11. You Are Not Here, home page.

12. You Are Not Here, home page.

13. You Are Not Here, home page.

14. You Are Not Here, home page.

15. I am grateful to Saidiya Hartman's theorizing of the witnessing of suffering in these terms.

16. You Are Not Here, home page.

17. You Are Not Here, home page, emphasis mine.

18. Gaza Mom, "You Are NOT Here."

19. Gaza Mom, "You Are NOT Here."

20. Gaza Mom, "You Are NOT Here."

21. Gaza Mom, "You Are NOT Here."

22. Gaza Mom, "You Are NOT Here."

23. Awad, "Nostalgia for the Future."

24. Bourdain, *Parts Unknown*, Season 2, episode 1, "Jerusalem, the West Bank, and Gaza."

25. Bourdain, *Parts Unknown*, Season 2, episode 1, "Jerusalem, the West Bank, and Gaza."

26. Zayid, "Watching Anthony Bourdain in Palestine."

27. Zayid, "Watching Anthony Bourdain in Palestine."

28. Bourdain, *Parts Unknown*, Season 2, episode 1, "Jerusalem, the West Bank, and Gaza."

29. Puar, "On Torture," 13.

30. Zahr, "Anthony Bourdain, Will You Marry Me?"

31. Zahr, "Anthony Bourdain, Will You Marry Me?"

32. Zahr, "Anthony Bourdain, Will You Marry Me?"

33. Zahr, "Anthony Bourdain, Will You Marry Me?"

34. Bourdain, *Parts Unknown*, Season 2, episode 1, "Jerusalem, the West Bank, and Gaza."

35. Bourdain, *Parts Unknown*, Season 2, episode 1, "Jerusalem, the West Bank, and Gaza."

36. Zayid, "Watching Anthony Bourdain in Palestine."

37. Kane, "Celebrity Foodie Anthony Bourdain's Trip to Palestine."

38. Bourdain, *Parts Unknown*, Season 2, episode 1, "Jerusalem, the West Bank, and Gaza." Cited in Kane, "Celebrity Foodie Anthony Bourdain's Trip to Palestine."

39. Associated Press. "Israel Used 'Calorie Count' to Limit Gaza Food During Blockade."

40. Khan, "You Can't Discuss Palestinian Food without Talking about the Occupation."

41. Kane, "Celebrity Foodie Anthony Bourdain's Trip to Palestine." The problems he notes are that Bourdain's episode does not mention the Nakba or return. Bourdain also gives voice to Israelis in the aftermath of rockets fired from Gaza but omits any mention of Israel's bombing campaigns in Gaza in 2008–2009 and 2012.

42. Thomsen, "TV Chef Sums up the Problems in Gaza."

43. Thomsen, "TV Chef Sums up the Problems in Gaza."

44. See Estrin, "Palestinian Pleasures."

45. Estrin, "Palestinian Pleasures."

46. Estrin, "Palestinian Pleasures."

47. Estrin, "Palestinian Pleasures."

48. Estrin, "Palestinian Pleasures."

49. Estrin, "Palestinian Pleasures."

50. Ziadah, "We Teach Life, Sir."

51. Banksy, "Welcome to Gaza."

52. Banksy, "Welcome to Gaza."

53. Banksy, "Welcome to Gaza."

54. Banksy, "Welcome to Gaza."

55. Banksy, "Welcome to Gaza."

56. Banksy, "Welcome to Gaza."

57. Banksy, "Welcome to Gaza."

58. Banksy, "Welcome to Gaza."

59. Banksy, "Welcome to Gaza."

60. Banksy, "Welcome to Gaza."

61. Ryall, "Banksy Goes Undercover in Gaza."

62. Banksy, "Welcome to Gaza."

63. Gaza Parkour Team, *After Banksy*.

64. Gaza Parkour Team, *After Banksy*.

65. Gaza Parkour Team, *After Banksy*, emphasis mine.

66. Gaza Parkour Team, *After Banksy*.

67. Gaza Parkour Team, *After Banksy*.

68. Gaza Parkour Team, *After Banksy*.

69. Gaza Parkour Team, *After Banksy*.

70. Gaza Parkour Team, *After Banksy*.

71. Gaza Parkour Team, *After Banksy*.

72. Gaza Parkour Team, *After Banksy*.

73. McIntosh and Alfaleet, "Envisioning a Tourism of Peace in the Gaza Strip," 217.

74. Institute for Middle East Understanding (IMEU), "50 Days of Death and Destruction."

75. IMEU, "50 Days of Death and Destruction."

76. IMEU, "50 Days of Death and Destruction."

77. IMEU, "50 Days of Death and Destruction."

78. IMEU, "50 Days of Death and Destruction."

79. IMEU, "50 Days of Death and Destruction."

80. McIntosh and Alfaleet, "Envisioning a Tourism of Peace in the Gaza Strip," 218.

81. McIntosh and Alfaleet, "Envisioning a Tourism of Peace in the Gaza Strip," 218.

82. McIntosh and Alfaleet, "Envisioning a Tourism of Peace in the Gaza Strip," 218.

83. McIntosh and Alfaleet, "Envisioning a Tourism of Peace in the Gaza Strip," 219.

84. McIntosh and Alfaleet, "Envisioning a Tourism of Peace in the Gaza Strip," 219. A central actor in this looting was Israeli general—and amateur archaeologist—Moshe Dayan, who claimed that he would license a Palestinian fighter pilot before he would ever license a Palestinian tour guide. For Dayan, there is power in narration and cultural artifacts, both of which he sought to make sure Palestinians could not access.

85. McIntosh and Alfaleet, "Envisioning a Tourism of Peace in the Gaza Strip," 220.

86. McIntosh and Alfaleet, "Envisioning a Tourism of Peace in the Gaza Strip," 220.

87. McIntosh and Alfaleet, "Envisioning a Tourism of Peace in the Gaza Strip," 222.

88. McIntosh and Alfaleet, "Envisioning a Tourism of Peace in the Gaza Strip," 222.

89. McIntosh and Alfaleet, "Envisioning a Tourism of Peace in the Gaza Strip," 223.

90. McIntosh and Alfaleet, "Envisioning a Tourism of Peace in the Gaza Strip," 225.

91. Assali, "Postcard from a Liberated Gaza."

92. Assali, "Postcard from a Liberated Gaza."

93. Assali, "Postcard from a Liberated Gaza."

94. Assali, "Postcard from a Liberated Gaza."

95. Assali, "Postcard from a Liberated Gaza."

Chapter Seven. Witnesses in Palestine

1. An abridged and augmented version of this chapter appears as "Subjection and Performance: Tourism, Witnessing, and Acts of Refusal in Palestine," *Feminist Formations* 32, no. 2 (2020): 79–110.

2. On archaeology, see Abu El-Haj, *Facts on the Ground*; Masalha, *The Bible and Zionism*. On before and after the Nakba, see Khalidi, *Before Their Diaspora*; Said, "Permission to Narrate"; Khalidi, *All That Remains*; Masalha, *The Palestine Nakba*; and Seikaly, *Men of Capital*. On the refusal of the United States as an honest broker, see Said, *Orientalism*; Said, *Peace and Its Discontents*; and Khalidi, *Brokers of Deceit*. On the West Bank, see Makdisi, *Palestine Inside Out*; and Shehadeh, *Palestinian Walks*. On the racialized and gendered violence of Zionism, see Shalhoub-Kevorkian, *Militarization and Violence against Women in Conflict Zones in the Middle East*; Abdo, *Women in Israel*; and Abdulhadi, Alsultany, and Naber, *Arab and Arab American*

Feminisms. On Palestinian women and reproduction, see Kanaaneh, *Birthing the Nation*. On Palestinian citizens in Israel, see Nassar, *Brothers Apart*. On international law, see Erakat, *Justice for Some*.

3. Said, *Out of Place*; Karmi, *In Search of Fatima*; Abu Saif, *The Drone Eats with Me*; Barghouti, *I Saw Ramallah*; Karmi, *Return*.

4. For a small sampling of fiction on displacement, see Kanafani "Returning to Haifa"; Habiby, *The Secret Life of Saeed*; Abulhawa, *Mornings in Jenin*; Alyan, *Salt Houses*.

5. Baltzer, *A Witness in Palestine*.

6. Sharif, "Vanishing Palestine."

7. For more on this analogical tendency, see Salamanca et. al, "Past Is Present."

8. Again, I am grateful to A. Naomi Paik for helping me think through this distinction.

9. On imagined geographies, see Said, *Orientalism*.

10. Said, "Permission to Narrate."

11. Cole, "Alice Walker."

12. Lory, interview by author, October 4, 2013.

13. Lory, interview by author, October 4, 2013.

14. Negrón, interview by author, November 25, 2014. Here, she refers to the 1985 hijacking of the Italian MS *Achille Lauro* and the murder of Leon Klinghoffer by the Palestine Liberation Front.

15. Stoler, panelist, "Anthropologists and Controversial Engagements."

16. Cole, "Alice Walker."

17. My flagging of the solidarity tropes evident in Walker's report-back is neither an endorsement of all of her work nor a claim that solidarity tourists in any way echo her other sentiments, particularly those that are antisemitic (see Grady, "The Alice Walker Anti-Semitism Controversy Explained"). Instead, I share her remarks on *Democracy Now!* as an example of the formula many solidarity tourists engage to make sense of what they witness in Palestine. Antisemitism is in no way part of this formula.

18. For more on colonial knowledge production in Palestine/Israel, see Shohat, "Notes on the Post-colonial."

19. Goff, interview by author, September 14, 2013.

20. Green, interview by author, July 31, 2013.

21. Alzanoon, interview by author, November 22, 2014.

22. Negrón, interview by author, November 25, 2014.

23. Macy, interview by author, October 14, 2014.

24. Macy, interview by author, October 14, 2014.

25. Macy, interview by author, October 14, 2014, emphasis mine.

26. For a touchstone text in this genre, see Abdulhadi, Alsultany, and Naber, *Arab and Arab American Feminisms*.

27. For canonical pre- and post-9/11 critiques of Islamophobic feminisms that share this logic, see Mohanty, "Under Western Eyes"; Mohanty, *Feminism without Borders*; Abu Lughod, "Do Muslim Women Need Saving?"; Shohat, *Talking Visions*; and Mahmood, *The Politics of Piety*.

28. Macy, interview by author, October 14, 2014.

29. Ruth Wilson Gilmore's definition of racism as "the state-sanctioned or extralegal production and exploitation of group-differentiated vulnerability to premature death" is instructive here (Gilmore, *Golden Gulag*, 28).

30. Alzanoon, interview by author, November 22, 2014.

31. Lory, interview by author, October 4, 2013.

32. Turtle Island is one Indigenous name for North America.

33. I borrow this formulation from Nikhil Singh in his work *Black Is a Country*.

34. Lory, interview by author, October 4, 2013.

35. Cole, "Alice Walker."

36. Kane, "A Level of Racist Violence I Have Never Seen."

37. Mbembe, "On Palestine," viii.

38. Soske and Jacobs, *Apartheid Israel*, viii.

39. The e-book, *Apartheid Israel: The Politics of an Analogy*, edited by Jon Soske and Sean Jacobs, was meant to begin discussion and encourage the African Studies Association to endorse an academic boycott of Israeli universities (Soske and Jacobs, *Apartheid Israel*, 1). It was first published by Africa Is a Country (https://africasacountry.com/2014/11/the-apartheid-analogy) in the wake of the American Studies Association's February 2014 endorsement of a boycott of Israeli academic institutions—itself made possible by organizing on the heels of the US Academic and Cultural Boycott of Israel's solidarity tour of Palestine that hosted members of the American Studies Association's National Council—and in conjunction with the November 2014 African Studies Association meeting in Indianapolis, Indiana.

40. Soske and Jacobs, *Apartheid Israel*, 1.

41. Soske and Jacobs, *Apartheid Israel*, 1.

42. Soske and Jacobs, *Apartheid Israel*, 1.

43. On the arms trade and sectarianism, see Vally, "Solidarity with Palestine." On neoliberalism, see Clarno, "Neoliberal Apartheid." On the flattening of historical difference and the question of analogy, see Tallie, "The Historian and Apartheid." On BDS, see Hassim, "Academic Freedom and Academic Boycotts."

44. Kelley, "Apartheid's Black Apologists," 31.

45. Qutami, "Moving Beyond the Apartheid Analogy in Palestine and South Africa."

46. Tallie, "The Historian and Apartheid," 16.

47. Tallie, "The Historian and Apartheid," 17.

48. For more on the Piscataway Conoy Tribe and Piscataway Indian Nation, see Piscataway Conoy Tribe, home page.

49. The infographic included an image by Polypod and Philippe Ghabayen and drew on statistics from "Olive Harvest Fact Sheet."

50. See Canadians for Justice and Peace in the Middle East, "If #Canada were #Palestine..how would you feel? #JSIL" [sic]. Twitter, November 5, 2014, https://twitter.com/CJPME/status/530074712618323969.

51. Xero (@LMoiseiwitsch), Twitter, accessed December 5, 2014.

52. For a sustained discussion of the past and present of Black-Palestine solidarity, see the "Black-Palestinian Transnational Solidarity" special issue of the *Journal of Palestine Studies* 48, no. 4 (2019), including Erakat and Hill, "Black-Palestinian

Transnational Solidarity"; Nassar, "Palestinian Engagement with the Black Freedom Movement Prior to 1967"; Webb, "Troubling Idols"; pieces on global solidarity movements by Robin D. G. Kelley ("From the River to the Sea to Every Mountain Top") and Russel Rickford ("To Build a New World"); a roundtable on Black-Palestine solidarity delegations (Abuznaid et al., "Roundtable"); and a review essay on Fischbach's *Black Power and Palestine* (Bishop, "Review"). See also Erakat, "Geographies of Intimacy," where she details what she calls "structures of intimacy" forged between Black and Palestinian activists in and after Ferguson. In their essay, "Reciprocal Solidarity: Where the Black and Palestinian Queer Struggles Meet," Sa'ed Atshan and Darnell L. Moore call this intimacy reciprocal solidarity, a space of friendship and shared struggle forged through "mutual recognition and radical love" (690).

53. For more on the origins of policing, regionally understood, see Harring, *Policing a Class Society*. For more on the carceral state, see Gilmore, "Abolition Geography and the Problem of Innocence"; Gilmore, *Golden Gulag*; Davis, *Are Prisons Obsolete?*; Browne, *Dark Matters*; Ngai, *Impossible Subjects*; Walia, *Undoing Border Imperialism*; Chase, *Caging Borders and Carceral States*; Rodríguez, *Forced Passages*; and Hernández, *Migra!*

54. Elia, "Solidarity Means Fighting for Black Lives." The United States and Israel share settler solidarities that function through shared technologies of violence (the Israeli military trains US police departments), shared weaponry (the United States provides Israel with weapons that Israel uses against Palestinians, including ammunition and tear gas), and shared settler logics (from the theft of Indigenous land to the logic of the chosen to sanctify that theft). It is critical, however, to retain historical context and specificity as we launch our critiques and fortify our organizing. For more on these training programs and shared technologies of violence, see Researching the American-Israeli Alliance and Jewish Voice for Peace, "Deadly Exchange."

55. RL, interview by author, August 23, 2019.

56. RL, interview by author, August 23, 2019.

57. RL, interview by author, August 23, 2019.

58. RL, interview by author, August 23, 2019.

59. RL, interview by author, August 23, 2019.

60. Farasha, interview by author, August 23, 2019.

61. Farasha, interview by author, August 23, 2019.

62. Farasha, interview by author, August 23, 2019.

63. Farasha, interview by author, August 23, 2019.

64. Farasha, interview by author, August 23, 2019.

65. Farasha, interview by author, August 23, 2019.

66. Alzanoon, interview by author, November 22, 2014.

67. Farasha, interview by author, August 23, 2019.

68. Farasha, interview by author, August 23, 2019.

69. Farasha, interview by author, August 23, 2019.

70. Farasha, interview by author, August 23, 2019.

71. Farasha, interview by author, August 23, 2019.

72. Farasha, interview by author, August 23, 2019.

73. Green, interview by author, July 31, 2013.

74. Dean MacCannell details the appeal to the authentic in *The Tourist*.

75. Green, interview by author, July 31, 2013.

76. Green, interview by author, July 31, 2013.

77. See Dean MacCannell's classic *The Tourist* for an extended meditation on how leisure structures tourism.

78. al-Zubaidy, interview by author, September 6, 2012.

79. For an extended meditation on politically ambiguous "ugly" feelings like shock and boredom, see Ngai, *Ugly Feelings*.

80. Green, interview by author, July 31, 2013.

81. Negrón, interview by author, November 25, 2014.

82. Negrón, interview by author, November 25, 2014.

83. See, for example, Kincaid, *A Small Place*; Walcott, *What the Twilight Says*; and Alexander, *Pedagogies of Crossing*.

84. Naiman, "Welcome to Palestine." It is worth mentioning that while this statement underscores the isolation to which Israel subjects Palestinians, prisoners in multiple geopolitical contexts, particularly in Israel, are often *not* allowed visits. In defiance of international law, Israel banned visits entirely for prisoners from Gaza in 2007–2012 and has continued to severely restrict them even after the ban was lifted. The prison metaphor, moreover, is hardly a metaphor, since—as tourists hear repeatedly—some 70 percent of Palestinians have had a family member imprisoned for resisting the occupation. See Hass, "Otherwise Occupied."

85. I am grateful to Kathleen Stewart for encouraging me to look at solidarity tourism "prismatically," or through and from multiple different, even competing, angles.

86. Ahmed, "Evidence." In this piece, Sara Ahmed discusses the accumulation of evidence on sexual harassment in university settings where both colleagues and administrators pretend it does not exist.

87. One example of how Israel restricts Palestinian movement in Jerusalem is Israel's 1988 "center of life" Supreme Court judgment, which requires Palestinian residents of Jerusalem—who are not Israeli citizens—to prove that their "center of life" is Jerusalem to not have their residency revoked. For more on this, see Jefferis, "The 'Center of Life' Policy."

Conclusion

1. Trump White House, "Peace to Prosperity."

2. Trump White House, "Peace to Prosperity."

3. Hawari, "Trump's 'Peace' Deal."

4. On relational readings in colonial contexts broadly, and in Palestine/Israel particularly, see Shohat, "Sephardim in Israel"; Shohat, "Notes on the Post-colonial"; Shohat, *Talking Visions*; and Shohat, "The Shaping of Mizrahi Studies."

5. See Nguyen, *The Gift of Freedom*.

6. Kokaly, interview by author, August 22, 2012.

7. Abu Hassan, interview by author, August 30, 2012.

8. Abu Hassan, interview by author, August 30, 2012.

9. Allen, *The Rise and Fall of Human Rights*, 16.

10. For some examples of companies with working relationships with Palestinian farmers that were established on tours to Palestine, and particularly on harvesting and planting initiatives, see Perfect Potion (https://www.perfectpotion.com.au) and Harvest Peace (https://harvestpeace.com). For an example of working relationships constructed between Palestinian archivists and librarians and information workers from the United States, Canada, Sweden, Trinidad and Tobago, and Palestine, see Librarians and Archivists with Palestine (https://librarianswithpalestine.org), which began as a delegation to Palestine in the summer of 2013.

11. For more on the friendships constructed through solidarity delegations and the work of reciprocal solidarity, see Atshan and Moore, "Reciprocal Solidarity."

12. In thinking about the potential and danger of hope in the face of despair, I am guided by the work of José Esteban Muñoz in *Cruising Utopia: The Then and There of Queer Futurity* and Lauren Berlant in *Cruel Optimism*.

13. In considering the refusal of the logic of intractability and the concurrent demand for the impossible, I am indebted to Dean Spade's *Normal Life: Administrative Violence, Critical Trans Politics, and the Limits of the Law* and "Impossibility Now: A Trans* Politics Manifesto."

BIBLIOGRAPHY

Abdelnour, Samer, Alaa Tartir, and Rami Zurayk. "Farming Palestine for Freedom." *Al-Shabaka*, July 2, 2012. https://al-shabaka.org/briefs/farming-palestine -freedom-policy-brief.

Abdo, Nahla. *Women in Israel: Race, Gender and Citizenship*. New York: Zed Books, 2011.

Abdulhadi, Rabab, Evelyn Alsultany, and Nadine Naber, eds. *Arab and Arab American Feminisms: Gender, Violence, and Belonging*. Syracuse, NY: Syracuse University Press, 2011.

Abowd, Thomas. "The Moroccan Quarter: A History of the Present." *Journal of Palestine Studies* 7 (2000): 6–16.

Abu El-Haj, Nadia. *Facts on the Ground: Archaeological Practice and Territorial Self-Fashioning in Israeli Society*. Chicago: University of Chicago Press, 2001.

Abu Hassan. Interview by author. East Jerusalem, Palestine. August 30, 2012.

Abu Saif, Atef. *The Drone Eats with Me: Diaries from a City under Fire*. Manchester, UK: Comma Press, 2015.

Abu Zulof, Ayman. Interview by author. Beit Sahour, Palestine. August 22, 2012.

Abu-Lughod, Lila. *Do Muslim Women Need Saving?* Cambridge, MA: Harvard University Press, 2002.

Abu-Lughod, Lila. "Palestine: Doing Things with Archives." *Comparative Studies of South Asia, Africa and the Middle East* 38, no. 1 (2018): 3–5.

Abulhawa, Susan. *Mornings in Jenin*. New York: Bloomsbury, 2010.

Abuznaid, Ahmad, Phillip Agnew, Maytha Alhassen, Kristian Davis Bailey, and Nadya Tannous. "Roundtable: On Solidarity Delegations." *Journal of Palestine Studies* 48, no. 4 (2019): 92–102.

"Academics Refute Israeli Claims," *Al Fajr: Jerusalem, Palestinian Weekly* 9, no. 411 (April 3, 1988): 8–9. Freedom Archives. Collection: Palestine. Box: Academic, Students, and Thinkers on Palestine. San Francisco, CA.

Ahmad, Halah. "Tourism in the Service of Occupation and Annexation." *Al-Shabaka*, October 12, 2020. https://al-shabaka.org/summaries/tourism-in -service-of-occupation-and-annexation.

Ahmed, Sara. "Evidence." *Feministkilljoys*, July 12, 2016. https://feministkilljoys.com /2016/07/12/evidence/.

Ahmed, Sara. "Making Feminist Points." *Feministkilljoys*, September 11, 2013. https:// feministkilljoys.com/2013/09/11/making-feminist-points.

Aikau, Hōkūlani K., and Vernadette Vicuña Gonzalez, eds. *Detours: A Decolonial Guide to Hawai'i*. Durham, NC: Duke University Press, 2019.

Ajanebed Out: The Tragedy of Foreigners in Palestine. "Need a Purpose in Life? Visit Palestine." *Ajanebed Out*, November 6, 2013. https://ajanebedout.tumblr.com /post/66218396535.

Ajanebed Out: The Tragedy of Foreigners in Palestine. "Palestine: For All Your Professional and Academic Career Needs!" *Ajanebed Out*, November 6, 2013. https://ajanebedout.tumblr.com/post/66018243185.

Al-Ghubari, Umar. Interview by author. Zochrot, Tel Aviv, Israel. September 12, 2012.

Al-Haq. "Residency Revocation: Israel's Forcible Transfer of Palestinians from Jerusalem." *Al-Haq*, July 3, 2017. http://www.alhaq.org/advocacy/6331.html.

Al-Zubaidy, Yazan. Interview by author. Beit Sahour, Palestine. September 6, 2012.

Alcalay, Ammiel. *After Jews and Arabs: Remaking Levantine Culture*. Minneapolis: University of Minnesota Press, 1992.

Alexander, M. Jacqui. *Pedagogies of Crossing: Meditations on Feminism, Sexual Politics, Memory, and the Sacred*. Durham, NC: Duke University Press, 2005.

Alin, Erika. "Dynamics of the Palestinian Uprising: An Assessment of Causes, Character, and Consequences." *Comparative Politics* 26, no. 4 (1994): 479–98.

Allen, Lori. *The Rise and Fall of Human Rights: Cynicism and Politics in Occupied Palestine*. Stanford, CA: Stanford University Press, 2011.

Alqasis, Amjad. "Israel's Grip on the Palestinian Tourism Economy." +972 *Magazine*, June 5, 2015. https://972mag.com/israels-grip-on-the-palestinian-tourism -industry/107445.

Alsaafin, Lina. "Palestinian Protests in Israel Showcase Unprecedented Unity." *Al Jazeera*, May 16, 2021. https://www.aljazeera.com/news/2021/5/16/palestinian -protests-in-israel-showcase-unprecedented-unity.

Alternative Museum. *Occupation and Resistance: American Impressions of the Intifada*. New York: Athens Printing Company, 1990. Freedom Archives. Collection: Palestine. Box: Human Rights in Palestine. San Francisco, CA.

Alyan, Hala. *Salt Houses: A Novel*. Boston: Houghton Mifflin Harcourt, 2017.

Alzanoon, Sarah. Interview by author. Skype. November 22, 2014.

Amiry, Suad. *Golda Slept Here*. New Delhi: Women Unlimited, 2014.

Amram, Azri. "Digesting the Massacre: Food Tours in Palestinian Towns in Israel." *Gastronomica: The Journal for Food Studies* 19, no. 4 (2019): 60–73.

Anidjar, Gil. *The Jew, the Arab: A History of the Enemy.* Stanford, CA: Stanford University Press, 2003.

Anonymous. Interview by author. Beit Sahour, Palestine. August 2, 2012.

Anonymous. Interview by author. Beit Sahour, Palestine. September 2, 2019.

Aparicio, Eitan Bronstein. "Most JNF-KKL Forests and Sites Are Located on the Ruins of Palestinian Villages." *Zochrot*, April 2014. https://www.zochrot.org/en/article/55963.

Arnaóut, Abdelraouf, and Ahmed Asmar. "Israel Demolishes al-Araqib Village for the 184th Time." *Anadolu Agency*, March 11, 2021. https://www.aa.com.tr/en/middle-east/israel-demolishes-al-araqib-village-for-184th-time/2172306.

Art Forces. "Vision and History." *Art Forces*, accessed December 9, 2019. https://artforces.org/about/vision-and-history.

Aso, Michitake. *Rubber and the Making of Vietnam: An Ecological History, 1897–1975.* Chapel Hill: University of North Carolina Press, 2018.

Assali, Hadeel. "Postcard from a Liberated Gaza." *+972 Magazine*, December 25, 2020. https://www.972mag.com/postcard-from-a-liberated-gaza.

Associated Press. "Israel Used 'Calorie Count' to Limit Gaza Food during Blockade, Critics Claim." *Guardian*, October 17, 2012. https://www.theguardian.com/world/2012/oct/17/israeli-military-calorie-limit-gaza.

Atanasoski, Neda. *Humanitarian Violence: The US Deployment of Diversity.* Minneapolis: University of Minnesota Press, 2013.

Atshan, Saéd, and Darnell L. Moore. "Reciprocal Solidarity: Where the Black and Palestinian Queer Struggles Meet." *Biography* 37, no. 2 (2014): 680–705.

Austin, J. L. *How to Do Things with Words.* Cambridge, MA: Harvard University Press, 1975.

Aviv, Caryn. "The Emergence of Alternative Jewish Tourism." *European Review of History: Revue européenne d'histoire* 18, no. 1 (2011): 33–43.

Awad, Michel. Interview by author. Siraj Center for Holy Land Studies, Beit Sahour, Palestine. August 16, 2012.

Awad, Nadia. "Nostalgia for the Future." *New Inquiry*, March 22, 2015. https://thenewinquiry.com/nostalgia-for-the-future.

"After Banksy: The Parkour Guide to Gaza." Cited in Orhan Ayyüce, *Archinect News*, March 11, 2015. http://archinect.com/news/article/122663096/after-banksy-the-parkour-guide-to-gaza.

Azeb, Sophia. "Who Will We Be When We Are Free? On Palestine and Futurity." *The Funambulist* 24 (July–August 2019). https://thefunambulist.net/magazine/24-futurisms/will-free-palestine-futurity-sophia-azeb.

Azoulay, Ariella. *The Civil Contract of Photography.* New York: Zone Books, 2008.

Azoulay, Ariella. *Civil Imagination: The Political Ontology of Photography.* London: Verso, 2012.

Azoulay, Ariella. *From Palestine to Israel: A Photographic Record of Destruction and State Formation, 1947–1950.* London: Pluto Press, 2011.

Azoulay, Arielle. *Potential History: Unlearning Imperialism.* London: Verso, 2019.

BADIL. "End Israel's Policy of Discriminatory Child Registration in Jerusalem." *United Nations*, August 27, 2014. https://unispal.un.org/DPA/DPR/unispal.nsf /0/17D5ADBE503A562985257D4F00578495.

BADIL. "The Jewish National Fund." *Al-Majdal* 34 (Summer 2007). https://www.badil .org/en/publication/periodicals/al-majdal/item/429-the-jewish-national-fund -jnf.html.

BADIL. "BADIL Officially Launched the new 'Ongoing Nakba Education Center' in Bethlehem." Accessed July 8, 2022. https://www.badil.org/press-releases/1070 .html.

BADIL-Zochrot. "Study Visit to Cape Town." *Zochrot*, January 2012. https://zochrot .org/en/article/54464.

Baltzer, Anna. *A Witness in Palestine: A Jewish American Woman in the Occupied Territories*. London: Routledge, 2007.

Banksy. "Welcome to Gaza." *Banksy.com*, February 25, 2015. https://youtu.be /3e2dShY8jIo.

Barakat, Rana. "The Jerusalem Fellah: Popular Politics in Mandate-Era Palestine." *Journal of Palestine Studies* 46, no. 1 (2016): 7–19.

Barakat, Rana. "Lifta, the Nakba, and the Museumification of Palestine's History." *Native American and Indigenous Studies* 5, no. 2 (2018): 1–15.

Barakat, Rana. "Writing/Righting Palestine Studies: Settler Colonialism, Indigenous Sovereignty and Resisting the Ghost(s) of History." *Settler Colonial Studies* 8, no. 3 (2018): 349–63.

Barclay, Ahmad. "Exile and Return to Miska." *Sedek: A Journal on the Ongoing Nakba* 6 (May 2011): 11–20.

Barghouti, Mourid. *I Saw Ramallah*. Translated by Ahdaf Soueif. New York: Anchor Books, 2003.

Barnard, Ryvka. "Colonization and Resistance at Bethlehem's Manger Square." *Radical History Review* 129 (2017): 125–43.

Barraclough, Laura, Wendy Cheng, and Laura Pulido. *A People's Guide to Los Angeles*. Berkeley: University of California Press, 2012.

Barsamian, David. *Louder Than Bombs: Interviews from "The Progressive" Magazine*. Cambridge, MA: South End Press, 2004.

Beiler, Ryan Roderick. "US-Made Weapons Used on Bethlehemites . . . and a Cartridge in a Pear Tree!" *Ryanrodrickbeiler.com*, December 6, 2013. https://blog .ryanrodrickbeiler.com/2013/12/06/us- made-weapons-used-on-bethlehemites-and-a-cartridge-in-a-pear-tree (link now defunct).

Beiler, Ryan Roderick, and ActiveStills. "PHOTOS: This Tear Gas Brought to You by the U.S.A." *972Mag*, December 6, 2013. https://www.972mag.com/photos-this -tear-gas-brought-to-you-by-the-u-s-a/.

Beinin, Joel, and Zachary Lockman, eds. *Intifada: The Palestinian Uprising against Israeli Occupation*. Cambridge, MA: Middle East Research and Information Project, 1989.

Bel'Hassen, Yaniv, Natan Uriely, and Ortal Assor. "The Touristification of a Conflict Zone: The Case of Bil'in." *Annals of Tourism Research* 49 (2014): 174–89.

Bennett, Brett. "Naturalising Australian Trees in South Africa: Climate, Exotics and Experimentation." *Journal of South African Studies* 37, no. 2 (2011): 265–80.

Bennett, Brett. *Plantations and Protected Areas: A Global History of Forest Management*. Cambridge, MA: MIT Press, 2015.

Berkowitz, Terry. "Somebody's Brother, Somebody's Son." In *Occupation and Resistance: American Impressions of the Intifada*, edited by Alternative Museum, 62. New York: Athens Printing Company, 1990. Freedom Archives. Collection: Palestine. Box: Human Rights in Palestine. San Francisco, CA.

Berlant, Lauren. *Cruel Optimism*. Durham, NC: Duke University Press, 2011.

Bhandar, Brenna, and Rafeef Ziadah, "Acts and Omissions: Framing Settler Colonialism in Palestine Studies." *Jadaliyya*, January 14, 2016. https://www.jadaliyya.com/Details/32857.

Bhungalia, Lisa. "'From the American People': Sketches of the US National Security State in Palestine." *Jadaliyya*, September 18, 2012. https://www.jadaliyya.com/Details/2706.

Bhungalia, Lisa. "Managing Violence: Aid, Counterinsurgency, and the Humanitarian Present in Palestine." *Environment and Planning* 47, no. 11 (2015): 2308–23.

Bisharat, George. "Rite of Return to a Palestinian Home." *San Francisco Chronicle*, May 18, 2003. http://www.sfgate.com/opinion/article/Rite-of-return-to-a-Palestinian-home-2647312.php.

Bisharat, George. "Talbiyeh Days: At Villa Harun ar-Rashid in Jerusalem." *Jerusalem Quarterly* 30 (Spring 2007): 88–98.

Bishop, Elizabeth. "Review of *Black Power and Palestine: Transnational Countries of Color* by Michael R. Fischbach." *Journal of Palestine Studies* 48, no. 4 (2019): 123–25.

Black, Ian. "Remembering the Nakba: Israeli Group Puts 1948 Palestine Back on the Map." *Guardian*, May 2, 2014. http://www.theguardian.com/world/2014/may/02/nakba-israel-palestine-zochrot-history.

Bloom, David. "Letter from Jayyous." *The Nation*, March 8, 2004. http://www.thenation.com/article/letter-jayyous.

Bourdain, Anthony, writer and host. *Parts Unknown*. Season 2, episode 1, "Jerusalem, the West Bank, and Gaza." Directed by Sally Freeman. Aired September 15, 2013, on CNN. https://www.youtube.com/watch?v=riZic8b49w8.

Bousac, Julien. "L'archipel de Palestine orientale." Originally drawn for *Le Monde Diplomatique* (2009) and cited in Mackey, "The West Bank Archipelago."

Bouteldja, Houria. *Whites, Jews, and Us: Toward a Politics of Revolutionary Love*. Cambridge, MA: MIT Press, 2017.

Brannon, Susan. "Hebron Settlers." *Electronic Intifada*, July 29, 2002. https://www.electronicintifada.net/content/hebron-settlers/3709.

Braverman, Irus. *Planted Flags: Trees, Land, and Law in Palestine*. New York: Cambridge University Press, 2009.

Braverman, Irus. "Planting the Promised Landscape: Zionism, Nature, and Resistance in Israel/Palestine." *Natural Resources Journal* 49, no. 2 (2009): 317–65.

Braverman, Irus. "Uprooting Identities: The Regulation of Olive Trees in the Occupied West Bank." *PoLAR: Political and Legal Anthropology Review* 32, no. 2 (2009): 237–64.

Break the Silence Mural Project. In *Occupation and Resistance: American Impressions of the Intifada*, edited by Alternative Museum, 75. New York: Athens Printing Company, 1990. Freedom Archives. Collection: Palestine. Box: Human Rights in Palestine. San Francisco, CA.

Brin, Eldad. "Politically-Oriented Tourism in Jerusalem." *Tourist Studies* 6, no. 3 (2006): 215–43.

Brodkin, Karen. *How Jews Became White Folks and What That Says about Race in America*. New Brunswick, NJ: Rutgers University Press, 1998.

Browne, Simone. *Dark Matters: On the Surveillance of Blackness*. Durham, NC: Duke University Press, 2015.

Brownsell, James. "Resistance Is Fertile: Palestine's Eco-War." *Al Jazeera*, November 2, 2011. https://www.aljazeera.com/indepth/features/2011/08/2011823152713716742.html.

Brunner, Benny, dir. *The Great Book Robbery. Al Jazeera, Witness* series, May 24, 2012. https://www.aljazeera.com/program/witness/2012/5/24/the-great-book-robbery.

B'Tselem. "Hebron City Center." *B'Tselem*, November 11, 2017. https://www.btselem.org/hebron.

B'Tselem. "Olive Harvest 2013: 27 Cases of Abuse of Harvesters and Property-Damage Indicate Military's Preparation Inadequate." *B'Tselem*, December 25, 2013. https://www.btselem.org/settler_violence/20131225_olive_harvest.

B'Tselem. "Statistics on Demolitions of Houses Built without Permits in East Jerusalem." *B'Tselem*, May 9, 2010. https://www.btselem.org/jerusalem/demolitions_by_neighborhoods.

B'Tselem. "Taking Control of Land and Designating Areas Off-Limits to Palestinian Use." *B'Tselem*, accessed November 20, 2013. http://www.palestineportal.org/wp-content/uploads/2016/10/BTselem_TakingLand_OffLimitsToPalestinianUse.pdf.

Butler, Judith. *Bodies That Matter: On the Discursive Limits of Sex*. New York: Routledge, 2011.

Butler, Judith. *Gender Trouble: Feminism and the Subversion of Identity*. New York: Routledge, 2006.

Campos, Michelle. *Ottoman Brothers: Muslims, Christians, and Jews in Early Twentieth-Century Palestine*. Palo Alto, CA: Stanford University Press, 2010.

Campt, Tina. *Listening to Images*. Durham, NC: Duke University Press, 2017.

Canadians for Justice and Peace in the Middle East. "If #Canada were #Palestine.. how would you feel? #JSIL" [*sic*]. Twitter, November 5, 2014. https://twitter.com/CJPME/status/530074712618323969.

Carby, Hazel. "The Multicultural Wars." *Radical History Review* 54 (1992): 7–18.

Center for Constitutional Rights, National Lawyers Guild, and ACLU of Southern California. "Charges Dropped in the 20-Year-Old Case against Palestinian Activists." *Electronic Intifada*, October 13, 2007. https://electronicintifada.net/content/charges-dropped-20-year-old-us-case-against-palestinian-activists/784.

Chase, Robert T. *Caging Borders and Carceral States: Incarcerations, Immigration Detentions, and Resistance*. Chapel Hill: University of North Carolina Press, 2019.

Clarke, Richard. "Self-Presentation in a Contested City: Palestinian and Israeli Political Tourism in Hebron." *Anthropology Today* 16, no. 5 (2000): 12–18.

Clarno, Andy. *Neoliberal Apartheid: Palestine/Israel and South Africa after 1994*. Chicago: University of Chicago Press, 2017.

"Code of Conduct for Tourism in the Holy Land: A Palestinian Initiative." *Green Olive Tours*, accessed February 5, 2014. https://greenolivetours.com/a-code-of -conduct-for-tourism-in-the-holy-land/.

Cohen, Shaul Ephraim. *The Politics of Planting: Israeli-Palestinian Competition for Control of Land in the Jerusalem Periphery*. Chicago: University of Chicago Press, 1995.

Cohen-Hattab, Kobi. "Zionism, Tourism, and the Battle for Palestine: Tourism as a Political-Propaganda Tool." *Israel Studies* 9, no. 1 (2004): 61–85.

Cohen-Hattab, Kobi, and Yossi Katz. "The Attraction of Palestine: Tourism in the Years 1850–1948." *Journal of Historical Geography* 27, no. 2 (2001): 166–77.

Cole, Juan. "Alice Walker: Palestinians Face Oppression Much Worse Than Jim Crow of Old South." *Informed Comment*, September 29, 2012. https://www.juancole .com/2012/09/alice-walker-palestinians-face-oppression-much-worse-than-jim -crow-of-old-south.html.

Cook, Jonathon. "Coexistence in Israel's 'Mixed Cities' Was Always an Illusion." *Informed Comment*, May 22, 2021. https://www.jonathan-cook.net/2021–05–22 /israel-mixed-cities-illusion.

Cruz, Cynthia. "Silence Is Enough: On Emily Jacir." *Hyperallergic*, August 7, 2014. https://hyperallergic.com/142225/silence-is-enough-on-emily-jacir/.

Dajani, Magda. "Mona Lisa Minus the Forbidden Colors of the Palestinian Flag." In *Occupation and Resistance: American Impressions of the Intifada*, edited by Alternative Museum, 63. New York: Athens Printing Company, 1990. Freedom Archives. Collection: Palestine. Box: Human Rights in Palestine. San Francisco, CA.

Dallasheh, Lena. "Persevering through Colonial Transition: Nazareth's Palestinian Residents after 1948." *Journal of Palestine Studies* 45, no. 2 (2016): 8–23.

Dallasheh, Lena. "Troubled Waters: Citizenship and Colonial Zionism in Nazareth." *International Journal of Middle East Studies* 47, no. 3 (2015): 467–87.

Darwish, Mahmoud. "The Earth Is Closing on Us." In *Victims of a Map: A Bilingual Anthology of Arabic Poetry*, by Adonis, Mahmoud Darwish, and Samih al-Qasim, 13. Translated by Abdullah al-Udhari. London: Al-Saqi Books, 1984.

Davidson, Lawrence. "Christian Zionism as a Representation of American Manifest Destiny." *Critique: Critical Middle Eastern Studies*, 14, no. 2 (2005): 157–69.

Davis, Angela Y. *Are Prisons Obsolete?* New York: Seven Stories Press, 2011.

Davis, Rochelle. *Palestinian Village Histories: Geographies of the Displaced*. Stanford, CA: Stanford University Press, 2010.

Decolonizing Architecture Art Research (DAAR). "About." *Decolonizing.ps*, accessed September 5, 2014. http://www.decolonizing.ps/site/about.

Decolonizing Architecture Art Research (DAAR). "DAAR/Studio in Exile: 01 Present Returns." *Decolonizing.ps*, July 2, 2014. http://www.decolonizing.ps/site/2014/06 /daarstudio-in-exile-01-present-returns.

Democracy Now!. "Kerry: Settlement Expansion Doesn't Threaten Peace Talks," August 14, 2013. http://www.democracynow.org/2013/8/14/headlines#8144.

Denson, Roger. "Know Thine Enemy." In *Occupation and Resistance: American Impressions of the Intifada*, edited by Alternative Museum, 6–17. New York: Athens Printing Company, 1990. Freedom Archives. Collection: Palestine. Box: Human Rights in Palestine. San Francisco, CA.

Doumani, Beshara. "Rediscovering Ottoman Palestine: Writing Palestinians into History." *Journal of Palestine Studies* 21, no. 2 (1992): 5–28.

Ein Hod Artists' Village. Home page. *Ein Hod Artists' Village*, accessed February 12, 2020. https://ein-hod.info.

El-Haddad, Laila. "You Are NOT Here." *Gaza Mom*, November 17, 2009. http://www .gazamom.com/2009/11/you-are-not-here-2 (link now defunct).

Elia, Nada. "Looking Beyond 'Women and Children' in Gaza's Casualties." *Mondoweiss*, November 15, 2019. https://mondoweiss.net/2019/11/looking-beyond -women-and-children-in-gazas-casualties.

Elia, Nada. "Solidarity Means Fighting for Black Lives." *Mondoweiss*, June 4, 2020. https://mondoweiss.net/2020/06/solidarity-means-fighting-for-black-lives.

Eng, David. *The Feeling of Kinship: Queer Liberalism and the Racialization of Intimacy*. Durham, NC: Duke University Press, 2010.

Enloe, Cynthia. *Bananas, Beaches, and Bases: Making Feminist Sense of International Politics*. Berkeley: University of California Press, 1989.

Erakat, Noura. "Geographies of Intimacy: Contemporary Renewals of Black-Palestinian Solidarity." *American Quarterly* 72, no. 2 (2020): 471–96.

Erakat, Noura. *Justice for Some: Law and the Question of Palestine*. Palo Alto, CA: Stanford University Press, 2019.

Erakat, Noura, and Mark Lamont Hill. "Black-Palestinian Transnational Solidarity: Renewals, Returns, and Practices." *Journal of Palestine Studies* 48, no. 4 (2019): 7–16.

Esmeir, Samera. *Juridical Humanity: A Colonial History*. Palo Alto, CA: Stanford University Press, 2012.

Essa, Azad. "Sheikh Jarrah: How the US Media Is Erasing Israel's Crimes." *Middle East Eye*, May 7, 2021. https://www.middleeasteye.net/opinion/sheikh-jarrah -israel-palestine-us-media-erasing-crimes.

Estrin, Daniel. "Israel Accused of Revoking Thousands of Jerusalem Residency Permits from Palestinians." npr, January 6, 2018. https://www.npr.org/sections /parallels/2018/01/06/574678148/israel-accused-of-revoking-thousands-of -jerusalem-residency-permits-from-palesti.

Estrin, James. "Palestinian Pleasures." *New York Times: The Lens*, January 7, 2014. https://lens.blogs.nytimes.com/2014/01/07/palestinian-pleasures.

Evans, Gabe, Nick Mitchell, and Taylor Wondergem. "Scenes from the Wildcat Strike: A Documentary History." Special issue, *Critical Ethnic Studies* 6, no. 2 (Fall 2020).

Farasha, Noelle. Interview by author. Jerusalem, Palestine. August 23, 2019.

Feldman, Ilana. *Governing Gaza: Bureaucracy, Authority, and the Work of Rule, 1917–1967*. Durham, NC: Duke University Press, 2008.

Feldman, Ilana. *Life Lived in Relief: Humanitarian Predicaments and Palestinian Refugee Politics*. Oakland: University of California Press, 2018.

Feldman, Keith. *A Shadow over Palestine: The Imperial Life of Race in America*. Minneapolis: University of Minnesota Press, 2015.

Fields, Gary. *Enclosure: Palestinian Landscapes in a Historical Mirror*. Oakland: University of California Press, 2017.

Fischbach, Michael. *Black Power and Palestine: Transnational Countries of Color*. Palo Alto, CA: Stanford University Press, 2019.

Foley, Malcolm, and J. John Lennon, *Dark Tourism: The Attraction of Death and Disaster*. Andover, UK: Cengage Learning EMEA, 2000.

Foucault, Michel. *Discipline and Punish: The Birth of the Prison*. Translated by Alan Sherida. New York: Vintage, 1977.

Gaza Parkour Team. After Banksy: The Parkour Guide to Gaza, March 11, 2015. Accessed July 18, 2022, https://youtu.be/DhSdo6HTAso.

Gilmore, Ruth Wilson. "Abolition Geography and the Problem of Innocence." In *Futures of Black Radicalism*, edited by Gaye Theresa Johnson and Alex Lubin, 225–40. London: Verso, 2017.

Gilmore, Ruth Wilson. *Golden Gulag: Prisons, Surplus, Crisis, and Opposition in Globalizing California*. Berkeley: University of California Press, 2007.

Gilroy, Paul. *Postcolonial Melancholia*. New York: Columbia University Press, 2005.

Gluck, Sherna Berger. *An American Feminist in Palestine: The Intifada Years*. Philadelphia: Temple University Press, 1994.

Gluck, Sherna Berger. Interview by author. Santa Monica, CA. April 27, 2019.

Goff, Maggie. Interview by author. Skype. September 14, 2013.

Gonzalez, Vernadette Vicuña. *Securing Paradise: Tourism and Militarism in Hawai'i and the Philippines*. Durham, NC: Duke University Press, 2013.

Gonzalez, Vernadette Vicuña, and Laurel Mei-Singh. "DeTours: Mapping Decolonial Genealogies in Hawai'i." *Critical Ethnic Studies* 3, no. 2 (2017): 173–92.

Gordon, Neve. "Uprooting the Bedouins of Israel." *The Nation*, December 2, 2010. https://www.thenation.com/article/156822/uprootingbedoins-israel.

Grace, Anne. "The Tax Resistance at Bayt Sahur." *Journal of Palestine Studies* 19, no. 2 (1990): 99–107.

Grady, Constance. "The Alice Walker Anti-Semitism Controversy Explained." *Vox*, December 20, 2018. https://www.vox.com/culture/2018/12/20/18146628/alice-walker-david-icke-anti-semitic-new-york-times.

Grassroots Jerusalem. *Wujood: The Grassroots Guide to Jerusalem*. Jerusalem: Grassroots Al-Quds, 2016.

Green, Addis. Interview by author. Skype. July 31, 2013.

Greene, Susan. "I Witness Silwan: Who Is Watching Whom?" *Jerusalem Quarterly* 82 (2020): 154–67.

Gregory, Derek. *The Colonial Present: Afghanistan, Palestine, Iraq*. Hoboken, NJ: Wiley-Blackwell, 2004.

Griffin, Maryam S. *Vehicles of Decolonization: Public Transit in the Palestinian West Bank*. Philadelphia: Temple University Press, 2021.

Günel, Gökce, Saiba Varma, and Chika Watanabe. "A Manifesto for Patchwork Ethnography." *Society for Cultural Anthropology*, June 9, 2020. https://culanth.org/fieldsights/a-manifesto-for-patchwork-ethnography.

Habiby, Emile. *The Secret Life of Saeed: The Pessoptimist.* Translated by Salma Khadra Jayyusi and Trevor Le Gassick. Northampton, MA: Interlink Publishing Group, 2001.

Haddad, Toufic. *Palestine Ltd.: Neoliberalism and Nationalism in the Occupied Territory.* New York: I. B. Tauris, 2016.

Hamad, Saida, and Reem Nuseibeh. "BZU Discusses Uprising." *Al Fajr: Jerusalem, Palestinian Weekly* 9, no. 412 (April 10, 1988): 8–9. Freedom Archives. Collection: Palestine. Box: Academic, Students, and Thinkers on Palestine. San Francisco, CA.

Hanegbi, Haim, and Tzachi Ostrovosky. "Palestinian Houses in West Jerusalem: Stories and Photographs." *Zochrot,* October 2008. https://zochrot.org/uploads /uploads/27dc322c9367a805c2bc69ef0ad1039d.pdf.

Harding, Susan. *The Book of Jerry Falwell: Fundamentalist Language and Politics.* Princeton, NJ: Princeton University Press, 2001.

Harring, Sidney L. *Policing a Class Society: The Experience of American Cities 1865–1915.* Chicago: Haymarket Books, 2017.

Harris, Emily. "In Little Town of Bethlehem, US Aid on Display at Christmas Market." NPR, December 29, 2013. https://www.npr.org/2013/12/24/256890160/in -little-town-of-bethlehem-u-s-aid-ondisplay-at-christmas-market.

Hartman, Saidiya. *Scenes of Subjection: Terror, Slavery, and Self-Making in Nineteenth Century America.* New York: Oxford University Press, 1997.

Hass, Amira. "It's Not the Olive Trees." *Haaretz,* January 11, 2006. https://www .haaretz.com/1.5313890.

Hass, Amira. "Otherwise Occupied: For Israel, It Seems Goliath Was the Victim." *Haaretz,* July 27, 2015. https://www.haaretz.com/.premium-goliath-the-victim-1 .5379470.

Hassan, Boudour Yousef. "African-Palestinian Community's Deep Roots in Liberation Struggle." *Electronic Intifada,* July 10, 2015. https://electronicintifada.net /content/african-palestinian-communitys-deep-roots-liberation-struggle /14682.

Hatuqa, Dalia. "Saving the West Bank's Shuhada Street." *Al Jazeera,* March 8, 2013. https://www.aljazeera.com/features/2013/3/8/saving-the-west-banks-shuhada -street.

Hawari, Yara. "Radical Futures: When Palestinians Imagine." *Al-Shabaka,* March 24, 2020. https://al-shabaka.org/commentaries/radical-futures-when-palestinians -imagine.

Hawari, Yara. "Trump's 'Peace' Deal Flagrantly Tramples on Palestinian Rights and Freedoms." *Guardian,* January 30, 2020. https://www.theguardian.com /commentisfree/2020/jan/30/trump-peace-deal-palestinian-rights-israel -international-law.

Hazbun, Waleed. *Beaches, Ruins, Resorts: The Politics of Tourism in the Middle East.* Minneapolis: University of Minnesota Press, 2008.

Hernández, Kelly Lytle. *Migra!: A History of the US Border Patrol.* Berkeley: University of California Press, 2010.

Herzl, Theodor. *Altneuland.* Princeton, NJ: Markus Weiner Publishers: 2000.

Hilo, Baha. Interview by author. Joint Advocacy Initiative, Beit Sahour, Palestine. July 23, 2012.

Hiltermann, Joost R. "Israel's Strategy to Break the Uprising." *Journal of Palestine Studies* 19, no. 2 (1990): 87–98.

Hutnyk, John. *The Rumour of Calcutta: Tourism, Charity, and the Poverty of Representation.* London: Zed Books, 1996.

Ibrahim, Noor. "Olive Groves in the West Bank Have Become a Battleground. That's Why Volunteers Come from around the World to Help at Harvest Time." *Time*, November 1, 2019. https://time.com/5714146/olive-harvest-west-bank.

Imada, Adria. *Aloha America: Hula Circuits through the US Empire.* Durham, NC: Duke University Press, 2012.

Imwas Human Society. *Emwas Will Never Go into Oblivion: The Story of Imwas.* Pamphlet. Last accessed February 13, 2020, www.imwas.org (link now defunct).

Institute for Middle East Understanding (IMEU). "50 Days of Death and Destruction." *Institute for Middle East Understanding*, September 10, 2014. https://imeu .org/article/50-days-of-death-destruction-israels-operation-protective-edge.

International Middle East Media Center. "Palestinian Popular Resistance in Hebron." *IMEMC News*, June 9, 2015. https://imemc.org/article/71865.

International Middle East Media Center. "The Practicalities of the Palestinian Right of Return." *IMEMC News*, July 13, 2015. https://imemc.org/article/72236.

Ir'Amim. "Jerusalem Municipality Budget Analysis for 2013: Share of Investment in East Jerusalem." *Ir'Amim*, December 2014. http://www.ir-amim.org.il/sites /default/files/PL_Investment%20in%20East%20Jerusalem%20December%20 2014–2%2025%2015.pdf.

Ir'Amim. "Permanent Residency: A Temporary Residency Set in Stone." *Ir'Amim*, January 6, 2012. http://www.ir-amim.org.il/en/report/permanent-residency -temporary-status-set-stone.

Isaac, Rami K., Vincent Platenkamp, Freya Higgins-Desbiolles, and C. Michael Hall. "Giving Palestinian Tourism(s) a Voice." In *The Politics and Power of Tourism in Palestine*, edited by Rami K. Isaac, C. Michael Hall, and Freya Higgins-Desbiolles, 244–49. London: Routledge, 2015.

Jacir, Emily. "Ex Libris 2010–2012." *Alexander and Bonin*, 2021. https://www .alexanderandbonin.com/exhibition/188/exhibition_works/1682.

Jailer, Todd, and Melani McAlister. "The Israeli-Palestinian Conflict and the US Peace Movement." In *Intifada: The Palestinian Uprising against Israeli Occupation*, edited by Joel Beinin and Zachary Lockman, 275–99. Cambridge, MA: Middle East Research and Information Project, 1989.

Jayyusi, Salma Khadra, ed. *Anthology of Modern Palestinian Literature.* New York: Columbia University Press, 1992.

Jean-Klein, Iris E. F. "Alternative Modernities, or Accountable Modernities? The Palestinian Movement(s) and Political (Audit) Tourism during the First Intifada." *Journal of Mediterranean Studies* 12, no. 1 (2002): 43–79.

Jefferis, Danielle C. "The 'Center of Life' Policy: Institutionalizing Statelessness in East Jerusalem." *Jerusalem Quarterly* 50 (Summer 2012): 94–103.

Johnson, Walter. *Soul by Soul: Life Inside the Antebellum Slave Market*. Cambridge, MA: Harvard University Press, 2009.

Kadman, Noga. "Acting the Landlord: Israel's Policy in Area C, the West Bank." *B'Tselem*, June 2013. https://www.btselem.org/download/201306_area_c_report _eng.pdf.

Kadman, Noga. *Erased from Space and Consciousness: Israel and the Depopulated Palestinian Villages of 1948*. Bloomington: Indiana University Press, 2015.

Kadman, Noga, Tomer Gardi, Umar al-Ghubari, and Aviv Gros-Allon, eds. *Once Upon a Land: A Tour Guide to Depopulated Palestinian Villages and Towns* (Hebrew and Arabic). Tel Aviv: Zochrot/Pardes Publications, 2012.

Kanaaneh, Rhoda Ann. *Birthing the Nation: Strategies of Palestinian Women in Israel*. Berkeley: University of California Press, 2002.

Kanafani, Ghassan. "Returning to Haifa." In *Palestine's Children: Returning to Haifa and Other Stories*. Translated by Barbara Harlow and Karen E. Riley, 149–95. Boulder, CO: Lynne Rienner, 2000.

Kane, Alex. "A Level of Racist Violence I Have Never Seen: UCLA Professor Robin D. G. Kelley on Palestine and the BDS Movement." *Mondoweiss*, February 16, 2012. https://mondoweiss.net/2012/02/a-level-of-racist-violence-i -have-never-seen-ucla-professor-robin-d-g-kelley-on-palestine-and-the-bds -movement.

Kane, Alex. "Celebrity Foodie Anthony Bourdain's Trip to Palestine Highlights Gaza Blockade, Racist Settlers." *Mondoweiss*, September 16, 2013. https://mondoweiss .net/2013/09/celebrity-foodie-anthony-bourdains-trip-to-palestine-highlights -gaza-blockade-racist-settlers.

Kaplan, Amy. *Our American Israel: The Story of an Entangled Alliance*. Cambridge, MA: Harvard University Press, 2018.

Kaplan, Caren. *Aerial Aftermaths: Wartime from Above*. Durham, NC: Duke University Press, 2018.

Karmi, Ghada. *In Search of Fatima: A Palestinian Story*. New York: Verso Books, 2009.

Karmi, Ghada. *Return: A Palestinian Memoir*. New York: Verso Books, 2015.

Kassis, Bisan. Interview by author. Joint Advocacy Initiative, Beit Sahour, Palestine. September 3, 2012.

Kassis, Rami. "The Struggle for Justice through Tourism in Palestine." In *Peace through Tourism: Promoting Human Security through International Citizenship*, edited by Lynda-ann Blanchard and Freya Higgins-Desbiolles, 225–40. London: Routledge, 2013.

Kelley, Robin D. G. "Apartheid's Black Apologists." In *Apartheid Israel: The Politics of an Analogy*, edited by Jon Soske and Sean Jacobs, 125–42. Chicago: Haymarket Books, 2015.

Kelley, Robin D. G. "From the River to the Sea to Every Mountain Top: Solidarity as Worldmaking." *Journal of Palestine Studies* 48, no. 4 (2019): 69–91.

Kelley, Robin D. G. "Why Did You Fire Steven Salaita?" *Jadaliyya*, August 13, 2014. https://www.jadaliyya.com/Details/31098/Why-Did-You-Fire-Professor-Steven -Salaita.

Kelly, Jennifer Lynn. "Israeli Gay Tourist Initiatives and the (In)visibility of State Violence." *GLQ: A Journal of Lesbian and Gay Studies* 26, no. 1 (2020): 160–73.

Kelly, Jennifer Lynn. "Locating Palestine within American Studies: Transitory Field Sites and Borrowed Methods." In *Theorizing Fieldwork in the Humanities: Methods, Reflections, and Approaches in the Global South*, edited by Shalini Puri and Debra A. Castillo, 95–107. New York: Palgrave Macmillan, 2016.

Kelly, Jennifer Lynn. "On Being There: One Palestine Solidarity Tour in Focus." *Dalia Association*, September 2019. https://dalia.ps/news/being-there-one-palestine -solidarity-tour-focus.

Kelner, Shaul. *Tours That Bind: Diaspora, Pilgrimage, and Israeli Birthright Tourism.* New York: New York University Press, 2010.

Khalidi, Walid. *All That Remains: The Palestinian Villages Occupied and Depopulated by Israel in 1948.* Washington, DC: Institute for Palestine Studies, 1992.

Khalidi, Walid. *Before Their Diaspora: A Photographic History of the Palestinians.* Washington, DC: Institute for Palestine Studies, 1984.

Khan, Yasmin. "You Can't Discuss Palestinian Food without Talking about the Occupation." *Literary Hub*, February 5, 2019. https://lithub.com/you-cant-discuss -palestinian-food-without-talking-about-the-occupation.

Kincaid, Jamaica. *A Small Place.* New York: Farrar, Straus and Giroux, 1988.

Klinker, Mary Jo, and Heidi Morrison. "On the Pedagogy of 'Boomerangs': Exposing Occupation through Co-implication." *Radical Teacher: A Socialist, Feminist, and Anti-racist Journal on the Theory and Practice of Teaching* 117 (2020): 40–47.

Koensler, Alexander, and Christina Papa. "Political Tourism in the Israeli-Palestinian Space." *Anthropology Today* 27, no. 2 (2011): 13–17.

Kokaly, Samer. Interview by author. Alternative Tourism Group, Beit Sahour, Palestine. August 22, 2012.

Kozol, Wendy. *Distant Wars Visible: The Ambivalence of Witnessing.* Minneapolis: University of Minnesota Press, 2014.

Kudaimi, Ramah. "Join Virtual Delegation to Palestine." *US Campaign for Palestinian Rights*, July 26, 2017. https://uscpr.org/virtualdelegation.

Laderman, Scott. *Tours of Vietnam: War, Travel Guides, and Memory.* Durham, NC: Duke University Press, 2009.

Lampman, Jane. "Mixing Prophecy and Politics." *Christian Science Monitor*, July 7, 2004. https://www.csmonitor.com/2004/0707/p15s01-lire.html.

Lisle, Debbie. "Consuming Danger: Reimagining the War/Tourism Divide." *Alternatives: Global, Local, Political* 25, no. 1 (2000): 91–116.

Long, Joanna C. "Rooting Diaspora, Reviving Nation: Zionist Landscapes of Palestine-Israel." *Transactions of the Institute of British Geographers* 34, no. 1 (2009): 61–77.

Long, Joanna Claire. "(En)planting Israel: Jewish National Fund Forestry and the Naturalisation of Zionism." Master's thesis, University of British Columbia, 2005. https://open.library.ubc.ca/soa/cIRcle/collections/ubctheses/831/items/1 .0092127.

Lorber, Ben. "Keren Kayemet LeYisrael and Environmental Racism in Palestine." *Earth First!* 32, no. 3 (2012): 28–32.

Lory, Yvonne. Interview by author. Skype. October 4, 2013.

Love Under Apartheid Team. "'Love Under Apartheid' Tells the Story of Palestinians Fighting for the Right to Love." *Mondoweiss*, February 14, 2012. https://mondoweiss.net/2012/02/love-under-apartheid-project-tells-story-of-palestinians-fighting-for-the-right-to-love.

Lowenstein, Andrea Freud. "Confronting Stereotypes: Reading Maus in Crown Heights." *College English* 60, no. 4 (1998): 396–420.

Lubin, Alex. *Geographies of Liberation: The Making of an Afro-Arab Political Imaginary.* Chapel Hill: University of North Carolina Press, 2014.

Lubin, Alex, Les W. Field, Melanie Yazzie, and Jakob Schiller. "The Israel/Palestine Field School: Decoloniality and the Geopolitics of Knowledge." *Social Text* 31, no. 4 (2013): 79–97.

MacCannell, Dean. *The Ethics of Sightseeing.* Berkeley: University of California Press, 2011.

MacCannell, Dean. *The Tourist: A New Theory of the Leisure Class.* New York: Schocken Books, 1976.

Mackey, Robert. "The West Bank Archipelago." *The Lede: New York Times Blog,* May 7, 2009. https://thelede.blogs.nytimes.com/2009/05/07/the-west-bank-archipelago.

Macy, Marietta. Interview by author. Skype. October 14, 2014.

Mahajneh, Alaa. "Situating the JNF in Israel's Land Laws." *Al-Majdal* 43 (Winter–Spring 2010). https://www.badil.org/en/publication/periodicals/al-majdal/item/1404-mahajneh-jnf-and-israeli-law.html.

Mahmood, Saba. *The Politics of Piety: The Islamic Revival and the Feminist Subject.* Princeton, NJ: Princeton University Press, 2011.

Mahrouse, Gada. *Conflicted Commitments: Race, Privilege, and Power in Transnational Solidarity Activism.* Montreal: McGill-Queen's University Press, 2014.

Makdisi, Saree. *Palestine Inside Out: An Everyday Occupation.* New York: W.W. Norton Company, 2008.

Manalansan, Martin, IV. *Global Divas: Filipino Gay Men in the Diaspora.* Durham, NC: Duke University Press, 2003.

Manof, Einat. "Countermapping Return." *Sedek: A Journal on the Ongoing Nakba,* no. 6 (May 11, 2011). http://zochrot.com/uploads/uploads/3ef901cb0371ba8f6b731f884fadc939.pdf.

Mary (pseudonym). "From the Diary of an American in Occupied Palestine." *The Link* 22, no. 5 (1989): 1–13. Freedom Archives. Collection: Palestine. Box: Americans for Middle East Understanding. San Francisco, CA.

Masalha, Nur. *The Bible and Zionism: Invented Traditions, Archaeology and Post-Colonialism in Israel-Palestine.* New York: Zed Books, 2007.

Masalha, Nur. *The Palestine Nakba: Decolonising History, Narrating the Subaltern, Reclaiming Memory.* New York: Zed Books, 2012.

Massad, Joseph. "The Persistence of the Palestinian Question." *Cultural Critique* 59 (2005): 1–23.

Mbembe, Achille. "On Palestine." In *Apartheid Israel: The Politics of an Analogy*, edited by Jon Soske and Sean Jacobs, vi–vii. Chicago: Haymarket Books, 2015.

McAlister, Melani. *Epic Encounters: Culture, Media, and US Interests in the Middle East since 1945*. Berkeley: University of California Press, 2005.

McAlister, Melani. *The Kingdom of God Has No Borders: A Global History of American Evangelicals*. New York: Oxford University Press, 2018.

McAlister, Melani. "Prophecy, Politics, and the Popular: The *Left Behind* Series and Christian Fundamentalism's New World Order." *South Atlantic Quarterly* 102, no. 4 (2003): 773–98.

McIntosh, Ian S., and Jamil Alfaleet. "Envisioning a Tourism of Peace in the Gaza Strip." In *The Politics and Power of Tourism in Palestine*, edited by Rami K. Isaac, C. Michael Hall, and Freya Higgins-Desbiolles, 217–27. London: Routledge, 2015.

Meibers, Marylu. "Untitled." In *Occupation and Resistance: American Impressions of the Intifada*, edited by Alternative Museum, 68. New York: Athens Printing Company, 1990. Freedom Archives. Collection: Palestine. Box: Human Rights in Palestine. San Francisco, CA.

Middle East Children's Alliance. "History." *Middle East Children's Alliance*, accessed November 29, 2021. https://www.mecaforpeace.org/history/.

Middle East Children's Alliance. "Staff, Board, and Advisors." *Middle East Children's Alliance*, accessed November 29, 2021. https://www.mecaforpeace.org/staff -board-and-advisors/.

Middle East Children's Alliance. "Break the Silence Mural Project." *Middle East Children's Alliance*, accessed June 30, 2017. mecaforpeace.org/partners/break-the -silence-mural-project (link now defunct).

Mikdashi, Maya. "Can Palestinian Men Be Victims? Gendering Israel's War on Gaza." *Jadaliyya*, July 23, 2014. https://www.jadaliyya.com/Details/30991.

Mitchell, Timothy. *Colonising Egypt*. Berkeley: University of California Press, 1991.

Mitchell, Timothy, and Anupama Rao. "Editor's Note." *Comparative Studies of South Asia, Africa and the Middle East* 38, no. 1 (2018): 1–2.

Mohanty, Chandra Talpade. *Feminism without Borders: Decolonizing Theory, Practicing Solidarity*. Durham, NC: Duke University Press, 2003.

Mohanty, Chandra Talpade. "Under Western Eyes: Feminist Scholarship and Colonial Discourses." *boundary 2* 12, no. 3 (1984): 333–58.

Morita, John. "House Demolition II," In *Occupation and Resistance: American Impressions of the Intifada*, edited by Alternative Museum, 70. New York: Athens Printing Company, 1990. Freedom Archives. Collection: Palestine. Box: Human Rights in Palestine. San Francisco, CA.

Mostafanezhad, Mary. *Volunteer Tourism: Popular Humanitarianism in Neoliberal Times*. London: Ashgate, 2014.

Moughalian, Sato. *Feast of Ashes: The Life and Art of David Ohannessian*. Stanford, CA: Stanford University Press, 2019.

Mullen, Jethro, and Ben Wedeman. "'They Went to the Beach to Play': Deaths of 4 Children Add to Growing Toll in Gaza Conflict." cnn, July 17, 2014. https:// www.cnn.com/2014/07/17/world/meast/mideast-conflict-children/index.html.

Muñoz, José Esteban. *Cruising Utopia: The Then and There of Queer Futurity*. New York: New York University Press, 2009.

Muñoz, José Esteban. *Disidentifications: Queers of Color and the Performance of Politics*. Minneapolis: University of Minnesota Press, 1999.

Murphy, Jay. "The Intifada Makes Many Artists." *Occupation and Resistance: American Impressions of the Intifada*, edited by Alternative Museum, 29–39. New York: Athens Printing Company, 1990. Freedom Archives. Collection: Palestine. Box: Human Rights in Palestine. San Francisco, CA.

Naiman, Robert. "Welcome to Palestine: 'Even Prisoners Are Allowed Visits.'" *Al Jazeera*, April 14, 2012. https://www.aljazeera.com/opinions/2012/4/14/welcome-to-palestine-even-prisoners-are-allowed-visits.

Naser-Najjab, Nadia, and Ghassan Khatib. "The First Intifada, Settler Colonialism, and 21st Century Prospects for Collective Resistance." *The Middle East Journal* 73, no. 2 (2019): 187–206.

Nassar, Maha. "Palestinian Engagement with the Black Freedom Movement Prior to 1967." *Journal of Palestine Studies* 48, no. 4 (2019): 16–32.

Nassar, Maha. *Brothers Apart: Palestinian Citizens of Israel and the Arab World*. Palo Alto, CA: Stanford University Press, 2017.

Nassar, Maha, Ilana Feldman, Zachary Lockman, Noura Erakat, and Joel Beinin. "Fifty Years of Occupation." *Middle East Research and Information Project*, June 5, 2017. https://merip.org/2017/06/fifty-years-of-occupation.

Nassar, Tamara. "Fight to Save Jaffa's Last Muslim Cemetery from Israeli Bulldozers." *Electronic Intifada*, June 1, 2018. https://electronicintifada.net/blogs/tamara-nassar/fight-save-jaffas-last-muslim-cemetery-israeli-bulldozers.

Negrón, Olga. Interview by author. New York. November 25, 2014.

Ngai, Mae M. *Impossible Subjects: Illegal Aliens and the Making of Modern America*. Princeton, NJ: Princeton University Press, 2004.

Ngai, Sianne. *Ugly Feelings*. Cambridge, MA: Harvard University Press, 2007.

Nguyen, Mimi Thi. *The Gift of Freedom: War, Debt, and Other Refugee Passages*. Durham, NC: Duke University Press, 2012.

Nguyen, Thuy. "Coal Mining, Forest Management, and Deforestation in French Colonial Vietnam." *Environmental History* 6, no. 2 (2021): 255–77.

Noy, Chaim. "The Political Ends of Tourism: Voices and Narratives of Silwan/The City of David in East Jerusalem." In *The Critical Turn in Tourism Studies: Creating an Academy of Hope*, edited by Irena Ateljevic, Nigel Morgan, and Anette Pritchard, 27–41. London: Routledge, 2011.

Obenzinger, Hilton. *American Palestine: Melville, Mark Twain, and Holy Land Mania*. Princeton, NJ: Princeton University Press, 1999.

"Olive Harvest Fact Sheet." UN Office for the Coordination of Humanitarian Affairs. October 19, 2011. https://reliefweb.int/report/occupied-palestinian-territory/olive-harvest-fact-sheet-october-2011.

"Oxfam Briefing Paper: The Road to Olive Farming." *Oxfam International*, October 15, 2010. https://www.oxfam.org/en/research/road-olive-farming.

Paik, A. Naomi. *Rightlessness: Testimony and Redress in US Prison Camps since World War II*. Chapel Hill: University of North Carolina Press, 2016.

Palestine Remembered. "Welcome to Salama." *Palestine Remembered*, December 19, 2007. https://www.palestineremembered.com/Jaffa/Salama/index.html.

Palestinian Campaign for the Academic and Cultural Boycott of Israel. "Do No Harm! Palestinian Call for Ethical Tourism/Pilgrimage." *BDS*, March 12, 2019. https://bdsmovement.net/pacbi/ethical-tourism.

Palestinian Liberation Organization Negotiation Affairs Department. "The Annexation of Tourism: Israel's Policies and their Devastating Effects on Palestinian Tourism." *Palestinian Liberation Organization Negotiation Affairs Department*, March 24, 2016. https://www.nad.ps/sites/default/files/annexation_of_tourism .pdf.

Palestinian News and Information Agency (WAFA). "Virtual Reality App Gives Users Access to Everyday Life in Palestine." *Palestinian News and Information Agency* (WAFA), October 13, 2019. http://english.wafa.ps/page.aspx?id =QEKrPsa113917220076aQEKrPs.

Pappé, Ilan. "More Oslos: The Two-State Solution Died Over a Decade Ago." *Palestine Chronicle*, September 26, 2013. http://www.palestinechronicle.com/more -oslos-the-two-state-solution-died-over-a-decade-ago.

Pappé, Ilan, and Samer Jaber. "Ethnic Cleansing by All Means: The Real Israeli 'Peace' Policy." *Mondoweiss*, October 17, 2014. https://mondoweiss.net/2014/10 /ethnic-cleansing-israeli.

Parks, Lisa, and Caren Kaplan, eds. *Life in the Age of Drone Warfare*. Durham, NC: Duke University Press, 2017.

Peled-Elhannan, Nurit. *Palestine in Israeli Schoolbooks: Ideology and Propaganda in Education*. New York: I. B. Taurus, 2012.

Pennock, Pamela. *The Rise of the Arab American Left: Activists, Allies, and Their Fight against Imperialism and Racism, 1960s–1980s*. Chapel Hill: University of North Carolina Press, 2017.

Peteet, Julie. *Space and Mobility in Palestine*. Bloomington: Indiana University Press, 2017.

Piscataway Conoy Tribe. Home page. *The Official Piscataway Conoy Tribe*, accessed May 30, 2021. http://www.piscatawaytribe.org.

Pratt, Mary Louise. "Arts of the Contact Zone." *Profession* (1991): 33–40.

Press, Michael. "How a Mark Twain Travel Book Turned Palestine into a Desert." *Hyperallergic*, September 20, 2017. https://hyperallergic.com/400528/how-a -mark-twain-travel-book-turned-palestine-into-a-desert.

Puar, Jasbir. "On Torture: Abu Ghraib." *Radical History Review* 93 (2005): 13–38.

Puar, Jasbir K. *The Right to Maim: Debility, Capacity, Disability*. Durham, NC: Duke University Press, 2017.

Qutami, Loubna. "Moving Beyond the Apartheid Analogy in Palestine and South Africa." *Middle East Research and Information Project*, February 3, 2020. https://merip.org/2020/02/moving-beyond-the-apartheid-analogy-in-palestine -and-south-africa-trump.

Rabiyeh, Said. Introductory Comments at Grassroot Jerusalem's *Wujood: The Grassroots Guide to Jerusalem* Book Launch. Educational Bookshop, Jerusalem, Palestine, August 4, 2019.

Radai, Itamar. "Qatamon, 1948: The Fall of a Neighborhood." *Jerusalem Quarterly* 46 (2011): 6–14.

Rashid, Khalidi. *Brokers of Deceit: How the US Has Undermined Peace in the Middle East*. New York: Beacon Press, 2014.

Raz-Krakotzkin, Amnon. "On the Right Side of the Barricades: Walter Benjamin, Gershom Scholem, and Zionism." *Comparative Literature* 65, no. 3 (2013): 363–81.

Remembering. "iNakba: The Invisible Land." V. 2.4.8. Remembering, October 4, 2017. https://apps.apple.com/us/app/inakba/id864050360.

Researching the American-Israeli Alliance and Jewish Voice for Peace. *Deadly Exchange: The Dangerous Consequences of American Law Enforcement Trainings in Israel*. New York: Researching the American-Israeli Alliance, 2018. https://deadlyexchange.org/wp-content/uploads/2019/07/Deadly-Exchange-Report.pdf.

Reuters. "US House Democrats Offer Resolution Blocking $735 Million Israel Weapons Sale." *Retuers*, May 19, 2021. https://www.reuters.com/business/aerospace-defense/us-house-democrats-offer-resolution-blocking-735-million-israel-weapons-sale-2021-05-19.

Rickford, Russel. "'To Build a New World': Black American Internationalism and Palestine Solidarity." *Journal of Palestine Studies* 48, no 4 (2019): 52–68.

RL. Interview by author. Jerusalem, Palestine. August 23, 2019.

Robins, Margo, and Valentin Lopez. "A Conversation on Wildfire Ecologies." *Berkeley Center for New Media*, March 1, 2021. http://bcnm.berkeley.edu/events/22/history-theory/4242/a-conversation-on-wildfire-ecologies.

Robinson, Shira. *Citizen Strangers: Palestinians and the Birth of Israel's Liberal Settler State*. Palo Alto, CA: Stanford University Press, 2013.

Rodinson, Maxime. *Israel: A Colonial-Settler State?* Atlanta, GA: Pathfinders Press, 1973.

Rodríguez, Dylan. *Forced Passages: Imprisoned Radical Intellectuals and the US Prison Regime*. Minneapolis: University of Minnesota Press, 2006.

Ryall, Jenni. "Banksy Goes Undercover in Gaza, Releases a Mini-Documentary." *Mashable*, February 25, 2015. https://mashable.com/archive/banksy-gaza-documentary.

Rybnicki, Avi. "To Gaza and Back." Special Report: Physicians for Human Rights, in "Comparing the Incomparable: Naomi Chazan considers Israel and South Africa," *New Outlook: Middle East Monthly* 31, no. 6 (June 1988). Freedom Archives. Collection: Palestine. Box: Academic, Students, and Thinkers on Palestine. San Francisco, CA.

Saadeh, Raed. "Experiential Community-Based Rural Tourism Potential in Palestine: Challenges and Potentials." In *The Politics and Power of Tourism in Palestine*, edited by Rami K. Isaac, C. Michael Hall, and Freya Higgins-Desbiolles, 95–112. London: Routledge, 2015.

Said, Edward. *After the Last Sky*. New York: Columbia University Press, 1998.

Said, Edward. *From Oslo to Iraq and the Road Map: Essays*. New York: Vintage Press, 2005.

Said, Edward. "One State Solution." *New York Times*, January 10, 1999. https://www
.nytimes.com/1999/01/10/magazine/the-one-state-solution.html.

Said, Edward. *Orientalism*. New York: Pantheon Books, 1978.

Said, Edward. *Out of Place: A Memoir*. New York: Vintage, 1999.

Said, Edward. *Peace and Its Discontents: Essays on Palestine in the Middle East Peace Process*. New York: Vintage Press, 1996.

Said, Edward. "Permission to Narrate." *Journal of Palestine Studies* 13, no. 3 (Spring, 1984): 27–48.

Said, Edward. *The Politics of Dispossession: The Struggle for Palestinian Self-Determination, 1969–1994*. New York: Vintage, 1994.

Said, Edward. *The Question of Palestine*. New York: Times Books, 1999.

"Salama 1987." *Palestine Remembered*, accessed September 8, 2021. https://www
.palestineremembered.com/Jaffa/Salama/Picture17574.html.

Salamanca, Omar Jabary, Mezna Qato, Kareem Rabie, and Sobhi Samour. "Past Is Present: Settler Colonialism in Palestine." *Settler Colonial Studies* 2, no. 1 (2012): 1–8.

Saliba, Therese. Review of *An American Feminist in Palestine, Women and the Israeli Occupation*, and *Gender and the Israeli-Palestinian Conflict*. *Signs* 22, no. 3 (1997): 753–56.

Saranillio, Dean Itsuji. "Colonial Amnesia: Rethinking Filipino 'America' Settler Power in the US Colony of Hawai'i." In *Positively No Filipinos Allowed*, edited by Antonio T. Tongson, Edgardo V. Gutierrez, and Ricardo V. Gutierrez, 124–41. Philadelphia: Temple University Press, 2004.

Save Lifta. "About Lifta." *Save Lifta*, accessed September 8, 2021. http://savelifta.org
/about-lifta.

Schama, Simon. *Landscape and Memory*. New York: Knopf, 1995.

Schneider, Emily. "'It Changed My Sympathy, Not My Opinion': Alternative Tourism to the Occupied Palestinian Territories." *Sociological Focus* 53, no. 4 (2020): 378–98.

Schulman, Sarah. "A Documentary Guide to Brand Israel and the Art of Pinkwashing." *Mondoweiss*, November 30, 2011. https://mondoweiss.net/2011/11/a
-documentary-guide-to-brand-israel-and-the-art-of-pinkwashing.

Segal, Rafi, and Eyal Weizman, eds. *A Civilian Occupation: The Politics of Israeli Architecture*. London: Verso, 2003.

Seikaly, Sherene. "How I Met My Great-Grandfather: Archives and the Writing of History." *Comparative Studies of South Asia, Africa and the Middle East* 38, no. 1 (2018): 6–20.

Seikaly, Sherene. *Men of Capital: Scarcity and Economy in Mandate Palestine*. Palo Alto, CA: Stanford University Press, 2016.

Shalhoub-Kevorkian, Nadera. *Militarization and Violence against Women in Conflict Zones in the Middle East: A Palestinian Case-Study*. Cambridge, UK: Cambridge University Press, 2009.

Sharif, Lila. "Savory Politics: Land, Memory, and the Ecological Occupation of Palestine." PhD diss., University of California, San Diego, 2014. https://escholarship
.org/uc/item/485943qz.

Sharif, Lila. "Vanishing Palestine." *Critical Ethnic Studies* 2, no. 1 (2016): 17–39.

Sharpley, Richard, and Philip R. Stone. *The Darker Side of Travel: The Theory and Practice of Dark Tourism*. Bristol, UK: Channel View Publications, 2009.

Shehadeh, Raja. *Palestinian Walks: Forays into a Vanishing Landscape*. New York: Scribner, 2007.

Shehadeh, Raja. "The Plight of the Palestinian Olive Tree." *New York Times*, November 13 2012. https://latitude.blogs.nytimes.com/2012/11/13/the-plight-of-the -palestinian-olive-tree.

Shireen Hassim, "Academic Freedom and Academic Boycotts." In *Apartheid Israel: The Politics of an Analogy*, edited by Jon Soske and Sean Jacobs, 101–4. Chicago: Haymarket Books, 2015.

Shlaim, Avi. *The Iron Wall: Israel and the Arab World*. New York: W. W. Norton and Company, 2001.

Shohat, Ella. "The Invention of the Mizrahim." *Journal of Palestine Studies* 29, no. 1 (1999): 5–20.

Shohat, Ella. "Notes on the Post-colonial." *Social Text* 31/32 (1992): 99–113.

Shohat, Ella. *On the Arab-Jew, Palestine, and Other Displacements*. London: Pluto Press, 2017.

Shohat, Ella. "Sephardim in Israel: Zionism from the Standpoint of Its Jewish Victims." *Social Text* 19/20 (1988): 1–35.

Shohat, Ella. "The Shaping of Mizrahi Studies: A Relational Approach." *Israel Studies Forum* 17, no. 2 (2002): 86–93.

Shohat, Ella. *Taboo Memories, Diasporic Voices*. Durham, NC: Duke University Press, 2006.

Shohat, Ella Habiba, ed. *Talking Visions: Multicultural Feminisms in a Transnational Age*. Cambridge, MA: MIT Press, 2001.

Siddiqui, Usaid. "Outrage after Jeopardy Host Rules Bethlehem Not in Palestine." *Al Jazeera*, January 14, 2020. https://www.aljazeera.com/news/2020/01/jeopardy -episode-palestine-question-uproar-200111165110124.html.

Silverstein, Shel. *Where the Sidewalk Ends: Poems and Drawings*. New York: Harper-Collins, 1974.

Simpson, Audra. *Mohawk Interruptus: Political Life across the Borders of Settler States*. Durham, NC: Duke University Press, 2014.

Singh, Nikhil. *Black Is a Country: Race and the Unfinished Struggle for Democracy*. Cambridge, MA: Harvard University Press, 2005.

Sion, Brigitte. *Death Tourism: Disaster Sites as Recreational Landscape*. London: Seagull Books, 2014.

Siraj Center for Holy Land Studies. Home page. *Siraj Center for Holy Land Studies*, 2021. https://www.sirajcenter.org/index.php/en/.

Sizer, Stephen. *Christian Zionism: Road Map to Armageddon?* London: Inter-Varsity Press, 2004.

Slyomovics, Susan. *The Object of Memory: Arab and Jew Narrate the Palestinian Village*. Philadelphia: University of Pennsylvania Press, 1998.

Smith, Shawn Michelle. *Photography on the Color Line: W. E. B. Du Bois, Race, and Visual Culture*. Durham, NC: Duke University Press, 2004.

Somerville, Siobhan. *Queering the Color Line: Race and the Invention of Homosexuality in American Culture.* Durham, NC: Duke University Press, 2000.

Soske, Jon, and Sean Jacobs, eds. *Apartheid Israel: The Politics of an Analogy.* Chicago: Haymarket Books, 2015.

Spade, Dean. "Impossibility Now: A Trans* Politics Manifesto." *S and F Online* 11, nos. 1–2 (Fall 2012/Spring 2013). https://sfonline.barnard.edu/gender-justice -and-neoliberal-transformations/impossibility-now.

Spade, Dean. *Normal Life: Administrative Violence, Critical Trans Politics, and the Limits of the Law.* Rev. ed. Durham, NC: Duke University Press, 2011.

Spivak, Gayatri Chakravorty. "Can the Subaltern Speak?" In *Marxism and the Interpretation of Culture*, edited by Cary Nelson and Larry Grossberg, 271–313. Basingstoke, UK: Macmillan Education, 1988.

Spivak, Gayatri Chakravorty. "Righting the Wrongs." *South Atlantic Quarterly* 103, no. 2/3 (2004): 523–81.

Stamatopoulou-Robbins, Sophia. "The Joys and Dangers of Solidarity in Palestine: Prosthetic Engagement in an Age of Reparations." *CR: The New Centennial Review* 8, no. 2 (2008): 111–60.

Stamatopoulou-Robbins, Sophia. *Waste Siege: The Life of Infrastructure in the West Bank.* Palo Alto, CA: Stanford University Press, 2019.

Stanton, Andrea. "Locating Palestine's Summer Residency: Mandate Tourism and National Identity." *Journal of Palestine Studies* 47, no. 2 (2018): 44–62.

Stanton, Andrea. *"This Is Jerusalem Calling": State Radio in Mandate Palestine.* Austin: University of Texas Press, 2013.

Stein, Rebecca. "Dispossession Reconsidered: Israel, Nakba, Things." *Ethnologie Française* 45, no. 2 (2015): 309–20.

Stein, Rebecca. "Israeli Routes through Nakba Landscapes: An Ethnographic Meditation." *Jerusalem Quarterly* 43 (2010): 6–17.

Stein, Rebecca. *Itineraries in Conflict: Israelis, Palestinians, and the Political Lives of Tourism.* Durham, NC: Duke University Press, 2008.

Stoler, Ann Laura, panelist. "Anthropologists and Controversial Engagements: The Boycott of Israeli Academic Institutions." Panel at the American Anthropological Association Annual Meeting, Washington, DC, December 4, 2014.

Stoler, Ann Laura. *Imperial Debris: On Ruins and Ruination.* Durham, NC: Duke University Press, 2013.

Stoler, Ann Laura. "Imperial Debris: Reflections on Ruin and Ruination." *Cultural Anthropology* 23, no. 2 (2008): 191–219.

Stoler, Ann Laura. "Intimidations of Empire: Predicaments of the Tactile and Unseen." In *Haunted by Empire: Geographies of Intimacy in North American Empire*, edited by Ann Laura Stoler, 1–22. Durham, NC: Duke University Press, 2006.

Stoler, Ann Laura. "Memory Work in Java: A Cautionary Tale." In *Carnal Knowledge and Imperial Power: Race and the Intimate in Colonial Rule*, 162–203. Berkeley: University of California Press, 2002.

Stoler, Ann Laura, and Karen Strassler. "Casting for the Colonial: Memory Work in 'New Order' Java." *Comparative Studies in Society and History* 42, no. 1 (2000): 4–48.

"Stop Israel's Forced Displacement of Palestinians from East Jerusalem!" *Every action.com*, accessed May 9, 2021. https://secure.everyaction.com /wUAYmd6RzEacXxN3WQuYQQ2.

Strickland, Patrick. "Israel Plans to Reintroduce Ban on Palestinian Flag." *Electronic Intifada*, December 1. 2014. https://electronicintifada.net/blogs/patrick -strickland/israel-plans-reintroduce-ban-palestinian-flag.

Tallie, T. J. "The Historian and Apartheid." In *Apartheid Israel: The Politics of an Analogy*, edited by Jon Soske and Sean Jacobs, 81–86. Chicago: Haymarket Books, 2015: 81–86.

Tamari, Salim. *Jerusalem 1948: The Arab Neighbourhoods and Their Fate in the War*, 2nd ed. Jerusalem: Institute of Jerusalem Studies and BADIL Research Center, 2002.

Tamari, Salim. "Tourists with Agendas." *Middle East Report* 196 (1995): 24.

Taylor, Steve, Peter Varley, and Tony Johnston, eds. *Adventure Tourism: Meanings, Experience, and Learning*. New York: Routledge, 2013.

Teaiwa, Teresia. "Reading Gauguin's *Noa* with Hau'ofa's *Nederends*: Militourism, Feminism, and the 'Polynesian' Body." In *Inside Out: Literature, Cultural Politics, and Identity in the New Pacific*, edited by Vilsoni Hereniko and Rob Wilson, 249–63. Boulder, CO: Rowman and Littlefield, 1999.

Teaiwa, Teresia. "Reflections on Militourism, US Imperialism, and American Studies." *American Quarterly* 68, no. 3 (2016): 847–53.

Teisch, Jessica B. *Engineering Nature: Water, Development, and the Global Spread of American Environmental Expertise*. Chapel Hill: University of North Carolina Press, 2011.

Teves, Stephanie Nohelani. *Defiant Indigeneity: The Politics of Hawaiian Performance*. Chapel Hill: University of North Carolina Press, 2018.

Thomas, Deborah. *Political Life in the Wake of the Plantation: Sovereignty, Witnessing, Repair*. Durham, NC: Duke University Press, 2019.

Thomas, Lynell. *Desire and Disaster in New Orleans: Tourism, Race, and Historical Memory*. Durham, NC: Duke University Press, 2014.

Thomsen, Simon. "TV Chef Sums Up the Problems in Gaza More Than Most Diplomats." *Business Insider*, July 25, 2014. https://www.businessinsider.com.au/tv -chef-anthony-bourdain-sums-up-the-problems-in-gaza-better-than-most -diplomats-2014-7.

Trump White House. "Peace to Prosperity: A Vision to Improve the Lives of the Palestinian and Israeli People." *WhiteHouse.gov* (archives), January 2020. https://trumpwhitehouse.archives.gov/wp-content/uploads/2020/01/Peace-to -Prosperity-0120.pdf.

Twain, Mark. *Innocents Abroad*. Hartford, CT: American Publishing Company, 1867.

UNESCO. "Lifta (Mey Naftoah): Traditional Mountain Village." UNESCO, accessed February 13, 2020. https://whc.unesco.org/en/tentativelists/6061.

Unruly. Home page. *Unruly*, accessed September 8, 2021. http://jocsm.org.

Urry, John. *The Tourist Gaze*. New York: SAGE, 1990.

Vally, Salim. "Solidarity with Palestine: Confronting the 'Whataboutery' Argument and the Bantustan Denouement." In *Apartheid Israel: The Politics of an Analogy*, edited by Jon Soske and Sean Jacobs, 43–52. Chicago: Haymarket Books, 2015.

Visualizing Palestine. "Jerusalem: A City for All?" (infographic). *Visualizing Palestine*, April 2017. https://visualizingpalestine.org/visuals/city-for-all.

Visualizing Palestine. "Since 1967 Israel Has Razed over 800,000 Palestinian Olive Trees, the Equivalent to Destroying Central Park 33 Times Over." *Mondoweiss*, October 10, 2013. https://mondoweiss.net/2013/10/palestinian-equivalent -destroying.

Visualizing Palestine. "Uprooted" (infographic). *Visualizing Palestine*, October 2013. https://visualizingpalestine.org/visuals/olive-harvest.

Walcott, Derek. *What the Twilight Says*. New York: Farrar, Straus and Giroux, 1988.

Walia, Harsha. *Undoing Border Imperialism*. Chico, CA: AK Press, 2014.

Webb, Taurean J. "Troubling Idols: Black-Palestinian Solidarity in US Afro-Christian Spaces." *Journal of Palestine Studies* 48, no. 4 (2019): 33–51.

Weiss, Phillip. "Jeff Halper Tours Ma'ale Adummim Pointing Out Stolen Olive Trees." August 13, 2012. YouTube video, 0:04:25. http://www.youtube.com/watch?v =oIm1GzjKNhY.

Weitz, Joseph. *Forests and Afforestation in Israel*. Translated by Shlomo Levenson. Edited by Isaac Arnon. Jerusalem: Massada Press, 1974.

Weizman, Eyal. *Hollow Land: Israel's Architecture of Occupation*. New York: Verso, 2007.

Wexler, Laura. *Tender Violence: Domestic Visions in an Age of US Imperialism*. Chapel Hill: University of North Carolina Press, 2000.

Willis, Deborah. "Mothers and the Shebab." In *Occupation and Resistance: American Impressions of the Intifada*, edited by Alternative Museum, 74. New York: Athens Printing Company, 1990. Freedom Archives. Collection: Palestine. Box: Human Rights in Palestine. San Francisco, CA.

Wolfe, Patrick. *Settler Colonialism and the Transformation of Anthropology: The Politics and Poetics of an Ethnographic Event*. New York: Bloomsbury Academic, 1998.

Wood, Amy Louise. *Lynching and Spectacle: Witnessing Racial Violence in America 1890–1940*. Chapel Hill: University of North Carolina Press, 2009.

Xero (@LMoiseiwitsch). Twitter. Accessed December 5, 2014 (account currently suspended).

You Are Not Here. Home page. *You Are Not Here*, accessed September 7, 2017. http:// youarenothere.org.

Zahr, Amer. "Anthony Bourdain, Will You Marry Me?" *Civil Arab*, September 13, 2013. https://www.civilarab.com/anthony-bourdain-will-you-marry-me.

Zayid, Maysoon. "Watching Anthony Bourdain in Palestine." *Daily Beast*, September 19, 2013. https://www.thedailybeast.com/watching-anthony-bourdain-in -palestine.

Zerubavel, Yael. *Recovered Roots: Collective Memory and the Making of Israeli National Tradition*. Chicago: University of Chicago Press, 1995.

Ziadah, Rafeef. "We Teach Life, Sir." November 12, 2011. YouTube video, 0:04:38. https://www.youtube.com/watch?v=aKucPh9xHtM.

Ziv, Oren. "Israeli Police Determined to Escalate the Violence in Jerusalem." *+972 Magazine*, May 7, 2021. https://www.972mag.com/jerusalem-police-violence -sheikh-jarrah.

Zochrot. "'Ayn Hawd." *Zochrot*, accessed February 12, 2020. https://www.zochrot.org
    /en/village/49423.
Zochrot. "Dayr Yasin." *Zochrot*, accessed January 15, 2020. https://zochrot.org/en
    /village/49106.
Zochrot. "Lifta." *Zochrot*, accessed February 12, 2020. https://zochrot.org/en/village
    /49239.
Zochrot. "Miska." *Zochrot*, accessed November 15, 2021. https://zochrot.org/en
    /village/49248.
Zochrot. "Salama." *Zochrot*, accessed February 10, 2020. https://zochrot.org/en
    /village/49897.
Zochrot. "Truth and Redress." *Zochrot*, accessed June 18, 2021. https://www.zochrot
    .org/video/all?category=3.
Zonzsein, Mairav. "Jewish National Fund Resumes Forestation Project in Al-Arakib."
    +972 Magazine, May 7, 2012. https://www.972mag.com/jewish-national-fund
    -resumes-forestation-project-in-al-arakib/.

INDEX

Page numbers in italics refer to figures.

al-Khader, 89, 107, 110–11
Allen, Lori, 249
Allende, Salvador, 262n96
almond trees, 88, 95, 100, 150, 152
al-Mughayer, 47–48
AlQassab, Abdallah, 202–3
Al-Qissariya Market, 183
al-Rashid, Harun, 119
al-Shabaka, 64
al-Sharafi, Fida, 30–31, 32, 50
Al-Shati Refugee Camp (Beach Camp), 42, 183, 279n4
Alternative Museum, 41, 51, 183; *Occupation and Resistance: American Impressions of the Intifada*, 36, 45, 52–55
Alternative Tourism Group (ATG): Olive Tree Campaign, 66, 89–94, 102, 107–11, 141, 219, 227, 238, 242, 262n98
alternative tourism sector, 6, 13, 64–65
al-Walaja, 90, 111
Alzanoon, Sarah, 80–81, 218, 221–23, 228, 231–32, 236, 265n52, 266n65
al-Zubaidy, Yazan, 85, 107, 109, 155, 238, 241, 262n98
Amah Mutsun Tribal Land, 17
Ambassador Hotel, 41
American Colony Hotel, 40
American Israel Public Affairs Committee (AIPAC), 34
American studies, 12, 97, 257n45
American Studies Association, 227; BDS endorsement (2014), 283n39
A. M. Qattan Foundation: Centre for the Child, 183, 191
'Anata, 59
Angola, 34
annexation, 54, 63, 75, 88–89, 93–94, 245
anticolonialism, 33, 146, 241–42, 247–48, 250; and citational politics, 87; and Indigeneity, 229–30; and intifadas, 38, 260n40; language of, 64; and methodology of book, 11–12, 15; solidarity tourism as, 2, 4–6, 15–16, 20, 72, 80, 143, 208, 215
Anti-Defamation League, 34
Antigua, 12
anti-imperialism, 34
antiracism, 12
antisemitism, 27, 38, 117
anti-Zionism, 43, 116, 129, 137, 145, 224, 247, 250, 275n57
apartheid, 115; Israeli, 77–78, 82, 109, 226, 245, 283n39; South African, 163, 165, 222–24, 226, 277n58

Applied Research Institute of Jerusalem (ARIJ), 90, 92, 263n6
Apricot Liberation Front, 100, 103, 110
apricot trees, 100, 103–4, 110
Arab Americans, 34, 219
Arab-Jews, 28
Arab Orthodox Christians churches, 173
Arafat, Yasser, 24, 44–45, 47, 258n1
archaeology, 18, 114–15, 129, 134, 205, 207, 212, 281n84
archipelago, 3, 60; Palestine as, 5, 59–62, 86, 246, 254n10, 263n2, 263n6
archives, 6, 22, 48, 141, 152, 158, 163, 178, 274n44; digital, 8, 167, 174, 181, 184; of displacement, 212, 276n4; familial, 145–46, 174; and report-back genre, 33, 35, 37, 41, 45
Area A/B/C system, 62–63, 69–70, 75–76, 90, 265n42
Armenian genocide, 121, 131
Armenian Palestinians, 131, 136
Ar-Ram, 59
arrests, 1, 34, 54, 83
Art Forces, 56
Arts and Crafts Village, 183, 279n4
Ashkenazi Jews, 15, 38, 118
Asian American studies, 12
Assali, Hadeel: "Postcard from a Liberated Gaza," 208–9
Atshan, Sa'ed, 283n52
At-Tuwani, 9
Australia, 229, 268n16, 268n18
Avraham, Tamar, 117–18, 135
Awad, Michel, 64–69
Awad, Nadia, 188, 205
'Ayn Hawd/Ein Houd, 5, 18, 95, 104, 139, 148–49, 152–53, 267n5, 270n45
Azeb, Sophia, 127–28, 164
'Azzun, 105

back casting, 207
BADIL Resource Center for Palestinian Residence and Refugee Rights, 90, 92, 167, 170, 181, 205, 224–25; Ongoing Nakba Project, 255n19; "Study Visit to Cape Town," 164–66; "The Practicalities of Return," 162–63
Bakr, Ismail, Zakaria, Ahed, and Mohamed, 46
Balfour Declaration (1917), 90
Banksy, 180, 208; *After Banksy* (Gaza Parkour Team), 202–205; *Welcome to Gaza*, 199–201
Bantustans, 223, 263n17
Barahmeh, Salem, 178
Barakat, Rana, 127, 156, 254n5
Barcelona Peace Park, 183

imagining otherwise, 206, 210
Immigration and Nationality Act/McCarran-Walter Act (1952), 34
Indiana, 218–20; Indianapolis, 205, 208, 283n39
Indiana University, 205
Indigenous Peoples, 14, 17, 114, 115, 156, 164, 284n54; Indigenous feminism, 265n52; land stewardship by, 98, 144–45, 149; in settler colonial narratives, 98, 145, 225, 229–30; in Turtle Island, 222, 225–30, 283n32. *See also* First Nations Peoples; Native Americans
Indigenous studies, 14, 254n5
inheriting loss, 88–94, 107, 110, 121, 204, 210, 274n44
Institute for Middle East Understanding, 115
interdisciplinarity, 11–12, 16, 257n45, 267n2
Interfaith Peacebuilders. *See* Eyewitness Palestine
International Solidarity Movement (ISM), 8, 255n26
intifada gardens, 21
intifadas. *See* first intifada (1987–93); second intifada (2000–2005)
invitation (term), 3
Israeli Arab discourse, 28, 50, 275n2
Iraq, 33, 56, 170
Ireland, 89
Irgun, 98, 174
Islamic fundamentalism, 25, 66
Islamophobia, 216, 219
islands, Palestine as, 5, 59–63, 86, 254n10. *See also* archipelago
Israel Defense Forces (IDF), 93, 110–11, 130, 230, 269n21, 275n57
Israeli Army, 149
Israeli Border Patrol, 32
Israeli Committee Against House Demolitions (ICAHD), 103, 132
Israeli Ministry of the Interior, 116
Israeli Ministry of Tourism, 77, 134
Israeli Navy, 191
"Israeli-Palestinian conflict" discourse, 28, 86, 153, 186, 191, 245, 252
Israeli Supreme Court, 120, 285n87
Israel Land Authority, 100, 155, 268n14
Israel Lands Authority Law (2009), 268n14
iTunes, 174

Jab'a, 94, 219
Jabali, Muhammed, 171–72
Jabalya Refugee Camp, 28, 33
Jacir, Emily: *Ex Libris*, 274n44
Jacobs, Sean, 224

Jaffa/Yafa, 112, 135, 137, *140*, 235, 262n96, 270n45; as "mixed city," 18, 139, 173
Jalat family, 118
Jamjum, Hazim, 164–65
Janco, Marcel, 149, 152
Japanese occupation of China, 262n96
Jawdat (Gluck's host), 31, 39
Jayyous, 100, 103
Jenin, 149, 173, 178, 218, 231, 234–35, 237
Jeopardy!, 267n77
Jericho, 29, 59, 71–72, 75, 77, 133, 137
Jeries, Raneen, 176
Jerusalem, 40, 52, 73, 91, 98, 139, 145, 157, 208, 230, 234, 248; and afforestation, 270n40; Al-Buraq Wall/Western Wall, 128, 130; al-Khalil Gate, 117; Al-Suwana, 129; Al-Tur, 129; Armenian Quarter, 131; Ar-Tur, 134; in Bourdain's work, 188–90, 192; and "center of life" judgement, 285n87; Damascus Gate, 115, 130; displacement in, 110, 112–13, 117–1128; Dome of the Rock, 177; Dung Gate, 134; East, 5, 15–17, 27, 38, 41, 47, 74, 76–77, 99, 113–16, 129, 136, 167, 179, 227, 231, 272n2; Gaza Street, 117; German Colony, 134; in Gluck's work, 27, 31–32; Jaffa Gate, 117; Jaffa Road, 130; Jewish Quarter, 129, 275n58; Mahane Yehuda, 153; Mamilla corridor, 130; Mea Sharim, 153; Moroccan Quarter (Al-Magharbeh), 128, 130; as multiple occupied, 114–17; Muslim Quarter, 129–30; Old City, 18, 27, 77, 114, 128–32, 136, 173, 177, 188, 275n58; and Oslo Accords, 64, 76; Qatamon, 123–26; Ras al-Amud, 129; segregation in, 74–80, 86, 90, 102, 178, 179, 227, 270n45; Separation Wall in, 114, 132–33; Sheikh Jarrah, 114, 129, 138, 174, 270n45, 272n3; Silwan, 114, 129, 134, 262n109; and "suburbs" discourse, 153; Talbiya, 118, 125; Temple Mount, 134; and tourism, 68; tours in, 68–69, 72, 112–37, 140, 149, 205–6, 210, 244, 247; US depictions of, 239; Wadi Joz, 129; West, 18, 99, 114, 117, 126, 128, 135–36, 173, 272n2; Western Wall Plaza, 130
Jerusalem Municipality, 155
Jesus Christ, 75
Jewish Agency, 269n21
Jewish Americans, 23, 34–35, 38, 257n42, 258n2
Jewish Iraqis, 170
Jewish National Fund (JNF), 95, 97–99, 102, 104, 149, *150*, 157, 268n14, 269n33; Zochrot's Jewish National Fund (JNF) Erasure of Palestine Tour, 143–48, 171
Jiddah, Ali, 130–31, 275n58
Jiftliq, 29

Michael, Sami, 170
Middle East Children's Alliance (MECA), 56
Middle East Report, 25
Middle East studies, 97
Mikdashi, Maya, 26
militarism, 79, 130, 196, 255n27; feminist
   critiques of, 14, 256n33; racially gendered,
   38–39; and tourism, 3, 12, 256n33. *See also*
   militourism
militarization, 7, 63, 78, 79, 100, 141, 240,
   264n26, 266n58; and masculinity, 39; racial-
   ized, 78, 222. *See also* militourism
Military Order 1015 (1982), 100
militourism, 12, 256n33
Min, Yong Soon, 52
Minoan artifacts, 207
Miska, 162–63, 167–72
Mitchell, Timothy, 146
"mixed cities," 19, 138–39, 173–74
Mohr, Jean: *After the Last Sky*, 48
Molavi, Shourideh, 172
Moore, Darnell L., 283n52
Morita, John, 52; *House Demolition II*, 54
Morris, Benny, 29
Moss, Rayna, 33
Mount Carmel, 149
Mount of Olives, 129, 134
Mount of Temptation, 64, 75
Mousa, Nabhan, 89, 107, 110
MS *Achille Lauro*, 216, 282n14
multiculturalism, 65, 73, 148, 172–73,
   277n41
Muñoz, José Esteban, 253n1, 286n12
Murphy, Jay, 52
Mycenaean artifacts, 207

Nabi Saleh, 1–2, 235
Nablus, 44, 69, 72, 135, 173, 211, 231, 234–35,
   242, 245
Nakba, 16, 122, 125, 212–14, 231, 269n33, 280n41;
   archiving, 141; definition, 255n19; and depopulation, 174; and displacement, 153, 155–56,
   164–65; iNakba (Zochrot), 174–78; ongoing,
   7, 76, 92, 101, 110–11, 170, 248, 255n19; and
   theft, 135. *See also* depopulation; displacement; dispossession; expulsion
Naksa, 110, 128, 141
Native Americans, 148, 222, 226. *See also* Indigenous Peoples
Native friendliness, 11, 240
Natour, Salman: *Memory*, 170
Navi Daniel, 89
Nazareth, 19, 72, 125, 135, 138–39, 173, 220

necropolitics, 225
Needle, Katie, 267n77
Negev Desert, 104
Negrón, Olga, 218, 239
neoliberalism, 224, 265n50
Netanyahu, Benjamin, 264n22
Netherlands, 89
New Left, 34
Newton, Huey, 258n1
New York City, 52, 54, 115, 120, 181, 218; Manhat-
   tan, 227
New York Times, 193
Ngai, Sianne, 47
Nickard, Gary, 46
9/11, 66, 230
+972 *Magazine:* New Futures project, 208
1967 War (Six-Day War), 38, 99, 129, 157,
   275n2
nongovernmental organizations (NGOs), 10, 73,
   256n27, 265n50, 272n1; NGO-ization, 72
North America, 24, 97, 222, 226. *See also* Turtle
   Island
Norway, 89
nostalgia, 21, 57–58, 139, 183, 250; for the future
   (Awad), 184, 188, 205
Nuweser, Luft: "Uncle Matta," 170

Occupation Bootcamp, 155, 235–36, 241
occupation tourism, 180, 238, 247
Occupied Territories, 5, 19, 23, 46, 254n10.
   See also Gaza; Golan Heights; West Bank
Odeh, Ibrahim, 31–32
Odeh, Yacoub, 153–56
Ohanessian, David, 121
olive trees, 69, 75, 127, 150, 152, 203, 233, 251,
   267n1, 272n59; Israeli uprooting of, 54, 88,
   94, 98–103, 106–11, 154, 170, 224, 227, 248,
   271n65, 272n71; planting/harvesting, 18, 66,
   85, 87–113, 136, 141, 144–45, 170, 213, 219, 227,
   238, 242, 250, 262n98; planting programs, 18,
   88; and Separation Wall, 103, 106. *See also*
   deforestation
Omar, Ilhan, 177
Operation Cast Lead (2008–9), 180–81, 206–7,
   210
Operation Nachshon, 98, 269n21
Operation Pillar of Defense (2012), 180, 207,
   210
Operation Protective Edge (2014), 180, 200,
   205, 207, 210
Organization of Arab Students (OAS), 34
Orientalism, 3, 14, 22, 66, 87, 216, 219, 256n38,
   257n44

West Bank, 1, 37, 75, 86, 126, 128, 135, 148, 162–63, 166, 169, 178–80, 193, 211–12, 235, 244, 247, 275n2; afforestation in, 99–100; and art, 51–52, 55, 59; in Banksy's work, 200, 204; in Bourdain's work, 188–91; in Denson's work, 36, 46; fragmentation of, 5–6, 24, 59–64, 74, 76, 113, 116, 131, 205, 237, 241, 263n2, 263n6, 263n17, 270n45; in Gluck's work, 24–25, 39–40, 44; and Historic Palestine, 138–39, 167; land theft in, 263n7; and methodology of book, 15–17; NGOs in, 72, 265n50; olive tree planting/harvesting in, 18, 87, 90–95, 100–113, 141, 144–45, 250; Palestinian Authority in, 272n72; refugee camps in, 57, 95, 153; in report-back genre, 36–42; segregation in, 222–24, 240, 248, 270n54; settlements in, 254n10; tours in, 5–9, 15–19, 21, 47–48, 51, 68, 74–81, 139–41, 149, 157–59, 186, 220, 227, 238, 245, 276n9; US depictions of, 239; water theft in, 218

WhatsApp, 234

white savior narratives, 8

Wietz, Yosef, 99

Willis, Deborah, 36–37, 42, 52, 54–55

witnessing *vs.* witnessing to, 255n27

womenandchildren, 26

Women of Color and Indigenous Feminist Delegation (2011), 265n52

women's and gender studies, 257n45

"World Communism," 34

World War I, 13

World War II, 262n96

World Zionist Organization (WZO), 268

Yafa. *See* Jaffa/Yafa

Yalo, 157

"Your work is not here" (invitation), 11, 74, 131, 252

Yugoslavia, 163, 166

Zahr, Amer, 190, 199

Zahra Hotel, 192

Zayid, Maysoon, 189–90, 192–93

Zayyad, Tawfiq: "The Olive Tree," 101, 105

Zer-Aviv, Mushon: You Are Not Here (YANH), 180–88, 206, 208, 245, 279n4

Ziadah, Rafeef, 48, 199, 212

Zimbabwe, 166

Zionism, 140–42, 167, 189, 255n27; and "balance" discourse, 33; Christian, 104, 272n3; and "conflict" discourse, 28; and de/afforestation, 18, 88–89, 92, 94–98, 103–4, 107, 110–11, 248; and displacement, 34, 88, 111, 113, 137, 149, 153, 248, 268n14; and permission to narrate, 22; racially gendered violence of, 212, 219; resistance to, 39, 43, 116, 129, 137, 145, 163, 171, 224, 247, 250, 275n57; and settler colonialism, 254n5; and theft, 116–29, 136; and tourism, 13, 149, 247

Zobidy, Adnan, 52, 262n98

Zochrot, 118–27, 135, 140–42, 153–54, 157, 159, 167–69, 172, 181, 205, 224–25, 273n15, 274n44, 276n9, 278n64; "From Truth to Redress: Realizing the Right of Return of the Palestinian Refugees" conference (2013), 172; iNakba, 174–78; Jewish National Fund (JNF) Erasure of Palestine Tour, 143–48, 171; *Once Upon a Land*, 117, 276n4; *Sedek*, 170; "Study Visit to Cape Town," 164–66; "The Practicalities of Return," 162–63

zone sous surveillance, 60

Zreiqat, Loay, 83

Zurayk, Rami, 271n59